Puritan Conquistadors

Puritan Conquistadors
Iberianizing the Atlantic,
1550–1700

Jorge Cañizares-Esguerra

STANFORD
UNIVERSITY
PRESS

Stanford,
California

Stanford University Press
Stanford, California

This book has been published with the assistance of a University Cooperative Society Subvention Grant awarded by The University of Texas at Austin.

Printed in the United States of America on acid-free, archival-quality paper

Library of Congress Cataloging-in-Publication Data

Cañizares-Esguerra, Jorge.
  Puritan conquistadors : iberianizing the Atlantic, 1550-1700 / Jorge Cañizares-Esguerra.
    p. cm.
Includes bibliographical references and index.
  ISBN -13: 978-0-8047-4279-5 (cloth : alk. paper)
  ISBN -10: 0-8047-4279-0 (cloth : alk. paper)
  ISBN -13: 978-0-8047-4280-1 (pbk. : alk. paper)
  ISBN -10: 0-8047-4280-4 (pbk. : alk. paper)
  1. America—History—To 1810—Religious aspects—Christianity.   2. America—Civilization—European influences. 3. Colonization—Religious aspects.   4. Puritans—New England—Intellectual life.   5. Spaniards—America—Intellectual life. 6. Demonology—America—History.
7. Indians, Treatment of—America—History.   8. Devil in literature.   9. English literature—Early modern, 1500–1700—History and criticism.   10. Spanish American literature—To 1800—History and criticism.   I. Title.
E18.82.C36   2006
970.01—dc22   2006005162

Typeset by BookMatters in 10/13 Electra

For my dad, whose life first taught me to see our continent whole
For Jeff Speicher, whose mind and friendship I cherish

Contents

Contents

Illustrations

Illustrations

Acknowledgments

The day we went to the health care center, my father was scared. While visiting the United States, he had suddenly developed double vision, a neuropathy of the sixth cranial nerve pair typical of diabetics. Fortunately for all of us, he once had served in the U.S. Army and was entitled to medical care from the Department of Veterans Affairs. My father is a veteran of the Korean War. After moving to the United States from Ecuador at age twenty in 1950, he was drafted. The war proved a blessing for him, because the GI Bill allowed him to pay for college and go to Mexico to study. In Mexico, he obtained a degree in medicine and a doctorate in cellular biology. He soon became a professor and full-time researcher at the Universidad Nacional Autónoma de México (UNAM). In the meantime, he met my mother, a Colombian studying architecture in Mexico, got married, and had children (myself included). In 1968, my father signed documents supporting the student movement of Tlatelolco, and since foreigners were not supposed to get involved in national politics, UNAM did not renew his contract. So, in 1969, after having lived in Mexico for fourteen years, he (we) left for Quito, his hometown. In Ecuador, my father went on to (re)build a successful career. Although he was never good at making money, he was good at creating institutions. He established a blood bank and a hematology service from scratch and over the years created a sophisticated laboratory of hematological research; working under adverse conditions, he managed to publish several articles in leading hematological journals. Over the years, he saw three of his four children leave Ecuador, just as he had once left. Now, he travels all over the world visiting his children. The day he suddenly developed double vision, he was visiting me. Being relatively poor by U.S. standards, he could not afford specialized private medical care, so we turned to the Veterans Administration.

My father is short, thin, and looks "Hispanic," and the VA doctor who saw him immediately jumped to the conclusion that this was a case of badly managed diabetes in a poor, uneducated Hispanic man. He brusquely asked my father about Ecuador: Are you "primitive" there? Do you have cars? Buildings? Highways? TVs? My father and I smiled, half puzzled and half amused, and said nothing. This book, in part, seeks to answer the doctor's questions. It is also meant to be a tribute to my father, that most pan-American of men.

Many people have helped me complete this book. Jeffrey Speicher has always been there for me. He has read drafts of every chapter, offering stylistic suggestions and witty criticism. Richard Kagan read a version of the entire manuscript, and his thoughtful advice prompted me to reorganize the book. I got a good deal of research done while I was a fellow at the Charles Warren Center for American History at Harvard (2001–2). At the center, Joyce Chaplin and Charles Rosenberg nourished me intellectually, while Pat Denault took care of my everyday concerns. Lino Pertilo (master) and Sue Weltman and Francisco Medeiros (administrators) offered my family and myself housing at Eliot House and made our stay at Harvard memorable. The unparalleled resources and knowledgeable librarians of the Fine Arts, Houghton, and Widener Libraries at Harvard proved a blessing. Part of the research and writing was done at the Huntington Library on an Andrew Mellon Fellowship (2003–4). I not only enjoyed the splendid gardens there but also the support of a most professional staff of librarians. I owe an especial debt of gratitude to Roy Ritchie, director of research. The remainder of the writing was done at the University of Texas at Austin, where I enjoyed a Harrington Faculty Fellowship (2004–5), and I am grateful to Larry Faulkner, president of University of Texas, for his generous invitation. I also owe a debt of gratitude to Susan Dean-Smith, Christin Marcin, John Dollard, and Victoria E. Rodriguez. Now that I am permanently at the University of Texas I have felt welcomed by my new colleagues at the History Department. But this book could not have been written without the emotional and professional support of my former colleagues at the State University of New York, Buffalo (SUNY–Buffalo). Erik Seeman in particular has been an endless source of information on Puritan studies, and Jim Bono has been unsparing in his friendship.

Bernard Bailyn, Ralph Bauer, Patricia Gardina Pestana, Richard Godbeer, Jean Howard, Brian Levak, and Erik Seeman read different drafts carefully, offered guidance and countless references, and often forced me to rethink all or parts of my argument. Jim Sidbury, John Slater, John Smolenski, Dan Usner, and Walter Woodward provided key references at different times in the evolution of my research. Alison Frazier and Neil Kamil opened their graduate seminars at the University of Texas to try out my argument, lending a sympathetic ear. I also owe thanks for feedback on various chapters to the following friendly audiences: the USC–Huntington Early Modern Studies seminar; the History Department at the University of Texas–Austin Brown Bag (Bruce Hunt, Dolora Wojciehowski, James Sidbury, Michael Stoff, and Mauricio Tenorio-Trillo); the "Imperial Identity: Construction and Extension of Cultural Community in the Early Modern World" conference at the University of Minnesota (Ted Farmer); the "Beyond the Line: The North and South Atlantics and Global History, 1500–2000" conference at SUNY–Buffalo; the Latin American Studies Program at Miami University of Ohio (Charles Ganelin); the History Department of Florida State University, Tallahassee (Robinson Herrera, Matt Chides, and Joan Cassanovas); the History Department at the University of Pittsburgh (Donna Gabaccia, Marcus Reddiker, and John Markoff); the History Department of the University of California, San Diego (Clinton D. Young; Erick van Young); the Institute for Advanced Historical Studies, University College, London (Felipe Fernández-Armesto and David Brading); the Center for History, Society and Culture at the University of California, Davis (William Hagen, Tom Halloway, Charles Walker, and Andrés Reséndez); the Humanities and Social Science Division at the California Institute of Technology (Mordechai Feingold); the History Department at Johns Hopkins University (Richard Kagan, John Pocock, and David Nirenberg); the Center for Early Modern Studies at the University of Washington, Seattle (Benjamin Schmidt); the History Department at Pennsylvania State University (Londa Schiebinger and Mathew Restall); the workshop "Witnessing in Latin America: Interdisciplinary Conversations" at Princeton University (Michelle Cohen and Chris Garcés); the Kaplan Lectures, University of Pennsylvania (Catalina Muñoz, Nancy Farris, Roger Chartier, and Barbara Fuchs); and the University of Miami (Laura Matthews, Mary Lindemann, Guido Ruggiero, and Richard Godbeer).

For the concluding chapter on historiography, I received sympathetic readings, references, and helpful suggestions from Jeremy Adelman, Anthony Grafton, Jack P. Greene, John Markoff, Jaime Rodríguez O., Erik Seeman, and Eric Van Young. Thanks to Jordana Dym for an invitation to present the argument of this chapter to a sympathetic audience at Skidmore College, and to Erik Slaughter and Lisa Voigt for their invitation to air my views at the conference "In Comparable Americas" organized by the Newberry Library and the University of Chicago..

Had I relied on my own knowledge of Latin, this book would have been plagued with errors of all kinds. Fortunately, David Lupher came to my aid at the last minute. He double-checked most of my transcriptions and transla-

Acknowledgments

tions and generously offered corrections, which I have followed. All remaining errors are, of course, my own. I received help from many people during the process of securing permission to publish images, including Jaime Cuadriello, Enrique Florescano, Illona Katzew, Alexandra Kennedy, Doña Lydia Sada de González, and Vit Ulnas. A University Cooperative Society Subvention Grant awarded by the University of Texas at Austin helped defray part of the costs of publication. At the Stanford University Press, Norris Pope and Anna Eberhard Friedlander skillfully guided me through the process of publication, while Peter Dreyer lent his erudition and meticulous reading skills to turn a half-baked text into a publishable manuscript.

As always, Sandra C. Fernández created the emotional and intellectual environment that made writing possible for me. Sebastián and Andrea will one day turn to this book to make sense of their father. May you find his soul in these pages. Sandra, Sebastián, Andrea: your smiles and love have kept me warm over the years, making tolerable even the coldest of winters.

Puritan Conquistadors

Introduction

On Sunday, September 19, 1649, multitudes gathered along the roads between the Franciscan convent of Lima and the city's cathedral to witness the relocation of the holiest of relics, a sliver of Christ's Cross donated by the late pope Urban VIII (1568–1644) to the Peruvian Church. The event was timed to coincide with the launching of a new campaign to extirpate idolatries in the archbishopric of Lima. Seven of the most learned priests and missionaries in the capital had been charged by the recently appointed archbishop, Pedro de Villagómez (1585–1671), with spearheading this campaign. These seven now waited for the order to march into the hinterlands. They carried white pennants, each with a green cross, bearing the mottoes "Levate signum in gentibus" (Set ye up a standard among the nations) and "Ecce Crucem Domini, fugite partes adversae" (Behold the Cross of the Lord, flee ye enemies) in scarlet letters.[1] As Villagómez explained in a pastoral letter addressed to all the clergy in his archdiocese, these *visitadores* were soldiers of Christ about to begin the second chapter of an ongoing epic struggle against the devil in Peru. Drawing on Paul's letters to the Ephesians (6:10–17), Villagómez asked both *visitadores* and parish priests to be knights of the Lord: "Finally, my brethren, be strong in the Lord, and in the power of his might. Put on the whole armour of God, that ye may be able to stand against the wiles of the devil. For we wrestle not against flesh and blood, but against principalities, against powers, against the rulers of the darkness of this world, against spiritual wickedness in high places. Wherefore take unto you the whole armour of God, that ye may be able to withstand in the evil day, and having done all, to stand. Stand therefore, having your loins girt about with truth, and having on the breastplate of righteousness; And your feet shod with the preparation of the gospel of peace; Above all, taking the shield of faith, wherewith ye shall be able to quench all the fiery darts of the wicked. And take the helmet of salvation, and the sword of the Spirit, which is the word of God."[2]

This crusading spirit was necessary, Villagómez thought, because the New World had long been under Satan's control. A trickster and master of deceit,

F IG . 1.1. Anonymous, Cuzco school of painting (seventeenth century), *The Conquest of Peru*. Colección Poli, Lima. Taken from José de Mesa and Teresa Gisbert, *Historia de la pintura cuzqueña*, 2: 507. The conquest of Peru is presented here as a cosmic epic battle pitting God against the devil. In heaven, the struggle is overseen by the Virgin Mary and a crusading Santiago Matamoros (St. James the Moor-Killer), while the archangel Michael slays Satan. On earth, two legions of Spaniards (one lay, the other religious) advance to take on the Inca armies of Atahualpa.

the devil had for centuries enjoyed absolute mastery over the easily duped natives of Peru. This uncontested sovereignty, however, had been challenged with the arrival of the armies of Francisco Pizarro. The conquistadors had begun the process of liberating the natives from Satan's brutal, unrelenting, tyrannical rule, but the devil did not stand by idly; he fought back (fig. 1.1).

Although the natives had already received the Gospel, it was clear that Satan was still very much alive in the coastal valleys and highlands of Peru, where Amerindians still continued to worship rivers, mountains, lightning, rainbows, and all sorts of sacred objects in the landscape. Pablo José de Arriaga (1564–1622), a Jesuit whose 1621 work on idolatries Villagómez greatly admired, had already described the scale of this satanic, idolatrous worship. A member of one of three extirpating teams between 1616 and 1618, Arriaga reported that in less than eighteen months, his party alone had managed to elicit 5,694 confessions; to identify some 750 wizards; and to gather, smash, and burn in autos-da-fé 603 *huacas* (sacred objects worshipped by a community), 3,140 *canopas* (household deities), and at least 1,100 mummified ancestors, to say nothing of dozens of corpses of infant twins kept in jars and hundreds of other holy curiosities.[3]

In this epic struggle over sovereignty in Peru, *visitadores* were first and foremost exorcists. For example, Villagómez, who decried the use of torture and considered exile the harshest acceptable punishment, reserved for unrepentant wizards, ordered his spiritual knights to exorcise each repentant idolater on holy ground after preaching to and eliciting confessions from him or her. Thus Villagómez advised *visitadores* to gather the population in the local church and deliver the following incantation: "In the name of the Almighty God, and Jesus Christ his son, and the Holy Spirit I exorcise you filthy spirits. Withdraw [filthy spirits] from these servants of God, whom God our Lord [wishes to] free from your error and bewitchment."[4]

Facing the daunting task of uprooting the devil from Peru, Villagómez turned to the Cross (see fig. 1.2). He therefore timed the departure of the seven knights to coincide with the transference of the relic of the Cross (given originally by Patriarch Nicephorus [758–829] to Pope Leo III [795–816]),[5] because he thought that in Peru the Cross would work against idolatry in the same way that the Ark of the Israelites had destroyed the image of the Philistine god Dagon (1 Sam. 5: the Philistines rout the Israelites in battle, capture their holy Ark, and take it to the temple of Dagon). Peru was like the temple of Dagon, a space temporarily inhabited by both the devil and God.[6] As explained by Blas Dacosta, the learned Franciscan to whom Villagómez had entrusted the sermon that would cap the day's festivities, the Cross was designed by God to be "the fatal knife of all idolatries."[7] Drawing on the interpretation by Tommaso de Vio Cajetan (1469–1534) of John 12:31–32 ("Now is the judgment of this world: now shall the prince of this world be cast out. And I, if I be lifted up from the earth, will draw all men unto me"), Dacosta argued that the devil was a tyrannical prince and

FIG. 1.2. The Cross protects Franciscan friars from demons. From Diego Muñoz Camargo (1529–99), *Descripción de la ciudad y provincia de Tlaxcala*. Muñoz Camargo was a mestizo. According to Fernando Cervantes (1994), the indigenous peoples of central Mexico quickly embraced European ideas about the devil. Like Christ's twelve apostles, twelve Franciscan missionaries were dispatched to Mexico in 1523 to oust the devil. The Franciscan minister-general, Francisco de los Angeles, sent off the twelve as the vanguard of an army of knights, saying: "Go . . . and armed with the shield of faith and with the breastplate of justice, with the blade of the spirit of salvation, with the helmet and lance of perseverance, struggle with the ancient serpent which seeks and hastens to lord himself over, and gain the victory over, the souls redeemed with the most precious Blood of Christ" (Francisco Angelorum, "Orders Given to 'the Twelve' [1523]," in *Colonial Spanish America: A Documentary History*, ed. Mills and Taylor, 64).

that Christ had come to dispossess the devil from this position by means of the Cross.[8]

But Villagómez demanded more from the clergy under his command, for he thought that the struggle in Peru was not merely about "rooting out, destroying, mowing down, and dispersing" (ut evellas, et destruas, et disperdas et dissipes) the forces of Satan in Peru by wielding the Cross; it was also about "building and planting" (et aedifices et plantes).[9] Thus Villagómez asked his subordinates to be gardeners, "turning into smooth valleys the rugged landscape that was the wilderness in the hearts and customs of the Indians."[10] Priests and *visitadores* were destined to "cultivate this orchard that God planted in a sterile desert, dry and out of the way." These farmers needed to be cautious, however, for just as God acted as "fertilizing rain," Satan behaved as "[hail and gale], scorching, drying, and destroying the fruit of virtue growing in the hearts and souls of the Indians."[11] In its original struggle against the devil in Peru, Villagómez explained, the Church had overextended itself, creating a vineyard whose vines' shallow roots could not withstand the withering force of Satan's freezing rain and gales. It was now time to create a sturdy plantation in Peru.[12] By manipulating a number of common early modern European tropes about the devil, which have not received sufficient attention from historians, Villagómez connected demonology in the New World to the idioms of epics, the crusades, and gardening.

The 1649 episode in Lima summarizes in a nutshell the themes I seek to explore in this book, namely, that demons were thought to enjoy great geographical mobility and extraordinary power over people and Nature; that the devil was considered to rule over the natives as a tyrannical lord, for he had chosen the New World as his fiefdom; that colonization was perceived as an ongoing epic struggle against a stubbornly resistant Satan; and that the New World was imagined either as a false paradise or as a wilderness that needed to be transformed into a garden by Christian heroes. Although paradigmatically captured in the story of Villagómez's staged campaign of spiritual knights who both wield crosses to slay the dragon of idolatry and use plows to root out weeds and plant orchards, these themes should not be assumed to be typical of Iberian colonization alone.

Iberians, we have often been told, saw themselves as crusading heroes engaged in an expansionist campaign of *reconquista*, first against the Moors and later against the Amerindians. So Villagómez's image of knightly priests battling Satan fits in well with this stereotype of Iberian expansionism. There is no denying that the crusading and chivalric played a crucial role

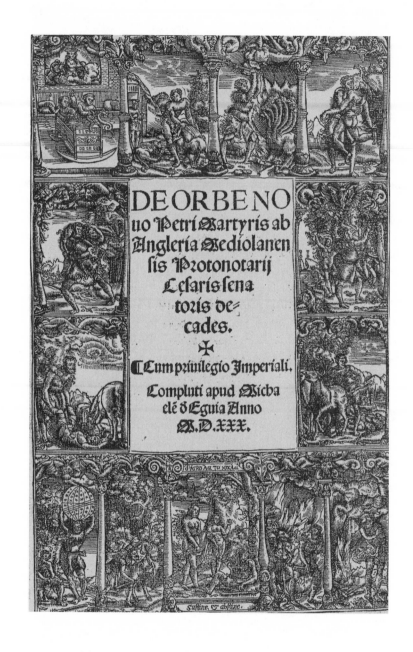

DE ORBE NO
uo Petri Martyris ab
Angleria Mediolanen
sis Protonotarij
Cęsaris sena
toris de=
cades.

✠

❡ Cum priuilegio Imperiali.

Compluti apud Micha
elé d'Eguia Anno
M.D.XXX.

in early modern Iberia. Recent works by Felipe Fernández-Armesto on Columbus, Sanjay Subrahmanyam on Vasco da Gama, and Peter Russell on Prince Henry the Navigator demonstrate in vivid detail how the crusading and chivalric acted as driving forces in the Spanish and Portuguese colonization of the New World, Africa, and India.[13] Conquistadors set sail into the unknown hoping to find treasure and allies so as to launch, yet again, a crusade to recapture Jerusalem. By the same token, conquistadors set sail hoping to establish their own fiefdoms through sheer chivalric prowess. The fourteenth- and fifteenth-century conquest of the Canaries, Azores, Madeira, and the Cape Verde islands gave vassals and lands of their own to Iberian, Italian, and French fortune seekers with chivalric names like Lancelot and Gadifer (see fig. 1.3).[14]

Yet the ethos of the crusading and the chivalric has been used to separate the Iberian Catholic colonial expansion from the British Protestant one. William Prescott, for example, made popular among nineteenth-century U.S. audiences the image of Spanish conquistadors as both benighted medieval throwbacks and chivalric heroes, explaining why Spanish America had developed so differently from British America.[15] This book seeks to

F IG. 1.3. *(opposite)* The twelve labors of Hercules. From Pietro Martire d'Anghiera, *De orbe novo* (Alcalá de Henares, 1530). Courtesy of the Huntington Library, San Marino, California. This image first appeared in *Heredoti libri nomen* (Cologne, 1526). The frontispiece allegedly represents all of Hercules' labors. This is the first explicit visual document that ties the European colonization of America to the discourse of the demonological and the epic. In the imagination of Miguel de Eguia, the editor of this posthumous edition of the chronicle written by Anghiera (1457–1526), the Spanish conquest of the New World promises to bring the conquistador-hero untold riches (here represented by the golden apples of the Hesperides). Yet to get this wealth (material as well as spiritual), the hero needs first to slay the multiheaded dragon of idolatry, defeat the giant Antaeus, and fool Atlas. I have identified the following scenes clockwise from the top left: Hercules, with his half brother Iphicles, plays with serpents in his cradle (not a labor); first labor, Nemean Lion; second labor, Lernean Hydra; eleventh labor, Hercules defeats Antaeus; eleventh labor, Hercules in the Hesperides; tenth labor, Cattle of Geryon; Hercules' self-immolation in a pyre (not a labor); twelfth labor, Cerberus; ninth labor, Hippolyte's Belt; third labor, Hind of Ceryneia; eleventh labor, Atlas and Hercules; eighth labor, man-eating horses of Diomedes; fourth labor, Erymanthean boar. The fifth (Augean Stables), sixth (Stymphalian Birds), and seventh (Cretan Bull) labors are not represented. Tellingly, three of the images on this frontispiece chronicle Hercules' pursuit of the golden apples of the Hesperides.

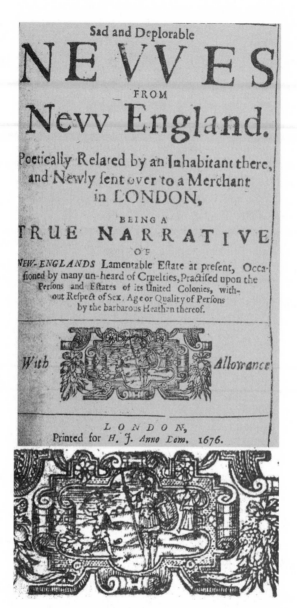

F IG . 1.4. David and Goliath. Frontispiece detail from Benjamin Tompson, *Sad and Deplorable Newes from New England*. Courtesy of the Huntington Library, San Marino, California. Tompson's book is an epic poem on King Philip's War. Like Edward Johnson, Tompson presents the natives as Satan's minions, who, like demons in hell, dismember bodies. The settlers, on the other hand, appear as epic heroes like David, who slew the demonic Philistine giant Goliath. This illustration points to the importance of typology in the colonization of the New World.

overcome such distinctions and to demonstrate that some justifications for colonization in Puritan colonial Massachusetts were really not that different from those espoused in, say, Catholic colonial Lima. It postulates that British Protestants and Spanish Catholics deployed similar religious discourses to explain and justify conquest and colonization: a biblically sanctioned interpretation of expansion, part of a long-standing Christian tradition of holy violence aimed at demonic enemies within and without.

Around the time Villagómez sent his spiritual knights to uproot Satan from the Peruvian Andes, for example, the Puritan divine Edward Johnson (1599–1672) published a remarkably similar epic of Christian heroes battling the devil in the New World (fig. 1.4). Johnson's history of the New England colonies (1654) opens with a call to arms to his Puritan comrades: "You are called the faithfull Souldiers of Christ . . . pulling downe the Kingdome of Antichrist . . . take up your Armes and march manfully on till all opposers of Christ Kingly power be abolished . . . be not daunted at your small number, for every common Souldier in Christ Campe shall be as David who slew the great Goliath."[16] Johnson wanted his Puritan knights to be armed and prepared for battle with Satan, for "the people of Christ ought to behave themselves in war-like Discipline. . . . Store your selves with all sorts of weapons for war, furbish up your Swords, Rapiers and all other piercing weapons."[17]

This martial, epic tone surfaces throughout Johnson's narrative. Before departing for the New World, Johnson's Puritans first have to confront Satan in the shape of Papists and Antinomian sectarians.[18] Once at sea, they engage in pitched battles with the devil. Soon after lifting anchor with her Puritan cargo destined for Massachusetts, the flagship *Arbella* is threatened by demon-induced storms. God, however, intervenes: "many of these people amazed finde such opposition in nature . . . [and grow sick and disenchanted] but he who is very sensible of his peoples infirmities, rebukes the winds and Seas for their sakes."[19] Fearing the arrival of the millennium, when he will be chained in hell, and "seeing how these resolved Souldiers of Christ in New England with indefatigable paines laboured, not only the finall ruine of Antichrist, in both, but also the advance of Christs Kingdom," Satan "sets upon a new way to stop (if it were possible) this worke of Reformation" by stimulating among the colonists the emergence of such sectarians as Gortenists, Familists, Seekers, Antinomians, Anabaptists, Arminians, Arians, and Formalists, whose "heads of Hydra" will fortunately be "cut off" by the "sharpe sword of the Word."[20]

But Satan had more than Protestant dissenters to threaten the survival of the New Israelites in the American Canaan, for his true minions were the

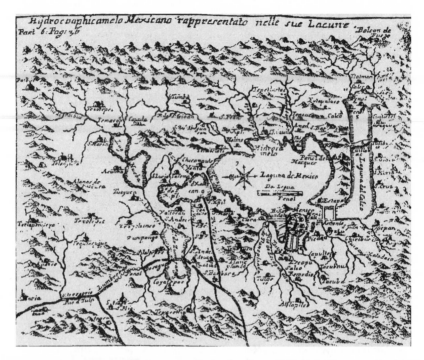

FIG. 1.5. The Beast of the Apocalypse represented in the lakes of the central valley of Mexico. From Gemelli Careri, *Giro del mondo* (Naples, 1699–1700). Courtesy of the John Carter Brown Library, Brown University, Providence, R.I. The image rather vividly captures Edward Johnson's claim that the American landscape itself was one of four allies of Satan in the New World (the others being the Amerindians, ocean storms, and Protestant dissenters). Gemelli Careri was an Italian traveler who visited Mexico in the 1690s on the last leg of a trip that also took him to Siam, China, and Japan. In Mexico, he was given this map representing the drainage system of the central valley at the time of the European arrival. The rivers in the valley drained into a collection of small and large lakes, one of which, the Lake of Mexico, often flooded Tenochtitlán, the Aztec capital. Early seventeenth-century Flemish civil engineers drew the map while developing a system to open sluices through the surrounding mountains to dry the valley and thus end Mexico City's periodic floods. Later in the century, Creole Mexican scholars concluded that this hydrographic map of the valley demonstrated beyond reasonable doubt that Satan himself had carved out the Mexican landscape: the rivers draining into the upper end of Lake "Calco" (Chalco) represented the horns of the beast; the elongated Lake Calco its neck; the round lake of Mexico, the beast's belly; the rivers "San Juan," "Escoputulco," and "Taneplanda," its legs and claws; and the rivers of "St. Gioan" and "Papalo," its wings. In confirmation of this view of Mexico's alliance with Satan as revealed in the basin's drainage system, Creole scholars offered Careri cabalistic readings of the names of the ten Aztec monarchs from "Acamapichtli" to "Quauhtimoc" (Cuauhtemoc), the combined numerical value of which added up to 666, the number of the Beast.

Amerindians. Thus the Puritans first face the "Tarratines," who, like demons devoted to dismembering bodies in hell, would "eat such Men as they caught alive, tying them to a Tree, and gnawing their flesh by peece-meals off their Bones."[21] However, the Puritans' most formidable Amerindian enemies were the Pequot, who, like the Tarratines, "feasted [on] their corps in a ravening manner." War broke out between the settlers and the Pequot in 1636–37. The quarrel, Johnson thought, was "as antient as Adams time, propagated from that old enmity betweene the Seede of the Woman, and the Seed of the Serpent, who was the grand signor of this war."[22] Clearly, the Pequot were "not onley men, but Devils; for surely [Satan] was more then ordinaryly present with this Indian army."[23] According to Johnson, the most threatening enemies among the Pequot were their shamans, who were capable of manipulating nature and producing "strange things, with the help of Satan."[24]

Satan, Johnson argued, had the Puritans completely surrounded on the American battlefield. To the one side (the right), he had aligned "the damnable Doctrines" of the Antinomians, "as so many dreadful engines set by Satan to intrap poore soules." In front of the Puritan troops, Satan had positioned the "barbarous and bloudy people called *Peaquods*." In the rear, the ocean, the devil had demons setting off tempests so as to cut off any possible route of escape. Finally, to the other side of the settlers (the left), Satan had placed the "Desert and terrible Wildernesse" of America.[25] Along with storms at sea, Dissenters, and satanic attacks by the Amerindians, the very landscape itself was allied with the devil in the struggle to uproot the settlers (see fig. 1.5).[26]

Why then would anyone "passe the pretious Ocean and hazard thy person in battell against thousands of Malignant Enemies there?"[27] Johnson answered that question by simply pointing to "wonder-working providence," for in the epic battle against Satan, God was on the side of the settlers. To keep the Puritans from starving and drowning, God sends rain in time of drought and calms the storms unleashed by Satan at sea. In short, for every obstacle thrown by Satan in the Puritans' way, God steps in to rescue the settlers from hardship. This providential logic is often carried to extremes. In Johnson's scheme, famines and plagues wreaking havoc among the Amerindians appear as God's means to clear the land for the Puritans to enjoy.[28]

The epic element in Johnson's history far outdoes that in Villagómez's pastoral letters. Whereas Villagómez's heroes are anonymous *visitadores* wielding the Cross as sword and swearing by Christ, Johnson's heroes far surpass Hercules, Aeneas, and Ulysses. Unlike these classical heroes, who gave in to the temptations the flesh, the Puritan warriors do not pay attention to the "pleasant embraces . . . and syren songs" of the "lady of Delights." "Such Souldiers of Christs, whose aymes are elevated by [God]," Johnson concluded, "[are] many Millions above that brave Warrier Ulysses."[29] John Winthrop, "eleven times governor" of New England, appears in Johnson's history as a knight armed with a sword leading the elect against Babylon.[30]

Even the crusading spirit supposedly typical of Iberian colonization makes its appearance in Johnson's narrative. In his account of the Pequot War, the Mohawks are transformed into a satanic enemy whom the Puritans must slay: the *Moor*-hawks.[31] Readers might be tempted to argue that Johnson was an oddity, so disoriented and lost in a crusading world of his own as to find Moors in New England. But he was not alone. Take, for example, the case of the anonymous account of the history of King Philip's War (1675–76) titled *News from New England* (1676). After sketching a satanic portrayal of the Amerindians, the author coolly adds the following entry to his tally of the dead in battle: "At Woodcock 10 miles from Secouch on the 16th May was a little Skirmage betwixt the *Moors* and Christians, wherein there was of the later three slain and two wounded and only two Indians kild."[32] These examples seem to give the lie to the historiographical tradition that, since Prescott, has sought to exaggerate the cultural differences between Anglo-Protestant and Catholic-Iberian discourses of colonial expansion in the New World. It is clear that the Puritans were also willing to launch a *reconquista* against the devil in America to recover the continent for God.

While typical of their age, the ideas of Villagómez and Johnson confront us with mental structures that jar our modern sensibilities, for theirs was a world in which demons roamed the earth unleashing tempests and possessing entire peoples.[33] By the mid seventeenth century, colonists of European descent were absolutely certain of the overwhelming presence of demons in the New World. Satan appeared to the settlers as a tyrannical lord, with castles and ramparts all over America, whose subjects were willing to go down fighting to the last man (see fig. 1.6).

After having lorded it over the continent for centuries, Satan was suddenly facing an unexpected onslaught by a determined vanguard of Christian knights. For the settlers, colonization was an ongoing epic battle. In the world of the Europeans, demons were real, everyday physical forces, not figments of the imagination or metaphors standing for the hardships of colonization, as we might condescendingly be prone to assume.[34] Plainly put, in the eyes of European settlers, colonization was an act of forcefully

FIG. 1.6. Luis de Riaños, *The Road to Hell* (ca. 1618–26). Church of Andahuailillas, Department of Cuzco, Peru. Taken from José de Mesa and Teresa Gisbert, *Historia de la pintura cuzqueña*, 2: 399. The mural is a copy of an engraving by Jeronimus Wierix (1553–1619) illustrating Psalm 106 (on the idolatrous corruption of the nation of Israel among the Canaanites). Notice that the road to hell leads to a fortified castle with a moat, drawbridge, and archers.

expelling demons from the land. Whether it was by defeating external plots devised by Satan to weaken colonial settlements (by means of, say, pirates, heretics, indigenous religious revivals, frontier wars, imperial policies seeking to weaken colonial autonomy, etc.) or by physically casting out demons using charms such as crosses (Catholics/Anglicans) or Bibles (Puritans), one way that Europeans saw colonization was as an ongoing battle against the devil. This simple yet powerful insight has often been assumed, but rarely adequately explored, for historians have focused rather on elucidating the European legal discourses of territorial possession.

Historians have been only partially right to argue that the British were more "modern" than the Spaniards when justifying territorial possession. It is now common to maintain that the British deployed Lockean theories of property: land and objects belonged to those who had transformed them through labor. Since the British colonists did not find traces of "labor" in the New World, they considered the lands of the natives empty and ripe for the picking. Spaniards, on the other hand, were more "medieval." They justified territorial possession by claiming that the pope had *dominium* and *imperium* over pagan territories. As the pope had transferred that sovereignty to the Spanish kings, the latters' vassals felt entitled to the newfound lands.[35] This distinction not only blurs important chronological differences (Puritan colonization was launched some 150 years after the Spaniards first arrived in the New World), it also leaves out the more important biblical foundations of European colonial expansion. For Puritans and Catholics alike, colonization was an act foreordained by God, prefigured in the trials of the Israelites in Canaan. Just as the Israelites had fought against the stiff resistance of Satan's minions, the Philistines, Puritans, and Spanish clerics felt entitled to take over America by force, battling their way into a continent infested by demons. Ultimately, the objective of both religious communities became to transform the "wilderness" into blossoming spiritual "plantations."

This common demonological discourse is the subject of this book. But before plunging into it, a question needs to be answered: Why specifically compare the Puritans of New England, rather than some other group in British America, to the Spanish Catholics? Given that Jack Greene has demonstrated that New England's politics, culture, and economy were not representative of the British American experience, it would appear to make more sense to study the ideologies of colonization in the middle and southern British American colonies.[36] In fact, as the work of Edward L. Bond suggests, the crusading discourse of colonization as an epic battle against the devil seems to have run as deeply in seventeenth-century Virginia as it did in

Puritan New England.[37] But the findings of scholars like Greene have not yet dislodged the Puritans from the public imagination as the quintessentially "American" colonists. This reason alone justifies my choice: I want to reach and challenge a wide audience. Furthermore, there is the issue of sources. Simply put, Puritans left behind a far larger cache of primary sources than other English colonists. I have nevertheless not completely overlooked other British colonies, particularly Virginia.

At first sight, positing resemblances between the Puritan and Spanish clergies makes little sense, for the literature on the Reformation has familiarized us only with the differences. The Puritans were followers of John Calvin (1509–64), whereas the Spaniards were staunch defenders of the pope, leaders of the Counter-Reformation. These two communities therefore developed very different views of God, salvation, Church organization, and conversion. As followers of Calvin, for example, the Puritans believed that God was an almighty sovereign whose plans for humanity were inscrutable. In their view of things, Catholics, who thought that it was up to them to work out their own salvation (by either practicing virtues or praying to God), were deluded. Catholics had a ridiculous view of God as a petty merchant whose will could be bought (by buying indulgences, for example) or bent at will (through confession and prayers). According to the Puritans, however, salvation was a preordained act of God, and nothing humans did could change the outcome. Catholics had deviated from the original message of God as revealed in the Old and New Testaments. Over the centuries, Catholics had added institutions and ceremonies never mentioned in the Bible. The Puritans in fact owed their name to their efforts to "purify" the Church of these inventions and live according to the religious, social, and political institutions found in the Bible. For the Puritans, Catholic "inventions" were not really products of the human imagination but demonic deceptions: Counter-Reformation Spain stood for the Antichrist.[38]

These theological differences manifested themselves concretely in the ways these two religious communities approached colonization. Spanish Catholics, for example, had a more inclusive idea of Church membership, along with a more hierarchical understanding of how to communicate with God. Spaniards therefore approached conversion by demanding that indigenous peoples conform to certain rituals and external behaviors, but allowed great variations in practice. This attitude toward conversion allowed for the multiplication of micro-Catholicisms all across the empire. The Puritans, however, saw things differently. For them, conversion implied God's election: the individual had to be touched by God's grace after protracted "preparation." God acted like a seal on the wax of the body and soul (justi-fication), transforming them forever (sanctification). To belong to a Puritan Church, individuals needed to prove, through protracted interviews and testimonials (which could last several months), that they had in fact been touched by the grace of God. When the Puritans arrived in the New World, they instituted such strict rules of conversion that not even the children of the Church elders were guaranteed membership. Although the Puritans did seek to convert Amerindians to hasten the arrival of the millennium, in practice native converts were few and far between.[39] In short, whereas by the seventeenth century, there were thousands, if not millions, of Amerindians in Spanish America practicing their own versions of Catholicism, only a handful of Amerindians in New England could bear witness to the grace of God.

It is clear that there were important differences separating the Puritans from the Spanish Americans. But there were also significant resemblances, and the scholarship on the Atlantic world has paid little attention to them, because it has imagined that world in largely national terms. In the pages that follow, I explore the discourse of demonology and spiritual gardening and argue that British American Puritans and Spanish American Catholics in fact saw the world of colonization in remarkably similar terms.

But before plunging into the substance of this book, let me provide some clarifications about my approach. Although Europeans had been confronting Satan for millennia and thought that demons hovered over the entire world, their battle with them in the New World was thought to be qualitatively dif-ferent. It was not that the New World was afflicted with more demons than Eurasia. Europeans believed that there were millions of good angels and bad angels, organized as armies, all over the world. The problem was one of entrenchment. The devil and his minions had exercised uncontested sover-eignty over the New World for 1,500 years, ever since Satan took a group of Scythians, his own elect, to colonize the empty land that was America right after or around the time the Gospel began to spread in Eurasia. Thus the devil had had time to build "fortifications" in the New World and set deep roots both in the landscape and among the people. The Europeans therefore battled an external enemy, not only the devil within, whom they knew well. Suffering, sin, temptation, and possession had long been considered mani-festations of demonic power laying siege to the individual soul. To be sure, the battle to overcome satanic temptation and to avoid sin would continue in the New World, and Satan's attacks on the individual soul, often mani-fested themselves as outright external physical aggression, especially when he targeted females.[40] It is also true that for the Puritans, as Richard Slotkin has noticed, fears of satanic external enemies, particularly Amerindians and the wilderness, were simply projections of dark Calvinist views of the inner soul: rotten, postlapsarian human nature.[41] The struggle of individual souls to achieve sanctity or salvation in the Indies is partly the focus of this book, especially as both Puritans and Iberians sought to transform their souls and the colonies into spiritual gardens. Yet I am also concerned with the battles that pitted Europeans against powerful "external" enemies — both human and nonhuman — dedicated to destroying the polity: storms, earthquakes, epidemics, pirates, foreign enemies, heretics, witches, imperial bureaucrats, Amerindians, and African slaves.

It has been my priority throughout to reconstruct the logical structure, the grammar, of a discourse. Each of the myriad sources I discuss emerged in unique social and political contexts and was devised to persuade particular audiences and to address particular agendas. I have not sought to reconstruct these various contexts. Rather than historicizing each source, I have sought to reconstruct a worldview (of demonology as it pertains to colonization). At every turn, however, I have avoided anachronistic, condescending readings of the past. Like Brad S. Gregory, who has masterfully reconstructed the alien world of martyrdom among early modern Christian communities (Protestant, Anabaptist, and Catholic), marked by a willingness to kill and to be killed that offends our modern views of toleration and psychological "normality," I seek to reconstruct a worldview that is equally violent, alien, and offensive to our modern sense of what is physically possible.[42]

Another important element to keep in mind while reading this book is that the discourses of demonology and gardening were only two of many in the Atlantic bazaar of ideas.[43] I am aware that I deal mostly with the ideas of the learned (clergy and laity). We should not, however, dismiss the study of the discourse I have identified on account of its being both elite and one of many. By the end of this book, it will be clear, I hope, that demonology and gardening are discourses scholars need to treat seriously if we want to gain a deeper understanding of early modern European colonialism.

Third, I am aware that using categories such as "Iberians" and "Puritans" is a reductive stance toward these historical actors. There were to be sure many strands within the so-called orthodox Puritan tradition (to say nothing of the variations at the fringes of this Reformed movement), and that a similarly mind-boggling array of doctrinal positions can easily be discerned in the "Iberian" sources.[44] In the case of demonology, one could, for example, cite the debate over toleration between the "Puritans" Roger Williams (1604?–1683) and John Cotton (1584–1652) in the 1630s in Massachusetts. Williams argued that heretics were weeds in the garden of the Church, but that the Bible did not authorize their being rooted out. Moreover, Williams argued that the weapons with which to battle the devil were not physical but spiritual. Thus, according to Williams, toleration was the orthodox position to take. John Cotton, on the other hand, found biblical passages that allowed him to claim the opposite, namely, that heretics were both weeds to be cleared from the enclosed garden of the Church and agents of Satan to be fended off physically, not spiritually.[45] This controversy alone shows that there were important differences when it came to the thinking of the devil as an external enemy of the New England polity. It should be noticed, however, that Williams was so far outside the pale that he was excommunicated. When it came to the threat represented by Satan as enemy of the polity, there was indeed a "Puritan" orthodoxy. This is also true of all the other groups discussed in this book.

Fourth, I assume that the satanization of the American continent gained momentum in the seventeenth century. Most of the sources I use in this book originated in this period. Many explanations have been offered as to why Europeans grew more fearful of the devil in the seventeenth century. John Bossy, Fernando Cervantes, and Stuart Clark have argued that the Reformation altered the conception of sin. As morality came to be organized around the Ten Commandments, rather than around the cardinal virtues (the avoidance of social sins), the Deuteronomic sanction against false worship turned the triad "heresy, idolatry, and witchcraft" into a continuum of crimes against religion. Such focus heightened fears of the power of Satan. Cervantes and Clark have also argued that the rise of nominalism contributed to bolstering the image of a powerful deity ruling over a cosmos unrestrained by natural laws. Belief in the preternatural and the supernatural, therefore, gained ground. It should be noticed that the preternatural was not only the realm of the occult and marvels but also the domain of the devil.[46]

Finally, I rely throughout on images as primary sources. Images are often used by historians simply as illustrations to enliven their narratives. My intention has been rather to present images as additional evidence to written sources. Many of the images therefore have long captions and should be read as extended footnotes. In some cases, images are the sole extant source available to elucidate an argument. It will become obvious that with a few exceptions most of the images discussed in this book are from the Iberian world. This imbalance would seem to point to a major difference between

Spanish and British America, the former allegedly a culture that privileged the visual and the oral and the latter one that relied on the printed word. But such dichotomies oversimplify the past. It is not only that Spanish America enjoyed a thriving printing industry but also that British America possessed lively scribal and oral cultures, particularly in the Chesapeake. More important, the mental re-creation of biblical imagery was central to Puritan piety, meditation, and prayer. Extant Puritan sermons are laced with striking visual imagery, remarkably similar to the images discussed in this book.[47]

I am concerned both with changes over time and with the persistence of the discourse of demonology and colonization. The devil as an external enemy changed strategies over time. In the case of the Spanish American sources I study, Amerindians were originally seen as Satan's most powerful allies in the New World, but once the colonial regime was established in places like Mexico and Peru, the main demonic enemy became somebody else. In the case of the Spiritual Franciscans in Mexico, the twelve "apostles" arrived loaded with three centuries of accumulated Joachimite apocalyptic predictions in a ruined Tenochtitlán. The friars thought that the preaching of the Gospel to hitherto unknown peoples whom the devil held in bondage was the long-anticipated sign of the beginning of the millennium. To them, the Aztecs were Satan's elect. Satan had long been known for his parodies of God. Over the course of the Middle Ages, it was increasingly believed that the Antichrist was an exact inverted replica of Christ: a false prophet, performer of miracles, bound to have his own Annunciation and Resurrection. In Mexico, the Franciscans found no Antichrist but Satan's ultimate mockery of God, namely, a society whose history and institutions seemed to be an inverted mirror image of those of the Israelites. According to the Franciscans, Satan had picked the Aztecs to recapitulate each and every one of the episodes of the history of the Israelites: exodus to a Promised Land, settlement amid Canaanites, David- and Solomon-like monarchies, the building of a temple, and prophecies of doom and imminent destruction. Lucifer's mockery of the Eucharist and the miracle of transubstantiation, on the other hand, took place every week on the steps of the temple of Huitzilopochtli, where the bodies and hearts of sacrificed warriors were served to the masses to enjoy as morsels. Not surprisingly, the Franciscans regarded Hernán Cortés (1485–1547) as a providential figure, a "General of Christ" who had waged the first battle in the epic struggle to hasten the millennium. Franciscans saw colonization as a spiritual holy war and built their massive mission compounds in central Mexico with large crenellated walls as symbolic battlements against the devil (the Augustinians, preaching to the Otomies in Ixmiquilpan, Hidalgo, and seeking to represent the ongoing spiritual struggles between good and evil, had murals of bloody battles between their new Otomi charges and their neighbors, the savage, demonic Chichimecs, including beheadings, painted in the very mission church itself). Yet all these compounds were also built with the layout of the New Jerusalem in mind (see fig. 1.7). This very millenarian narrative allowed these Franciscans to embrace the natives as God's new elect. In creating his inverted mirror image of the Church of Israel, Satan had chosen the Aztecs for their single-minded devotion and piety. Seeking to outshine the priestly legislation of Moses' Leviticus, Satan selected a people whose willingness to abide by disciplinary rules of penance and sacrifice far outdid those of the average Christian. These were precisely the virtues that the early Franciscans needed to create a New Jerusalem in the Indies: if properly catechized, the natives could easily become large communities of saints. Thus the Franciscan Toribio de Benavante, aka Motolinía (1482?–1569), maintained in his *Historia de los Indios de Nueva España* (ca. 1550) that the natives were so pious, so Spartan in their needs, so detached from the pursuit of wealth, so meek, humble, and willing to endure suffering and sacrifice that they did not have "any hindrance that would keep them from reaching heaven, unlike the many obstacles we Spaniards have and that keep us down."[48] Curiously, once the friars embraced the natives as the ideal pliable clay with which to build the Church of the millennium, and once the friars began to vie with the settlers for control of the bodies (not the souls) of the natives, the Franciscans became more prone to see the wiles of Satan in the New World manifested in the actions of the very descendants of the "General of Christ," the lay settlers. Fray Juan de Zumárraga (1468–1548), a Franciscan and first archbishop of Mexico, denounced *encomenderos* as "repulsive and disgusting" non-Christians, who gave out an "evil smell" that contrasted dramatically with the "heavenly smell of these poor Indians."[49] The Franciscans were not alone. Bartolomé de las Casas (1474–1566) tirelessly argued that conquistadors were demons and the colonial regime was hell. By the end of the sixteenth century, as the Spanish Crown sought to strengthen the secular Church (clergy not belonging to religious orders) and curtail the hegemony the religious orders had over spiritual ministration to the Amerindians, the Franciscans most likely found Satan incarnated in the ecclesiastical establishment.[50]

In the following chapters, it will become clear that the main satanic enemy of both the Iberians and the English in the New World was a moving target, constantly shifting according to the party involved and the circumstances. The Mexican Creoles, I argue, passionately embraced the cult of

FIG. 1.7. "Emblem of things the friars do in the Indies [*tipus eorum que frates faciunt in Novo Indiarum Orbe*]" from Diego Valadés, *Rhetorica christiana* (1579). Courtesy of the John Carter Brown Library, Brown University, Providence, R.I. Led by Martin Valencia and St. Francis himself, twelve Franciscans carry the Holy

(continued)

Our Lady of Guadalupe because they found in their typological readings of the image a fulfillment of Revelation 12:7–9, that is, of battles waged between the Dragon and the archangel Michael in heaven. This text, they thought, was a prophecy of the conquest of the Aztecs by Cortés. But the Creoles were even more fascinated by Revelation 12:13–17, for these passages described the battles of the Dragon against the Woman of the Apocalypse and her descendants on earth. According to the Creole clergy, in Revelation, St. John had anticipated the sufferings of the heirs of the conquistadors in America at the hands of satanic peninsular upstarts. Spanish American Creoles liked to imagine the peninsular newcomers (including *conversos*, merchants, and centralizing Crown officers) as Satan's allies.

Peninsulars, in turn, demonized the Creoles, presenting them as corrupt, degenerate Amerindians. More important, peninsulars identified the battles against Satan in the New World as part of a much larger geopolitical

FIG. 1.7 *(continued from previous page)*
Roman Church into the New World for the first time ("primi sanctae romane aeclesie [*sic*] in novo indiarum orbe portatores"). The Lord has foreordained their task in Genesis 28:14–15: "And thy seed shall be as the dust of the earth, and thou shalt spread abroad to the west, and to the east, and to the north, and to the south . . . And, behold, I am with thee, and will keep thee in all places whither thou goest" (dilatarebis ad orientem, occidentem, septentrionem, ac meridiem et ero custos tuus et tuorum). The Church the twelve Franciscans carry is inhabited by the Holy Spirit ("spiritus santus abitat in ea"), corresponding to the millennial, third spiritual age of Joachim de Fiore. The Church in the Novo Indiarum Orbe is a walled garden, a New Jerusalem: its walls rest on twelve stone foundations bearing the names of the twelve apostles of the Lamb (Rev. 21:14) (the twelve small rectangles scattered on the ground seem to be both the tombs of the original Franciscan apostles and the stone foundations of the new millennial Church). The Holy Spirit that descends from the throne of God fertilizes a path of trees where the infirm (*infirmi*) are taken to be healed. The trees in the Franciscan compound thus seem to correspond to the Trees of Life of the New Jerusalem whose leaves are "used as medicine to heal the nations" (Rev. 22:2). In this New Jerusalem, the friars mete out justice, bury the dead, perform the sacraments (confession, communion, last rights, baptism, matrimony, penance, and the Eucharist), and teach the Indians music and to read and write. The Gospel is also taught through the use of images. Notice, however, that besides books and images, the friars use Nature, in the form of a tree, to instruct their charges in doctrine (*examen matrimonii*). On the millennial architecture in the mission compounds built by Franciscans, Augustinians, and Dominicans in sixteenth-century Mexico, see Jaime Lara (2004) and Samuel Edgerton (2001).

struggle pitting God against Lucifer. Pedro Calderón de la Barca's 1651 *auto sacramental* (a theatrical genre performed during Corpus Christi) *La semilla y la cizaña* (The Wheat and the Tares) typifies the attitude of Spanish intellectuals in Madrid. Calderón interprets Matthew 13 as a prefiguration of the fate of the Gospel in the four continents (each standing for a type of soil) and has Christ dressed as a farmer and the devil as a weed. Seeking to prevent the seed planted by Christ from ever flourishing with the help of theatrical characters clad like demons/Furies representing hurricanes (Cierzo [North Wind]), a swarm of locusts (Ira [Fury]), and fog (Niebla), the devil (Cizaña) stumbles upon characters that stand for each of the continents and their main religions. One of four continents where Christ the farmer plants seeds is "America" (with thorny soil, where seedlings are choked by weeds), who appears wearing a feather dress, riding an alligator, and accompanied by the lackadaisical "Idolatry." The other three are "Asia" (rocky soil, where some plants grow without deep roots), who appears dressed as a Jew, riding an elephant, and under the supervision of "Judaism"; "Africa" (a footpath, where seeds are easily picked up by birds), who appears dressed as a Moor, riding a lion, and overseen by "Paganism"; and "Europe" (good soil, where seed multiplies hundredfold), who appears dressed like a Roman, riding a bull, and led by "Gentilism." As the play unfolds, the devil successfully manages to kill the harvest everywhere, except in Europe. Tellingly, the devil assigns a continent to each Fury: "Cierzo" uproots the plants of Asia, "Ira" picks up the seeds of Africa, and "Niebla" seeks to kill off the harvest in Europe, sowing *neguilla* (869), the corncockle, *Agrostemma githago*, a noxious weed that grows along with wheat, in the lands where Protestantism is born. The devil himself, Cizaña, is in charge of America and has beautiful-looking fields appear; on closer inspection, however, the fields of flowers turn out to be weeds. Two things are clear from Calderón's reading of Matthew 13. First, the struggle between God and Satan is for control of the entire earth. Second, America is the continent that most fully belongs to the devil, despite its misleading paradisiacal looks. Clearly, the play exemplifies the early modern Spanish demonological global imagination. The satanic epic in the New World reveals these global sensibilities particularly in the characters of the pirates and the Moors.[51]

Lope de Vega's *La Dragontea* (1598), an epic poem by another giant of the Spanish Golden Age, is representative of how the Spanish intelligentsia managed to cast the battles against Satan in the New World as episodes in a global struggle in which both Muslim pirates in the Mediterranean and English privateers in the Caribbean played their parts. As Milton would later do with the devil, Lope transforms Francis Drake (1542–96) into a satanic hero worthy of admiration: Draco, the very Dragon of the Apocalypse (fig. 1.8). Drake is a creature of Satan who unsuccessfully wreaks havoc in Panama and the Caribbean, seeking to weaken the Spanish empire in the same way that Muslim Barbary corsairs with names like "Chafer, Fuchel, Mamifali, and Morato" are doing in the Mediterranean (1.23). Eventually, the satanic hero dies, after having been unable to capture Nombre de Dios (God's Name), the strategic port in Panama where silver from Peru was accumulated to be sent back to Spain. Having presided over the death of the Antichrist himself, Philip III turns out to be a harbinger of the millennium, free now to crush the Muslim corsairs (10.689–91, 695, 719–32).[52] The 1711 epic poem *Vida de Santa Rosa de Lima* (Life of St. Rose of Lima) by Luis Antonio de Oviedo y Herrera (1636–1717) is also representative of how Satan was thought to operate globally, mobilizing not only earthquakes and Amerindians but also Protestant pirates. In this, the Peruvian Santa Rosa of Lima (1586–1617) is presented as a godly heroine, who, to save Lima from destruction, fights great preternatural battles against earthquakes induced by Lucifer, calls by Yupanqui (Lucifer's Inca ally in the poem) for the Amerindians of Peru to rebel and for the Araucanians to join in Dutch attacks, and Protestant pirates' raids.[53] Demons fly all over the world lining up English, Dutch, and Amerindian allies to expel the Iberians.[54]

Clearly, the Amerindians were not the only allies of the devil in the New World. In fact, the first great battle pitting the Inquisition against the devil in Peru, for example, did not involve the natives but prominent Spanish religious figures in Quito, Lima, Cusco, and Potosí. In 1572, the newly created Inquisition of Lima arrested a group of friars led by the prestigious Dominican theologian Francisco de la Cruz for having communicated with demons through séances that masqueraded as meetings to exorcise the maiden María Pizarro. A trial-investigation that lasted six years forced the provincial of the Dominicans to flee, caused the death in prison of the Dominican Pedro Toro, and led in 1578 to the burning at the stake of de la Cruz in an auto-da-fé that also included others parading in penitential garb. The drama began when a group of learned Jesuits, Theatines, and Dominicans, who eventually spread all over the viceroyalty, sought to expel the demons possessing María. The clergy, however, came across evidence that María was also visited by good spirits of saints and archangels. The archangel Gabriel liked to chat with de la Cruz in particular, for the latter was a magus who cast horoscopes and dabbled with talismans. Soon the archangel handed down to the Dominican amulets to exorcise demons and

FIG. 1.8. "Tandem aquila vincit" (The Eagle Wins at Last) from Lope de Vega, *La Dragontea* (1598). Lope de Vega casts Francis Drake as the Beast of the Apocalypse, which is finally slain by the archangel Michael/Philip II. God protects the Habsburg, enabling him to "trample down lions and poisonous snakes ... to crush fierce lions and serpents under your feet [*conculcabis leonem et draconem*]" (Vulg. Ps. 90). Engaged in a global battle against the forces of God, Lucifer finds allies not only among the Indians but also among Protestant and Moorish pirates.

to protect the wearer from committing sins. The archangel also gave de la Cruz a blueprint for a new millenarian Church in the Indies. Suddenly, the former leading orthodox theologian found himself advocating the end of celibacy for priests; the spread of polygamy among the laity; the uselessness of the sacrament of confession and inoffensiveness of idolatry among the Amerindians; the restitution of the feudal rights that Charles V had taken away from the conquistadors and their heirs in the mid sixteenth century; the impending collapse of the corrupt Church of Rome; and the restoration in the New World of the ancient Israelite Church. De la Cruz himself would become the new David, head of both the state and the Church, pope and emperor at the same time. The Inquisition insisted that the priests who communicated with the archangel Gabriel through María had failed to "discern" that the spirits dwelling in the young woman were all demons intent on engineering a coup in Peru against the new viceroy, Francisco de Toledo (r. 1569–81). The devil was determined to uproot the authority of Spain and the Catholic Church in the Indies, working this time through a group of influential priests led by the lascivious, self-aggrandizing de la Cruz, who turned out to be a satyr, tirelessly having sex with both pious women and men and impregnating hapless victims like María. The devil set no limits as to whom he recruited as allies to undermine the Catholic regime in the Indies.[55]

By the time the Puritans arrived in New England, the colonists of Spanish America had already drastically changed their perceptions of who were the preferred minions of the devil in the New World. It is very revealing that the Holy Office of the Inquisition was set up in America in 1571 by Philip II not to persecute Satan's followers among the Amerindians but to stem the demonic plots of *conversos* (falsely converted Jews), *alumbrados* (those whose emphasis on silent prayers and direct communication with God suspiciously resembled Lutheran notions of grace), and witches, blasphemers, and sexual offenders within the "Hispanic" urban communities. Although inquisitors in the Indies did find their share of *conversos* and *alumbrados* to prosecute and punish, they acted on the assumption that the devil privileged the sins of promiscuity, blasphemy, and petty witchcraft over all others in the New World.[56] It is worth mentioning, however, that in the Spanish empire, by and large, witches were not seen as devil worshippers akin to learned necromancers like de la Cruz, that is to say, as members of a threatening heretical sect, but rather as traditional practitioners of amorous and harming spells. In the minds of the inquisitors, bigamy, sodomy, blasphemy, and non-learned witchcraft were more prevalent in the New World due to the contaminating influences of Native Americans and Africans.[57] The devil operated in the New World by eroding the racial and social hierarchies of the well-ordered polity that the Spanish state had sought to establish, causing the pious to be easily trapped.

Mestizaje—interbreeding—was perceived as one of the weapons deployed by the devil to undermine the spread of Christianity in America. The art of determining whether the spirits that visited the expanding communities of mystics among hermits, friars, nuns, and *beatas* (beguines) in the Indies were godly or satanic, for example, was linked to the threat of *mestizaje*.[58] Besides the traditional emphasis on probing the theological soundness of women's visions, always inherently suspect, inquisitors in the Indies were moved to evaluate not only the racial and social status of the alleged mystics themselves but that of their followers and confessors as well. Those who experienced the typical preternatural manifestations of mystics (i.e., visions, dreams, stigmata, levitation, torturing by demons, and bilocation) and whose origins or relations were closest to the poor, *castas*, Amerindians, and blacks became immediately suspected of being agents of the devil, not God.[59] Blacks and mulattoes in particular were considered potential allies of the devil. On May 2, 1612, for example, on the grounds that they had long been planning an uprising, 35 blacks and mulattoes were hanged in Mexico City, and their bodies were either quartered or decapitated. The planned uprising was deemed part of a larger strategy by Satan to wreak havoc. Reportedly groups of urban blacks and mulattoes seeking to create an "African monarchy" would poison and kill all male Spaniards and keep Spanish women and Amerindians as slaves. According to one account, the plot had been concocted by an old black slave, Sebastian, and his disciples: a band of "witches" and "sorcerers," masters of the "black arts."[60]

It is clear that the process of colonization in Spanish America unfolded amid evidence of ongoing demonic threats carried out by all sorts of enemies, including frontier Amerindians, pirates, heretics, false mystics, and African slaves. And the multipronged attack by the devil caused the colonists to develop a siege mentality. Evidence of this siege mentality also surfaces in the Protestant versions of the satanic epic, particularly in Puritan ones.

English Protestants first found the devil in America among the Spaniards, not the Amerindians. Later, however, the satanic epic, as originally conceived by the Spaniards, was embraced by the Protestants. The satanic epic was a literary tradition that first evolved in Portuguese and Spanish America. It lionized Iberian colonization as a battle that pitted Catholic heroes against Satan's minions, the Amerindians, and against Leviathan in the sea. Although the trope of the satanic epic was quickly adopted all over Europe, Protestants (especially the Dutch) first organized their epic narratives around battles pitting Protestant heroes against satanic Spaniards.[61] In Elizabethan England, the figure of the privateer, a pillaging soldier of fortune who, like the Spanish conquistador, sought treasure and entry into the ranks of the grandees, became the equivalent of the Spanish conquistador battling Satan. Ruthless, plundering, lowly hidalgos like Francis Drake appeared in numerous satanic epics as heroes bleeding the Spanish Antichrist white.[62]

But by the time of the arrival of the Puritans in the New World, the English had begun to see Amerindians, not the Spanish, as the main ally of the Devil in the New World. This shift coincided with the 1622 slaughter of settlers in Virginia and the Pequot War (1637), which dramatically changed English perceptions of the Amerindians; thereafter the natives became Satan's minions. Scholars like Joyce Chaplin and Karen Ordahl Kupperman have shown that Elizabethan sources originally tended to be respectful and even admiring of Native American societies, but later English views of the Amerindians in North America soured.[63] As Alfred A. Cave has persuasively demonstrated, demonology played a significant role in turning a petty squabble in the Connecticut River valley among the Dutch, English, Mohegan, Narragansett, and Pequot over access to pelts, wampum, and regional hegemony into a Manichean battle pitting the godly Puritans against Satan's minions, the Pequot. The view of the Pequot as demonic moved the Puritans to collect scalps and hands of enemy warriors as trophies and to regard burning Indian children and women alive as heroic.[64] Not surprisingly, the Puritan satanic epic came to resemble those first introduced by the Iberians. Spaniards, to be sure, did not lose their status as satanic agents. The narrative of the Spanish conquest as a demonic butchery was paradoxically kept firmly in mind as Puritans struggled to justify in writing their own barbarous acts against their newfound demonic enemies. As Jill Lepore has shown, Puritan narratives of King Philip's War (1675–76) were aimed at justifying unusual acts of cruelty by demonizing the Wampanoag and other Algonquian groups, all the while seeking to clear the Puritans of charges of Spanish-like demonic savagery.[65]

Approaching Puritan studies from the perspective of "siege" contributes to the larger historiography on Puritan views of the devil as an external enemy who threatened the polity. Richard Godbeer's and, more recently, Mary Beth Norton's studies of the Salem witchcraft outbreak have shown that the crisis can be explained only if we are willing to enlarge our vision of whom the Puritans considered their satanic enemies to be. Godbeer has argued that the Puritan laity brought witches to trial often but without much success. It was only in 1692 that the laity succeeded in having magistrates and ministers punish and even execute witches on a large scale (there were, to be sure, other isolated cases before). This unusual behavior of the Puritan clergy, Godbeer argues, can only be explained in the context of the siege mentality that began to develop in Essex County in the wake of King Philip's War. For two decades, Puritans experienced all sorts of setbacks, including epidemics, loss of political autonomy vis-à-vis the English Crown, Quaker encroachment, failed campaigns against the French, and constant frontier warfare with the natives. Puritan magistrates, for the first time, were willing to see Satan as an enemy not only working within the soul but also harassing the community from without. Thus the clergy during the Salem crisis found themselves willing to punish as demonic anybody deemed to be an outsider (spinsters with connections to Quakers and to the Amerindian frontier).[66] Norton has more recently made a similar argument. According to Norton, Salem's witches were deemed by Puritans to be allies of the Amerindians or the French and thus Satan's minions in the larger struggle for control of the northeastern frontier.[67]

This Puritan siege mentality was part and parcel of who the Puritans were. It was precisely this siege mentality that rendered the Puritans so uncompromising in their negotiations with the Pequot, leading to the war of 1637, which happened in the context of the Antinomian controversy (in which Anne Hutchinson and her followers were seen as demonic agents) and in the wake of attempts at court, led by Sir Ferdinando Gorges, to take the colony's charter away. The Puritans read these three events as part of a demonic plot to oust them from America.[68] The Puritan version of the satanic epic demonstrates that from the very beginning, Puritans saw themselves threatened by a Satan bent on attacking the polity through the agency of Spaniards, storms, the wilderness, Amerindians, heretics, witches, and royal bureaucrats.

The study of the structure and evolving nature of the satanic epic shows that despite national (Spanish-English) and confessional (Catholic-Protestant) differences, variances in the genre were only superficial. One important goal of this book is to demonstrate the common religious world informing all European colonial discourses, particularly Spanish and English ones. Like John Bossy, I do not see the Reformation as a radical break with the medieval past.[69] Despite the undeniable impact of the Reformation and the new dynastic early modern states in creating emerging national differences, early modern Europeans enjoyed a long history of shared cultural values, harkening back millennia.

The commonalities largely stemmed from a shared Christian culture, for Christianity from its inception had understood the history of the elect to be an ongoing spiritual and physical battle against hostile demonic enemies, including heretics, pagans, Jews, and Muslims, part of a cosmic confrontation between good and evil. Countless texts in the Old and New Testaments cast religious life in militaristic terms. Recent scholarship on the crusades, for example, has shown that they were not an aberrant variety of religious violence. Tradition has misleadingly reduced the crusades to five campaigns against Islam that took place between 1095 and 1229, aimed at recapturing Jerusalem, but we now know that the crusades were a peculiar form of religious piety, second only to monasticism, and that their violence was regarded as penitence and charity. War as pilgrimage was considered to be a form of sacrifice and atonement aimed at sympathetically re-creating Christ's suffering. Religious warriors who died in battle were regarded as martyrs, and their bodies became relics. All crusading warriors, not only those who belonged to the military-religious orders, took vows (by taking the Cross) and enjoyed the spiritual and temporal immunities of the clergy. More often than not, their enemies were pagans, heretics, and other Christians, not Muslims in the Holy Land. It was crusading Germanic military orders who in the thirteen and fourteenth centuries spearheaded the colonization and settlement of the Baltic region, battling pagan Slavs, allies of the devil. This peculiar form of organized religious violence slowly went out of style as the transnational power of the papacy dwindled, although plenty of "crusades" continued to be launched in the sixteenth and seventeenth centuries.[70]

Yet the biblical interpretations of conversion, salvation, and the history of the elect as epic spiritual and military confrontations between good and evil did not go away. From at least the fifteenth century on, holy wars ceased to be experienced as forms of monastic penitence, a way to earn clerical immunities. The new religious wars became wars pitting Israelites against Canaanites. The Hussites, the French, and the Spaniards, among many others, justified violence against external enemies in providential, eschatological terms, launching wars of national election to hasten the arrival of the millennium. As they did so, they imaginatively transformed their local landscapes into Holy Lands, sacred spaces, New Jerusalems.[71] This book contributes to the literature on medieval and early modern religious violence by demonstrating, through concrete examples, how the discourses of eschatology, providential-national election, and holy landscapes worked together to justify expansion and colonization. The devil, I argue, was the linchpin that in the early modern New World held all these discourses together.

I seek to highlight resemblances over differences. Even in areas where strong differences should be expected, we in fact find similarities. Take, for example, the case of the demonization of the Spaniards in the Protestant epic. As I have already mentioned, this inversion was in fact an idea first introduced by the Spaniards themselves. Take also the case of millenarian discourses of national election underpinning such discourses as the "City on the Hill" and the "Errand into the Wilderness." Creole patriots in Spanish America, for example, interpreted the miracle of Our Lady of Guadalupe in the same epic, providential, and apocalyptic terms that Elizabethans had used decades before to articulate a notion of national election, or that Puritans would use to voice their hope of creating the first Church of visible saints modeled solely on biblical examples. I also argue that given these similarities of the satanic epic, it would perhaps make sense to study John Milton's *Paradise Lost* (1667) with an eye to resemblances to the Iberian genre.

Sixteenth- and seventeenth-century Europeans were obsessed with demons, and they thought that the devil had made the New World his fiefdom. Chapter 2, "The Satanic Epic," shows that among both English Protestants (Anglicans and Puritans) and Iberian Catholics, colonization was understood to be an ongoing epic struggle to dislodge Satan from the continent. Both northern Protestant and southern Catholic settlers felt threatened and surrounded by the devil, who allegedly attacked their polities by unleashing storms, earthquakes, and epidemics, and by loosing heretics, tyrannical royal bureaucrats, foreign enemies, and Amerindians on them. I argue that we need to turn to the rich tradition of the New World Iberian "satanic epic" to make sense of the Puritan siege mentality that historians are now using to explain such events as the Pequot War, King Philip's War, and the Salem witchcraft crisis of 1692. This chapter demonstrates that a wider pan-American perspective can upset the most cherished national narratives of the United States, for I maintain that the Puritan colonization of New England was as much an epic, crusading act of *reconquista* (against the devil) as was the Spanish conquest. My emphasis on the pan-Atlantic history of the satanic epic also sheds light on possible and unacknowledged influences on Milton's *Paradise Lost* (1667). Finally, and so as not to exaggerate the centrality of Spanish America to any narrative of the Atlantic, I locate that most typical of colonial Mexican cultural phenomena, the exegesis of the miracle of Our Lady of Guadalupe, itself part of the narrative of the satanic epic, within Elizabethan apocalyptic traditions.

Chapter 3, "The Structure of a Shared Demonological Discourse," refines our understanding of the demonological in colonization by paying careful attention to the structure of this shared discourse. I argue that only by turning to Iberian sources can the structure of Puritan demonology be understood, and vice versa. I build on the expanding historiography on early modern demonology in both Europe and the New World to explore the building blocks of this shared discourse: the geographical mobility of demons; the geopolitical battles pitting God against Satan for full or partial control of the planet; the understanding of Amerindian ritual cannibalism as part of a larger theology of hell (i.e., dismemberment of bodies); the despotic, enslaving, feudal, and tyrannical rule of Satan; the collective demonic corruption of Amerindians as a manifestation of collective effeminate degeneration; colonization as an act of liberation; the mockery and inversion of Christian religious institutions introduced by Satan in the New World; the Amerindians as Satan's elect; and the use of "typological" readings of the Bible to structure narratives of colonization.

Chapter 3 also builds bridges linking the historiographies of colonial British and Spanish America to shed new light on old subjects. I use the well-developed historiography of Puritan typology (the understanding of colonization as a fulfillment of events prefigured in the Bible) to understand Iberian typological readings of colonization.[72] The Iberian clergy, for example, assumed that Satan had used typology to organize the history of the continent. Franciscans in particular maintained that Satan had sought to mimic the narrative of the Pentateuch in the New World. Thus, according to this view, if the Israelites were the chosen people of God, the Aztecs were Lucifer's elect. Franciscans like Juan de Torquemada transformed the history of the Aztecs into an inverted version of the history of the Israelites in the Old Testament. According to this Franciscan narrative, the Aztecs had experienced an exodus and had their own ark, tabernacle, and Moses. Upon arrival in their promised land, the Aztecs also experienced an age of subordination to "Canaanites," followed by an age of monarchies (the Aztecs had Davids and Solomons of their own, who built a temple) and an age of prophets. Finally, like the Israelites, the Aztecs saw their temple leveled and their capital destroyed by foreign powers. Even today, this is still the way historians narrate the history of the Aztecs: migration, settlement, subordination, monarchy and empire, and foreordained doom and collapse.

Chapter 4, "Demonology and Nature," explores how the discourse of demonology and colonization encouraged both demonological and providential perceptions of the landscape and nature. Again, I argue that to understand British America, one needs to turn to Spanish America, and vice versa. Despite all their differences, intellectuals in both the British and Iberian Atlantics saw Satan as enjoying control over the weather, plants, animals, and landscapes in the New World. Iberian demonological views of nature, therefore, should inform any interpretation of William Shakespeare's *The Tempest* (first performed in 1611, printed in 1623) as a colonial text. Finally, I argue that demonological views of nature and colonization encouraged a particular perception of the American landscape among Europeans: the New World often came to be seen as a false paradise that to be saved needed to be destroyed by Christian heroes. This epic and domineering attitude toward Nature informed early modern European forms of knowledge-gathering more generally.

Chapter 5, "Colonization as Spiritual Gardening," shows how the trope of gardening allowed both Puritan and Spanish clergies to imaginatively transform America from satanic continent to holy land. Both groups tapped into an age-old tradition of interpreting sanctification as an amorous liaison with God in a sealed garden. The Song of Songs informed the way both Puritans and Spaniards understood the growth of both the individual soul and the corporate Church. Both groups understood God to be a gardener and the soul and the Church to be a garden. The struggle of individuals and communities was to keep weeds out of the soul and the Church. Puritans and Spaniards were obsessed with keeping their gardens "hedged," safe from satanic attacks. Satan could attack the soul through sinful temptation or outright possession. But Satan was also an enemy who could strike from outside, battering and destroying the Church itself. Satan laid siege to both Spanish and Puritan colonies by unleashing tempests, earthquakes, epidemics, encroaching Crown bureaucrats, heretics, foreign enemies, and Amerindians. This chapter discusses how saints in Spanish America and New England strove to be flowers in the garden of the new Church. Both Catholics and Calvinists in the New World thought themselves ideally positioned to produce more and better flowers and gardens than their European brethren. Both groups sought to establish a New Jerusalem in the Indies by multiplying blossoming gardens: individual souls of outstanding piety and well-tended collective spiritual vineyards. Colonial saints in Spanish America took the names of flowers (St. Rose of Lima and St. Mariana, the Lily of Quito, to cite just two examples). Relics and the bodies of saints were thought to give off flowery smells. Spanish American colonial churches were designed as vineyards. Working within the tradition of biblical typology, the colonial Church itself was thought to be the antitype of the Garden of

Eden. Puritans had no relics, no cult of saints, and no holy spaces, yet they also used the trope of gardening promiscuously. This chapter thus suggests that although the Reformation and the rise of dynastic centralizing states introduced significant national and confessional differences, centuries of a shared medieval culture conferred uniformity onto most early modern European colonial experiences.

Chapter 6, "Toward a 'Pan-American' Atlantic," is historiographical. It seeks to explain why the literatures of the British and Spanish Atlantics have gone their separate ways. It puts the blame squarely on an ideological and scholarly tradition that has sought to present the United States and Latin America as two ontologically different spaces. The narrative of "Western" civilization has contributed to highlighting the differences rather than the resemblances. The political stakes in this exercise are huge. *Puritan Conquistadors* should be read as a reply to Samuel Huntington's influential *Who Are We? The Challenges to America's National Identity* (2004). A professor of political science at Harvard, Huntington is best known for his controversial *The Clash of Civilizations and the Remaking of World Order* (1996), in which he argues that the civilizational chasm that had long separated the Christian West from the Muslim East became so deep in the wake of the Cold War that conflict was inevitable. Huntington's blatant essentialism contributed to heightening the Western rhetoric of war, particularly in the wake of September 11, and his prophecies became self-fulfilling. Writing as a self-confessed patriot, Huntington has found a new enemy in *Who Are We?*: Hispanics belong culturally and linguistically to a radically different civilization, one that threatens America's unity and identity and undermines the Anglo-Protestant values and institutions upon which the United States has prospered. Views such as Huntington's are fueling the current political debate over Mexican illegal immigration. Hispanics in our midst are increasingly being portrayed as a threat to the integrity of the nation, a peril second only to "Arab terrorists." By showing the common roots of Spanish and British American discourses of colonization, I seek to cut Huntington's much vaunted culture of Anglo-Protestant exceptionalism down to size.

The Satanic Epic

The frontispiece to Juan de Castellanos's epic *Primera parte de las elegías de varones illustres de Indias* (Elegies for Illustrious Great Men of the Indies, Part One) (1589) is extraordinarily revealing (fig. 2.1). In it the conquest appears as the fulfillment of various biblical passages, an act of charity setting the natives free from the clutches of Satan. The image typifies the use of typology in the Spanish colonization of the New World. The faithful maiden Spain ("Hispania Virgo fidelis"), bearing the Cross and the Bible, slays the dragon Leviathan ("dan [Vulg., Dan. 14:26] io diruptus est draco"), which has prevented the crossing of the Atlantic. The dragon bites its own long tail, which encircles both the ocean and the two continents, and its Amerindian allies shoot arrows at Hispania, who stands on a shell in the middle of the ocean. Angels and the Holy Spirit descend on the New World. The Spanish king's coat of arms unites the two halves of the composition, in which the fauna and flora of the Old and New Worlds stand at opposite sides. The words around the coat of arms proclaim "Philip II, Catholic and pious king" as the "Defender of the Church over seas and lands" ("Super maria terrasque Eae [Ecclesiae] De[Defensor] Philip 2 Rex Catholicus atque pi[us]"). A crucified Christ stands on top of the coat of arms and is flanked by references to Rev. 19:15–16: "Rex regum et Dominus dominantium," King of kings and Lord of lords: a vengeful lord with a "sharp sword" for mouth who is about to "smite the nations" of the New World ("And out of his mouth goeth a sharp sword, that with it he should smite the nations: and he shall rule them with a rod of iron: and he treadeth the winepress of the fierceness and wrath of Almighty God./And he hath on his vesture and on his thigh a name written, KING OF KINGS, AND LORD OF LORDS"). Right at the center of the composition, there is a quotation from Ps. 33(32):5: "Misericordia Domini plena est terra" (the earth is full the goodness of the LORD). The escutcheon of Hispania is held up by an Old World lion and by what appears to be an American "tiger." For every Old World animal, there is one from the New; thus the peacock stands opposite the turkey (palms, monkeys, parrots, and turkeys stand for America).

On the ground, right, below the escutcheon and next to the European rabbit, lies a dismembered Amerindian corpse, a symbol of the terrors that Hispania must overcome. Hispania arrives with a message of liberation, for written on the leaves and trunks of the American palm there are passages from Ps. 40:1–3 (Vulg. 39:2–4): "Expectans expectavi Dominum et intendit mihi./Et exaudivit preces meas et eduxit me de lacu miseriae et de luto fecis et statuit super petram pedes meos et direxit gressus meos./Et inmisit in os meum canticum novum carmen Deo nostro videbunt multi et timebunt et sperabunt in Domino" (I waited patiently for the LORD; and he inclined unto me, and heard my cry./He brought me up also out of an horrible pit, out of the miry clay, and set my feet upon a rock, and established my goings./And he hath put a new song in my mouth, even praise unto our God: many shall see it, and fear, and shall trust in the LORD). References to other psalms adorn the Old World olive tree: Ps. 52:8 (51:10): "ego autem sicut oliva fructifera in domo Dei" (But I am like a green olive tree in the house of God); Ps. 86(85):9: "omnes gentes quascumque fecisti venient et adorabunt coram te Domine et glorificabunt nomen tuum" (All nations whom thou hast made shall come and worship before thee, O LORD; and shall glorify thy name); and Ps. 98(97):2: "notum fecit Dominus salutare suum in conspectu gentium revelavit iustitiam suam" (The LORD hath made known his salvation: his righteousness hath he openly shewed in the sight of the heathen). Engraved around the escutcheon are passages from the New Testament: "Venite ad me omnes" (Come unto me, all ye that labour and are heavy laden, and I will give you rest [Matt. 11:28]), and "Alias oves habeo que non sunt ex hoc ovili et illas oportet me adducere et vocem meam audient" (And other sheep I have, which are not of this fold: them also I must bring, and they shall hear my voice; and there shall be one fold, and one shepherd [John 10:16]). Right on top of Hispania, there are fragmented references to Isa. 49:18: *omnes isti congregati* ("leva in circuitu oculos tuos et vide omnes isti congregati sunt venerunt tibi vivo ego dicit Dominus quia omnibus his velut ornamento vestieris et circumdabis tibi eos quasi sponsa" [Lift up thine eyes round about, and behold: all these gather themselves together, and come to thee. As I live, saith the LORD, thou shalt surely clothe thee with them all, as with an ornament, and bind them on thee, as a bride doeth]) and Ps. 45:3–4 (Vulg. 44:5): *intende prospere* ("specie tua et pulchritudine tua et intende prospere procede et regna propter veritatem et mansuetudinem et iustitiam et deducet te mirabiliter dextera tua" [O most mighty, with thy glory and thy majesty./And in thy majesty ride prosperously because of truth and meekness and righteousness; and thy right hand shall teach thee terrible things]).

FIG. 2.1. The faithful maiden Spain ("Hispania Virgo fidelis"), bearing the Cross and the Bible, slays the dragon Leviathan. This image typifies the use of typology in the Spanish colonization of the New World. From Juan de Castellanos, *Primera parte de las elegías de varones illustres de Indias* (1589). Courtesy of the Huntington Library, San Marino, California.

This frontispiece makes explicit the biblical inspiration for the holy violence unleashed by the Spaniards on the natives. Colonization becomes a fulfillment of Biblical, apocalyptic prophecies, an act of liberation and wrathful divine punishment. But there were more than biblical roots to the Spanish colonization, which was also mediated by classical texts. The classicism inspiring the frontispiece and Castellanos's work more generally is further elucidated by an accompanying poem by the Dominican Alberto Pedrero, who lionizes Castellanos (1522–1607) for outdoing both Homer and Virgil. Whereas Virgil misleadingly presented the narrow and provincial adventures of the hero Aeneas as having earth-shattering significance, and whereas Homer dealt with heroes and monsters who were in fact fictional, Castellanos wrote about real heroes whose terrifying adventures were truly global. Unlike Hercules, who faced three-headed monsters and visited fictional gardens, the heroes of Castellanos, according to Pedrero, battled the

Great Dragon of the Ocean. The devil had prevented Europeans from crossing the Atlantic and had kept America's native peoples tyrannized and the resources and marvels of the New World hidden.[1] Castellanos himself made that point explicit in a poetic interpretation of the image: Hispania the warrior maiden had launched an assault on the dragon Leviathan guarding the New World. The dragon was a huge serpent biting its own tail, a tail so long that it circled the ocean at both ends. It had fallen to Philip II to preside over the slaying of this monstrous serpent.[2]

Castellanos's confidence that the navigational prowess of Habsburg Spain had finally broken the back of Leviathan comes through again in another image, published in Madrid some forty years later. In the frontispiece to Juan de Solórzano Pereira's 1629 study of the laws of the Indies, *Disputationem indiarum iure*, Philip IV (r. 1621–65) appears as a mighty ruler who has subdued the oceans, depicted in the form of the sea god Neptune. Philip's power reaches to the very border of the heavens ("subdidit Oceanum sceptris et margine coeli clausit opes"). To confirm the epic nature of the composition, the frontispiece includes, under the banner "Domat omnia virtus" (Virtue Tames All), an image of Hercules clubbing the multiheaded Hydra to death (fig. 2.2).

Dozens of epics of colonization were first written in Portuguese and Spanish America. It is a little-noticed fact that these are actually theological epics, in which Christian heroes battle satanic ones. In this chapter, I examine the description of colonization and settlement as an epic struggle against the devil and deconstruct the genre into a set of tropes that circulated widely across the Atlantic.

The Iberian Satanic Epic

Juan de Castellanos, a parish priest in Tunja, a city in the Colombian Andes, was a typical poet of his age. Like so many disenfranchised Creoles of the sixteenth and early seventeenth centuries, he thought nostalgically of his conquistador ancestors, and he wrote to keep alive the memory of the heroes of the conquest, drawing scrupulously on texts and witnesses. He first wrote a long history of the conquest in prose, intending to translate it into poetry, but he managed to publish only the first installment, dealing with the conquest

F I G. 2.2. *(opposite)* Philip IV subdues Neptune. Juan de Solórzano Pereira, *Disputationem indiarum iure* (Madrid, 1629). Courtesy of the John Carter Brown Library, Brown University, Providence, R.I.

and colonization of Hispaniola, Cuba, Puerto Rico, Trinidad, the Orinoco, and Margarita. In any event, his 1589 *Elegías de varones illustres* is organized around the premise that the "discovery" and settlement of America pitted the forces of evil against the conquistador Christian heroes. Although many interesting and useful studies of Spanish and Portuguese early modern imperial epics are now beginning to appear, they seem not to have noticed the prominent role played by Satan in most of the plots.[3] In this section I go over some of the numerous epics written in the late sixteenth and seventeenth centuries in various regions in Portuguese and Spanish America. Rather than being comprehensive, I seek to identify the demonological ideas at the core of these epics. The reader should notice that in many of these epics the allies of Satan in the New World are not only Amerindians but also Spaniards, *conversos*, pirates, and Nature itself.

The first epic about the New World that I know of was published in Coimbra, Portugal, in 1563; it came from the pen of José de Anchieta (1534–97), a Jesuit whose sanctity gave him the preternatural ability to control the weather and the fauna of Brazil. In *De gestis Mendi de Saa*, Anchieta turns the third governor-general of Brazil, Mem de Sá (r. 1557–72), into a Christian Ulysses determined to oust Satan from the New World. Unsurprisingly, the devil surfaces in Anchieta's poem as a tyrannical lord, who presides in Brazil over hordes of demonic Amerindians, creatures devoted to dismembering bodies.[4] The devil also appears as a powerful lord capable of unleashing storms to keep the new Portuguese Church authorities from landing.[5] In Anchieta's epic, Mem de Sá is God's instrument for setting Brazil free from Satan's tyrannical rule.[6] There are, of course, scenes in which the Cross expels demons, shamans lose preternatural power as they move from the wilderness into the civilized missions, and heroes slay dragons that guard the entrance to the New World.[7]

The conquest of Mexico attracted the attention of more poets than that of Brazil. In the late sixteenth century, the nostalgic Creole heirs of the conquistadors (led in 1519 by Hernán Cortés) produced a spate of epics: Gabriel Lobo Lasso de la Vega (1558–1615) published *Mexicana* in 1594, and Antonio de Saavedra y Guzmán *El peregrino indiano* (The Creole Pilgrim) in 1599. Both works in fact seem to have been inspired by Francisco de Terrazas's lost poem *Nuevo Mundo y conquista*, written in the late sixteenth century. Fortunately for the historian, parts of Terrazas's poem survived in a manuscript by Baltasar Dorantes de Carranza, *Sumaria relación de las cosas de la Nueva España* (Summary Relation of the Things of New Spain) (1604). In the pages of Dorantes de Carranza's scrapbook, filled with references to New

World marvels and poems lionizing the heroic ancestors of leading Creole Mexican families, Terrazas's lyrical voice can still be heard.

Terrazas (d. ca. 1604) describes the surprising discovery by Cortés in Cozumel of two surviving Spanish captives of a previous expedition, for example: Gonzalo Guerrero, who embraced the ways of the Maya and fought the Spaniards to the death, and Jerónimo Aguilar, who played a significant role alongside Malinche as translator in Cortés's Mexican expedition. Terrazas recounts in gory detail the capture of a party of twelve soldiers by the bloody cannibal leader Canetabo. Five of the Spaniards have their hearts ripped out, and their bodies are dismembered and eaten. The remaining seven are kept in cages to be fattened for later cannibal consumption. Canetabo appears as an agent of Satan, ruling over an "infernal kingdom" (*reino infernal*), the epitome of hell.[8] Canetabo himself is a satanic monster: huge, fat, with hands drenched in blood and blackened with smoke, and a striped black-red face with red mouth and teeth, spilling blood.[9] Canetabo offers the hearts of his victims to demons, but the demons cannot receive these pure hearts, which are destined solely for God.[10] Terrazas's epic contains the standard scene in which the hero (Cortés) is threatened by storms unleashed by demons while crossing the sea. The demons are determined not to allow the hero to land in America, but God calms the waters.[11] Finally, Terrazas presents the conquest as an act of liberation, in which the Spanish knights, ancestors of the handful of surviving leading Creole families, confronted Satan in pitted battles in Mexico.[12]

Gabriel Lobo Lasso de la Vega reproduced every one of these tropes in his *Mexicana*, published in Madrid in 1594 to correct his earlier 1588 youthful indiscretion, the epic *Cortés valeroso*, which appeared to the complete indifference of critics.[13] *Mexicana* opens with the ubiquitous demonic scene: aware of Cortés's departure from Cuba to conquer Mexico, Satan/Pluto strikes back with unusual fury, for he knows that this "General of Christ" is about to plant the Cross and thus challenge his own undisputed tyrannical rule over Mexico. Satan orders Neptune to unleash a tempest to sink Cortés's fleet: "May your fury be unleashed on [the newcomers]. May they experience the violence of the stormy, blinding, confusing sea! Do not allow the bloody Cross where Christ laid his back to be seen by the Indians. May your power not allow [these intruders] to sow what I have weeded out. Pull their ships down into the abyss, for these ships carry within them God and God's laws."[14]

Cortés, to be sure, is not alone. God dispatches the archangel Michael to guide him. From this moment on, the epic is transformed into a cosmic battle pitting the archangel Michael against Satan. The archangel supports both

Cortés at sea (again dispersing a storm off the coast of Tabasco) and on land (breaking down fierce indigenous resistance in battles in both Tabasco and Tlaxcala). Satan backs the Amerindians by unleashing new storms, putting the cacique of Tabasco on guard through dreams about the new arrivals, helping the Tabascans to organize an ambush, and encouraging the Tlaxcalans to take on the Spaniards.[15] The Amerindians are at every turn cast as the minions of Lucifer, largely because they dismember bodies just as demons do in hell.[16]

In Lasso de la Vega's *Mexicana*, Satan not only manipulates the Amerindians, he also uses some Spaniards. So Satan/Pluto visits the Furies and has one of them, Megaera, the Fury who represents grudges, possess members of Cortés's army. The demonically infected soldiers denounce the hero and call on everyone to go back to Cuba before it is too late; that is, before the Spaniards are dismembered and eaten barbecued on skewers. This plot fails because Cortés finds out and persuades those being intimidated to push on.[17] Undaunted, Megaera continues to undermine Cortés's vision by eliciting jealousy among the Spanish enemies of the "General of Christ" back in Cuba, who send an army to capture and discipline the hero.[18] Lasso de la Vega's *Mexicana* would most likely have continued to explore the struggles between God and Satan in Mexico, but it ends abruptly with Cortés fleeing Tenochtitlán, the Aztec capital, during the so-called Noche Triste. *Mexicana* typifies the colonial satanic epic, for the enemies of the hero are found not only without but also within the Spanish community.

Antonio de Saavedra y Guzmán also chose the cosmic struggle between Satan and God in the conquest of Mexico for the plot of his *El peregrino indiano* (1599), an epic lionizing his ancestors, which begins with Cortés's departure from Cuba and ends with Cuahtemoc's capture and execution after the siege and destruction of Tenochtitlán.[19] Saavedra y Guzmán, a provincial magistrate (*corregidor*) in Zacatecas, was a Creole patriot, a self-taught astronomer, and a relative by marriage of Cortés's infamous lieutenant Pedro de Alvarado.

It would require too much space and time to go over the many passages of *El peregrino indiano* that present the natives as satanic cannibals, the conquest as the substitution of the Cross for the devil, and colonization as an act of liberation from Satan's tyranny.[20] But in every account of battles pitting Spaniards against Amerindians, Saavedra y Guzmán has the souls of slaughtered natives go straight to hell.[21] Native warriors appear at every turn moved by satanic furor.[22] Finally, Saavedra y Guzmán includes numerous passages that dwell on the pacts struck between the natives and Satan, as well as on indigenous demonic worship.[23]

To make sure that this demonological message was not lost on the reader, and using terms and ideas that could have come from Castellanos's frontispiece, Saavedra y Guzmán opens his epic with Cortés's traumatic ocean crossing from Cuba to Yucatan fighting storms unleashed by demons: "Ever since the malicious arrogant Lucifer saw himself expelled from the heavenly sacred empyrean into the dark abyss of the ocean, he has sought to establish his own kingdom on earth; a state devoted to praise his miserable pettiness [and] jealousy of the greatness of heaven. As soon as he learned that the enterprising fleet [of Cortés] was coming to set the souls [of the Amerindians] free, which this malevolent prince had enslaved, [Satan] summoned his legions and powers to resist and not to lose his sovereignty over this dark kingdom and monarchy. Thus from the four cardinal points, he called on the winds to come together . . . to destroy [Cortés's] fleet, to [cause it to] sink it and be swallowed by the sea."[24] Providence steps in at this point and saves Cortés and his crew.[25] Conquest thus becomes a charitable act of liberation. Holy violence thus is not only reasonable but also mandatory.

Saavedra y Guzmán introduces the stereotypical character of the shaman: wielder of great preternatural powers and allowed by Satan to peek into the future. Lifting whole pages from the second installment of Alonso de Ercilla's *La Araucana*, published in 1578, in which a shaman, Fitón, brings the knight into a hellish laboratory to see both the future victories of the Holy League against the Turks at Lepanto and the global geography of the Spanish empire in a crystal ball, Saavedra y Guzmán retails the story of an elderly Tlaxcalan witch, Tlantepuzylama, who predicts the Spanish triumph over Satan in America. Peeking into a crystal ball in her cavernous underground laboratory, which contains collections of poisons, blood, corpses, teeth, fat, and brains of all sorts of creatures, including hydras, scorpions, bats, dragons, frogs, panthers, alligators, owls, sharks, pregnant monkeys, boys, and infant girls, Tlantepuzylama reveals to the Tlaxcalan senate the full imperial might backing Cortés. The visions of the witch persuade the Tlaxcalan senate to switch sides in the battle between God and Satan, for the Spaniards will soon rule Mexico.[26]

This satanic plot continued to surface in epics written in Mexico during the seventeenth century. Take, for example, the case of the *Historia de la Nueva México* (History of New Mexico) (1610) by Gaspar Pérez de Villagrá (1555–1620), which is typical of the genre. Pérez de Villagrá lionizes Juan de Oñate (1549–1624), whose 1596 expedition finally allowed the Spanish to settle the lands of the Pueblos. The crusading logic underlying the early modern European colonial expansion is cast here in Virgilian and Homeric idioms. Oñate appears engaged in a great struggle against Satan, a tyrannous lord who had enjoyed absolute sovereignty over the natives of New Mexico. God, to be sure, sides with Oñate in his efforts to oust the devil and set the natives free. In the process, however, Oñate slaughters hundreds of Amerindians, Lucifer's allies.[27]

In Pérez de Villagrá's eyes, Mexico was a society threatened, not only by Satan's frontier natives, but also by the demonic envy of upstart peninsular authorities. Pérez de Villagrá describes in detail, for example, how the new viceroy Gaspar de Zúñiga y Acevedo (1560–1606), count of Monterey, sought to replace Oñate as leader of the expedition with one of his own minions. The ancien régime logic of this Creole discourse is reinforced in the poem when Pérez de Villagrá blames a century of failures in the colonization of New Mexico on the effeminate nature of the new peninsular arrivals. Unlike the original line of conquistadors, who had never allowed the harrowing trials of the frontier to intimidate them, the new arrivals were easily cowed, returning to the Spanish urban centers as soon as they encountered difficulties. These newcomers had polluted blood and were most likely effeminate *conversos*.[28] It was Oñate's old Christian blood and thus his willingness to endure hardships that was responsible for the recent Spanish triumphs on the northern frontiers. Yet what is remarkable about this epic is that Pérez de Villagrá presents Oñate as noble "mestizo," a proud relative of Moctezuma.[29] In Pérez de Villagrá's epic, the crusading knight Oñate appears as typical of the Creole noble elites, rooted in both Christian hidalgo and Aztec blood.

Whether the Creoles confront northern frontier natives or upstart, degenerate *conversos*, the main villain in Pérez de Villagrá's *Historia* is always Satan. Pérez de Villagrá opens the poem with a description of the Aztec migration from the north. Satan takes on the appearance of an old witch with pendulous breasts and a huge mouth with canine teeth.[30] The witch carries an eight-ton iron rock, dumps it on the ground, and orders the rearguard of the indigenous caravan, standing to one side of the iron mound, to go back north to establish the Pueblo settlements of New Mexico. Then the witch orders the other half, the vanguard standing on other side of the mound, the Aztecs, to continue south to build Tenochtitlán in the central valley of Mexico. According to Pérez de Villagrá, the huge iron mound in the northern Mexican landscape once left behind by Satan as a boundary between the Pueblo and the Aztecs was endowed with strange, preternatural powers. Pérez de Villagrá describes how this mark in the landscape kept Spanish horses away by driving them crazy, until a Catholic priest exorcised the mound.[31] Not surprisingly Pérez de Villagrá considered it as providential that the "spring" of Christian saints, nuns, and martyrs that was Mexico City had replaced the "horrible hell" that had been Tenochtitlán, where every year 100,000 victims were ritually sacrificed to Satan.[32]

The genre of satanic epic had an influence beyond clerical intellectuals in Brazil, Colombia, and Mexico. Of all the poets in Iberian America who wrote epics of the conquest as a cosmic battle, it was a bard in Chile, Alonso de Ercilla (1533–94), who was destined to receive the recognition of posterity. Along with *Os Lusíadas* (1572) by Luis Vaz de Camões (1524–80), which describes the heroic deeds of the Portuguese led by Vasco da Gama in Africa and India, *La Araucana*, published by Ercilla in three installments (1569, 1578, and 1589), has long been considered the single most important Iberian epic poem of the early modern period. In fact, and to the detriment of countless other poems, *La Araucana* still receives the lion's share of attention. It is not entirely clear why this should be so, for *La Araucana* is remarkably similar in length and argument to dozens of early modern Iberian epic poems of colonization. Be that as it may, modern critics such as David Quint have sought to present *La Araucana* as a poem that, although written by a Spaniard, represented the views of the Araucanians, the Amerindian "losers."

Paying attention to the digressive, open-ended structure of the poem, Quint has argued that *La Araucana* lacks the teleological structure that organizes such epics of the victors as Virgil's *Aeneid*. *La Araucana*, according to Quint, has no clear narrative arc leading to a final triumphal resolution, no denouement, no final Spanish victory, no single Spanish hero around whom the narrative is organized. In fact, Quint has argued, in structure, the poem resembles Lucan's *Pharsalia*, an ironic critique of the genre of imperial epics. *La Araucana* has no distinguishable Spanish heroes, save for Ercilla himself, who often ventures into the wilderness to meet grieving Araucanian heroines and cunning shamans. In fact, Ercilla's heroes are Araucanian warriors such as Caupolicán and Lautaro.[33]

Although provocative, this interpretation of *La Araucana* flies in the face of much contrary evidence within the poem itself. James Nicolopulos has recently restored the imperial pedigree of the epic. According to Nicolopulos, the 1579 second installment (cantos 16 to 29) of *La Araucana*, in which pastoral romance, magi, prophecies, and visions are for the first time introduced in the poem, represents Ercilla's effort to outdo Camões's *Os Lusíadas*, an unabashed paean to Portuguese colonial adventures in Africa and Asia. Thus *La Araucana*, Nicolopulos persuasively concludes, presented a marginal Spanish frontier war as part of a much larger imperial expansionist narrative, including the triumphs of Philip II against both the French in Saint Quentin and the Turks at Lepanto. According to Nicolopulos, and Quint notwithstanding, *La Araucana* is overwhelmingly an imperial poem.[34]

My reading of *La Araucana* demonstrates the truth of Nicolopulos's assertion. To go over all the references to demonology in *La Araucana* would be tiresome. The poem has all the tropes that since Anchieta's *De gestis Mendi de Saa* had become a staple of the genre: the storm unleashed by demons (which attacks the fleet sailing from Peru to Chile with Ercilla and the new governor of Chile, García Hurtado de Mendoza [1535–1609], son of the viceroy of Peru); the all-powerful warrior who is the embodiment of Lucifer (Tucapel); the countless cannibal scenes (including Araucanians' urge to gnaw the bodies of Spanish soldiers during battle); the migration to hell of all the souls of Araucanians killed in combat; the shaman (Fitón) who has command over the elements (particularly the weather) and whose hellish underground cave contains collections of bodily fluids and the corpses of hydras, harpies, amphisbaenas (serpents with heads at both ends), infant girls, dragons, griffons, scorpions, and sharks; and the foundational pact binding the natives to Satan with which the poem kicks off.[35]

Typical of Ercilla's sensibility is his description of Araucanian religion: "These are Godless and lawless people, who nevertheless respect the one who was expelled from heaven. In their hymns, they celebrate [Lucifer] as powerful and as a great prophet and curry favor with him through false chants. They call [on Satan] to preside over all their activities and take as certain every one of his predictions, whether ominous or propitious. And when they are about to wage war, they communicate with and seek guidance from him. If [the devil's] predictions are ominous, they do not engage in battle, regardless of their desire to do so. There is no case of importance in which they do not invoke [Satan]. They call him Eponamón and often give this name to anyone who is courageous."[36] Also typical of the poem are scenes in which the natives communicate with Satan/Eponamón, who helps them destroy the Spaniards by manipulating the weather.

Needless to say, God steps in at the last minute to save the Spanish elect. Consider the case of the Araucanian siege of Imperial, a Spanish frontier town. As the Araucanians dig in around the Spanish settlement, the weather suddenly changes: darkened skies, gales, torrential rain, hail, and lightning descend upon the embattled town. Satan then makes his appearance in the sky as a "horrible, ugly dragon with a tail coiled and enveloped in fire" and tells the natives that the time to unleash the final attack on the city has arrived. Just when the Araucanians are about to do so, however, the sky clears up and the storm ends as suddenly as it began. A woman whose head is as blindingly brilliant as a star makes her appearance, borne on the clouds. She orders the natives to scatter, go home, and not to advance on Imperial. The bedazzled natives obey the Virgin, sparing the settlers a gruesome death.[37]

Between the 1589 publication of the last installment of *La Araucana* and 1660, eight lengthy epic poems were written in the southern part of the continent to describe the continuous frontier war of attrition there.[38] It is curious that most studies of Ercilla have managed to study his poem without paying much attention to this massive subsequent outpouring of epic verse. It is not my intention to fill the gap here; to do so would take a separate study. My intention rather is to emphasize the continuity in the demonological narrative that Ercilla's *Araucana* inspired. Take, for example, the case of Pedro de Oña's *Arauco domado* (Tamed Araucanian), published in Lima in 1596. Most commentary on this poem maintains that Oña (1570–1643) sought to distance himself from Ercilla by identifying a clear Spanish hero, the son of the viceroy of Peru and governor of Chile, García Hurtado de Mendoza (1535–1609), who in *La Araucana* plays a somewhat marginal role, largely because Ercilla had once been condemned to death by Hurtado de Mendoza (although later pardoned). Oña's poem misleadingly presents Hurtado de Mendoza as a conqueror who at last "tamed" the Araucanians, for the Mapuche continued to put up a fight well into the nineteenth century.

Oña's *Arauco domado* repeats each and every one of the demonological tropes in the original *Araucana*. The poem opens with a dramatic account of Spanish defeat. The Araucanians have managed to bring hell back to a land that seemed to have been liberated from Satan. In the wake of successful attacks that destroyed several frontier towns and killed the governor of Chile, Pedro de Valdivia (1500–1554), the Araucanians are determined to exterminate all Christians and bring down the "fires of hell" on the settlers' towns.[39] As they roam over a land soaked red in Spanish blood, where the impaled heads of Europeans are proudly displayed, the Araucanians ready themselves to take over the entire globe. The victorious Araucanians in fact seem poised to attack heaven itself. It is at this point that Providence steps in. First, Lautaro, the leader of the Araucanians, dies. Then a hero is chosen in Lima to lead the *reconquista*: the aristocratic youth Hurtado de Mendoza.

This eloquent hero moves hundreds of settlers in Peru to action, and a liberating expeditionary army is soon created. The fate of the Araucanians is thus sealed, and they know it. The natives gather in general council, and their shamans summon the devil, Eponamón. An old shaman begs Satan to emerge from hell to help, for the Araucanians have dutifully sacrificed to Lucifer by bleeding corpses white, drinking blood, and eating bodies.[40] Satan does show up, shaking the earth and unleashing a tornado. His voice thunders from the middle of the twister announcing the arrival of Hurtado de Mendoza. Satan predicts defeat and departs, leaving a sulfurous stench behind. Rengo, an Araucanian hero, denounces the devil for instilling fear among the Araucanians, bids "this false Eponamón go visit others,"[41] and persuades the natives to fight. Despite his own advice, the devil nevertheless intervenes and unleashes tempests to keep Hurtado Mendoza from reaching Chile by sea.[42]

I have briefly summarized cantos 1 to 4 of *Araucano domado*, which accurately capture the tone and argument of the remaining fifteen. Like Ercilla's *Araucana*, Oña's poem casts the Amerindian hero Tucapel as the embodiment of Satan himself; shows that the souls of Amerindians killed in battle go straight to hell; presents native warriors as possessed by demonic fury; and includes numerous references to Araucanian cannibalism.[43]

Like their peers in Brazil, Mexico, and Chile, clerical intellectuals in Peru and Argentina also wrote long poems in which the devil appears in many disguises to oppose the hero. Juan de Miramontes Zuázola left behind *Armas antárticas* (ca. 1608), recounting not only the conquest of Peru and civil wars among the conquistadors but also attacks on Caribbean and Pacific ports by the English pirates Francis Drake (1542–96) and John Oxenham (d. 1580), Satan's allies.[44] In 1602, Martín del Barco Centenera (1535–1605) published a lengthy epic poem of twenty-eight cantos, *Argentina y conquista del rio de la Plata*, limning the Spanish and Portuguese triumphs in the River Plate against the devil.[45]

There were also poems written in Latin, like Anchieta's. Take, for example, the poem *De mira novis orbis detectione* (On the Marvelous Discovery of the New World), widely thought to have been written in 1530 by Alvar Gómez de Ciudad Real (b. ca. 1488), but actually penned by Gonzalo Navarro Castellanos in 1667. This short poem casts Christopher Columbus's "discovery" of America as an epic battle between Satan and God. In it, Columbus becomes "Christum ferens," the bearer of Christ, who lands in America to liberate the Amerindians from Lucifer's tyranny.[46] Satan shows up in the poem at every turn, throwing obstacles in Columbus's path and using courtiers to mock his plans when Columbus is invited to speak before Ferdinand and Isabella. Satan also unleashes tempests when Columbus is crossing the ocean.

I could continue almost endlessly my analysis of the dozens of epic poems written about Iberian America in the late sixteenth and early seventeenth centuries, describing the historical adventures of the liberating Christian conquistador heroes struggling against Indians, Spaniards, *conversos*, pirates, and Nature. All of them, however, follow the same basic structure, with the conquest of the New World cast as a cosmic struggle pitting God against Satan. These poems reinvent the genre inaugurated by Homer and carried on by Virgil. As in classical epics, in these poems, heroes of rival parties abound; so too do classical deities who lend their support to one of the two embattled parties. What is distinctive about the Iberian satanic epic, however, is that both heroes and deities work for two clearly delineated cosmic forces. The messy epics of the classical past, with their multitude of morally ambiguous gods, give way in the Iberian poems to two main characters: God and Satan.[47]

This Manichean structure affected all Iberian epics of colonial expansion and is at the very core of Camões's *Os Lusíadas* (1572), which recounts the Portuguese expansion into Africa and India, not Brazil. Of all the epic poems that I have discussed *Os Lusíadas* most resembles the *Iliad*. Like the *Iliad*, *Os Lusíadas* begins with an assembly of classical deities taking sides. Feeling his own cult in India threatened by the spread of Christianity, the powerful Bacchus marshals the help of several deities and throughout the poem attacks Vasco da Gama, the Portuguese Achilles. Bacchus is not da Gama's only enemy among the gods, however. The monstrous Adamastor, transformed into the Cape of Good Hope when he seeks to rape the beautiful Thetis, goddess of the sea, unleashes the most terrifying storms when da Gama rounds the Cape. Fortunately, da Gama can count on the help of Venus and Mars, who repeatedly dissolve the ubiquitous tempests and ambushes organized by the allies of Bacchus, the Moors. But despite the many deities in the plot, *Os Lusíadas* remains at the core a struggle between God and Satan.

I do not pretend to imply that the poems' quasi-Manichean structure of two great cosmic powers engaged in battle over the control of the New World (and, in the case of Camões, Africa and India) leaves no place for the heroic and the chivalric even among the so-called defeated. On the contrary, the poems are full of beautiful Amerindian heroines who love and mourn fallen comrades and handsome Spanish enemies. The poems are also replete with courageous natives whose prowess in battle puts that of any conquistador to shame. By the same token, Satan finds allies not only among the Amerindians but also often among Spanish conquistadors, pirates, and *conversos*. But these complexities, which in some cases include mestizo heroes related to noble Amerindian and Castilian families, as with Juan de Oñate, should not obscure the basic underlying structure of the poems: Satan and God are locked in battle for control of the New World.

The Satanic Epic in the Catholic Atlantic

Readers might be tempted to see these epics as uniquely Iberian, representative of the spirit of crusading *reconquista*. But again readers would be wrong, for the satanic epic became a staple of the wider Catholic world. At about the same time that Anchieta, Castellanos, Terrazas, Lasso de la Vega, Saavedra de Guzmán, Pérez de Villagrá, Ercilla, Oña, Miramontes de Zuázola, Barco Centenera, and Navarro Castellanos, to name only a few, were writing their epics, Italian humanists were busily writings theirs. In Torquato Tasso's *Gerusalemme liberata* (1581), for example, the hero is kidnapped by a satanic temptress and taken to an island off the coast of America, where he is seduced by effete luxury. But more important for the argument of this chapter are the epics by Lorenzo Gambara (1506–96), *De navigatione Christophori Columbi libri quattuor* (1581) and by Giulio Cesare Stella (1564–1624), *Columbeidos libri priores duo* (1589). The latter poem in particular traces in excruciating detail the plots of the devil to make Columbus fail.[48]

The notion that the devil plotted to make it difficult for explorers to "discover" and colonize new territories became a common trope. The Portuguese Pedro Fernández de Quirós sought support for years in Spain and Rome to put together a fleet in the Pacific to discover the *Quarta pars incognita*, a continent expected to exist in the antipodes to keep the planet in balance. Quirós began his search for patronage right after he was hired as pilot major of Alvaro Mendaña's 1595–96 second expedition to the Solomon Islands (first discovered in 1568) to locate Solomon's Ophir (1 Kings 9:26–28). Quirós's Joachimite, millenarian, crusading expectations did not go down well in Madrid, so he turned to Rome for support. After many years of courting Clement VIII, Quirós finally secured backing from the pope and returned to Spain, where he got Philip III to open the Crown's purse strings. In December 1605, Quirós sailed in search of the mythical Terra Australis, and the following year, he discovered a large island, which he named "La Australia del Espíritu Santo," intending thus to honor the Austrian dynastic roots of his Habsburg patron. Quirós presented himself as the "Christum-ferens" of Terra Australis, the bearer of Christ to this new world. He portrayed both the difficulty he had had in obtaining court patronage in Madrid and Rome and his subsequent travails as a plot by the

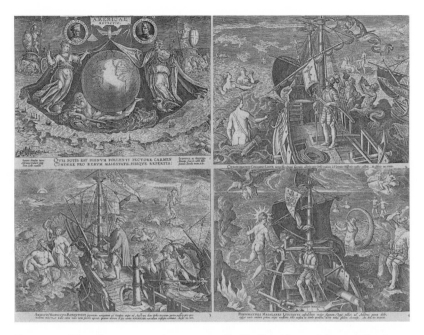

FIG. 2.3. Three heroes cross the ocean, guided by Providence. Johannes Stradanus (designer), Adrainus Collaert (engraver), and Ioannes Galle (printer), *Americae Retectio* (ca. 1589). From Straet, *New Discoveries* (1953). Courtesy of the Burndy Library, Dibner Institute for the History of Science and Technology, MIT.

devil to slow the arrival of the millennium and stop the spread of the Gospel on a continent Satan had ruled as sole sovereign for centuries.[49]

"Christum-ferens," an epic hero bringing the liberating message of Christ into a land long in the hands of Satan, became a staple of the Catholic Atlantic. A series of four engravings of Christopher Columbus, Fernão de Magalhães (Ferdinand Magellan) (d. 1521), and Amerigo Vespucci (1451–1512), entitled *Americae Retectio* (the Rediscovery/Unveiling of America) and originally designed in 1589 by the Flemish painter Jan van der Straet (1523–1605), who worked in Italy under the latinate name Johannes Stradanus, reveals the popularity of the Iberian epic genre, including its millenarian expectations, in both Italy and the Low Countries (fig. 2.3).

This series of four engravings depicts the voyages of Columbus (from Liguria), Vespucci (from Florence), and Magellan (from Portugal). The first image in the series (upper left corner) has the Holy Spirit pulling off a veil with the help of both Janus (a god who faces both East and West and who therefore represents Liguria, including Genoa, Savona, Albiziola, Cogoreto, Porto Fino, La Spezia, and Porto Venere) and Flora (the goddess who represents Vespucci's Florence and its satellites, Massa, Pisa, and Livorno). The unveiling exposes not one but *two* new worlds (America and Africa) and a new ocean (the Atlantic). The god Oceanus now lies supine, no longer obstructing navigation in the Atlantic. Columbus is flanked by a chariot-riding Neptune, the patron of Florence, while Vespucci has Mars, patron of Florence, at his side. The Latin caption expresses skepticism that anyone would ever be able to compose a song capable of capturing the majestic significance of this discovery.[50]

In the next engraving (upper right corner), Columbus has become the "Christum-ferens," the bearer of Christ, a fully armored knight, the harbinger of the millennium. Although surrounded by the monsters of the sea, Columbus's ship is led by the dove of the Holy Spirit. Diana, who as Selena/Luna has control over the tides, holds tight to her bow and arrows to keep approaching sea monsters at bay. She carries Columbus to the safety of the three Caribbean islands on the horizon. Genoa's patron, Neptune, ruler of the seas, rides in his chariot near Columbus, while the Tritons blow spiral conch-shell trumpets to calm the stormy waters and scare marine monsters away. Amorous sea-nymphs linger quietly in the background, ready to gratify the hero sexually. Neptune, Diana, and Triton acknowledge that "Christum-ferens" is God's elect and help Columbus defeat Leviathan. The caption in Latin partially explains the meaning of the image: "The Ligurian Christopher Columbus added to the crown of Spain nearly another world, which he discovered by overcoming the terrors of the ocean."[51]

The third engraving (bottom left hand) has Vespucci making astronomical observations with a quadrant. Next to him is a banner bearing the Cross, a reminder that Vespucci first described the constellation of the Southern Cross. A broken mast reminds the viewer that the knight-cosmographer has managed to survive a tempest. Vespucci's enemies are not the sea monsters that surround Columbus's ships but a hybrid Hera/Scylla goddess and her lover, Glaucus. Stradanus creates a formidable rival to the hero by combining into a single feminine deity the attributes of Hera (represented here by the peacock, whose feathers Hera created out of the eyes of the slain monster Argus), Hercules' main rival (and thus carrying Hercules' club), and Scylla, the beautiful nymph transformed by Circe into a multiheaded cannibal monster with snake and scorpion tails. Like a Hercules under the spell of Queen Omphale, Vespucci has taken his armor off and runs the risk of being emasculated. Fortunately for the hero, Athena, Hercules' friend and protector, appears, clad in full armor and bearing Medusa's head on her shield. Florence's patron Mars also accompanies Vespucci. Although the hero Vespucci is ready to crush the cannibals, Athena hands them a lily, a gesture of peace. The ubiquitous sea-nymphs witness this scene, waiting to shower the hero with sexual favors. Again the caption underneath the image partially gives some clues as to how to interpret the image: "By means of an amazing voyage to the West and South, the Florentine Amerigo Vespucci opened up *two* unknown parts of the world, which are greater in size than the one we inhabit. One of these two parts is by universal consensus named after him, America."[52]

The final image (lower right hand) represents Ferdinand Magellan crossing the straits (represented here by a Patagonian giant, who swallows an arrow, to the right, and the Land of Fire, to the left) that unite the Atlantic and the South Seas. Led by Apollo, the sun god, carrying a lyre, and helped by Aeolus, the god of the winds, Magellan appears as a knight clad in full armor who charts the heavens with an armillary sphere, a lodestone, and a compass. Clearly, Magellan faces great dangers while following the sun in his circumnavigation: a broken mast signifies the tempests he has overcome, and the frightful bird Roc, typical of the Indian Ocean and capable of lifting elephants, signifies future terrors in the unknown South Seas.[53] The Latin caption underneath commemorates the deeds of a hero whose name was immortalized in the straits he discovered and who had emulated the sun god Apollo by rounding the globe.[54]

It is common among experts on the genre of early modern epics to point out the wide European impact of Matteo Maria Boiardo's *Orlando innamorato* (1483), Ludovico Ariosto's several versions of *Orlando furioso* (1516, 1521, 1532, and 1545), and Tasso's *Gerusalemme liberata* (1581) on such writers as Ercilla, Camões, Spenser, and Milton. What seems to be missing in this approach is curiosity about how the Iberian satanic epic might have influenced Italian clerical intellectuals. It is not only a matter of chronological priorities, for Tasso's *Gerusalemme liberata*, after all, appeared in the wake of the extraordinary successes of Ercilla's first two installments of *La Araucana* and Camões's *Os Lusíadas*. It is also a matter of fact that direct borrowing can easily be traced. Stella's *Columbeidos libri priores duo* and Stradanus's illustrations, for example, took the idea of Columbus as "Christum-ferens," the bearer of the Cross in a satanic New World, from Bartolomé de las Casas. It was Las Casas's *Historia de las Indias* (1552–61), which circulated in manuscript, that first portrayed the life of Columbus in epic terms by elucidating all the obstacles the devil threw in the hero's path. Overtaken by millenarian dreams, Columbus himself took to signing his name as "Christum ferens," but it was Las Casas who cast that insight into a narrative of endless satanic interventions against the hero.[55]

The Elizabethan Satanic Epic

This epic view of the European expansion into the New World as a confrontation pitting God against Satan was also shared by Protestants. Take, for example, the case of Richard Eden (1521–76), who, seeking to please Philip II, joint sovereign of England from 1554 to 1558 as the husband of Mary I, contended in his influential 1555 translation into English of the first three decades of Pietro Martire d'Anghiera's De orbe novo (1516) that the Spanish conquest had freed millions of natives from Satan's tyranny. Everybody should rejoice, Eden argued, "to see the kingdom of God to be so far enlarged upon the face of the earth, to the confussion of the Devil and the Turkish Antichrist." There are no Christian men, he continued, who "do not rejoice with the Angels of heaven for the deliverance of trewe our brothers, our flesh, and our bones from the hands of our common enemy the ovide serpent who had so long had them in his possession."

According to Eden, the feat of liberating millions was largely due to Spanish navigational prowess, for their sailors had "excelled the voyage of Jason and the Argonauts to the region of Colchos, or all that ever were before." For Eden, the key to the Spanish breakthrough lay in the Spanish ability to outsmart Satan, who had bedazzled all Europeans into ignorance of how to cross the ocean. Finally, the Spaniards had also defeated the lock Satan had on the sea itself. "It had suffered the great serpent of the sea leviathan." Eden argued, "to have such dominion of the Ocean and to cast such mist in the eyes of men that since the creation of the world in the year before named, there had been no passage from our known parts of the world to these new lands."[56]

The reader should be reminded that at the time Eden published his translation of Martire d'Anghiera's three first decades, the son of Hernán Cortés himself, Martín Cortés, marques del Valle, was in England in the retinue of Philip II, busily advertising the glories of his father and profoundly influencing Tudor chivalric culture.[57] But it was not only Protestant sycophants who embraced this portrayal of epic heroes who were greater than Ulysses and Aeneas and had been led by God to defeat Leviathan at sea; it was also dear to one of the most rabid critics of the Spanish colonization of the New World, Theodore de Bry. The four images designed by Stradanus in 1587 appeared

im as a saint: "Erect his statue whereas hers hath beene; Make
our Saint, and make the shrine herse his" (B7v). The ancients
ve also preferred Drake to Neptune given the former's greater
ural hold over the seas; this alone would have placed Drake "in thy
 of saints" (C3r). Not surprisingly, before a hero of such caliber,
wers in fear: "Spaine trembled at the thunder of his name,/And
se Giants proudlie did rebell,/No thunder-bolt had needed but
/Their hawtie-minded forces to quell,/And send them by whole
into hell" (C5r). It is Philip II, the "Tartessian Caligula," who most
ke "and hides his doating head for very horrour." The very sound of
ame causes this modern Caligula to "lie astonish'd with uncouth
xhaling forth his gasping breath with dolour,/While DRAKE (our
les) vanquished this Spanish Hydra's ever-growing head" (C5r).
r Raleigh was also lionized by Elizabethan poets for slaying the
Antichrist. George Chapman (1559–1634), the celebrated translator
r, wrote an "epic poem on Guiana," *De Guiana carmen epicum*
at typifies Elizabethan views of Raleigh. Published in a volume
Raleigh's learned lieutenant Lawrence Kemys (d. 1618) recounts
d trip to the coast of Guiana in 1596 to recover samples of gold (a
ndertaken immediately on the heels of Raleigh's first trip in 1595),
's poem sings the praises of Raleigh the hero.[63] A man like Raleigh,
with founding an English empire in the New World at the expense
II's empire, appears in Chapman's poem as the antithesis of the
a hero who knows the true meanings of virtue, honor, and piety
is able to deliver a bloodless conquest: "Riches, and Conquest, and
e I sing,/Riches with honour, Conquest without bloud" (A1v). In
n, both Raleigh and Elizabeth stand for England, the opposite of
ian Neptune."
man urges Queen Elizabeth (1533–1603) to continue to support
dreams of displacing the Spaniards from Guiana, a land that
in the poem as a beautiful maiden "whose rich feet are mines
/Whose forehead knocks against the roofe of Starres," but who
ever been held in "heretofore savage corruption. . . . In barbarous
by the greedy Spaniards (A1v). Chapman in fact requests Elizabeth
ve up on Raleigh's plans and urges Elizabeth not to behave like a
ve yet passing hurricane against the mighty "Iberian Neptune."
n, the poet suggests, should rather be like a steady river, which grows
as it runs its course, able to join the Ocean as an equal.
man presents the Spanish as anti-heroes engaged in reckless, mur-

FIG. 2.4. The hero confronts Leviathan at sea with the help of God. From
Theodore de Bry, *Americae pars quarta* (1594).

(albeit inverted and without the Latin captions) in de Bry's *Americae pars
quarta*, a translation into Latin of the first volume of Benzoni's voyages (fig.
2.4). The epic message of Stradanus's images was reinforced by de Bry's
choice of frontispiece in the very volume where hero-cosmographers battle
Leviathan: an orchard-garden with frolicking natives worshipping the devil
(see fig. 4.13).

De Bry was not the only Protestant who tapped into Iberian epic models
for inspiration. All Elizabethan paeans of colonizing merchant-adventurers
ultimately built on the very Iberian models Elizabethan writers despised so
much. For all their ferocious critique of the Spanish conquistador and the
Spanish conquest as a model to avoid and dread, Elizabethans fell back on
the model of the knight battling demons in the New World, albeit in this
case Satan not only controlled the sea but had the Spaniards, rather than the
Amerindians, as his minions.

The equivalent of the conquistador in Elizabethan England was the
pirate. Pirates followed the "business model" first introduced in the New

World by the marauding multinational parties of soldiers of fortune we like to call "Spanish" conquistadors, namely, the search for treasure through plunder. Like the conquistadors, these pirates-turned-privateers shared with the Crown any windfall profits in exchange for coats of arms and knighthoods. Typical of these pirate-conquistadors was Francis Drake. Born to an impoverished Protestant lay preacher, Drake spent his youth plying the waters of the English Channel in a small boat he inherited from a master fisherman he had served for several years. Later, he used his Plymouth family connections to the Hawkinses, who had made a fortune through illegal trade (including capturing and selling African slaves) and piracy off the coast of Venezuela, to escape his life as fisherman and embark on the business of piracy in the Caribbean. Drake excelled at raiding Spanish ports, as well as in his utter disregard for the fate of his partners, and having amassed a small fortune of his own in this way, he found himself at the center of a community of grandees, merchants, and cosmographers who were strategizing how to turn Elizabethan England into a maritime empire at Spain's expense. Along with John Dee (1527–1608), the two Richard Hakluyts, and Walter Raleigh (1554–1618), to name only a few, Drake designed ambitious plans to strangle the commerce of the Spanish empire. This strategic vision took Drake around the globe assaulting and plundering Spanish ports and fleets in both the Atlantic and the Pacific. In 1580, after having completed a circumnavigation that included an extraordinary successful campaign pillaging Spanish vessels and ports all along the Pacific coast, including Callao, Lima's port, the very heart of the Peruvian silver trade, Drake was knighted and received his own coat of arms from Queen Elizabeth herself. The seal included the image of a providential hand of God stretching out of the clouds to guide with a rope the *Golden Hinde*, Drake's sole surviving ship in the expedition, round the sphere of the earth. After a brief stint as a local potentate–turned–mayor of Plymouth, Drake continued his exploits with two separate campaigns: as admiral of a large fleet that in 1585 sacked every major Spanish port in the Caribbean, and as leader of a 1586 assault on Cadiz. His less than heroic exploits against the Spanish Armada in 1588 and his failed 1589 crusade to destroy the Spanish navy wintering in Portuguese and Galician ports marginalized him at court, however, and he died at sea in 1596 seeking to regain his prestige by leading another raiding operation aimed at Spanish ports in the Canary Islands and the Antilles, which was unsuccessful.[58]

For someone who came to be seen in Spain as at a minimum a satanic creature with great preternatural powers in battle or at worst as the dragon of the Apocalypse (see fig. 1.8), it is paradoxical that Drake was convinced

that it was Spain that represented the mu[...] good a businessman as Cortés, and like C[...] exploits to be part of a larger providentia[...] World. Unlike Cortés, however, Drake d[...] Aztecs; rather, he saw Satan as a Spaniard[...] crusading tradition of outrage over the "[...] ted by Spain in the New World. He and F[...] of knights moved to "Anger against the [...] Spaniards, whose Superstitions have exce[...] Abominations have excell'd those of Aha[...] Naboth, to obtain the Vineyard." These [...] revenge ("an eye for an eye"), chivalrously[...] natives to guard the garden that was Ame[...] and his crew considered the Spaniards t[...] nical rule over innocent natives by the ri[...] indiscriminate flogging as a sport. In Valpa[...] caught and dismembered one of Drake's c[...] preacher on board, Francis Fletcher, the S[...] hands of the sailor, ripped his heart out of[...] and to be devoured by "beast and foules." [...] of Spain against the Amerindians: "a mos[...] cruelty, so doth it declare to the world, in [...] holdeth the government of those parts."[60]

English poets understood Drake's ca[...] empire to be an epic battle against the d[...] to the 1589 failed expedition that Drake la[...] that had retreated to winter in Portugal and [...] Peele saw Drake as a knight "under the s[...] badge," setting sail to "to propagate religio[...] going beyond Portugal, all the way to Ro[...] Antechrist/And pull his Paper Walles and [...] poems written to honor Drake's epic strugg[...] Charles FitzGeffrey's *Sir Francis Drake: His[...] and his Tragicall Death's Lamentations* (15[...] after stanza, in a repetitive drumbeat, Fitz[...] as the battle of the archangel Michael agai[...] the poem, Drake is depicted as superior to [...] included Sir Guion (Gawain), Achilles, Aen[...] the ancients known Drake, they would have[...]

revered [...]
DRAKE [...]
would [...]
pretern[...]
catalog [...]
Spain [...]
when t[...]
his fan[...]
Myriad [...]
fears D[...]
Drake's [...]
terrour[...]
new *Al*[...]
Wal[...]
Spanis[...]
of Hon[...]
(1596), [...]
in whic[...]
his sec[...]
voyage [...]
Chapm[...]
obsesse[...]
of Phil[...]
Iberian [...]
and wh[...]
Renow[...]
the po[...]
the "Ib[...]
Cha[...]
Raleig[...]
appear[...]
of gold[...]
has ho[...]
Chaos[...]
not to [...]
destru[...]
Elizab[...]
might[...]
Cha[...]

derous self-interested pursuits. The rivals of these villains are the likes of Raleigh, "Patrician spirites that refine/your Flesh to fire, and issue like a flame." The English knights, unlike the Spaniards, know that they "cannot be Kings of Earth," superior to God, and so they are determined not to let "the Mynes of earth be Kinges" of them (A2v).

Chapman's heroes not only battle Satan's minions, the Spaniards, but also demons at sea. Chapman urges them to be daring and not to be cowed by Leviathan. Chapman's heroes know how to behave when the sea, jealous and aware of Elizabeth's mounting power, seeks to swallow their fleets. Swift as the wind, these Argonauts pierce through Leviathan's rage and soldier on to gain profit and renown.[64] In terms identical to those used by the Spanish bard Oña, who thought that the Iberian hero would "tame" the Araucanians, Chapman closes his poem arguing that the "savages" of Guiana will "fall tame before" the likes of Raleigh.

Three things stand out in Chapman's poem that seem to be distinct characteristics of the epic genre in Elizabethan England: the personification of Guiana as a maiden, the lover of the chivalrous knight; the association of knightly corruption with commercial self-interest; and the inversion of the satanic epic to describe Spanish colonialism in the New World. In the following pages, I describe each of these peculiar features of the genre in England.

Raleigh was a major ideological force in the colonization of "Virginia." Although his efforts between 1584 and 1589 to keep the Roanoke plantation alive proved futile, Raleigh was in fact responsible for christening the new territories "Virginia," in honor of his queen and rumored lover, Elizabeth. The name itself seems to indicate a peculiarly English contribution to the chivalric and epic Iberian-Mediterranean genre: a tendency to endow faraway lands with feminine attributes. In Chapman's epic, Raleigh the lover sets "glad feet on smooth Guianas breast" (A3v), never to allow Spanish syphilis to contaminate the maiden's blood again ("nor Gallique humours putrefie her bloud") (A4r). In *Eastward Hoe* (1605), Chapman (in collaboration with Ben Jonson and John Marston) has his drunkard sea captain, Seagull, who is about to cross the Atlantic along with the gullible, penniless knight Sir Petronel Flash in search of Raleigh's mythical gold in Virginia, rally his crew of adventurers Scapethrift and Spendall with the promise that "Virginia longs till we share the rest of her maidenhead."[65] Kemys, in whose work on Guiana Chapman celebrated Raleigh, thought of Guiana as a prostitute, lying supine for the hero to ravish: "Here whole shyeres of fruitfull rich groundes, lying now waste for want of people, doe prostitute themselves unto us, like a faire and beautifull woman, in the pride and floure of desired yeares."[66] Not surprisingly, Raleigh came to be considered the lover of "Virginia," as Richard Hakluyt (1552–1615) put it in his 1587 dedication to Raleigh of his edition of Martire d'Anghiera's *Decades*: "You freely swore that no terrors, no personal losses or misfortunes, could or would ever tear you from the sweet embraces of your own Virginia, that fairest of nymphs . . . whom our most generous sovereign has given you to be your bride. If you persevere only a little longer in your constancy, your bride will shortly bring forth new and most abundant offspring."[67] In his *Hakluytus posthumus, or Purchas His Pilgrimes*, Samuel Purchas (1577–1626), the other champion of English colonial expansion along with Hakluyt and Raleigh, thought of Virginia as a well-proportioned maiden in distress about to be raped by the Amerindians, but who deserved the best of husbands, namely, England: "But looke upon Virginia; view her lovely lookes (howsoever like a modest Virgin she is now vailed with wild Coverts and shadie Woods, expecting rather ravishment then Mariage from her native Savages) survay her heavens, Elements, Situation; her divisions by armes of Bayes and Rivers into so goodly and well proportioned limmes and members; her Virgin portion nothing empaired, nay not yet improved, in Natures best Legacies . . . and in all these you shall see, that she is worth the wooing and loves of the best Husband."[68]

Yet despite this rather unique transformation of medieval Marian sensibilities into chivalric libido aggressively projected onto the colonial landscape, English Protestants clung tenaciously to epic paradigms first introduced by the Iberians. There is, of course, the fact that the Elizabethans avidly read the Iberian epics of the New World that I have described above. George Carew Totnes, English governor in Ireland, for example, loosely translated Ercilla's *Araucana*.[69] Kemys turned to Castellanos's epic poem *Elegías de varones illustres* to identify the numerous Spanish expeditions to Guiana and thus to convince Elizabeth that there was something worth conquering in the New World.[70]

Along with many other goods then flooding English markets and wrecking English trades (including colonial dyes, silk, draperies, hats, and knives), Elizabethans avidly consumed the most successful of sixteenth-century Spanish exports, the chivalric romance, the first astute mass marketing of desire. Ever since Lope de Vega's *Conquista del Nuevo Mundo* (written ca. 1598–1603 and published in 1614), which ridiculed Columbus's chivalric visions as messianic illusions (see Chapter 3), there has been a tendency to associate the chivalric with a world of fantasies typical of the Iberian conquistadors. A scholarly view of Renaissance chivalry as a medieval anachronism, an institution with no clear function in an early modern world of centralizing monarchies and changing warfare, has reinforced this message.[71] This tendency was exacerbated among English speakers with the publication in 1949 of Irving Leonard's *Books of the Brave*, which depicts the conquistadors as dreamy knights living in the world of the chivalric romance *Amadis of Gaul*.[72] But we can surely do without misleading historiographies that present the ruthless conquistadors as living in a world completely of their own, isolated from the intellectual currents of the rest of Europe. It was anxiety over unemployment in England caused by the industrial-commercial success of the Spanish-Portuguese empire that moved Hakluyt, a representative of the clothworkers' guild, to depict Cortés as a savvy knight capable of privileging long-term strategy over instant gratification, a model for Raleigh to imitate.[73]

But despite Hakluyt's awareness that commercial success could not be dissociated from Spanish models of conquest, Elizabethan writers cultivated a distinction between knights and merchants that is hard to find in Spanish sources.[74] As one of the gentleman adventurers of the Virginia Company, Robert Gray, put it in *A good speed to Virginia* in 1609, when the Virginia Company was undergoing intense questioning in the face of repeated failure to deliver profits to shareholders, there were two types of men waiting to go to Virginia: namely, those "who have employed their best endevours in such virtuous and honourable enterprises, as have advanced the glorie of God, and inlarged the glorie and wealth of their countrie" and those who "preferred their money before vertue, their pleasure before honor, and their sensuall securitie before heroical adventures." The former, Gray argued, deserved "the immortalitie of your names and glorie," whereas the latter "shall perish with their money, die with their pleasures, and be buried in everlasting forgetfulness."[75] This rather medieval knightly, chivalric view of colonization that privileged service to God and honor over profits and mercantile pursuits had already gone out of fashion in Iberian America, where merchants, miners, and planters were firmly in control and the Creole heirs of the conquistadors nostalgically wrote epics to recall the forgotten deeds of their ancestors. It was such a distinction between knighthood and mercantile success that allowed Elizabethan writers (and Protestant writers like de Bry, as discussed in Chapter 4) to castigate Spanish colonization as demonic.

The anachronistic Elizabethan borrowing of Iberian chivalric models went beyond Raleigh's attempts to imitate Cortés or, more relevantly, Francisco de Orellana, the "discoverer" of the Amazon (Kemys christened the Orinoco the "Raleana," largely because the name "Orellana" was replacing "Amazon"). The very image of the Spanish colonization of the New World as satanic, as the symmetrical negative image of the good society, was an Iberian invention, as will become clear below. It was the Iberians themselves who first created epic narratives in which they cast America as a prelapsarian paradise, the Spanish colonial regime as hell, and the conquistadors as cannibalistic demons. The inversion of the satanic epic to castigate the conquest was a sixteenth-century Spanish original. In *De Guiana*, Chapman subtly plays with this inversion: Philip II appears as the Iberian Neptune, a surrogate of Leviathan.

The inversion of the satanic epic that damns the Iberians as the incarnation of Lucifer in the New World surfaces in Protestant sources throughout the long seventeenth century. This vision of Spain as demonic is at the core of Edmund Spenser's *Faerie Queene* (1590) (see Chapter 4), particularly the second canto, in which Guyon, the knight of Temperance, stands for all the values allegedly antithetical to the Spaniards. Spenser and Chapman were not alone in this either. Take, for example, the cases of two individuals closely associated with Raleigh's colonization attempts in Virginia: Sir Ralph Lane (1530–1603), who led the doomed 1585 attempt to set up a plantation on Roanoke Island, in what today is North Carolina, and Robert Johnson (fl. 1586–1626), who in 1609 wrote a pamphlet supporting the reorganization of Virginia.

Lane, the governor of Roanoke, understood the English colonization of Virginia as part of a larger epic struggle against satanic Spain, the tyrannous ruler of the Amerindians. For Lane, as for the Spaniards, colonization was an act of liberation that freed the Amerindians from Satan's tyrannical lordship. Yet for Lane the satanic tyranny was embodied in Spanish colonial rule, not in the idolatrous worship of the Carolina Algonquians: "Of such a kingdom as this is to the rest of her dominions, by means whereof likewise the Church of Christ throughout Christendom may by the mercy of God in short time find a relief and freedom from the servitude and tyranny that by Spain [being the sword of that Antichrist of Rome and his sect] the same hath of long time most miserably oppressed with."[76]

Robert Johnson also presented the English as avenging heroes, as Hercules willing to slay the tyrannous dragon that was the Spanish colonial regime, a regime of cannibals "devouring" millions of Amerindians bodies: "Honorauble I graunt is just Conquest by sword, and Hercules is fained to have had all his felicity in subduing and rooting out the Tyrants of the world, but unfainedly it is most honorable indeede, to subdue the tyranny of the roaring Lion, that devoures those poore soules in their ignorance and leads them to hell for want of light, when our Dominions shall be enlarged, and the subiects multiplied of a people so bought and ransomed, not by stormes of raging cruelties (as west India was converted) with rapiers point and musket shot, murdering so many millions of naked Indians . . . but faire and loving means, suting to our English natures."[77]

It is well worth noting that the inversion of the satanic epic, typical of Elizabethan England, suffered important transformations as the regime of the Tudors came to an end. The English then began to question their persistent failure to establish colonies and pragmatically set out to copy Spanish models of colonization, particularly in the middle colonies and the Caribbean. Bracketing this transformation are the writings of two Edwards: Hayes and Waterhouse.

The merchant-adventurer Edward Hayes penned an account of the failed expedition to Newfoundland led by Sir Humphrey Gilbert (1539–83), published by Hakluyt in 1589. Hayes assumes that the knight will succeed in the New World only if he becomes "an instrument to further [God's] cause and glory some way." According to Hayes, the "virtuous and heroycall minde" in the New World should have three clear motivations. First, the knight needed to think "chiefly [about] the honour of God" and thus strive to liberate the natives: those "poore Infidels captiveved by the devill, tyrannizing in most woonderfull and dreadfull maner over their bodyes and soules." Second, the knight had to work for the "advancement of his honest and well disposed countreymen." Finally, the chivalrous warrior needed to keep the "relief of sundry people within this realme distressed" firmly in mind. Since according to Hayes, the onset of the millennium was near, God was using the knight as an instrument to win over the Amerindians in the nick of time.

If this was true, why had Gilbert failed in his aimless expedition to Newfoundland? Hayes ultimately blamed the failure on Gilbert, who had behaved like a braggart Spanish knight. "Ambition or avaraice," Hayes thought, were the wrong motivations for colonization, and God had therefore not allowed the colonies that Gilbert had in mind to be built "upon so bad a foundation." According to Hayes, Gilbert was an intemperate commander, too easily given to fits of rage. Gilbert sought to please his crew by promising them untold riches. When he could not deliver, Gilbert took crucial decisions solely to save face. Clearly, he was an incompetent knight: "[Gilbert] was so incumbred with wants, and worse matched with many ill disposed people, that his rare iudgment and regiment premidatated for these affaires, was subieceted to tolare abuses, and in sundry extremities to holde on a course, mor to upholde credite, than likely in his own conceit happily to succeed."[78]

Like Hayes, Edward Waterhouse also wrote to explain the origins of colonial failure. But his *A declaration of the state of the colony and affaires in Virginia* appeared in a different context, namely, in the wake of the 1622 slaughter of 347 settlers in Virginia by a confederation of Tidewater

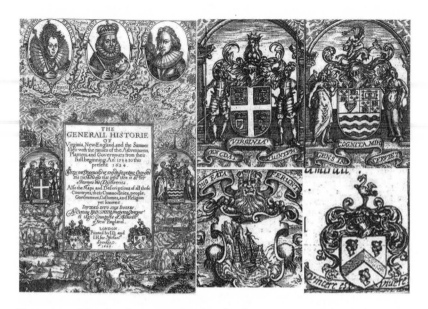

FIG. 2.5. John Smith as crusading knight. Frontispiece and details from John Smith, *The Generall Historie of Virginia, New England, and the Summer Isles* (London, 1624). Courtesy of the Huntington Library, San Marino, California. In this image, both the chivalric and crusading ethos and the discourse of the satanic epic behind the early modern English colonization of the New World come through. Elizabeth, James I, and Charles I preside over the colonies of Virginia, New England, and Bermuda, represented in the lower half of the frontispiece as luscious gardens abundant in game, fowl, fish, and plants. The coats of arms of Virginia, New England, and Bermuda shed some light on the epic narratives underlying the English colonization of America. Along with Scotland, England, Ireland (Hibernia), and "France," Virginia appears here as the fifth kingdom of James I: "En dat Virginia quintum" (Behold Virginia represents/gives the fifth [kingdom]). The arms of the Virginia Company bear a bust of Elizabeth/Virginia, flanked by two knights in full armor. New England's are no less telling. Neptune riding a seahorse announces the triumph of the English over the ocean terrors. Two maidens, one standing for England and the other for the New England (with an American bird on her shoulder) announce the Crown's acquisition of new vassals: "Gens incognita mihi serviet" (an unknown nation will serve me). "Quo fata ferunt" (Where destiny takes us) is the motto on the escutcheon of Bermuda, the monarchs' third colony. Finally, John Smith's mottoes "Accordamus" (Let us agree) and "Vincere est vivere" (To win is to live) identify him as a crusading warrior. The three Ottoman heads on his coat of arms signify not only Smith's captivity in Turkey in the 1580s but also his prowess in battle when he was in the pay of an Austrian prince seeking to contain the expansion of the Ottoman empire into eastern Europe.

Amerindians. For Waterhouse, the massacre represented the latest in a long series of English failures to establish viable colonies in the New World. Unlike Hayes, however, Waterhouse did not pin the failure on the mindless imitation of Spanish models of intemperance and greed, but rather on the irrational English resistance to following Spanish models of colonization.

Instead of trying to find Satan in the New World among the Spaniards, Waterhouse urged his fellow countryman seek the devil among the natives. Waterhouse pointed to Pizarro and Cortés as models of knighthood to imitate and encouraged settlers to introduce hounds against the Amerindians: "By pursing and chasing them with our horses, and blood-hounds to draw after them, and Mastives to teare them, which take this naked, tanned deformed Savages, for no other then wild beasts, and are so fierce and fell upon them, that they feare them worse than their old Devill which they worship, supposing them to be a new and worse kinde of devils than their owne."[79]

According to Waterhouse, it was the wrongful pursuit of chivalric dreams à la Raleigh, with an emphasis on the discovery of gold and maritime shortcuts to Asia, that had resulted in the persistent pattern of failure. Waterhouse therefore urged his English countrymen to imitate the Spanish colonies. Going against what for us are now centuries of accumulated Protestant wisdom about the Spanish colonies, Waterhouse insisted that Spain had long since abandoned colonial adventures that sought treasure and maritime shortcuts to Asia. The Spanish empire was organized around the pursuit of trade, agriculture, and commerce. Virginia should follow in the footsteps of the Spanish colonies, Waterhouse argued.

It is clear that after repeated English failures to consolidate a secure foothold in the New World, the old Elizabethan location of Satan among the Spanish, not the Amerindians, began to shift. The 1622 massacre in Virginia and the 1637 Pequot War in New England encouraged the settlers to embrace a satanic view of the natives. It is clear that in the 1620s and 1630s, a reorientation of the satanic epic in the English empire in the New World occurred. Take, for example, the case of John Smith (1580–1631).

Like Waterhouse, Smith represented a departure from Raleigh's paradigm of empire. Unlike Raleigh, Smith promoted the creation of colonies devoted to producing agricultural staples for Atlantic trade and openly criticized Raleigh's focus on plundering Spanish vessels and finding gold mines or shortcuts to Asia.[80] Yet for all his criticism of the earlier model, Smith saw himself, and his contemporaries saw him, as a crusading knight (fig. 2.5).

What is remarkable about Smith's sensibilities as a colonizer is not so much that he cast his life as that of a knight who had survived a crusading war against, and captivity under, the Ottoman Turks and who had opened up the American continent to the spread of the faith.[81] What is significant is that he stands for profound changes in English sensibilities toward the natives. As Karen Ordahl Kupperman has argued, Smith was a remarkable and sympathetic observer of things Amerindian in the early stages of his career. But back in England, as he transformed himself into an ideologue of colonization (particularly after the 1622 Virginia massacre), his view of the native Americans soured.[82] The change occurs precisely at the same time that Waterhouse was reflecting on the failures of Virginia. By the time Smith wrote his *General Historie,* the view of the Amerindians as the minions of Satan had become pervasive.

Smith is best known as the male protagonist in the romance of Pocahontas, who, we are told, pleaded with her father to spare him from being sacrificed to the gods in 1607. In fact, this picturesque story sheds light on the processes that allowed Smith and his fellow settlers to demonize the natives. In his 1624 *General Historie,* Smith recounts the story of his seven-week captivity. A tireless explorer, mapmaker, and cosmographer, Smith took it upon himself to map and survey the Chesapeake Bay region. In one of his many expeditions upriver, seeking to discover a route across Virginia to Asia, he was taken prisoner by Opechankanough, Pocahontas's uncle, to whom he immediately gave a compass, and whom he sought to teach Aristotelian physics. The compass saved Smith, for when Opechankanough saw the motions of the needle, he thought of Smith as a man of great preternatural power and invited him to a banquet (which the English captain took to be a sure sign that he was being fattened up to be cannibalistically consumed). Smith was even allowed to witnesses many "strange conjurations."[83]

Smith further enhanced his reputation as a great wizard by manipulating the technology of writing. Thereafter, he was paraded for weeks up and down the riverine towns of the Algonquians and introduced to countless demonic rituals. In one of them, "As if neare led hell/Amongst the devils to dwell," a fire was lit very early in the morning and a wizard, "a great grim fellow, all painted over with coale, mingled with oyle . . . with Snakes and Wesels skins stuffed with mosse" hanging from his head, came hopping out from a log house, singing "with a hellish voice and rattle in his hand." Many "more such like devils . . . painted halfe blacke, halfe red" joined in and a strange ceremony of songs and perorations ensued that lasted three whole days.[84]

Finally, Smith was taken to the king of the Powhatan, Pocahontas's father.[85] The grandees of the land got together in a log house to sacrifice Smith to the gods by braining him. At this point, Pocahontas thrust herself between the

FIG. 2.6. John Smith and the devil. John Smith, *General Historie of Virginia, New England, and the Summer Isles* (London, 1624) (left) (Courtesy of the Huntington Library, San Marino, California), and Theodore de Bry, *America primera pars* (Frankfurt a/M, 1590) (right). The images to the right come from de Bry's edition of John White's images of the Carolina Algonquians, whereas the image to the left is Robert Vaughn's montage, merging at least three of White's illustrations into one. Notice that in Vaughn's image, John Smith now appears seated around the bonfire next to a Medusa-like creature holding a rattle (see detail), the satanic wizard described in Smith's narrative.

club of the executioner and Smith's body, and Smith was spared. A few days later, Smith again encountered the king, who was painted black, "in the most fearfullest manner he could . . . more like a devil then a man."[86] Powhatan declared Smith an honorary son, however, and let him go. Once back in Jamestown, Smith sent gifts to Powhatan, who reciprocated by periodically sending provisions, which Smith used to consolidate his power.

This strange history of Smith's close encounter with Satan in the New World is made all the more interesting if close attention is paid to the engravings by Robert Vaughan that accompany Smith's account. Vaughan borrows images from John White's 1585 drawings of the Carolina Algonquians. What is fascinating about these borrowings is that the original drawings by White (fl. 1585–93), a colonist of Raleigh's failed Roanoke plantation, contain no reference to demonology. In the Elizabethan imagination, Satan was associated in the New World with the Spaniards, not the Amerindians. In Vaughan's rendition of White's images, however, Satan lives among the natives. Seated around the fire, the natives now appear with Medusa hairdos, engaged in a demonic Sabbath (fig. 2.6).

The Puritan Satanic Epic in America

That the Puritans embraced the satanic epic in the New World should not come as surprise. The devil was a formidable enemy for the Puritans as well. Like their Elizabethan predecessors, the Stuart Puritans inverted the Iberian genre, for central to Puritan self-identity was the satanization of popery and Spain. In fact, as Peter Lake has persuasively shown, anti-popery as a discourse of inversion allowed the Puritans, an extremist religious faction within the English ecclesiastical establishment, to take the initiative over more moderate and dominant Episcopal, Arminian (even Catholic) currents by the 1630s. Theologically, anti-popery represented Catholicism as the symmetrical negative image of the community of the godly: the natural religion of the fallen, in which the sovereignty of God had been replaced by the hubristic notion of salvation through good works, and the God-given sovereignty of Christian princes had been muzzled by the power of the pope. But to this discourse of demonic tyrannical usurpation Puritans added a powerful anti-foreign, populist, apocalyptic component. Anti-popery therefore became an epic patriotic narrative in which a foreign Antichrist (represented by the pope and his Spanish agents) battled the local community of the godly.[87]

One should therefore expect to find Spain as one of the demonic enemies of the Puritans in the New World. Yet Spaniards were one among many others laying siege to the Puritan Church in the New World, including Antinomians, officers of a centralizing British Crown, the wilderness, and, more important, the Amerindians. Puritans began to frame their own version of the satanic epic right at the time that Amerindian resistance took on a deadly character. The Puritan satanic epic began to be crafted as a result of the Pequot War, and Antinomians and Amerindians subsequently became the two most threatening satanic enemies in the Puritan imagination. I have already discussed Edward Johnson's *History of New England* in the Introduction. To further make my case, I would like at this point to discuss three texts representative of the Puritan experience in seventeenth-century New England: John White's *The Planters Plea* (1630); Benjamin Tompson's *Sad and Deplorable Newes from New England*, an epic poem on King Philip's War; and Cotton Mather's *Magnalia Christi Americana* (1702).

In 1630, John White (1575–1648) published a lengthy pamphlet in London to answer obvious potential objections from the Puritans to the colonization of New England, including claiming rights to a land already occupied by the natives. Although White found the land sparsely populated and thus vacant enough for Puritans to take, his main argument for colonization was not legal but "epic." Like his Iberian clerical predecessors in Brazil and Spanish America, White found the colonization of the New World to be "above the most glorious Conquests or successful enterprises that ever were undertaken by the most renowned men that the Sunne hath seene." That White used the term "conquest" to describe Puritan colonization should not surprise us, for the goal of setting up "plantation of colonies" in New England was first and foremost a military struggle to subdue Satan and to enlarge "Christs Kingdome."[88]

In terms almost identical to those of his Iberian cousins, the Puritan White maintained that "this Country of New England is destitute of all helpes, and meanes, by which the people might come out of the snare of Satan."[89] Since according to White the natives were the "bond-slaves of Sathan," the colonists needed to "erect a Church among them [the Amerindians, and] recover them out of the power of the Devill."[90] It was not lost on White that the Spaniards had already arrived in America to expel the devil, but for White this was not enough: God could not have intended colonization to have "no other scope but the satisfying of mens greedy appetites, that thirsted after the riches of that new found world." Nor could God have intended simply to use the Spaniards and their "barbarous cruelties as the world never heard of" to punish "the Atheisme and Idolatry of those heathen and brutish Nations," the Amerindians. According to White, it was the historical duty of the Puritans to complete the conquest of the New World that the Spaniards had so badly mismanaged. "Could any Conquest bee so glorious?" White wondered rhetorically, encouraging his Puritan brethren to cross the ocean to engage in epic battles of cosmic import.[91]

Writing some forty-five years after White, Benjamin Tompson (1642–1714) captured the drama of King Philip's War (1675–76) in two epic poems, *Sad and Deplorable Newes from New England* (1676) and *New-Englands Tears for her Present Miseries* (1676), seeking to present it as New England's Trojan War. In this American *Iliad*, the epic battle is not, however, between two matched sets of warriors, the Greeks and Trojans, but between Herculean settlers and filthy, satanic cannibal demons "with bloody hearts," whose victims they "butcher at their feet" like beasts.[92] The Amerindians brain their opponents with their clubs, wear Medusa-like hairdos, have the forests as their "fortifications" and "castles," belch fire like dragons, and use the blood and fat of white bodies to anoint themselves for their demonic ceremonies.[93] The demonic and the cannibal were intimately connected in America: in their raids on Puritan towns, the natives burned not only houses but people and cattle, because they wanted to feed the demonic spirits hovering over the land with smoke of roasted bodies.[94] King Philip himself appears in Tompson's epic as the devil presiding over hell.[95]

Cotton Mather also cast his history of the Puritan Church in New England in the same epic, cosmic terms. As Timothy Woodbridge, minister of Hartford, New England, put it in a praising, introductory poem, Mather's *Magnalia* was about tracing "out paths not known to mortal eye" of how Providence had guided "those brave [Puritan] men" through the terrors of Atlantic crossings and the ordeals of settlement: "Such were these *heroes*, and their *labours* such."[96] Woodbridge's poem accurately captures the pervasive epic tone of Mather's narrative, for Mather's history is about Herculean heroes pitted in battle against Lucifer in the New World.

The epic tone comes through everywhere in *Magnalia Christi Americana*. Book 1 describes the Atlantic crossing as an act of heroism against Leviathan, who had long enjoyed control over the ocean and kept Europeans in the dark about the existence of America.[97] Colonization itself is presented as an ongoing battle against the devil, who has his minions, the shamans, cause shipwrecks and poisonings as soon as the Puritans arrive.[98] Book 2, suggestively entitled "Ecclesiarum clypei" (Shields of the Churches), recounts the deeds and lives of Puritan leaders as modern Argonauts. Typical of Mather's biographies is that of Sir William Phipps (1650–95), captain-general and governor of Massachusetts. Mather presents Phipps as an English version of Francisco Pizarro, who through sheer chivalric prowess became both a marquis and the viceroy of Peru, although he was from lowly social origins.[99] Phipps appears as a hero who confronts the devil at every turn in New England. For example, Phipps abolishes the Salem trials because he is the first to realize that the devil is manipulating them by taking on the appearance of the innocent. Phipps also "saves the lives of many poor people from the rage of the diabolical Indians in the eastern parts of the country" by putting "those worse than Scythian wolves" to flight.[100] Hercules' labors were "pleasures" compared to Phipps's ordeals in America.[101] The final Book 7 is titled "Ecclesiarum praelia" (Battles of the Churches) and describes in exquisite detail all the enemies of the Puritans who for over a century sought to cause the plantations to fail. The battles against the devil in the guise of dissenting Antinomians such as Quakers and Familists take up most of this narrative. Chapters such as "Milles nocendi artes" (The Thousand Arts of Harming), on satanic temptations to weaken the Church, give way to chapters recounting the elimination of religious dissent such as "Hydra decapitata."[102] The last chapter of the book, "Arma virosque cano" (I Praise Arms and the Men), a slightly modified version of the introductory words of Virgil's *Aeneid*, is devoted to painstaking descriptions of the frontier battles against the satanic Amerindians: the Pequot, King Philip's, and King William's wars.[103]

This quick survey of the Puritan satanic epic in the Indies shows that there were remarkable similarities between how Iberian and Puritans understood their mission in the New World: both saw it as an epic struggle to uproot the devil. It should be clear by now that the English and the Iberians shared more than one thing when it comes to discourses of colonization. Seen from the perspective of demonology, colonization appeared as a battle pitting Christian heroes against the devil. In the case of the Elizabethans, the devil's original allies in the New World were the Spaniards. The demonization of Spanish colonialism, an idea first crafted in Spanish America by clerics like Las Casas and by Creole patriots, soon gave way to the demonization of the natives. It was the Stuart Puritans, not Tudor Elizabethans, who first embraced the Iberian satanic epic wholesale. Every demonological trope of the Amerindians first introduced by Anchieta's, Ercilla's, and Castellano's epics, to name only a few, surfaced later in Puritan histories of colonization and warfare in America.

The Spanish Conquest as Hell

I have argued that before their satanization of the natives, the English saw the Spaniards as the devil's minions in the New World. The representation of the Spanish colonial regime as hell and of conquistadors as demons was not, however, a Protestant creation. It is true that Protestants saw the pope and Spain as the Antichrist. Yet the projection of demonology onto the colonization of the New World was in fact first introduced by Spaniards. In the following pages, I show how a satanic view of Spanish colonialism emerged in Spanish America, first within clerical circles like that of Las Casas, but more forcefully among sixteenth- and early seventeenth-century Creole patriots. Finding themselves displaced by peninsular newcomers, and their power and status contested, Creoles readily invented a view of colonial society as hell and the *peninsulares* as demons.

In 1593, the Spanish humanist Juan Cristobal Calvete de Estrella published *De rebus Vaccae Castri*, his much-anticipated epic poem on the deeds of Cristóbal Vaca Castro (d. 1588), first viceroy of Peru, in Madrid. Since Vaca Castro had been sent by Charles V to put an end to the civil wars among conquistadors then ravaging Peru, it is not surprising that Calvete de Estrella's poem is about how the new viceroy brought the conquistadors to heel. To be sure, the poem includes staple references to Satan's attempts to halt the arrival of Vaca de Castro in America by unleashing storms. The poem also represents the local peoples and landscapes of the New World as satanic.[104] Yet what is remarkable is that Satan's main allies in the poem are neither the Amerindians nor the landscape but two Spanish conquistadors. The epic, it turns out, is a poem pitting Vaca Castro against Diego de Almagro and Pedro de Alvarado, the embodiments of Satan in the New World. At the promptings of Satan, one of the three Furies, Megaera, possesses Almagro and Alvarado, who become tyrannous usurpers. In the poem, these two conquistadors pillage, murder, and dismember people just as demons do in hell.[105]

Calvate de Estrella's inversion of the tropes of the Iberian satanic epic to describe the deeds of the Spanish conquistadors in the New World was by no means unique. Inca Garcilaso de la Vega, duly honored for his epoch-making history of the Incas, *Comentarios reales de los Incas* (1609), also manipulated and inverted the genre as he saw fit. Inca Garcilaso, for example, dedicated his *Historia general del Peru* (1617) to the Immaculate Conception, the woman of the apocalypse who with the help of the archangel Michael had confronted and defeated Satan. According to Inca Garcilaso, the Virgin was the Bellona/Minerva of the crusading Church, who had facilitated the Herculean labors of the Spanish conquistadors in the Indies. With her help the conquistadors had not only defeated the terrors of the sea but also performed "greater and more extraordinary heroic deeds than the Alexanders of Greece and the Caesars of Rome."[106] Not surprisingly, Inca Garcilaso thought his work to be a description of the "great battles and victories of the heroic Spaniards, true Christian Achilles and Hercules (Alcides)."[107] Yet for all his lionizing of the crusading, chivalric deeds of the Spanish conquistadors in the New World, Inca Garcilaso maintained, anticipating Milton by many decades, that Satan's minions were also heroes. Inca Garcilaso presented the Amerindians, the enemies of the Spaniards, as heroes, in part, because the natives themselves had "defeated the devil's sin and hell with the favor of heaven."[108] This tendency to turn the natives into heroes of the larger satanic epic, the conquest, allowed Inca Garcilaso at times to put indictments of the conquistadors as the devil into the mouths of native leaders.

Take, for example, the case of Inca Garcilaso's *La Florida del Inca* (1605), a history of Hernando de Soto's failed attempt to conquer and colonize what today is the southeastern United States. *La Florida* is organized as an epic in which both the Spaniards and the natives have great heroes who perform deeds of extraordinary chivalric prowess. At one point in the narrative, Inca

Garcilaso has a shortsighted Amerindian leader, Vitacucho (whose lack of prudence leads to the massacre of 1,000 of his best warriors), denounce the Spaniards as the minions of Satan. More defiantly than any of "the bravest knights in any of the works devised by the divine Ariosto and the most renowned and love-struck Matteo Maria Boiardo," Vitacucho challenges the council of his brothers and declares open war on Hernando de Soto.[109] Vitacucho prompts his Amerindian brethren not to be seduced by the Spaniards and to see them for what they actually are, namely, the spawn of Satan himself: "Should you be men of good judgment, you would see that the [Spaniards] in their deeds and works show themselves to be the children of the devil, not of the Moon and the Sun, our deities, for they go from land to land killing, plundering, pillaging everything in sight, taking woman and daughters that are not theirs."[110]

This flexible, chameleon-like ability to put the Spaniards on the side of either God or the devil in the satanic epic of colonization was first introduced by Bartolomé de las Casas. As I have already mentioned, it was Las Casas who first embraced Columbus's interpretation of himself as "Christum-ferens," a hero providentially elected to carry the message of Christian deliverance into the New World. For all his repeated criticism of the Spanish chivalric and crusading ideologies of colonization as a cover to exploit the natives, Las Casas organized his own failed colonial project in what today is the region of Venezuela (Cumaná) according to crusading values. Established around 1521, this colony in Cumaná was conceived by Las Casas as a place where settlers would trade with the natives for profits to be shared with the Crown and friars would convert the natives through gentle persuasion, not force. In fact, Las Casas requested the king to have all the settlers be part of the new crusading order of the "Knights of the Golden Spur" and wear crusaders' tunics.[111]

Despite these crusading values, or perhaps because of them, Las Casas repeatedly denounced the conquistadors as "the precursors of Anti-Christ and imitators of Mahomet, being thus Christian only in name," or as men "governed and guided by the Devil."[112] In fact, Las Casas soon came to see the conquest as an inversion of the satanic epic, in which America was a prelapsarian paradise, the conquistadors were demons, and the colonial regime was a stage for hell.

In his massive *Historia de las Indias* (completed 1552–61), a detailed history of Columbus's discovery of the Indies and of the early colonization of the Caribbean, Las Casas created an image of the Caribbean as prelapsarian paradise, located in a temperate climate and under the influence of numerous and most benign constellations. Not surprisingly, Las Casas endows this Eden with prelapsarian inhabitants, saying, "and I think [them] distinguished above all [the nations] of the world in gentleness, meekness, simplicity, humility, peace and quietude, and in other natural virtues; but that it would appear that Adam has not sinned in them."[113]

It is this prelapsarian paradise that the devil attacks through his agents, the Spanish conquistadors. The demonic character of the conquistador is revealed in his readiness to use dogs against the Amerindians: "Like many other exquisitely evil and most hurtful inventions against the human race that were created and fostered here [in the Caribbean] and that led to total destruction of the natives, [setting hounds loose to kill and dismember Amerindian bodies] was an invention first conceived, thought of, and sanctioned by the devil here."[114] But of all the institutions the satanic conquistadors introduced in the Caribbean, it was the *encomienda* (the assignment of entire communities to serve a given conquistador) that Las Casas most detested, because it had sanctioned a form of institutionalized cannibalism in which all settlers were allowed to "drink their [the natives'] blood and eat their bodies."[115] According to Las Casas, the *encomienda* bred satanic tyranny. In the same way that individuals trembled before the devil, the Caribbean natives cowered in front of the *encomendero*, whose fits of capricious wrath resembled Lucifer's.[116]

The discourse of inversion to chastise the colonial regime as satanic was not a monopoly of the critics of the conquistadors. In fact, the descendants of the conquistadors themselves deployed it to launch a furious critique of the new colonial regime that reformers like Las Casas had helped to establish in the 1550s. Take, for example, the case of the cleric Pedro de Quiroga, who died in anonymity in Cuzco sometime in the 1580s.

Quiroga's *Coloquios de la verdad* (ca. 1550–70) are fictional dialogues about the true nature of the new colonial regime that Las Casas had helped to establish. The dialogue is among three characters: the eremite Barchilon, the recently arrived Spanish soldier Justino, and a dispirited Inca, Tito, who is about to commit suicide. The characters collectively present Peru as a land that instead of being the replica of Spain the conquistadors had originally hoped to build was Spain's inverted negative image. It is the Amerindian Tito, in fact, who most forcefully presents the case of inversion when pressed by the inquiries of Barchilon and Justino to remember his past, including a trip to Spain: "When I was in Castile I found myself so fully human that I became convinced that those lands [Castile] breed humans, whereas ours breed irrational animals in the shape of humans."[117] For the friar Barchilon, Peru is a world upside down where the memory of the conquistadors has been forgotten and the priests live only to enrich themselves; where social orders and hierarchies are no longer respected; and where new arrivals from Spain "dare to think, speak, and do anything they please so as to outdo [the irreverence of] hell."[118] Tito complains that Spanish tyranny over the Amerindians is worse than that of the Incas and that the so-called sage, chivalrous, courageous, and godly Spaniards do unto the Amerindians exactly the opposite of what they preach should be done unto others. According to Tito, the Spaniards had contributed to disrupting indigenous social hierarchies, with disastrous moral results: decent, humble Amerindians emerged haughty and lascivious after stints in Spanish households. Like his contemporary Bartolomé de las Casas, Tito accuses the settlers of behaving like cannibals: "When you go back home loaded with treasure and gold, those in Castile are dazzled. Yet they don't realize that you also go back loaded with the skins of Indians flayed as in a butchery, and you also return soaked in the blood of those Indians who died for the sake of your new wealth."[119] Things are so bad in Peru that when Barchilon and Justino first encounter Tito, they think they are in a dialogue with the devil, because no Amerindian was expected to be so articulate. Facing all these reversals, Justino concludes that "this land weakens reason, affects the spirit and spoils and corrupts good customs. It engenders reverse conditions and transforms humans into their opposites. This happens not only in human bodies, but also even in animals and plants. This land transforms the good into bad."[120]

The same sense of profound alienation that led Quiroga to present Spanish Peru as hell moved Baltasar Dorantes de Carranza, a disenfranchised heir of the conquistadors, to argue in 1604 that Mexico was the negative, inverted image of Spain. It was Dorantes de Carranza's efforts to rescue all extant poetic epics about the heroic deeds of his ancestors that allowed parts of Terrazas's epic *Nuevo Mundo y conquista* to survive. Yet Dorantes de Carranza thought that the descendants of the conquistadors were being pushed aside and marginalized by new peninsular arrivals. For him, the New World had become a world upside down: "a procurer for the idle, a store of lies and deceit, . . . a brothel for the good, a bedlam for the sane, a dead-end for the nobility, a slayer of virtue."[121] The Indies, in short, were the "blueprint for hell" (*dibujo del infierno*), a place where Satan had fortified himself, eroding social hierarchies and breeding corruption, idleness, poverty, and disrespect.

It might seem paradoxical, but "Creole" patriotism in Spanish America was largely responsible for spreading the discourse of the colonial regime as demonic. I have already cited the works of Inca Garcilaso, Quiroga, and Dorantes de Salazar as typical of this genre. But it was the theologian Miguel Sánchez (1594–1671), the first to offer a patriotic exegesis of the millenarian significance of the miracle of Our Lady of Guadalupe, who sought to present the travails of Spanish Americans as caused by Lucifer's main allies, the peninsulars. This statement seems to fly in the face of all interpretations of Sánchez (that is, that he offered a typological reading of Revelation 12, in which the battles pitting the archangel Michael against the six-headed dragon had been fulfilled by Cortés's conquest of Mexico). But Sánchez also understood the battles of Michael and the woman against the devil as a war of attrition that did not end in 1521. Sánchez insisted that after being expelled from heaven by Michael, the dragon fell to earth and went after the woman and her son, unleashing a flood to drown them. For Sánchez, this earthly persecution stood for the travails of the Creole populations (the descendants of the woman). The evidence was there for all to see, for Mexico suffered regularly from floods. Although patristic scholarship had associated the dragon's attempts to drown the woman and the child with Christ's passion and Mary's pain, Sánchez maintained that they also signified the "passion" of being Creole in Mexico, that is, the continuous humiliations this population regularly endured at the hands of upstart *peninsulares*. According to Sánchez, peninsular newcomers had now become the main allies of the devil in the New World, not the Amerindians.[122]

It should become clear by now that at the time Elizabethans and Stuart Puritans were busily crafting an image of satanic Spanish colonization, Spanish settlers and friars had already fully fleshed out a discourse of the colonial regime as a demonic inversion.

Our "Elizabethan" Lady of Guadalupe

For all the confessional differences, the English and the Spaniards were ultimately cultural twins. Centuries of shared religious culture and exchanges did not simply disappear with the onset of the Reformation and dynastic national rivalries. There is perhaps no better example of the shared, common cultural world these two peoples inhabited than the way each created similar epic narratives of providential national election in England and Mexico. In the following pages, I argue that the millenarian discourse of national providential election that first appeared in England around the cult of Elizabeth also surfaced in Mexico around the cult of Our Lady of Guadalupe. Both were subsets of the genre of the satanic epic.

Thanks largely to the scholarship of Richard Bauckham, we know that

Elizabeth was welcomed by chiliast English writers as a sign of the imminent arrival of the millennium. Since the medieval chronicles of Geoffrey of Monmouth (1100?–1154), *Historia Regum Britanniae*, English history had been cast as an epic resembling that of the *Aeneid*, in which a wandering Brutus takes the place of Virgil's Aeneas as the founder of England. Through the agency of the moon goddess Diana, who has sway over both wilderness and tides, the exiled Brutus comes to the "empty" island of Britain, where he establishes a Trojan dynasty. According to this national mythology, England was both a wilderness and a potential new Rome. In the heady days of the Protestant Reformation, this national English myth took on new meanings in light of Protestant typology. Thus the English wilderness became Canaan, a promised land for the English, the New Israelites. With the rise of Elizabeth to the throne, the typological reading of English history received a boost, and the woman announced in Revelation 12:1–9 came to be read as a prefiguration of the queen: pregnant with Christ, persecuted by the popish Antichrist (personified in the Spanish Armada), and in pain, she is rescued by God, who removes her to the wilderness. According to these eschatological views, the reign of Elizabeth pointed to the imminent arrival of the apocalypse, as well as to England's providential election as the future location of the New Jerusalem.[123] This national millenarian epic is remarkably similar to that developed only a few decades later in Mexico, the only difference being that in Mexico, Our Lady of Guadalupe took the place of Elizabeth.

As my analysis of the poetry of Terrazas, Saavedra Guzmán, Lasso de la Vega, and Pérez Villagrá suggests, there was a predisposition among Creole intellectuals in Mexico to reinterpret their local history as an epic of cosmic significance. But it was the interpretation of the miracle of Our Lady of Guadalupe offered in 1648 by Sánchez that converted the earlier epic narratives into an eschatological tradition.

The miracle of the apparitions of the Virgin to an Aztec commoner, Juan Diego, allegedly took place in 1531 at Tepeyac, a hill near Mexico City. The Virgin had Juan Diego collect flowers in his cape to persuade a prelate to build the Virgin a church. When the Amerindian visited the bishop, the flowers transformed themselves into a painting of Our Lady of Guadalupe. Until the year Sánchez published his epochal interpretation, the miracle and the image remained just one of a great many Christian images with cults. The image itself was not unusual. Like all images of Our Lady of the Immaculate Conception, the icon of Our Lady of Guadalupe was thought to fulfill the woman prophesied in the Book of Revelation by St. John.[124] Indeed, it was a well-established tradition within the Catholic Church to

FIG. 2.7. The Miracle of Our Lady of Guadalupe as the fulfillment of St. John's vision of the woman of the Apocalypse. Anonymous eighteenth-century painter, *Saint Archangel Michael with Sword and Our Lady of Guadalupe Banner.* Courtesy of the Museo de la Basílica de Guadalupe, Mexico City.

claim that St. John's vision of a pregnant woman clad in the sun and stars and threatened by a multiheaded dragon was either a reference to the Virgin Mary or a symbol of a persecuted yet elected Church. In Revelation, God takes the newborn to his side, protects the woman by airlifting her into the desert, and sends the archangel Michael to oust the dragon from heaven.[125]

Taking this typical interpretation one step further in his *Imagen de la Virgen María Madre de Dios de Guadalupe* (1648), Sánchez claimed that St. John's vision of a woman clad in stars battling a dragon was, in fact, not a reference to the Immaculate Conception, but a prefiguration of the conquest and colonization of the New World, and of Mexico in particular. Every detail both of the woman in Revelation and of the image of Our Lady of Guadalupe supported this thesis, he argued. According to Sánchez, for example, the angel holding the Virgin up in the image was the same archangel, Michael, who had ousted the dragon from heaven. The dragon itself represented the sovereignty the devil had long enjoyed in the New World prior to the arrival of the Christian warriors. Sánchez insisted that the Spanish conquest did not guarantee that the devil had been beaten. Christianity in Mexico, he maintained, was engaged in an ongoing epic struggle against Lucifer, for according to Revelation, the dragon, after being beaten by the archangel Michael in heaven, descended to sow confusion on earth until the very end of time. More important, Sánchez presented the encounter between Juan Diego and the Virgin at Mount Tepeyac as the anti-type of that of Moses and God at Mount Sinai. The image of Our Lady of Guadalupe thus appeared as the new tablets of the Ten Commandments, a covenant written in indigenous hieroglyphs documenting God's election of the Mexican Church as the new Israelites.[126]

Sánchez's insight remained a staple of Creole colonial discourse in Mexico. As late as 1752, learned and powerful preachers were building on Sánchez's interpretation. For example, the rector of the episcopal college of Puebla, Mariano Antonio de la Vega, equated the archangel Michael with both Hercules and Mars and insisted that the battle of Revelation 12:7–9, in which Michael expels the dragon, had actually taken place in Mexico during the conquest. Moreover, de la Vega maintained that almighty God had tricked the devil, for God had used the coat of arms of the Aztecs, Satan's chosen, to depict in symbols the battle in Revelation. The coat of arms sported an eagle with a snake in its claws perched on a nopal cactus, which de la Vega argued represented the battle of the Herculean Spanish Michael against the serpentine Aztec troops. The satanic epic narrative of the history of Mexico allowed Sánchez and his clerical followers to claim a central role in universal history for Mexico.

The eschatological discourse of providential election that surfaced in mid-seventeenth-century Mexico is remarkably similar to that which arose in late sixteenth-century England around the cult of Elizabeth. Moreover, it bears close resemblance to the ideology crafted by seventeenth-century Puritans in New England. Ever since the pioneering studies of Perry Miller and Sacvan Bercovitch, it has become a truism that the trope of the "errand into the wilderness" was a creation of Puritan provincials to endow their marginal endeavors with cosmic, providential significance. By casting New England as a New Canaan, and the entire Old Testament as therefore a prefiguration of their history of settlement and colonization, the Puritans planted the seeds of the future doctrine of America's Manifest Destiny.[127] Miller's and Bercovitch's views have recently come under closer scrutiny. Reiner Smolinski and Theodore Dwight Bozeman have shown that the New England Puritans were in fact plagued with doubts as to the true location of the millennial New Jerusalem. More often than not, Puritans drew on well-established patristic and Calvinist traditions and found New Jerusalem located in places other than Massachusetts.[128] It is interesting to notice that none of these self-doubts ever seemed to have haunted the Mexican Creoles. Perversely, therefore, "Americans" need to look to Mexico for the true ancestors of the doctrine of Manifest Destiny.

Iberian Traditions in Milton's *Paradise Lost*

A good example of how Puritans embraced the genre of satanic epic is John Milton's *Paradise Lost* (1667). As J. Martin Evans has persuasively shown, Milton (1608–74) wove into his poetic rendition of Genesis a scathing critique of Spanish colonialism. Milton in fact has his Satan embark on a voyage of "discovery" from hell to a "New World" (paradise). In greed, ruthlessness, and cunning, Lucifer's voyage and "conquest" of paradise resembles that of the Spaniards in America. In short, Milton modeled his Satan on a Spanish conquistador. Like the Spanish conquistador, the devil brings the values of hell into the prelapsarian world of Adam and Eve, who at times are presented by Milton as noble savages. Yet Evans has also shown that Milton wove into his epic a view of the "New World" as controlled by Satan. Milton at times presents Adam and Eve as colonists whose duty is to eliminate the cannibalistic allies of Satan roaming the "plantation." According to Evans, *Paradise Lost* offered a program of positive Puritan colonization of New England.[129] Like their Elizabethan predecessors, Stuart Puritans were deeply ambivalent about where to find Satan in the New World. Convinced of their own anti-papal doctrine, Puritans like Milton embraced a satanic epic that found the minions of Lucifer in the New World among the Spaniards. Yet as they faced mounting Amerindian resistance in New England, which culminated in the Pequot War of 1637, these same Puritans began to find Satan in America increasingly among the natives.

Exactly how the genre of Iberian epic seeped into *Paradise Lost* remains to be explored, but it seems as though Milton was inspired by Spanish conquistadors or Amerindians to conjure up his Satan. This insight might help explain one crucial aspect of Milton's epic that has always confounded critics, namely, that Lucifer in *Paradise Lost* is not simply an enemy of God but a hero in his own right.[130] For this representation of Satan as hero, Milton might have simply tapped into two separate contemporary traditions of the epic available to him, both ultimately inspired by Iberian models. One was the Elizabethan satanic epic, which for all its criticism of the Spanish conquest as demonic nevertheless presented the conquistadors as heroic (see, for example, the cases of Hakluyt and Kemys cited above). The other source of inspiration available to Milton was the Iberian epic tradition itself, in which Satan repeatedly appears as hero.[131] Take the case of the warrior Tucapel, the embodiment of Satan in the epic poems on the Spanish colonization of Chile. Ercilla, for example, presents Tucapel as the single most important hero of *La Araucana*: daring, independent, extraordinarily brave, in short, a tireless warrior of unmatched chivalric prowess. It seems to me that *Paradise Lost* owes more than one motif and convention to the rich epic tradition inaugurated by the Iberians in the sixteenth century.

Conclusions

The Iberian satanic epic colored Italian, Flemish, and Dutch perceptions of colonization. More important, it helped frame English interpretations as well. I therefore first studied the genre of the satanic epic in Spanish (and Portuguese) America and then turned to explore the projections of the genre in countries like Italy, Flanders, Holland, and, above all, England. I show that in England, the satanic epic was first used to describe Spain's deeds in the New World, depicting Spanish colonialism as hell and the conquistadors as demons. This use of the satanic epic was, to be sure, part of the larger Protestant demonization of Catholicism, and particularly of Spain. Yet, paradoxically, the discourse of satanic Spain was in fact an Iberian invention.

Protestants borrowed the genre of satanizing Spain from peninsular sources. It was the Dominican Bartolomé de las Casas who first presented the conquest as hell and the conquistadors as Satan's minions.

Like their contemporary Dutch peers, the English changed their views of the natives in the 1630s and stopped considering the latter allies in the battle against a common satanic Iberian enemy.[132] Continous colonial failures in Virginia, along with indigenous resistance, particularly the 1622 massacre of Virginian settlers and the Pequot War, transformed English perceptions of the satanic epic. The writings of Captain Smith demonstrate how this shift took place. By the time the Puritans arrived in the Indies, the epic of colonization had been transformed into a battle pitting Christian heroes against Satan's new main allies, the natives. The satanic epic in England thus came full circle, back to Iberian models, because, paradoxically, the Puritans fully embraced every trope of the Iberian genre. I have suggested that this embrace helps shed light on similarities of Milton's *Paradise Lost* to the earlier Iberian satanic epic in the New World. But the similarities did not flow only in one direction. I have also argued that one important element of the Iberian satanic epic in the New World was the notion of national election and providential deliverance. Creole patriots in Spanish America interpreted the miracle of Our Lady of Guadalupe in terms of the satanic epic. The miracle appeared as a providential message of millenarian cosmic significance in the battle between God and Satan. This discourse hammered out in Mexico bears striking resemblance to the way the English had used the image of Elizabeth decades earlier to articulate a notion of national election — of the godly led by Elizabeth pitted in an epic struggle against the Spanish Antichrist.

Throughout this chapter, I have demonstrated not only the transnational circulation of ideas (English authors reading Iberian epics, for example, or the Protestant borrowing of Las Casas's inversion of the Iberian satanic epic), but also how all parties drew on a set of common tropes. The Reformation and the rise of aggressively centralizing states in the early modern period have helped mask similarities and caused scholars to emphasize national differences. Yet centuries of shared medieval Catholic culture should not be easily dismissed. A study of the satanic epic sheds light on a number of unsuspected similarities and shows them to be manifestations of a common cultural tradition.

The Structure of a Shared Demonological Discourse

In this chapter, I continue to explore how Iberian and Protestant Puritan theologies perceived the plots of the devil in the New World in strikingly similar ways. My main goal is to deconstruct the basic building blocks of the discourse of demonology and colonization: that demons enjoyed great geographical mobility as they and Satan engaged God in a geopolitics of evil (Satan migrated to America when the Gospel began to spread in Eurasia, for example, but moved again, including back to Europe, when the Europeans arrived in the New World); that Satan had enjoyed uncontested sovereignty and feudal control over the New World until the European arrival (including developing tyrannical rule and building "fortifications" that were difficult to uproot); that cannibalism was a reflection of the hellish world Satan had instituted in America; that the devil mimicked God both through Amerindian rituals and institutions that inverted Christian Church structures and through Amerindian historical narratives that perversely imitated those in the Bible; that Amerindians were collectively corrupted by the devil because they were collectively effeminate; that colonization was an epic act of liberation; and that colonization was about expelling demons from the land, for which either crosses or Bibles were used as charms.

If the previous chapter showed that the analysis of the tropes of the Iberian satanic epic can shed light on the nature of Puritan siege mentality (by enlarging current interpretations of Puritan demonology and the Salem witchcraft trials), this chapter looks through the other side of the glass by studying Puritan tropes to understand Iberian ones. Using the vast literature on Puritan "typology" (a reading strategy that found Old Testament narratives to be prefigurations of colonization: e.g., the Puritans as Israelites in a New Canaan) to explore Iberian sources, I argue that Catholics were every bit as interested in developing typological readings of colonization as were the Calvinists. A good but little understood example of how typology framed Spanish perceptions of the New World is the case of the Spanish historiography on the Aztecs. As the Spanish clergy interpreted native religious institutions as satanic inversions, the clergy came up with the idea that the Aztecs were the devil's elect: the inverted mirror image of the Israelites. Without much awareness of its roots, modern historiography still uses the Franciscan narrative of the Aztecs as the satanic "anti-type" of the Israelites (each people underwent an exodus, struggled to settle amid hostile "Canaanites," experienced ages of monarchies and of prophets, built a temple, and witnessed the destruction of its capital by foreign invaders). In the following pages, I study how this and other demonological narratives developed.

Satan's Tyranny

Epic narratives of colonization stemmed from a couple of simple notions, namely, that Satan had enjoyed uncontested lordship and sovereignty over the New World for centuries prior to the arrival of the Europeans, and that the devil had ruled as a tyrant, enslaving the natives. There is perhaps no more powerful statement of this dual vision than that offered in 1570 by Diego de Valadés (b. 1533), a mestizo Mexican friar who wound up representing the Franciscans in Rome, in an image he himself designed for his *Rhetorica christiana*. Valadés has his natives parade in shackles and pillories before a monstrous devil presiding over a court of obsequious demons and Amerindians (see fig. 3.1).

Valadés was convinced that Europeans had brought "freedom" to Mexico. But to do this, Europeans needed to attack the mechanisms used by the devil to ensnare and trap his victims. Standard theological doctrine held that the devil operated at an individual level. Free will made individuals originally responsible for their sins, but once they caved in to alluring temptations, they became Satan's indentured servants. Andrés de Olmos (1491–1570), a Franciscan in Mexico of an earlier generation, illustrated this process: "Demons do all they can to appropriate an individual to themselves, to be his owners, to humiliate him, to rule over him, to oppress him, to tie him up in chains in a dungeon."[1]

It was the Puritan Cotton Mather (1663–1728), however, who most keenly captured the stages toward individual moral serfdom first elucidated by the mestizo Valadés (see fig. 3.2). "The Devil first *enters* the heart of the sinner," Mather argued, "[and the] poor man delivers up the keys of the castle . . . [and] the devil gets [into] all the faculties of the soul [intellect, memory, and affections]." In the second phase, the devil *commands* the heart. It is at this stage that "the Devil can drag [the sinner] hither and thither and even do what he will with [the sinner]. The devil becomes the absolute commander

FIG. 3.1. The devil enslaves Amerindians. Diego de Valadés, *Rhetorica christiana* (Perugia, 1579). Courtesy John Carter Brown Library, Brown University, Providence, R.I.

FIG. 3.2. A sinner in chains. Diego de Valadés, *Rhetorica christiana* (Perugia, 1579). Courtesy of the John Carter Brown Library, Brown University, Providence, R.I. The sinner stands between an angel leading to heaven and demons leading to hell. Once an individual commits a sin of his own free will, he becomes a shackled beast of burden for the devil to ride.

of [the sinner's] undone Soul." Satan acts like a spider, Mather explained, and the sinner as a fly in a cobweb. It is here that the devil-spider "sucks out the heartblood of [the sinner-fly] when he pleases."[2] Thus, Mather concluded, "the devil is an Absolute Lord over the hearts of them that are not born again; he Rules and reigns like a Bloody Tyrant. . . . Come then, shake off the yokes of that Hellish Tyrant, by entering into Covenant with God in Christ."[3]

These theological principles did not apply fully to the Amerindians, however, for they, unlike other sinners who were tyrannized as individuals, were *collectively* enslaved by Satan. Just as much as Catholics, Protestants insisted that the natives were enslaved collectively. So in 1589, the merchant-adventurer Edward Hayes, long involved in seeking a northern passage to the China Sea, announced in his report on the 1583 voyage of Sir Humphrey Gilbert that Amerindians were "poore infidels captivated by the devil, tyrannizing in most wonderfull and dreadfull maner over their bodies and soules."[4] The archdeacon of Ely, in Cambridgeshire, England, Dr. Robert Tynley (1561–1616), concurred in 1609, referring to the natives of the New World as "those sillie, brutish, and ignorant soules, now fast bound with the chaines of error and ignorance, under the bondage and slavery of the Divell."[5] After having taught and converted natives from Bengal, India, the preacher Patrick Copland (ca. 1570–ca. 1655) announced in 1622 in London that the "Indians" of Virginia "groane under the burden of the bondage of Satan."[6] The indefatigable Samuel Purchas maintained in 1625, in the wake of the 1622 Virginia massacre in which 347 settlers lost their lives to an upris- ing of the Chesapeake natives, that the Amerindians of Virginia had proved to be "bad people, having little of Humanitie but shape . . . more brutish then the beasts they hunt, more wild and unmanly then that unmanned wild Countrey, which they range rather then inhabite; captivated also to Satans tyranny in foolish pieties, mad impieties, wicked idleness, busie and bloudy wickednesse." The role of the English in the New World, Purchas concluded, was to "deliver [the natives] from the power of darkness."[7] The Puritan John White, rector of Holy Trinity Church in Dorchester, in the county of Dorset, England, argued in 1630 that the Amerindians of New England were the "bondslaves of Sathan."[8] Finally, in 1653, the spiritual conqueror of native American souls, the Puritan John Eliot (1604–90), found the inhabitants of Massachusetts to be "poor captivated men (bondslaves to sin and Satan)."[9]

The Puritan Samuel Sewall (1652–1730) explored the nature of this col- lective serfdom in greater detail. Sewall saw the devil in America as a kind of Oriental despot, an absolute overlord: "For Satan was here as in his House strongly Fortified, and well Moted in. [He] was abundantly stored with Arms and Ammunition. Here [in the New World] he had his headquarters, his Palaces; his Throne, kept his Court; exercised an Universal, Unlimited, Unquestioned Jurisdiction." Like alienated serfs, the natives took the side of the devil, their slave master, in the epic struggle against the Europeans. "Being in love with Bondage," Sewall explained, "[Amerindians] take up Arms against their Deliverer; and strive with all their might to continue the Tyrant in quiet Possession. . . . He will not fail therefore to use all his Policy and Power, all his Methods and Stratagems of War against these recruits, coming over to reinforce the Invasion of his Dominions." Such an alliance of the slave and the slave master made the struggle all the more dangerous for the Europeans, for "Old and experienced Souldiers may be wounded and worsted in particular Encounters; specially in great Expeditions that are New and Unusual."[10]

Chapter 3

Cannibalism

There was something eerie about Satan's collective control of the natives. For one thing, it had made the Amerindians model their behavior on what demons do best in hell, namely, the processing and dismembering of bodies. As Carolyn Walker Bynum has elegantly shown, Christian patristic and medieval debates over hell and the Last Judgment were in fact arguments over the nature of the holy and the resurrected body. According to the theologians Bynum studies, holiness consisted of the avoidance of bodily change, decay, and putrefaction. All processes that dismembered and mixed human bodies, such cannibalism, quartering martyrs, and feeding them to the lions, threatened holy bodily resurrection. At the Last Judgment, however, God would put back together the bodies of the blessed, piece by piece, hair by hair, nail by nail. It is no wonder therefore that in medieval representations of hell, demons often appear busy mutilating and boiling bodies.[11] The first clear evidence that Europeans applied this conception of hell to Amerindian cannibalism appears in a Lisbon painting dating back to the 1550s, in which the anonymous Portuguese painter represents hell with the usual demons torturing, dismembering, and boiling bodies in cauldrons (fig. 3.3). The devil presiding over all these horrors is a Brazilian Tupinamba wearing a feather dress.

A closer look at Diego de Valadés's image of tyrannical oppression shows that for the Franciscan, the ritual dismemberment of bodies lay at the core of his conception of Amerindian collective servitude to the devil in Mexico. A clawed hydra with multiple arms presides over the natives as emperor. This monstrous Satan wears a necklace strung with skulls; at the bottom of the picture, demons boil and dismember bodies in hell, while two natives busily carry buckets of severed heads (see fig. 3.4).

For Valadés, the most radical expression of Satan's tyranny in the New World, compared to God's gift of free will to humankind, was that the devil demanded that the natives immolate their own children, deform their own bodies, and shed their own blood.[12] The Spanish friars had finally arrived to liberate these souls and bodies from Satan's intolerable oppression.[13]

The notion of an Amerindian collective servitude to the devil was closely linked to the idea that cannibalism was a widespread indigenous cultural institution.[14] As we have already seen, Edward Johnson saw the cannibal "Tarratines" as the embodiment of Satan himself. His Pequot warriors devoured animals like a pack of ravenous wolves, leaving the carcasses behind for their wives to eat. For Olmos, one of the first twelve Franciscans originally shipped

FIG. 3.3. Anonymous, *Hell* (detail), ca. 1550. Courtesy of the Museu de Arte Antiga, Lisbon.

FIG. 3.4. Cannibal detail. The devil enslaves Amerindians. Diego de Valadés, *Rhetorica christiana* (Perugia, 1579). Courtesy of the John Carter Brown Library, Brown University, Providence, R.I. The devil wears a necklace of skulls, and an Amerindian in hell carries a bucket full of heads.

off to Mexico in 1523 "armed with the shield of faith and with the breastplate of justice, with the blade of the spirit of salvation, with the helmet and lance of perseverance, [to] struggle with the ancient serpent,"[15] the connection between Amerindian satanism and cannibalism was clear: "Common folk used to be sacrificed to the demons. [Priests] used to butcher and hang these bodies as in a slaughterhouse. To satisfy the devil, they enacted harrowing sacrifices, bloodbaths, and crimes. Prior to the arrival of the Castilians, Satan's mansion in Mexico City, and everywhere else [in this land], was splattered with blood. They [the priests and the Devil] used to consume human meat together in front of the masses."[16]

To follow Pedro Cieza de León (1518–54), a chronicler of the early Spanish conquest and colonization of Peru, on his travels in the Colombian Andes, which he regarded as untouched by the civilizing effects of the Inca conquest, is like taking a tour of a house of horrors. Cieza de León spares no detail as he describes how in town after town, the Amerindians ate their neighbors as if the latter were farm animals (*animales campestres*). It was not only that some Colombian natives killed pregnant woman, sliced open their bellies, and ate their babies roasted; the Amerindians also had human slaughterhouses, with trunks, legs, arms, heads, and entrails dangling off the roofs like "bratwursts" (*morcillas*) and "salami" (*longanizas*) (see fig. 3.5). To

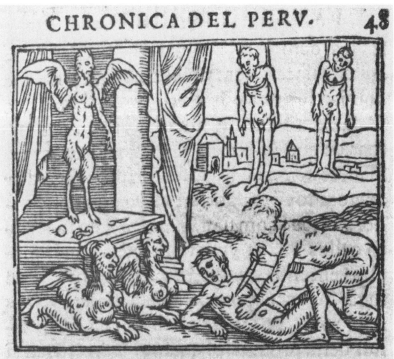

FIG. 3.5. Bodies hang like cattle in a Peruvian slaughterhouse. An Indian wielding a knife performs human sacrifice to the devil, who, satyrlike, with wings outstretched, blesses the act. Pedro Cieza de León, *La chrónica del Perú, nuevamente escrita* (Antwerp, 1554). Courtesy of the Huntington Library, San Marino, California.

Cieza de León's horror, a confused black soldier in the retinue of a conquistador had once entered a town and eaten these human body parts, thinking they were sausages. The confusion stemmed from the ability of the natives to stuff dismembered parts. Thus the Amerindians kept in the doorways to their houses the stuffed hands and feet of their victims. In some places, they flayed whole bodies, stuffed them with ashes, and then decorated them with wax heads and military insignia. But for all his disgust with the Amerindians for indulging in these practices, Cieza de León found the devil to be the real culprit. So, according to the Spanish chronicler, the dismembered bodies were usually located right next to altars to Satan. Satan himself occasionally possessed the stuffed bodies, animating them and scaring the natives to death.[17]

Wherever they went in the New World, the Europeans found a connection between cannibalism and collective demonic harassment. Andrés Pérez de Ribas (1576–1655), who in 1645 published an epic history of the spread of Jesuit missions in the northernmost frontiers of New Spain, found this connection even in the way Amerindians dispatched Jesuit martyrs. According to Pérez de Ribas, creating Christian "plantations" in the wilderness of Sinaloa, Topia, San Andres, Tepeguanes, and Parras involved transforming "beasts more ferocious than the lions and bears whose jaws David and Sampson had disjointed" into "gentle sheep."[18] These Amerindian beasts were given to "scalping their enemies and cutting off their heads and such parts as their feet and arms" while dancing and singing around the dismembered body. They did so "in such a way that such a scene resembled multitudes of demons in Hell, [the demons] who rule these people."[19] To be sure, the cracking of the jaw of the American beasts by the Jesuit Sampsons and Davids did not thrill the devil, who "grew enraged as he witnessed that the souls of [children] whom he had tyrannized for years no longer wound up in his infernal dungeons but went to heaven [after being baptized]." To establish precedent and to cow the Jesuits into fleeing, the devil moved against the "captain of the conquest" of his kingdom in Sinaloa, the Jesuit Gonzalo de Tapia. Pérez de Ribas describes in exquisite and gory detail the martyrdom of Tapia in 1594 by Satan's minions, the shaman Nacabeba and his followers, who, after seeking to convince the natives that baptism was the cause of the plagues that were wiping out the local native population, proceeded to hack Tapia to pieces.[20] In a typical demonic ceremony characterized by inversion and mockery of the holy, Nacabeba first tried to cook and ingest Tapia as a wafer while wearing the Jesuit's sacramental robes. Unfortunately for Nacabeba and the devil, the drunken cannibal orgy did not go smoothly, for God intervened repeatedly to put out the fire on which they were attempting to roast the Jesuit's body. Angered by this, Nacabeba tore off the arm with which the Jesuit had lifted the holy wafer during the sacrament of the Eucharist and performed a mockery of the mass, using Tapia's skull as chalice. Satisfied and drunk, the shaman then threw Tapia's arm away. According to Pérez de Ribas, at this point God intervened again, for the arm was found the following day lifting a Cross, with the fingers pointing to heaven. The intent of the devil and his minions, Pérez de Ribas concluded, "was to banish the preaching of the Holy Cross from Sinaloa. . . . In the end they failed, for the triumphant Cross of Christ was left standing."[21]

Lest the reader be tempted to discard this story of cannibalism and collective demonic harassment as merely typical Iberian medieval claptrap, let us turn to colonial New England for another illuminating example. If the Puritan literature on King Philip's War is remarkable for its anti-Amerindian virulence, Benjamin Tompson's accounts of it are breathtaking in their glorification of the settlers' violence.[22] As we saw in Chapter 2, Tompson sought to present the natives as demonic in his two epic poems, *Sad and Deplorable Newes from New England* (1676) and *New-Englands Tears for her Present Miseries* (1676).[23] Using strikingly vivid images, Tompson insisted that the demonic could not be dissociated from Amerindian ritual cannibalism. Thus for him, the natives burnt not only Puritan towns but also people and cattle, because they wanted to feed their deities with smoke of roasted bodies.[24] To clinch his argument, Tompson had King Philip himself figure as the devil presiding over hell.[25]

In this type of Puritan epic narrative, dissenters and atheists figure as monstrous, demonic cannibals along with the Amerindians. Edward Johnson, for example, attributed the birth of monsters to Anne Hutchinson, the leading "Antinomian" dissenter of the "free-grace" controversy of 1636–38, and to Hutchinson's follower Mary Dyer (who was allegedly delivered of a fetus with horn and claws) to Hutchinson's dabbling in satanically inspired midwifery and as God's punishment for the deviancy of these two women.[26] More to the point, Cotton Mather associated heretics with cannibalism. In his *Bateries upon the Kingdom of the Devil* (1695) Mather argued: "Atheists eat up the people of God as they eat bread. They destroy the People of God with open mouth; and they do it with as little remorse they do it with as much fury as much delight; as they can eat a meal when they are hungry. Such Cannibals doe the People of God often meet withal."[27]

The trope of cannibalistic consumption and satanic harassment was also used to present the Spaniards as satanic and to explain crucial events in the history of the continent. Take, for example, the case of Samuel Sewall, who was obsessed with millenarian theories. His *Phaenomena quaedam apocalyptica ad aspectum novi orbis configurata, or, Some few lines towards a description of the new heaven as it makes to those who stand upon the new earth* (1697) sought to dismiss the anti-American interpretations of the great English eschatologist Joseph Mede (1586–1638), who in his 1627 commentary on the Book of Revelation, *Clavis Apocalyptica* (translated as *The Key of the Revelation*), maintained, not surprisingly, that the devil had enjoyed absolute sovereignty over the New World prior to the arrival of the Europeans. Sewall did not take issue with this aspect of Mede's interpretation but with Mede's influential assertion that even after the second coming of Christ to inaugurate the millennium, America would not be able to shake off Satan's sovereignty. This theory suggested that the devil's lordship over the continent had not been dented by the arrival of the Europeans, and that the European effort to convert the natives was doomed. In fact, in Mede's reading of the future, the settlers would soon be part of Satan's elect, not of the New Jerusalem, as they fondly imagined. "I will hope," Mede confided to his friend the theologian William Twisse (1578–1646) in 1635, "[the Puritan settlers] shall not so far degenerate (not all of them) as time come in that Army of Gog and Magog against the Kingdome of Christ."[28] This threat of Creole degeneration moved Sewall to attack Mede's authoritative interpretation by challenging Mede's historical chronologies.[29]

To understand this rather technical point in the controversy, we need to remember that events in Revelation unfold in three phases as upheavals that succeed one another, with the opening of the seven seals followed by the blowing of the seven trumpets and the pouring of the seven vials. Mede argued in his *Clavis* that the first six seals corresponded chronologically to the history of the fall of Rome down to the barbarian invasions and to Rome's conversion under Constantine. The first four trumpets described the final collapse of Rome, and the last three the rise of Islam, the attack on the West by the Turks, and the rise of the anti-Christian popish state respectively. The events unleashed by the blowing of the seventh trumpet and the pouring of all seven vials, according to Mede, corresponded to contemporary events, including the Reformation and the massacre of Protestant martyrs in France, Holland, and Bohemia. The pouring of the seventh vial was drawing near, and it would finally lead to the removal of Satan to America for a millennium. After the millennium, however, the devil and the armies of demons of Gog and Magog would emerge from their exile in America to confront God one more time before the Last Judgment.[30]

Sewall altered these chronologies radically so that America would not remain the uncontested fiefdom of Satan until the very end of time. He argued, for example, that the opening of the fourth seal corresponded to the discovery of America, not to events in pre-Constantinian Rome, as Mede had suggested. According to Sewall, Revelation 6:7–8 ("And when he had opened the fourth seal, I heard the voice of the fourth beast say, Come and see. And I looked, and behold a pale horse: and his name that sat on him was Death, and Hell followed with him. And power was given unto them over the fourth part of the earth, to kill with sword, and with hunger, and with death, and with the beasts of the earth") prefigured the Spanish conquest of the New World. The conquistadors stood for the knight of Death bringing "hell" to America, taking over this fourth part of the earth, where they slaughtered the natives with swords, famine, and hounds. But this typological reading of Revelation had obvious flaws, because Mede, Sewall, and everyone else agreed that America had been Satan's kingdom at the time of the Spanish arrival. How could the Spaniards have brought hell to hell? It is here that the thesis of demonic cannibalism served Sewall well. In this particular context, the "hell" introduced by the rider Death, Sewall argued, was not the same hell over which the devil had presided in America, the fourth part of the earth. The hell introduced by the Spaniards signified the final destiny of the souls of millions of natives whom they had killed. The conquistadors had dispatched twenty million before having exposed them to the Gospel, and according to basic theological principles, all unconverted souls went straight to hell. More important from the perspective of this chapter, "hell" for Sewall signified how these slaughtered bodies had been disposed of. Torn to pieces by Spanish hounds, the bodies of the Amerindians had ended up dismembered and fragmented in the bellies of dogs.[31]

Collective Harassment and Amerindian Emasculation

The *selective* enslavement of entire peoples and their transformation into cannibal brutes who behaved like demons in hell, dismembering and boiling bodies, required an explanation, for according to standard theological views, no one was spared from the power of the devil. Lucifer had the extraordinary ability to manipulate Nature, appearing in disguises and potentially able to fool anyone, not only Amerindians. The devil also had command over the mind, potentially causing anyone (not only Amerindians) to take for real images what were in fact only phantasms of the imagination. Moreover, the structure of the physical world inhabited by humanity in the early modern period was one in which anyone (not only Amerindians) could potentially be deceived by Satan. This was a world organized around the Aristotelian distinction between "substance" (true, innermost nature) and "accident" (surface appearance), and according to Christian interpretations of Aristotelian physics "substance" and "accident" in a body did not necessarily overlap. Take, for example, the consecrated host. The host in its original state is white, round, and flat (which are "accidents"), but it is also "bread" (substance). After the miracle of the Eucharist, however, the "substance" of the host changes and becomes the body of Christ. The doctrine of transubstantiation points to a serious problem of credibility in human perception in a world ruled by the laws of Aristotelian physics. For unless one relied on the authority of a professional body of interpreters (i.e., the Church), there was no way of knowing whether the "accident" and "substance" of perceived objects overlapped. Thus one could be observing an object whose "accidents" indicated that it was, say, a cat, when in fact it was an animal with the "substance" of the devil.[32]

Epistemologically, this was a world in which anyone, not only Amerindians, could be deceived, a world in which the devil thrived. No one appreciated the impossibility of reaching certainty in a world in which demons could manipulate both objects and perception more than René Descartes (1596–1650). It could well be argued that the Cartesian method was every bit as much a reply to the Pyrrhonism of seventeenth-century humanists as an effort to sidestep the tricks of demons. Demons constantly make their appearance in Descartes's *Meditations* (1641) as the French philosopher seeks to find clear and distinct ideas, unassailable by the tricks of Satan.[33]

Although the devil had the ability to deceive anyone, he in fact focused his powers on harassing either the holiest or the weakest members of the human community. Satan assailed those whose spiritual powers he most feared. Thus he had once sought to tempt Christ (e.g., Matt. 4:1–11). His failure at this attempt did not keep Satan from going after friars, nuns, (Puritan) saints, and the pious in general. The devil also went after the weak, particularly women. Not surprisingly, demonologists agreed that holy males were capable only of being "obsessed" by the devil, whereas nuns and pious laywomen could be "possessed." The staunchest followers of the devil, after all, were witches.[34] As the Franciscan Olmos explained in his treatise on demonology in mid-sixteenth-century Mexico, it was women who the devil most easily deceived, because women were curious and, unlike men, wanted to know the secrets of Nature through shortcuts, without having to study. Moreover, women were more easily overcome by anger and jealousy and therefore were more willing to look to the devil to settle scores. Among women, spinsters and the poor were the most vulnerable, because they usually were alone and sought company and support. In fact, old single women were even willing to engage in sexual intercourse with demons.[35]

The claim that all Amerindians were spellbound by the devil suggests that European imaginations saw the natives as having a similar temperament and constitution to European females. The conclusions reached by Irene Silverblatt would seem to contradict this point, for she has argued that in the Peruvian campaigns against idolatry, the Catholic clergy zeroed in on female witches, as in Europe. But this interpretation is difficult to maintain, for the Europeans consistently thought that the most powerful allies of Satan in the New World were male shamans.[36]

There was something special about the power of the devil in the New World, for here he was capable of luring males as easily as he tricked females in Europe. When Pedro de Villagómez, the archbishop of Lima, sought to explain why it had become so difficult for the Church to extirpate idolatrous behavior in Peru, he had several explanations to hand: inter alia, that the natives were constantly reminded of their deities, since the latter were features of landscape itself; that the natives were reluctant to abandon religious traditions handed down to them by their elders, because those same elders would later be worshipped as mummies; that the devil was extraordinarily persuasive, a consummate trickster; that the division of labor among religious specialists in the Andes was so extraordinary that there were multitudes of shamans even in the smallest of communities; and that the Catholic parish priests in Amerindian towns were corrupt and ignorant. But despite his multi-causal theory, Villagómez most enjoyed laying the blame on the natives' psychological makeup, for they were *constitutionally* prone to be easily duped by the devil. Like European females, the natives were weak and naïve: "[The devil] deceives them with the greatest of ease, for [the natives] are childish [*incipientes*], slow in understanding, clumsy in reasoning, and lacking in knowledge of the secrets of the natural world [*experiencia*]. And since they lack the necessary Christian doctrine, these *miserables* have no capacity to see through the tricks of the devil, who, being more astute, skilful in moving and presenting himself, and with much greater knowledge of the secrets of Nature [than the Amerindians], deploys all his malice, strength and astuteness against them. [Amerindians] therefore easily surrender to worshipping [Satan]."[37] It is clear then that one way available to the Europeans to explain why the devil had been capable of enslaving the Amerindians as a whole was to claim that the latter were constitutionally naïve and simple-minded.

The Geographical Mobility of Demons: The Geopolitics of Evil

Another route taken by the Europeans was to argue that the devil had been completely unchallenged in the New World for centuries. Europeans thought that the devil moved around the globe picking and choosing his real estate carefully. Notwithstanding Ignacio de Loyola's influential view that "[the devil] summons innumerable demons, and scatters them, some to one city and some to another, throughout the whole world, so that no province, no place, no state of life is overlooked," early modern Europeans thought that the devil and his cohort of evil angels settled according to the law of least resistance.[38] Pierre de Lancre (1553–1631), an inquisitor in the Labourd area of the French Basque region, argued in 1612, for example, that the Basques were particularly prone to demonic worship. The males were rootless sailors, as "inconstant" as demons, who left behind vulnerable households headed by women for at least half the year when they went fishing. Moreover, the Basques had a long, well-established connection with the demon-ridden continent of America. They had long been trading with the Canadian natives, who refused, in fact, to "deal with the French in any language other than that of the Basque." Like the Amerindians of Hispaniola (and many other Europeans), Basques also smoked tobacco ("Petun or Nicotaine").[39] Yet despite all these predisposing factors, it was only in recent times that Labourd had witnessed collective devil worship. Why? The answer lay in the "devotion and effective pedagogical work of countless good missionaries [who] had chased the Demons and evil Angels away from the Indies, Japan and other places." Labourd was experiencing outbreaks of witchcraft because the retreating demons were now moving en masse into Christian lands, particularly into places like Labourd, where they "found a well-disposed people." "Slowly, after having driven away fathers and husbands to the New World and beyond, where there is no known religion, [demons] have become the masters of this country, taking control of the women, the children, and [even] the majority of priests and pastors."[40]

This very principle of the geographical mobility of demons served others to explain the arrival of the devil and his minions in the New World in the first place. Thus Mede, whose ideas on the millennial tenacity of the devil in the New World Sewall would loudly reject, argued in 1635 that

the Devil, being impatient of the sound of the Gospel and Cross of Christ in every part of this old world, so that he could in no place be quiet for it, and forseeing that he was like at length to lose all here, be thought himself to provide him of a seed over which he might reign securely. . . . That accordingly he drew a Colony out of some of those barbarous Nations dwelling upon the northern Ocean, (whither the sound of Christ had not yet come) and promising them by some oracle to show them a Country far better than their own, (which he might soon doe) pleasant, large, where never man yet inhabited, he conducted them over those desert lands and islands (which are many in that sea) by the way of the North into America; which none would ever have gone, had they not first been assured there was a passage that way into a more desireable country.[41]

The deafening sound of the Gospel in the Old World, according to Mede, had forced the devil to invite northern Scythians to settle and inhabit the New World.

This idea resonated down the seventeenth century with Puritan clerics. William Hubbard (1621–1704) and Cotton Mather used it repeatedly.[42] But Mather was also willing to build on Mede's insight. Mather argued that once his Scythian minions had crossed the land bridge from northern Asia to America, Satan had turned to the dragon of bewitchment to guard the "orchard" he had just captured, keeping the Europeans from learning how to use the lodestone to cross the Atlantic.[43] This was not to be Mather's only insight; he thought that when the devil had promised a New Canaan to the northern bands of Scythians in patristic times, as an escape from the barren deserts of northern Asia, Satan had lied. The devil in fact liked these deserts. King James I had already made this point in his fictional dialogue *Daemonologie* (1603), where a bewildered Philomathes asks Epistemone why incubi seemed to impregnate women more easily "in such wilde parts of the worlde, as *Lap.land*, and *Find-land*, or in our North *Iles of Orknay* and *Schet-land*." To which Epistemone replies: "where the Divell findes greatests ignorance and barbaritie, there assailes hee grosseliest."[44] Like James I, Mather thought that the devil enjoyed the uncultivated corners of the world. It stood to reason, then, that as the Puritan settlers moved like the Israelites into the wilderness, the devil would be forced to retreat ever deeper into the American frontier.[45]

The thesis of the geographical mobility of demons was widely applied by Europeans in the New World over the course of the sixteenth and seventeenth centuries. Thus in 1698, the Puritan divine Nicholas Noyes (1647–1717), who sided with Sewall against Mede's dismal views of the millennium in America, used this thesis to argue that when the Reformation had kicked the devil out of Europe, Satan sent his minions, the Spanish conquistadors and the popish Church, to America to secure him a beachhead to which to retreat.[46]

The Iberians had, in fact, long used a version of this very argument. In a letter addressed to Pope Paul III (r. 1534–49) in the late 1530s, the Dominican bishop of Tlaxcala, Julián Garcés (1452–1542), urged the pope not to spare support for the nascent Catholic churches both in Asia and America, for in Europe, the agents of the devil, the Turks, were taking over. "Let us snatch from the Devil more land in the Indies," Garcés concluded, "than he along with his Mohammedans stole from Europe. Let us shake the fortifications of the demons with a double battering-ram so as to free the [natives] from their ancient captivity."[47] In his massive 1615 history of Mexico, for example, the Franciscan Juan de Torquemada (ca. 1577–1664) maintained that there was a reason why Martin Luther (1483–1546) and Hernán Cortés (1485–1547) had both been born in 1485 (actually Luther was born in 1483), and why Luther's reformation had been launched the year Cortés conquered Mexico. According to Torquemada, God and Satan were engaged in a great geopolitical struggle, a give-and-take of territories. So, Torquemada added, Luther was born "to rattle the world and to bring under the banner of the devil those whose fathers and grandfathers had in the past been Catholic," whereas the "Christian Captain" Cortés had come into the world to "bring into the fold of the Catholic Roman Church the countless multitude of peoples who for untold number of years had been under the power of Satan." It was therefore clear "that whatever was lost on the one hand was recovered on the other, so as to break even according to God's accounting."[48]

In his history of the shrine to Our Lady of Copacabana in Peru (1621), Alonso Ramos Gavilán (b. ca. 1570) also sought to shed light on the nature of the celestial geopolitical reshuffling triggered both by the Reformation and by the conquest of America. Drawing on Matthew 21:43 ("Therefore say I unto you, The kingdom of God shall be taken from you, and given to a nation bringing forth the fruits thereof"), Ramos Gavilán tried to understand why English Protestants had smashed and destroyed so many holy images precisely in the years when the Amerindian natives were shedding their idolatry and embracing the cult of the image of Our Lady of Copacabana. "It seems," Ramos Gavilán argued, "that [Matt. 21:43] can be applied to the people of England . . . for we see that this region of Copacabana, which used to be the house of demons, is now steeped in religion, whereas England has become a new Babylon, the dumping ground of idolatry, confusion and death." "It is [therefore] reasonable to think," Ramos Gavilán concluded, "that holy images were taken away from England and given to these lucky little Indians [*estos venturosos Indezuelos*]."[49]

Satan: God's Ape in America

Mede's argument that during patristic times the devil had persuaded bands of northern barbarians to move from Asia into America resembles the narrative of the biblical books of Moses, for according to Mede, the devil had promised his chosen Scythians "by some oracle to show them a Country far better than their own, (which he might soon doe) pleasant, large, where never man yet inhabited, he conducted them over those desert lands and islands (which are many in that sea) by the way of the North into America; which none would ever have gone, had they not first been assured there was a passage that way into a more desireable country."[50] Just as God had led his elected Israelites to Canaan, Satan had conducted his wandering Scythians into the promised land of America. As Juan de San Pedro, one of the first twelve "apostles" sent by the Augustinians to Peru, came across an Andean history of creation that resembled the story of the Trinity, the friar argued: "Satan is God's simian," a primate constantly seeking to mimic God.[51]

Satan made a point of establishing a kingdom built on a parody of the Old and New Testaments in the New World. Is his account of the 1692 outbreak of witchcraft in Salem, Cotton Mather was astounded to discover how closely Satan had parodied God in America. It was not only that Satan had mocked the story of the Exodus in Mexico by leading the Aztecs into a southbound migration with a tabernacle and ark of their own, but also that "the Devil, which then thus imitated what was in the Church of the Old Testament, now among Us would imitate the Affayrs of the Church in the New." According to Mather, the witches in Salem were organized "much after the manner of Congregational Churches." They had "a Baptism and a Supper, and Officers among them, abominably Ressembling those of our Lord."[52] Besides seeking to imitate the rituals and principles of the original apostolic Church, Mather argued, Satan had also pursued these witches into "blasphemous Imitations of . . . things recorded about our savior or His Prophets, or the Saints of the Kingdom of God." Like Jesus, the Apostles, and the Blessed of the Last Judgment in the New Testament, Satan had enabled the witches to strike down "with fierce look"; "[make] the afflicted rise with a touch of their hand"; "[transport] themselves thro the Air"; "[travel] in spirit while their body is cast into trance"; "[enter] their names in a Book"; "[come] together from all parts at the sound of a Trumpet"; "[appear] sometimes clothed with light or fire"; and "[cause] cattle to run mad and perish."[53] When he leveled these charges against Satan's power to mimic God in America, Mather seemed to have had in mind such passages in the Bible as Matthew 8:32, in which Jesus, like the witches, causes livestock to go mad and perish ("And he said unto them [the demons], Go. And when they were come out, they went into the herd of swine: and, behold, the whole herd of swine ran violently down a steep place into the sea, and perished in the waters").

Mather's insight had long been recognized in Spanish America. The

Chapter 3

Franciscan Olmos in his mid-sixteenth-century demonological treatise insisted that whereas the Catholic Church had "sacraments," the devil performed "excraments" (*execramentos*), characterized by the employment of gross food, refuse, and dirt, as well as the use of gibberish verbal formulas and senseless speech.[54] As José de Acosta (1540–1600) maintained in 1590, in Mexico, the list of "excraments" was long and included baptism and, to the horror of everyone, the Eucharist and communion.[55] In Peru, the Catholic clergy were shocked to find that a "ghastly thing that these Indians also practice [is] the [sacrament] of oral confession."[56] Resemblances to Catholic practice and doctrine were everywhere to be found in Peru. The natives, for example, had the notion of "sentinel angels," charged with protecting and guarding nations from misfortune. "In all towns in this province," the Augustinian San Pedro complained, "the Devil, who mimics whatever he sees and who wants to pass as an angel of light, has persuaded the Indians to embrace a guarding angel, similar to the angels that according to our theologians take care of each nation and republic. The angels here, however, have been transformed into stone, for each town worships a *huaca*, or idol, that is, a large boulder."[57] There was also the practice among Andeans of keeping their nail and hair clippings, as if they were aware of the doctrine of bodily resurrection, for at the Last Judgment, God would reassemble each original body out of leftovers, including ashes, bones, and nail pairings.[58] Like Catholics who kept parts of saints' bodies as relics, the people of Cuzco had eviscerated the body of the Inca and kept his heart inside holy objects.[59] The preservation of mummified ancestors all over the Andes moved Cieza de León to argue that this was a satanic version of the Catholic cult of the saints and their relics.[60]

It is not surprising that Sor Juana Inés de la Cruz (1648–95), "The Tenth Muse" of the Spanish American baroque, found a place in her plays for the devil as a trickster and mime. In *El Divino Narciso* (Divine Narcissus), written in Mexico in 1688 to be performed as an *auto sacramental* in Madrid, Sor Juana, for example, reproduced each and every one of the tropes and motifs of early modern demonology I have described. The play begins with female "America" and male "Occident" worshipping the god of harvest (*dios de las semillas*), who is fed with the bodies and blood of humans. Satan makes sure to mimic the most sacred of Church sacraments, the Eucharist, so he has the Amerindians fashion images of the harvest god out of corn bread. The two Amerindians are soon confronted by female "Religion," who unsuccessfully seeks to persuade them to convert, and "Zeal," a knight who, after denouncing "Occident" as tyrant, has his army of Spanish soldiers attack the two natives. "Religion" persuades "Zeal" not to destroy the Amerindians without trying to reason with them again. This time, softened by the blows of "Zeal," "America" and "Occident" are more willing to listen, and "Religion" denounces the harvest god as Satan himself, a devil who seeks to mimic God and the sacrament of the Eucharist: "O God, help me! What images, what dark designs, what shadowing of truths most sacred to our Faith do these lies seek to imitate? O false, sly, and deceitful snake! O asp, with sting so venomous! O hydra, that from seven mouths pours noxious poisons, every one a passage to oblivion! To what extent, with this façade, do you intend maliciously to mock the mysteries of God?"[61]

After identifying Satan as an ape of God, "Religion" scrambles for ways to persuade the Amerindians. Believing that the natives are constitutionally incapable of being moved by oral arguments, "Religion" comes up with the idea of convincing the natives through images, that is, through a religious play (loa of auto, 401–12). To teach the natives about the true nature of Satan as a trickster, "Religion" concludes, the play should be about the Greek myth of Narcissus and the nymph Echo. In the play, "Narcissus" stands for Christ, who is seeking to find his lost reflection: humankind. "Echo," on the other hand, stands for the devil, who, spurned by Narcissus, keeps Narcissus's reflection (humankind) in chains (auto, 404–7). "Echo" accordingly presents herself as an ape of Narcissus, an echo of Narcissus's voice (auto, 355–57). Sor Juana elegantly summarized the sensibilities of her age.

The idea that Satan had sought to mimic the institutions of God in America found ringing confirmation in the history of the Aztecs. In 1606, the learned Dominican missionary Gregorio García (d. 1627) published a thick treatise seeking to explain the origin of the Amerindians. Unlike Mede, who emphasized a single Satan-led migration to America, García postulated many movements of people in which the devil had played no apparent role. Yet when it came to the Aztecs, García had no doubt that they had arrived in central Mexico led by the hand of Satan. García drew upon the ideas published by the Jesuit José de Acosta, who in 1590 made popular the notion that the Aztecs were Satan's elect. According to Acosta, with idolatry being "extirpated from the best and most noble part of the world [Europe], the devil decided to withdraw to the most isolated place, to rule over this other part of the globe," which "albeit much inferior in quality [nobleza] is much larger in size."[62] Acosta argued that the southbound migration of the Aztecs from Azatlan to central Mexico eerily resembled that of the Israelites from Egypt to Canaan. Like the Israelites, the Mexicans had carried a tabernacle and the ark of their deity, Huitzilopochtli.[63] García further fleshed out this narrative by explaining how Satan, mimicking the way God had fed the Israelites in the wilderness, had caused bread to rain from the sky and water to gush from rocks to feed the Aztecs during their own southbound migration.[64] Thus, García concluded: "Who is to deny that the departure and peregrination of the Mexicans resemble the departure from Egypt of the Children of Israel and their exodus? For the former, like the latter, were prompted to leave and go in search of a Promised Land. Both peoples took their Gods as guide, consulted the Ark and built a Tabernacle. Both drew advice and their laws and ceremonies [from these consultations]. And it took both a great number of years to reach the Promised Land. In these and many other things, the history of the Mexicans resembles the history of the Israelites according to Holy Scripture."[65]

Satan and Typology: The Aztecs' History as the Inverted Mirror Image of the Israelites'

García left "the many other" resemblances to the reader's imagination, but the Franciscan Juan de Torquemada filled in the blanks. Book 2 of Torquemada's massive history of Mexico, published in 1615, is devoted to exploring the analogies between the history of the Aztecs and that of the Israelites. Drawing upon a well-established patristic tradition that events and characters in the Old Testament were "types" or prefigurations of future history, Torquemada read the history of the Aztecs as the inverted, perverse fulfillment of the Old Testament.[66] In the following pages, I explore how our current narrative of Aztec history (northern migration; settlement under adverse conditions in central Mexico; triumph over neighboring ethnic rivals; and the fall of Tenochtitlán) emerged out of Franciscan typological readings of the Mexican past. Typology is usually attributed to Calvinist and, in the case of the New World, Puritan styles of thinking. There is to my knowledge only one study of Catholic uses of typology in colonization, whereas there are great many of New World Puritanism.[67] The evidence above shows that the inverted typological readings of the history of Mexico migrated into the writings of Puritan mainstream theologians like Mede via the publications of Acosta and Gregorio García. Mede used these views, in turn, to create the eschatological foundations of the genre of the "errand into the wilderness." Despite this evidence, British and Spanish American colonial studies have largely gone their own separate ways. In this section, I argue that Torquemada's history of Mexico should be read as the first typological study ever to appear in the New World. Torquemada fully fleshed out the history of the Mexica as the satanic mirror image of that of the Israelites. In his interpretation, the fall of Tenochtitlán was equivalent to the fall of Jerusalem, following an exodus, Canaanite oppression, and an age of monarchies and prophets.

According to Torquemada, the Aztecs were one of many peoples who over the course of the centuries had swept into central Mexico from the north. What was unique about them was that they were Satan's elect. Since Satan liked to mimic God, it stood to reason that the Aztecs shared with the Israelites more than an exodus through the wilderness. Like Acosta and García, Torquemada presented the Aztec migration from Azatlan to central Mexico as led and inspired by Satan. But being steeped in Amerindian historical sources, Torquemada was also able to find many other parallels. He identified the tribal leaders Huitziton and Tecpatcin as "the Moses and Aaron" of the Aztecs, for example. After taking their people on a decades-long southbound exodus, Huitziton and Tecpatcin had died in the "desert," just as had happened to the leaders of "the People of Israel during their migration through the wilderness. Moses and Aaron also died while leading them out of Egypt through the desert."[68] From the beginning Satan/ Huitzilopochtli sought to segregate his people from the larger group of Aztec tribes and ordered them to change their names: "Like my chosen ones, I want you to no longer be called Aztecs, but Mexica."[69] Satan then anointed them, gave them an ark, and sent them off to "defeat many enemies and lord it over vast provinces and kingdoms."[70] Like the God of the Israelites in the Old Testament, the Satan of the Mexica was a wrathful, punishing deity. He ripped out the hearts of those who once dared to challenge his order to keep moving south, announcing: "Do they seek to overlook and oppose my dictates and mandates? Tell them that I'll be revenged on them . . . for no one should dare dispute my orders. Everyone should understand that I am the only one to be obeyed."[71]

Once the Mexica arrive in central Mexico, Torquemada begins to consider them as equivalent to the Israelites buffeted and oppressed by Canaanites. As the Mexica get near the central valley of Mexico, they increase "like the Israelites under the Pharaoh" and become enslaved.[72] Here they endure a long "captivity" under the Aculhua, who systematically humiliate them; and the Mexica "mull over their afflictions and bad fortune, crying over their cramped [living conditions] and bad luck."[73] However, the devil promises them relief: "Don't grieve, Mexicans . . . I'll help you."[74] The Aculhua finally let them go, and the Mexica end up eking out a miserable existence in the marshes of the Mexican lakes, only to fall under the ruthless rule of the Tepanec of Azcaputzalco, who tax them unreasonably. At this point, Satan again promises relief: "I'll deliver you from hardship and affliction. I'll make things easy and smooth for you."[75] The ability of the Mexica to pay the exorbitant tribute exacted by the Tepanec causes the tyrant Tezozomoc, king of Azcaputzalco, to realize that the Mexica are Satan's elect, for "what they have done [i.e., pay the unrealistic taxes] is superhuman. I myself considered it impossible to meet the demands I put on them; . . . I want you to understand that these [Mexica] are favored by God [Satan in this case]. They are destined to rule over all the Nations."[76] Yet, "like the Pharaoh in the kingdom of Egypt, who, not finding the ordinary tribute of the children of Israel enough, kept piling hardships and burdens on them as the Israelites multiplied," Tezozomoc keeps on oppressing and harassing the Mexica, who keep on multiplying.[77]

Fortunately for the Mexica, the Tepanec overplay their hand with the Aculhua, who turn to the Mexica for help. Thus the Mexica and Aculhua form an alliance, defeat the Tepanec, and create an empire. In Torquemada's imagination, the Mexica at this point become the inverted satanic mirror image of the Israelites under the monarchies of Saul, David, and Solomon, no longer satanic Israelites in exodus and in captivity. Like the Israelites who built a temple to God once they acquired an empire, the Mexica erect one to Satan. The David of the Mexica is the first Moctezuma, Ilhuicamina; "the first thing he did under his rule was to lay [the foundation] of a Temple, a House to the Devil."[78] But he does not finish it. It is the Mexican Solomon, the emperor Ahuizotl who completes the "House and Temple to the Devil." Ahuizotl inaugurates the shrine to Huitzilopochtli by slaying 72,344 victims over the course of four days.[79] Not surprisingly the devil continues to deliver the Mexica from hardships and keeps them from starving during floods.[80]

Again like Israel in the age of the monarchies, the Mexica empire witnesses the rise of prophets, particularly among the rulers of the Aculhua, the main allies of the Mexica. In Torquemada's narrative, the Aculhua monarch Nezahualpilli emerges as a prophet, a closet deist, who nevertheless puts up with demonic human sacrifice. Largely because he is not Mexica, Nezahualpilli is one of the few capable of reading prophetic signs that announce the doom of the empire. Nezahualpilli understands that the sudden appearance of three crosses in the sky; the birth of monstrosities, including a bird with human head; the falling out of the sky of a stone column, which lands right next to the temple of Huitzilopochtli; the appearance of a hare that wanders unimpeded into the palaces; and a sudden increase of earthquakes and floods are all signs of things to come. Nezahualpilli prophesies that the end of the empire of Satan in Mexico is near, and that God's liberating army will soon arrive.[81]

Torquemada at this point in the narrative jumps to consider the capital of the Mexica, Tenochtitlán, as Satan's Jerusalem. Eerily, "like the Republic of Israel, to which we have compared it in various place of this history," Tenochtitlán witnesses most of the signs that the Jewish historian Flavius Josephus (37–100 CE) described had occurred in Jerusalem prior to the demolition of the Temple by the Romans.[82] In the years preceding Tenochtitlán's destruction by the Spaniards, the inhabitants of the city witness a light that blazes from east to west every night over the course of a year; a fire that has no natural cause, that cannot be put out, and that badly damages Huitzilopochtli's temple; a comet with three heads and a long tail that appears in the sky in plain daylight; a lake that suddenly begins to boil over and floods the city; two armies that appear in the sky; widespread famine; and a strange bird with a shining crown carved with images of armies.[83] The Mexica are paralyzed because they have no prophets of their own to interpret these signs (see fig. 3.6).

Unlike the Israelites in the Babylonian exile who had a Daniel and the Egyptians who had a Joseph to interpret ciphers (Genesis 37 and 40–41), the Mexica lack "true interpreters of dreams and natural signs. Their wizards were blind, ignorant men who waited for the king to make sense of the signs for them. Moctezuma did not have a Holy Prophet at hand to tell him the truth."[84] A Deborah-like prophetess (Judges 4–5) appears in Tenochtitlán on the eve of the conquest, however: Papan, the sister of Moctezuma, who, after experiencing a near-death episode, revives to tell the Mexica the meaning of her vision of a valley strewn with bones and heads and black men with horns and cloven hooves building a house, while a fleet approaches from the east. A good angel helps Papan understand that her vision represents things to come in Mexico, for the quarters that the demons are building in the valley is a charnel house to hold the bodies of those who will soon die battling the liberating fleet of God. Then the angel commands Papan to go back, wait for the army to arrive, and become a leader of the new converts. Papan acquiesces and from that day on leads a life of pious fasting. According to Torquemada, the case of Deborah/Papan represents yet another striking resemblance between the Israelites and the Mexica: "Heaven sends signs for people to reform and lead better lives. As Josephus says, God used to send signs to the People of Israel for them to wake up and look for ways to redeem themselves."[85]

After having presented the history of the Mexica as the satanic mirror

Indi prodigijs Montis igniuomi, Amnis arborem, mostrum que trahentis, Aquilarum iterum
tantūm Visarum, exercitus Hispani in aere de suo Victoris, paci conciliantur et Fidei in Chile.

image of that of the Israelites (including, along with the exodus, the Israelite oppression under the Canaanites and the age of monarchies, kingdoms, and prophets), Torquemada switches to a new analogy when he begins to describe the Spanish conquest. Now the Mexica become the Canaanites and the Spaniards the Israelites. Take, for example, Torquemada's account of Moctezuma's panic upon hearing that Cortés is about to cross the Sierra Madre on his way to Tenochtitlán. Like Balak, king of Moab, who ordered Balaam to cast a spell against the approaching Israelites (Numbers 22–24), Moctezuma orders his wizards to go to the mountain passes and stop the Spaniards by using a curse. Yet, like Balaam who actually blessed the Israelites instead of cursing them, Moctezuma's wizards prove unable to do anything against the approaching Israelite Iberians: "Because God, who has the power to muzzle the jaws of the lions seeking to reap the bodies of the saints, ties up the tongue of the Demons. God does not allow anything to hurt his vassals."[86]

Thus Torquemada presents the Spanish conquest as an act of exorcism.

FIG. 3.6. *(opposite)* Preternatural signs announce the defeat of the Chilean natives. According to Alonso de Ovalle's *Historica relación del reino de Chile*, prior to the arrival of the new Spanish governor Don Francisco de Zúñiga, the following signs appeared in Chile: armies in the sky (representing the triumph of the Spanish armies); bands of eagles nesting in the city (announcing the final triumph of the Habsburg); a volcanic eruption that caused floods and killed the fish in rivers (announcing famine and devastation); the sighting of an uprooted tree followed by a monster being carried away by the floods (representing the uprooting of idolatry and the devil). "It seems," Ovalle maintained, "that by divine Mercy the time has arrived to expel this beast by means of apostolic preachers, for whom these gentiles have great need. This beast has passed as the king and god [of the natives] and tyrannized this land. [The beast] will be uprooted and thrown out of his long-held possession into the mouth of the abyss, where it would be swallowed, digested, and torn into pieces by the teeth of furious waves and currents" (con que parece podemos esperar en la divina Misericordia se ha llegado ya el tiempo en que por medio de predicadores apostólicos, por quien clama ya este gentilismo, quiere que sea desterrada a despecho suyo esta bestia que ha tenido tiranizada como a su dios y a su rey esta tierra, y dando voces por verse desalojada y lanzada de su antigua posesión, abriendo el abismo su boca, la trague y consuma, despedazada entre dientes de sus furiosas olas y encendidas corrientes). Alonso de Ovalle, *Histórica relación del reino de Chile* (Rome, 1646; Santiago: Prensas de la editorial universitaria, 1969), bk. 7, ch. 9, p. 324. Courtesy of the John Carter Brown Library, Brown University, Providence, R.I.

His accounts of the foundation of the city of Puebla de los Angeles and of Mexico City itself under Spanish rule are very telling. The Spaniards had founded Puebla of the Angels at a spot where an indigenous town had been destroyed by internecine intertribal warfare. According to Torquemada, the new city had therefore been conceived as a monument to commemorate the utter destruction of the evil angels. With the foundation of Puebla, the victory of the good angels over the evil ones had moved from the heavenly to the terrestrial sphere: "[for the good angels] not only pursued the evil ones in heaven . . . but waged war on them on earth, always on the offensive without diminishing their zeal."[87] Built on the rubble of what used to be Tenochtitlán, the new Hispanic city of Mexico also celebrated the Iberian triumph over the devil. The cathedral occupied the ground where the Mexica temple to Huitzilopochtli had once stood. By the same token, the forty Christian churches of the capital had replaced the forty minor shrines surrounding Huitzilopochtli's temple. According to Torquemada, "it behooves God that the places where the devil has his throne be destroyed and that the banner of God's glorious victory be planted."[88] God was gratified by the new spectacle, for on the very spot in which "the sacrifice of human bodies to the devil" had once taken place, "now is offered the body and blood of Christ." Torquemada ended this account on a hopeful note, for he considered that Mexico now had "more good angels defending and protecting the city than the number of evil angels and demons" who used to rule the city under the Mexica.[89]

Driving out Demons with the Cross

When the twelve Franciscan "apostles" arrived in New Spain in 1523 clad in the armor of Christ, Tenochtitlán lay in ruins and was already on its way to becoming Mexico City. Busily, the Franciscans felled one of the sacred trees (most likely a gigantic *ahuehuete*, or Mexican cypress) in the forest of Chapultepec, Moctezuma's pastoral retreat, dragged it all the way back to the capital, and fashioned a cross for their new convent from it. Many natives gathered to help the Franciscans plant the Cross, but to no avail, for no matter how hard they tried, they could not lift it. Suddenly, an elderly Franciscan praying by the church choir had an illumination from God and was able to see what was transpiring in the convent's courtyard, where the devil was weighing down the Cross. Horrified, the Franciscan came running down, thrust everyone aside, and admonished the devil: "How can they raise this Cross with he who is seated on it? . . . Depart, accursed one, let the Cross of

Jesus Christ be raised and the standard of the faith be hoisted." Confronted, the devil fled, and in no time the natives pulled the Cross up.[90]

This Catholic use of crosses highlights an aspect of colonization that is often ignored, namely, that territorial possession was first and foremost an ongoing struggle against demons. We have already seen that, deploying typical crusading tropes, Pedro de Villagómez and Blas Dacosta thought that the Cross was the sword of the knight-*visitador* in the ongoing epic struggle to extirpate idolatries in Peru. In fact, once the twelve Augustinian "apostles" arrived in the Andes, the same scene was repeated with numbing regularity. In his history of the early Augustinian mission, San Pedro describes how every time the friars came across *huacas* (boulders the population worshipped as communal ancestor-deities who had miraculously turned into rocks), they removed them, "planting in the same spot crosses instead."[91] Upon arriving in Sinaloa, the Jesuit Gonzalo de Tapia, who was to die hacked to pieces by Satan's minions, although his dismembered arm triumphantly held on to the Cross, and whose skull was to be used as chalice in a mockery of the Eucharist, identified a tree under which an important regional idol was worshipped. So Tapia "rounded up a few natives, had a beautiful cross made, and went to this place [in procession] singing the Christian Doctrine. There he had the tree felled and to replace it had planted that most beautiful [tree] of the Holy Cross. Then he blessed the place to erase the memory of the former tree and its attendant superstitions."[92]

Crosses often saved the knights of Christ when waging war on the devil in the American wilderness. Take, for example, the case of Fray Pedro de Córdova, who, after having established the Dominican order in Hispaniola, decided to do battle with Satan on Margarita Island, off the coast of Venezuela. Córdova and a fellow friar tagged along with a private expedition, most likely made up of soldiers looking for slaves and plunder. Once on Margarita, the devil first greeted the Dominican with fierce Indian resistance. Then Satan turned to trickery. Pretending to accept the Spaniards as overlords, the Amerindians encouraged part of the expeditionary party to go in their vessels to bring more settlers. Not surprisingly, "the [remainder of] Spaniards [having] no means to escape, the devil ordered the Indians to kill them all." And so they did. Yet the two Dominicans escaped, for "each held in his hand a wooden cross, which miraculously let them get away from the hands of the Indians." Once on the beach, the two Dominicans managed to flee in a makeshift boat.[93]

There is also the case of the Dominican Francisco de la Asunción, whose relic of the Cross made him powerful. Asunción appears not to have been alone, for fragments of the True Cross seem to have circulated throughout Mexico. Asunción wore his sliver of the Cross everywhere he went. The relic not only saved him from drowning twice but also gave him power to cast out demons from his Mexican charges.[94]

But despite all the crosses planted, the devil refused to give in. As the Franciscan Olmos noted, Satan had, after all, long fought back, even in the cradle of Christianity itself. Simply put, Satan did not like to lose vassals. Whenever he saw someone he had had "in his claws" escape, he lashed back "full of jealousy, wrath, and rancor."[95] As both Iberian and Puritan settlers learned to their dismay, Satan did not sit idly by in America watching how "the light of Gospel and doctrine undoes and vanishes all his tricks and deceits and erodes his authority." He mobilized his armies and "with all his diligence, using the wizards as his agents, persuaded the natives to rise up in arms, return back into the wilderness to live unrestrained, [and] burn down the churches."[96]

But the devil not only got the natives to burn churches or, as it often happened, to misuse crosses.[97] Satan also went after the Europeans themselves and had them turn against the Cross. Take, for example, the case of the name of Brazil. "Brazil," as the outraged sixteenth-century Portuguese chronicler João de Barros (1496–1570) explained in 1552, would not have had that name but for the devil. In 1500, seeking to round the African Cape of Good Hope on his way to India, Pedro Alvares Cabral (1467–1520) had unexpectedly bumped into South America. Since it was typical for the Portuguese in the fifteenth century to plant crosses in new territories as they inched their way down the coast of West Africa, Alvares Cabral decided not only to plant a cross but also to call the newly "discovered" territory "Holy Cross."[98] According to Barros, Alvares Cabral and his motley crew felled a large tree, carved a cross, and put it on top of the largest tree possible. He then assembled the crew for mass, in what in all likelihood was a ramshackle ceremony of exorcism away from home, and christened the land Santa Cruz (Holy Cross). However, the Cross and the name of the new land were only to last a few years, for the devil, having "lost the dominion he had over us, through the passion of Jesus Christ that culminated in the cross," decided to strike back. Since the land of the Holy Cross was rich in the red wood called *pau-brasil*, from which Europeans extracted a red dye, the devil "worked to make this other name stick in the mouth of the people," and soon the name of Santa Cruz was completely forgotten, "as if the name of a wood for dyeing cloth were more important than that of the wood that gave color to all the sacraments by which we are saved, through the blood of Jesus Christ that was spilled on it." Feeling "that there is no other way for me to wreak vengeance on the devil," Barros sought to publicize the old name in his chronicle "to give back to this land the name that with so much solemnity was given it, on the pain of that same cross that will be revealed to them the Day of the Judgment, accusing them of being more devoted to *pau-brasil* than to it." It may have not escaped Barros that the instrument used by the devil to get the Cross replaced, namely, brazilwood, had itself long been known in Europe for yielding a "deceitful" product, just like the devil himself. The red dye extracted from this hard tropical hardwood of the East (and now West) Indies was known as "disceytfull brasell," because the satisfying deep red it at first produced quickly faded into a disappointing pinkish brown.[99]

The epic struggle over the substitution of the Cross for the devil gave way in Spain to a peculiar genre in seventeenth-century drama. Plays by two of the most influential early modern Spanish playwrights, Lope de Vega (1562–1635) and Pedro Calderón de la Barca (1600–1681), typify this genre. Lope de Vega's *El Nuevo Mundo* (written ca. 1598–1603 and published in 1614) is a complex play rich in characters but with a basic plot: the epic struggle between the devil and the Cross over the New World. The natives and their idolatrous practices stand on the side of the devil. Greedy picaresque soldiers of fortune and quixotic knights like Columbus carry the banner of the Cross. That Lope de Vega has self-serving, dishonest, greedy soldiers stand for the Cross seems counterintuitive. In fact, his portrayal of the supporters of the Cross is unexpectedly nuanced. To the demands for water and food from his crew during the terrifying first ocean crossing, for example, Columbus offers vague promises of chivalric fame comparable to that enjoyed by the crew of the *Argos*. Understandably, the motley crew does not react kindly to this hubris and mocks Columbus's Mosaic pretensions by asking him to have manna fall from the sky and water gush from the ships' hulls. In fact, they ridicule the age's chivalric ethos in terms similar to those used by Cervantes a few years later: "The world [Columbus] is looking for is completely imaginary, without foundations, a windmill."[100] More surprisingly, in the play, it is the devil himself who makes the natives realize that the Spanish Christian rhetoric is a cover for greed and plunder. "What a fool you are," the devil tells the native ruler Dulcan, whose beautiful fiancée has just been kidnapped by his alleged Spanish friends, "falling for such feigned friendship. Lusting after the gold of your Indies, they pass themselves off as saints. [While some] feign Christian decorum, others come to take all the treasure." Feeling betrayed, Dulcan also sees through the invaders' rhetoric: "What vile, inhuman beasts, denuded of piety, wearing the fleece of Christian law [these fellows are]!"[101]

But as the character standing for Idolatry in the play confronts Providence regarding the blatant contradiction between Spanish rhetoric and actions, Lope de Vega offers a solution to his mystifying decision to have anti-heroes represent the Cross. Providence argues for the indirect quality and sheer instrumentality of her decisions: "God judges the outcome," she tells Idolatry. If the final outcome is the salvation of Indian souls and the ultimate defeat of the devil in the New World, the nature of the instruments does not really matter.[102]

Despite all the Spanish treachery in America, the presence of the Cross guarantees Satan's defeat. The play is bracketed by scenes that display the power of the Cross. Although the Amerindians chop down the Cross planted by the Spaniards three times, it always miraculously grows back (see fig. 3.7). Finally, Satan flies down, accompanied by six demons, to admit defeat before a candlelit altar to the Cross, saying: "I am vanquished! You have won, Galilean. Yours is the glory, the triumph, the prize. I see you come down as host to take over this Indian kingdom. I surrender [the keys of the castle] into your holy hands as I go down to the dungeons of hell. I lived among these people as if with swine, for that's what you commanded me to do. Now you expel me from their bodies and cast me into the other dark ocean. I can no longer be called the eternal god [of the Amerindians], for today you have taken both this title and this kingdom from me. Yours is [this] world. You have redeemed [this] world!"[103]

The other play that typifies the genre is Pedro Calderón de la Barca's *La Aurora en Copacabana*, published in 1672, an epic story that celebrates the triumph of the Cross and the Virgin over the devil at Copacabana on Lake Titicaca, a spot where the Inca rulers had a temple to commemorate their own celestial origins as the terrestrial embodiment of the sun. The play has the devil represented by "Idolatry," a woman dressed in black, clothed with stars, and carrying a sword. Seeking to mimic the story of Christ, God's earthly embodiment, Satan persuades the Andeans to believe that the Inca is the son of the sun. When the Spaniards arrive in Peru, they plant a cross on top of a cliff. A bewildered Inca Guascar looses his most ferocious beasts on the new arrivals, but the animals, including a lion and a tiger, are transformed into the pets of the Spaniards at the sight of the Cross.

The Cross not only reins in the animals but also blinds and paralyzes an Indian who seeks to kill the standard-bearer of the Cross. When the devil sets fire to the Cross, it emerges unscathed from the flames. The confrontation between the devil and the Cross in the play comes to a head when two Indian lovers, Guacolda and Iupangui, are condemned by the Inca to be

FIG. 3.7. A hundred thousand Caribbean natives attack the Cross of la Vega, which is defended by Bartolomé Colón's Spanish troops and the Virgin herself (1495). Detail of frontispiece to Antonio de Herrera y Tordesillas's *Historia general de los hechos castellanos en las isles y tierra firme del mar océano, 1492–1531* (Madrid, 1601). Courtesy of the Huntington Library, San Marino, California. The legend beneath the image reads: "Los yndios procuran derribar y quemar la Cruz de la vega y el Adelantado pelea con ellos y los derrota" (The Indians strive to bring down and burn the Cross of la Vega. The *adelantado* [Bartolomé Colón] fights back and defeats them). One Indian carries a torch, two pull the Cross down with ropes, and another swings an ax. The Virgin, however, stands on top of the Cross and defends it from being desecrated. She and the infant Christ inspire the armies of Bartolomé Colón in battle.

sacrificed. The two cling to the Cross and miraculously cannot be removed. After having set the lovers free, the Spaniards are assisted in the final battle by Our Lady of Copacabana, who blinds the native armies, allowing the Europeans to win and take over.

Anglican Crosses/Puritan Bibles

Stories of crosses going up and of demons resisting or fleeing them abound in sixteenth- and seventeenth-century Iberian colonial sources, and the reader might be tempted to assume that this was a distinctively Iberian, or Catholic, phenomenon. There is evidence, however, that Anglicans deployed crosses as well. Take, for example, the case of Martin Frobisher (1535–94), who led three Arctic expeditions (1576, 1577, and 1578) to "Meta Incognita," establishing a mining camp on the present Kodlunarn Island, from where he ferried 1,500 tons of ore back to England, thinking he had found gold. Upon arrival on his second voyage, Frobisher ordered a stone cross put up and had his crew pray. Frobisher clearly thought he had arrived in a land where the devil ruled. Frobisher's men captured an elderly Inuit woman, "eyther a Divell, or a Witch," and "had her buskins plucked off, to see if she were cloven footed." When the English finally sailed home after sundry skirmishes and kidnappings, leaving behind a handful of stranded sailors, the Inuit took over their camps and appropriated the Cross for themselves.[104]

John Smith, who, with Pocahontas, is a figure of almost mythical proportions in the U.S. collective imagination, likewise went around erecting crosses on his cartographic expeditions in the Chesapeake Bay region of Virginia.[105] He was not alone in doing so either. Christopher Newport (ca. 1560–1617), Smith's nemesis, also erected a cross at the falls of the James River around the same time.[106] Clearly, Anglicans, like their Catholic peers, were anxious to plant crosses as they moved into hostile territory held by the devil. But what about the Puritans?

When the Anglican Thomas Morton (1575–1646) erected a huge, eighty-foot maypole in New England in 1627 to consecrate a heathen spot known to the Amerindians as "Passonagessit," and which he called "Merrymound," he created an uproar in the fledgling Puritan community. Puritans strongly took issue with Morton's "popish" efforts to render spaces holy, for according to Puritan doctrine, both time and space were homogeneously holy, and sacred calendars and churches were idolatrous. It is therefore not surprising that, to remind future generations of Morton's philistine, idolatrous behavior, the Plymouth Puritans decided to rename his Merrymound "Mount Dagon" (a reference to Dagon, the principal deity of the Philistines; cf. 1 Sam. 5). This was typical Puritan behavior. When the Welsh separatist John Hewes named a ford he had found across the Scituate marshlands Hewes' Cross, after himself, John Winthrop (1588–1649), the governor of Massachusetts, ordered the name changed to Hewes' Folly.[107] The Puritans were so set against the idolatrous use of the Cross that they refused to have the English flag, bearing the red cross of St. George, flown in New England until the 1680s, when a new governor, Edmund Andros, finally forced it upon them.[108]

These stories may give the impression that the Puritans did not buy into the Iberian and Anglican ceremonies of occupying new spaces in the New World that I have described above. It has been argued that "exorcism" was contrary to Puritan belief. As good Calvinists, Puritans conceded agency and sovereignty only to God, and they were thus naturally opposed to taking the battle against demons into their own hands. Yet Richard Godbeer has shown that despite clerical calls to use only fasting and praying to move God to act against the preternatural powers of witches and the devil, the laity were not shy about using counter magic to battle satanic trickery.[109] There is, of course, a difference between lay conjuring spells and ministers engaged in rituals of exorcism. But even at this level, it is prudent not to generalize. Cotton Mather's reputation, for example, suffered greatly when the divine Robert Calef denounced him in 1700 for having "rubbed" the stomach and breast of a possessed parishioner, Margaret Rule. Calef suggested lechery and immodesty on the part of the minister, Mather interpreted the act as a perfectly innocent attempt at expelling demons off Rule's fully clothed body.[110]

Exorcism was thus not wholly alien to the Puritans. When it came to expelling demons from the New World, the Puritans did consider the occupation of land as a battle over space in the New World that pitted them against demons. Puritans went about exorcising the land in two different ways: by using the Bible as a physical object in ways similar to the Catholic and Anglican use of the Cross, and by presenting the lands they settled as a New Canaan.

Although the Puritans rejected the Cross as idolatrous, they were willing to embrace the Bible as a charm. Although the Bible is an object, for the Puritans it was the living Word of God. Bibles were therefore often deployed as "arrows in a quiver to drive off enemies like Satan," just as the Cross was used among Catholics to scare demons away.[111] Puritans' belief in the Bible as a preternatural physical object in every way resembles the Catholic and Anglican use of the Cross. Take a case described by John Kingsley to the Connecticut War Council of May 5, 1676, during King Philip's War. As the Wampanoags prepared to launch an assault on a town, a Puritan colonist had furnished himself with a Bible and patiently waited for the Amerindians to attack, assuming that the mere physical presence of the Gospel would be enough to keep the minions of Satan away. He was unfortunately proven wrong.[112]

The exorcising logic of referring to New England as a New Canaan operated in more indirect ways. Thomas Morton, who was driven out of New England by the Puritans for his "popish" excesses, first made obvious the deeply contradictory nature of Puritan conceptions of colonization and space. Morton's *New English Canaan* (1637) is a scathing critique of Puritan uses of typology. It mockingly takes the Puritans to task for their self-aggrandizing pretension of reading the Pentateuch as a prefiguration of the settlement of New England.[113] That the Puritans saw their exile from England as a biblical exodus and the New World as the Promised Land, a New Canaan, points to the fact that, for all their claims to the contrary, the Puritans saw the occupation of space in America as an act of liberation, of expelling demons from the land. It is clear that the Puritans deliberately sought to take the holy out of the naming and colonization of spaces in New England. John Winthrop in his expeditionary errands enjoyed replacing Amerindian place-names with the names of his own friends and family, or even with the names of food he happened to have on hand (e.g., "Cheese Rock"). Yet this desacralization of local spaces was accompanied by the sacralization of the entire territory the Puritans colonized. In seeing New England as Canaan, they clearly understood the occupation of land as an epic struggle to rid the territories of both Canaanites and idolatry. Puritans represented New England as a potential New Jerusalem, the most holy of spaces in the new millennium.[114]

Conclusions

No analysis of early modern European colonization can afford to study Iberian and British sources separately (or French and Dutch ones for that matter). Yet the historiographies on the Iberian and British Atlantics seem to have developed in pristine isolation. This chapter has shown that the structure of the demonological discourse, for example, can only be untangled when the sources are studied together, for the learned in both societies shared similar theologies of how the devil went about oppressing peoples and taking over territories. Both imperial projects understood colonization to be an epic struggle of *reconquista* against the devil. Gaps in our understanding of the structure and grammar of the discourse of demonology and colonization can only be filled in when one is willing to assume that the seemingly different Puritan and Iberian sources are in fact of the same kind. It is clear, for example, that the "exorcism" of demons from the New World was not alien to Puritan sensibilities, Calvinist disclaimers to the contrary. By the same token, deploying typological readings to justify acts of colonization was not at all unfamiliar to the Spanish American clergy. In fact, typology seems to be at the heart of much of the Franciscan historiography on the

Aztecs, yielding a Pentateuch-like account of the precolonial history of central Mexico that has managed to survive over the centuries.

The similarities between Puritan and Spanish Catholic discourses of colonization stemmed from a shared, centuries-old tradition of Christian holy wars. Drawing on dozens of militaristic passages in the Bible, apologists justified the violence of holy wars largely as defense against vicious, demonic enemies. Crusaders, for example, understood their participation in war as penitential piety, an act of love aimed at defending the Church from both internal and external enemies, be they Jews, heretics (e.g., Cathars or Hussites), pagan Slavs, or Muslims. Wielding both swords and crosses, crusaders endured hardships as sympathetic reenactment of the suffering of Christ and saw pilgrimage and war as sacrifice and atonement, forms of monastic penitence to help move souls from purgatory to heaven. It is not surprising that crusaders took vows and came to enjoy clerical spiritual and temporal immunities.[115] But there were many other kinds of holy wars launched by the Christian churches both before and after the crusades. Holy warriors of the early modern period may not have taken vows or sought papal immunities, yet they continued to wage war against demonic enemies, be they Turks, Protestant Reformers, or popish Antichrists.[116] Europeans in the New World thus drew upon a store of medieval and early modern tropes of crusades and religious wars to justify colonization. Finally, the crusaders and soldiers of the Wars of Religion fought for control of local holy lands, not only of Jerusalem, the Holy Land. Christian warriors deployed typology to cast themselves as Israelites, their enemies as Canaanites, and their domains as New Jerusalems.[117] The same process took place in the New World, whose fauna and flora were originally presented as demonic. Chapters 4 and 5 study the parallel processes of the demonization and sacralization of Nature in America.

Demonology and Nature

The Jesuit José de Acosta's *Historia natural y moral de las Indias* (1590) immediately became a classic and was translated into many languages. Although Acosta's treatise has been hailed as an ambitious essay on comparative ethnography and a clear-eyed empirical study of the natural history of the New World, it is actually a treatise on demonology. Acosta was obsessed with demons and, as we saw in Chapter 3, sought to prove that the devil had introduced in the Indies all sorts of religious institutions that were satanic inversions of the Catholic sacraments: baptism, the Eucharist, the cult of saints, confession, and priesthood. Moreover, Acosta understood the historical narratives of the Aztecs to be Satan's mockery of the Pentateuch, an inversion of the history of the Israelites. The demonological character of Acosta's ethnography is well known.[1] What has not been noticed, however, is that his natural history is also colored by demonological concerns, for Acosta found Nature in the Indies to be "inverted" as well. Acosta thought that in America physical phenomena such as tides, seasons, and rainfall followed the exact opposite patterns of those in Europe. In his natural history, the Indies thus come across as a world upside down. Acosta sought to explain the inversions without reference to Satan, however. His natural history was actually an effort to deny the devil any agency over the structure of the natural world by explaining the seeming physical inversions of Nature in the Indies through the laws of Aristotelian physics and meteorology. Acosta's efforts to deny the devil any control over Nature in the New World was something to be expected of a natural philosopher. As Stuart Clark has argued, sixteenth- and particularly seventeenth-century natural philosophy was a concerted effort to deny the devil control over the preternatural (the realm of the occult beyond the purview of Aristotelian physics) by expanding the field of the knowable.[2] Since the devil was thought to manifest himself through the preternatural, people readily assumed that a continent as full of preternatural wonders as was America was also full of demonically induced natural phenomena. Having enjoyed uncontested sovereignty over America for centuries, the devil had also managed to gain dominion over Nature itself there.

In this chapter, I explore how the epic-crusading discourse of coloniza-tion encouraged demonological perceptions of the landscape and Nature. Paradoxically, it also encouraged providential readings of Nature. I argue that despite all their differences, Catholics and Protestants (Iberians and Puritans, in particular) went about "reading" Nature in very similar ways. Intellectuals of both parties argued that Satan had control over the weather, plants, animals, and landscapes in the New World. Both groups also con-ceded that Nature hid providential messages of liberation in the New World. It would seem that what scholars of early modern Catholicism have called the "baroque," scholars of Calvinism have called "typology," namely, exu-berantly allegorical reading of the Book of Nature. This chapter also dem-onstrates that Iberian demonological views of Nature should inform any interpretation of William Shakespeare's *The Tempest* (ca. 1611) as a colonial text. I close the chapter by showing that demonological views of coloniza-tion encouraged a particular perception of the American landscape among Europeans: the New World often came to be seen as a false paradise that to be saved needed to be destroyed by Christian heroes. The spiritual holy warriors found in nature a formidable ally of the devil. But the godly and the saintly were capable of overcoming Satan. The early modern spiritual holy war in America was thus waged over the control of the wilderness. This chapter partly explores how the slow process of turning a demonic landscape into a sacred holy land took place. In the next chapter I explore this point more fully.

The Tempest

There is no denying that Shakespeare had the New World in mind in more ways than one when he wrote *The Tempest*. It has long been argued that the play is partially based on William Strachey's account of the shipwreck that Sir Thomas Gates (d. 1621) suffered in 1609 off the coast of Bermuda on his way to becoming the new governor of Virginia. While stranded on Devil's Island for a year, Gates and his entourage experienced revolts by sailors determined to turn Elizabethan and Jacobean social hierarchies on their head.[3] *The Tempest* is full of references to America. Shakespeare puts into the mouth of Gonzalo words borrowed from Montaigne's essay "Des cannibales" ("Of the Cannibals" [1580]). Gonzalo imagines the temperate, lush island as a

Golden Age utopia, free of money, commerce, private property, technology, warfare, envious social hierarchies, and demanding labor (2.1.162–70).[4] The rabble represented by the drunken butler Stephano and the jester Trinculo take the shipwreck as an opportunity to become "viceroys" of the island (3.2.118), like the sailors under Gates or the soldiers of fortune who came to America during the Spanish conquest in search of fiefdoms of their own. Although represented as "a freckled whelp . . . not honored with a human shape" (1.2.335), a monster, half human, half fish, deformed by the influence of the moon (or a mooncalf), solitary and lacking articulate language, Caliban is also introduced as an Amerindian: an islander to be taken to London to be shown for money, a curiosity whose monstrosity resulted from his being struck by a thunderbolt (2.2.30–35). Moreover, the relationship between Caliban and Prospero is meant to evoke the relationship between Amerindians and Spanish missionaries and conquistadors. Caliban waxes lyrical about his first encounter with Prospero, who "made much of me" and taught "me too to name the bigger light and how the less." In return, he introduces Prospero to "all the qualities o'th' isle, the fresh springs, brine pits, barren place and fertile" (1.2.395–405). Soon, however, Caliban attempts to rape Miranda, Prospero's daughter, and compounds the offense by persuading Stephano and Trinculo to kill Prospero and take over the island. Like a good conquistador, Prospero responds in kind, sending hounds with names like "Mountain," "Silver," "Fury," and "Tyrant" after the culprits to "grind their joints" and "shorten their sinews" (4.1.282–86). As a result of his treachery, Caliban is enslaved by Prospero.

Some of these references to the colonization of the New World have prompted scholars to offer postcolonial readings of *The Tempest*. Yet for all its contribution, this new scholarship has ignored all the references to the preternatural and the demonological in the play and has thus failed to locate *The Tempest* in its appropriate historical context.[5] The colonial and the demonological are inextricably linked in *The Tempest*. The exiled Prospero arrives on an island that had long been in the hands of Sycorax, an Algerian witch so powerful that she was forced to live in isolation. On the island, Sycorax encounters Ariel, "a spirit too delicate to act her earthy and abhorred commands" (1.2.325–26), and imprisons him "into a cloven pine." Ariel remains trapped for twelve years, even after Sycorax has passed away. Sycorax, in the meantime, has intercourse with the devil and gets pregnant with Caliban. The savage monstrous Caliban is thus the son of a witch and the devil himself (1.2.384; 5.1.323–30). In fact, besides a monster or an Amerindian, Caliban is taken to be a demon in the play (2.2.58; 2.2.101).

Curiously, however, Caliban has no preternatural powers and comes across as a hapless creature destined to be a servant.[6]

Prospero is the one with power in the play. He has spent all his life reading books to master the preternatural, and upon arrival on the island, he releases Ariel from his imprisonment in exchange for the latter's service. It is through the indentured angel Ariel that Prospero deploys his powers. He sends Ariel to set off a storm to shipwreck those who expelled him from Milan: Antonio, Prospero's brother and counterfeit duke of Milan, and the king of Naples, Alonso. Throughout the play, Prospero commands the angel Ariel to become a nymph or a harpy or a pack of hounds or a set of characters in a masque, depending on the occasion. Ariel is so capable of mutating into any shape or creature that the besieged castaways end up admitting that the reports of travelers, often taken to be lies and fantasies, must be true (3.3.25–69). Like the spiritual intelligence that he is, Ariel moves through the sphere of air and visits distant places in an instant.

It is clear that in *The Tempest* America not only figures as an island on which to create utopias or as a space inhabited by monstrous primitives. Shakespeare considers America a space where great preternatural battles are fought between angels and demons for control of Nature. This was a well-established tradition by the time the play was performed.

Storms

It has become a scholarly truism to argue that Shakespeare's description of the storm Prospero unleashes on his enemies was taken from the account by William Strachey of Sir Thomas Gates's shipwreck off the coast of Bermuda. In an account to which Shakespeare reportedly had access, and that circulated in manuscript from 1610 until its publication by Samuel Purchas in 1625, Strachey reports the nature of the storm that sunk Gates's vessel: a tempest set off by demons near islands that deserved their name, namely, Devil's Islands.[7] This might well be the case. Yet, as I have shown already, the trope of storms caused by Satan to sink pious Europeans coming to America was a very well established literary convention among both Catholics and Protestants by the time Shakespeare wrote his play. It would be tiresome to revisit the many sixteenth-century Iberian epics discussed in Chapter 2 in which the hero is faced with storms unleashed by a Satan desperate to halt the arrival of the Christian knight in the New World. In this section, I simply go over other examples that suggest that this trope was widely held by both Catholics and Protestant European powers in the New World.

The century-old trope in the Iberian satanic epic of the hero battling storms in both the Atlantic and the Pacific oceans caused by the devil finds in Calderón de la Barca's *La Aurora en Copacabana* (see Chapter 3) its most riveting expression. There is a moment in Calderón's *auto sacramental* when Pizarro and his colleagues, after having planted the Cross and realized the scope of the civilization (and wealth) they have just "discovered," decide to go back to Panama to get reinforcements. At this point, the devil, who has just lost Mexico and fears that his lordship in Peru is about to end too, strikes back. Satan, who in the play inhabits the sphere of the air and speaks to the natives through the wind, orders demons to stir up a tempest to sink Pizarro's vessel: "With the magical horror of my horrors upset the spheres of earth and water. Before this vessel escapes with news of this newfound land, let's have the sea pursue, pound, and sink it."[8] Fortunately for Pizarro, the threat never materializes, for the Cross protects him and his crew from storms. In the Iberian imagination, the struggle between God and Satan in America was for control, not merely of the continent's human inhabitants, but also of Nature.

But these ideas did not belong solely to the Spaniards. French Jesuits in Canada also cast colonization as a struggle over Nature. The Jesuit Paul Lejeune (1591–1664) saw himself "as like the pioneers who go ahead to lay trenches for the next wave of brave soldiers to besiege and capture the place."[9] Lejeune spent much of his time in New France devising "great engines of war to destroy Satan's Empire," that is, plans to oust Satan from America.[10] To be sure, Lejeune's main enemies were the Iroquois, Satan's minions. He saw the French-Iroquois wars of the 1640s as part of a well-thought-out plan by the devil "to see demons return to their [former] empire."[11] Yet the Jesuit also saw Nature itself as part of the struggle. Lejeune tells of French supply ships loaded with grain coming from Europe in 1640 that were buffeted by storms let loose by demons, who "during most of the voyage stirred up the ocean, unleashed the winds, and provoked the most horrible and continuous tempests." Fortunately for the settlers, "Angels saved our fleet from the tempests demons unleashed to sink it."[12] In Lejeune's eyes, Canada was "a donjon of demons."[13] The forests, for example, were "guarded during the [humid] summer by small flying dragons," millions of blood-sucking insects let loose to bleed the French white.[14]

That Nature itself was considered a battleground was not simply a Catholic superstitious conceit. It was an idea that Protestants wholeheartedly embraced. We have already seen in Chapter 1 that Johnson considered the American landscape and tempests unleashed by demons to be instruments created by the devil to keep the Puritans from settling the New

World. It was typical in New England throughout the seventeenth century to present sea crossings in epic terms. On arrival in Massachusetts in 1633, the Puritan divine Master Welles, for example, wrote to his congregation back in Tarling, Essex, that "he and his family [had] passed the deepest and [were] alive and well . . . in spite of Divells and stormes."[15] In 1702, Cotton Mather explained that "tis very likely that the evil angels may have a particular energy and employment, oftentimes in the mischiefs done by thunder." Satan, he explained, "commands much of the magazine of heaven," instilling fear through "fiery meteors, thunder and lightening." The devil could "do wonders in the air," including, of course, setting off storms at sea.[16]

Mather saw New England as a land where demons harassed the godly, for lightning in the province mostly struck "the houses of God." New England seemed to be "a countrey signalized with mischiefs done by thunders, as much as perhaps most in the world. If things that are smitten by lightning, were to be esteemed sacred, this were a sacred country."[17]

In keeping with the Puritan preoccupation with Satan's control of ocean crossings to and from New England, Mather was able to identify one case of demonic harassment at sea in which the craft itself was attacked. In December 1695, a vessel headed to Barbados from Boston, Mather asserted, was suddenly struck by Satan. One by one, her crew of nine began to be "insensible carried away," suddenly evaporating into thin air. Satan had tempests rock the ship and unleashed winds to keep the three sailors who managed to survive from landing when they happened to be near a port. To top it off, Satan turned the vessel invisible every time it came near other vessels.[18] Sixteenth- and seventeenth-century British American (particularly Puritan) settlers repeatedly denounced the power of Amerindian shamans to communicate with the devil to unleash storms. These *pawwaws* were thought capable of shifting shoals and bringing forth fogs to cause shipwrecks. They also caused floods or droughts at will, and in wartime caused crops to fail to wipe out the settlers.[19]

That Mather continued to express these ideas in the early eighteenth century should not surprise us. Scholars in Europe did not cease to be puzzled by demonically induced storms even during the "age of reason." Take, for example, the case of the German natural philosopher Johann Zahn (1641–1707). In his 1696 *Specula Physico-Mathematico-Historica*, Zahn argued that "extraordinary winds and horrible tempests are the work of demons and the product of magic, as attested by the examples discussed and collected by several authors." Demons and their ministers (*malefici, praestigitores, incantatores*), he contended, had been allowed by God to have special power over the atmosphere.[20]

Chapter 4

Plants

But the devil did not only have special power over the sphere of air, from which he and his minions unleashed winds, lightning, and even meteors (see fig. 4.1).[21] Another idea widely shared by early modern Europeans was that the devil interacted with plants, precisely because he and the demons under his command were such aerial creatures. In his *Curiosa filosofía y tesoro de maravillas de la naturaleza* (1644), the great baroque polymath Juan Eusebio Nieremberg (1595–1658), explained that the demons were either naturally attracted to or repelled by physical objects. According to this Spanish Jesuit, anything that resembled the Cross repelled demons. Cinquefoil, Dioscorides' *pentaphyllon*, also known as *pie de Christo* (foot of Christ), Nieremberg argued, "shows an extremely well-defined cross anywhere you cut it. I am not surprised then that the devil flees this plant, because he flees the Cross."[22] By the same token, there were objects that attracted demons, such as women's hair, particularly when vain women spent too much time fixing it. By seeking to be voluptuous and attractive to men, these women, especially when they wore their hair uncovered, actually wound up attracting demons, who, like men, were lecherous creatures.[23] This attraction and repulsion between objects and demons also extended to kings. It was believed that the kings of England and France were capable of curing diseases such as gout and scrofula (*lamparones*) by simply being near the sick. Even more impressive, the king of Spain actually had the power to drive demons away.[24] Although Nieremberg attributed these skills to supernatural powers, he could have also attributed them to these kings' bodily vapors, for the Jesuit was convinced that the air plants gave off was enough to explain why some worked better in church to exorcise demons.[25] Demons transformed themselves into bodies by curdling the middle layer of the sphere of air in which they lived, and the smoke given off by certain plants "conditioned this [layer], making it impossible for the devil to take up bodily forms."[26]

Given these ideas, it should not be surprising to find that soon upon arrival in the New World, Europeans looked for plants to exorcise demons.[27] The royal physician Francisco Hernández (1517–87), sent by Philip II in the 1570s to America to systematically gather plants for the royal pharmacy, went beyond the call of duty and produced a massive natural history of central Mexico that included eleven volumes of illustrations and the description of 3,000 new plants, far surpassing classical sources such as Dioscorides, whose survey of Mediterranean plants did not exceed 500. Hernández, for example, was captivated by the *tlahuelilocaquahuitl*, or *caragna* tree, whose leaves had the shape of the Cross. Not surprisingly, Hernández argued, "there is a

FIG. 4.1. Aerial demons attacking Amerindians. Illustration of a passage in Theodore de Bry's translation of Jean de Léry's *Histoire d'un voyage fait en la terre du Brésil* (1578), in de Bry's *America*, vol. 3 (Frankfurt a/M, 1597).

belief among the natives that evil demons greatly fear and flee this tree and that it resists the casting of spells."[28] The tree was therefore "called the 'tree of insanity' because by driving off demons and preventing enchantment it cures those who are mad through the demons' wickedness."[29] Hernández was even able to find in Oaxaca a crystal capable of exorcising demons, known as *yztehuilotl*, or crystalline stone (*lapide crystallino*): "No other crystal is furnished with similar marvelous faculty. If the informants are telling the truth, the stone causes demons to flee. It also protects from the poison of serpents or any other venomous animal."[30]

Even more common among Europeans in America than looking for substances to exorcise demons was the search for plants and objects used by the devil. Fray San Pedro in his chronicle of the "spiritual conquest" of Peru, for example, describes all the natural and preternatural dangers that besieged the original twelve Augustinian apostles as they battled the devil in the Andes. It was not only that some of the *huacas* that communities worshipped as the fossilized remains of their original ancestors were capable of "shrinking the arms and legs" of unauthorized persons who "dared to come near them," but also that there were plants used to cast spells capable of putrefying the body and turning it into a pile of worms. Fortunately for these Augustinian soldiers of Christ, neither the *huacas* nor the plants could do anything to them.[31] San Pedro described the case of one native guide whose body had putrefied before the very eyes of the friars after a shaman had handed them and their guides drinks; however, the friars themselves had survived unscathed.[32] One friar even taunted a shaman by eating a fruit poisoned with the powder of a demonic herb. Citing Psalm 90(91):13 ("Thou shalt tread upon the lion and adder: the young lion and the dragon shalt thou trample under feet"), San Pedro concluded that the friars were literally capable of "walk[ing] over the snake and basilisk and tread[ing] upon the lion and dragon."[33]

The notion that there were "satanic" herbs was controversial. Rather than claiming that American herbs were demonic, the physician Juan de Cárdenas (1563–1609), who had been born in Spain but raised and trained in Mexico City, maintained, for example, that plants always acted on the body through natural means, either by manipulating the four elements, and thus the humors, or by occult sympathies. It was absurd to maintain, he argued, that there were plants that had satanic virtues themselves: "We absolutely deny that either herbs or medicinal drugs can produce any effect that goes beyond the limit of the natural action."[34] Those who believed "that it was through [the manipulation of an] herb that witches could turn invisible or move throughout the world in an instant or penetrate objects and return to the place from where they originally came" were dead wrong. All the actions were caused by "the art of the devil rather than the virtue of the plant."[35] All herbs could do, Cárdenas argued, was to create the natural conditions of confusion in the internal senses for the devil to establish communication through dreams and visions. But for all his disclaimers, Cárdenas identified a number of these herbs that made the deceiving powers of the devil easier, including peyote, *poyomate* (*Salvia divinorum?*), *hololisque* (the seeds of the morning glory), and *piciete* (tobacco).[36]

The reception of tobacco typifies the European tendency to link American plants to the operations of the devil. As early as 1535, the Spanish naturalist Gonzalo Fernández de Oviedo made explicit the connections between the use of tobacco in the Caribbean and shamanic communication with Satan.[37] Despite the steady growth in tobacco consumption in Europe as topical paste, snuff, or smoke, the physician Francisco de Aguilar y Leira (1478–1557) continued in *Desengaño contra el mal uso de tabaco* (1634) to present tobacco in the same terms as did Oviedo and Cárdenas, namely, as a plant that altered the internal senses to allow demonic possession through dreams and visions.[38] Addiction to tobacco was perceived as a typical symptom of the devil's power to do away with free will.[39]

This view of tobacco as demonic in certain Spanish quarters was transmitted to the rest of Europe. Take for example the case of King James I of England, the author of *Daemonologie*. In his 1604 *A Covnter-Blaste to Tabacco*, James portrays tobacco as a means for the devil to wreak havoc among the noble classes of his kingdom (he was less concerned about the populace consuming the wicked herb). Since James considered himself to be a physician of the body politic responsible for curing diseases of the commonwealth, he took it upon himself to identify the many dangers with which tobacco use threatened the polity. There were undoubtedly medical reasons to avoid tobacco, he observed. The lungs of many smokers had been found black upon death. The alleged dry and warm virtues of the plant that balanced the cold and wet properties of the brain, instead of clearing fumes from the brain, created "distillations" within, clouding perception. Claims by supporters of the herb that it was good for all ailments were nonsense. If left to their own devices, peddlers of tobacco would sell the drug to both papists and Puritans to exorcise demons: "And if it could by the smoke thereof chace devils, as the smoke of Tobias fish did (which I am sure could smel no stronglier) it would serve for a precious Relicke, both for the superstitious Priests, and the insolent Puritanes, to cast out devils withall."[40] The greatest danger of tobacco lay in addiction. Operating like the devil, tobacco caused users to surrender their free will: "no more then an old Drunkard can abide to be long sober" could they do without it. In fact, it induced states of "bewitchment."[41] The social consequences of tobacco consumption were also dismal. Tobacco led to emasculation: those who used it were "even at this day accounted as effeminate among the Indians themselves."[42] Thus, not only did gentlemen waste fortunes on a drug that resulted in stinking breath, but it also caused effeminacy—and at time when Britain needed courageous knights.

Seeking to explain why a drug that harmed the body and the polity was so popular, James found the cause in fashion. It was a herd mentality that had blinded the valorous and chivalrous gentleman of Britain into mimicking the natives of America: "Shall we, I say, without blushing, abase ourselves so farre, as to imitate these beastly Indians, slaves to the Spaniards, refuse to the world, and as yet alien to the holy Covenant of God? Why do we not as well imitate them in walking naked as they doe? In preferring glasses, f[e]athers and such toyes, to golde and precious stones, as they do? Yea why do we not denie God and adore the devil as they do?"[43] The source of tobacco should in itself have made the "sins and vanities" associated with it apparent to the British gentry. Practices that came from a continent whose peoples and nature were possessed by the devil could only encourage devilish consequences. After having established that tobacco had originally been used in America to cure syphilis, and after having damned the Amerindians for "the uncleanly and adust constitution of their Bodies" and "the intemperate heat of their Climate," James blasted those who overlooked the vile, venereal nature of the American continent and the satanic creation of the plant: "it seem as miracle to me, how a Custome springing from so vile a Ground, and brought in by a Father so generally hated, should be so welcome." Clearly, there was something satanic about the fumes of tobacco, which reminded James I of hell: "the blacke stinking fume thereof, nearest resembling the horrible Stigian smoke of the pit that is bottomelesse."[44]

The imprint of Satan could be found in Nature everywhere in the New World. Nicolás Monardes (1512–88), for example, discovered images of dragons inside the fruit of the *sangre de drago* tree (*Croton lechleri*) (fig. 4.2). Although the great naturalist Carolus Clusius (Charles de l'Écluse) (1526–1609) failed to verify Monardes's assertions after he planted the American *sangre de drago* in his botanical garden at the University of Leiden, scholars continued to speculate on the meaning of these mysterious images.[45]

Thus in a study of biblical references to reptiles published in 1595, Juan Bustamente de la Cámara maintained that the *sangre de drago* tree drew on the vital spirits left by corpses of dragons in the New World. The tree, like dragons and snakes, shed off its outer bark like scales. The tree was endowed with long roots that conducted the vital spirits of dragons up the trunk into the fruits or leaves where the image of these winged snakes were reproduced.[46] Bustamente de la Cámara should not be dismissed as an isolated crackpot or, worse, a naïve believer in dragons. Johann Faber, a German cleric who resided in Rome and who along with Galileo has recently been presented by David Freedberg as a leading member of the Academy of the Lynx, a harbinger of scientific modernity, offered a natural history of dragons in the New World in his commentary on the work of Francisco Hernández.[47] Faber reminds the reader that dragons had been spotted both in Africa and America by such impeachable witnesses as García de Orta, Antonio Pigaffeta, Odoardus Barbosa, Americo Vespucci, and Francis Drake.[48]

Johann Zahn was a firm believer in dragons.[49] Yet, like James I, his interest in the demonic in America was more centered on plants. In his massive 1696 *Specula Physico-Mathematico-Historica*, Zahn offered a brief survey of

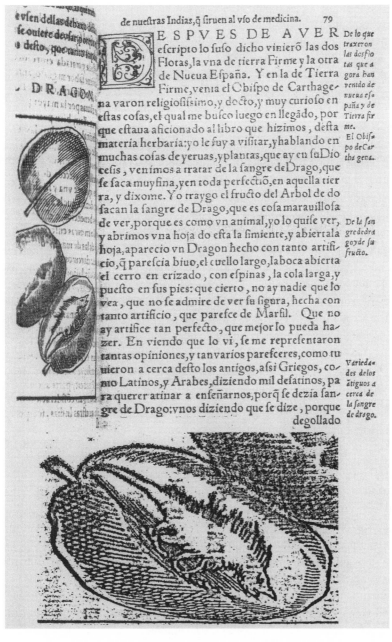

ESPVES DE AVER eſcripto lo ſuſo dicho vinierõ las dos Flotas, la vna de tierra Firme y la otra de Nueua Eſpaña. Y en la de Tierra Firme, venia el Obiſpo de Carthage- na varon religioſiſsimo, y docto, y muy curioſo en eſtas coſas, el qual me buſco luego en llegãdo, por que eſtaua aficionado al libro que hizimos, deſta materia herbaria: yo le ſuy a viſitar, y hablando en muchas coſas de yeruas, y plantas, que ay en ſu Dio ceſis, venimos a tratar de la ſangre de Drago, que ſe ſaca muy fina, yen toda perfectiõ, en aquella tier ra, y dixome. Yo traygo el fructo del Arbol de do ſacan la ſangre de Drago, que es coſa marauilloſa de ver, porque es como vn animal, yo lo quiſe ver, y abrimos vna hoja do eſta la ſimiente, y abierta la hoja, aparecio vn Dragon hecho con tanto artifi- cio, q̃ pareſcia biuo, el cuello largo, la boca abierta el cerro en erizado, con eſpinas, la cola larga, y pueſto en ſus pies: que cierto, no ay nadie que lo vea, que no ſe admire de ver ſu figura, hecha con tanto artificio, que pareſce de Marfil. Que no ay artifice tan perfecto, que mejor lo pueda ha- zer. En viendo que lo vi, ſe me repreſentaron tantas opiniones, y tan varios pareſceres, como tu uieron a cerca deſto los antigos, aſsi Griegos, co- mo Latinos, y Arabes, diziendo mil deſatinos, pa ra querer atinar a enſeñarnos, porq̃ ſe dezia ſan- gre de Drago: vnos diziendo que ſe dize, porque degollado

De lo que traxeron las dos ſlo tas que a gora han venido de nueua eſ- paña y de Tierra fir me.

El Obiſ- po de Car tha gena.

De la ſan grededra go y de ſu fructo.

Varieda- des delos ãtiguos a cerca de la ſangre de drago.

FIG. 4.2. Dragon image found inside the fruit of the *sangre de drago* tree. Nicolas Monardes, *Dos libros que tratan de las cosas medicinales de nuestra Indias occidentales* (Seville, 1574). Courtesy of the Huntington Library, San Marino, California.

the "admirable virtues, powers, and operations of certain plants."⁵⁰ Of the
sixty-four plants in his census of botanical marvels, fourteen hailed from
America; and all of them were poisonous. Zahn introduced the reader to the
aquapam, a Colombian tree whose shadow alone caused people to pass out
and to develop hives so large as to cause people to explode, dying with their
intestines splattered about; the manioc, or yucca, a Caribbean root that is
extremely poisonous if not cooked; a plant in Antequera, Oaxaca, so dangerous that it killed immediately even if ingested in tiny amounts and so powerful that it could be kept in storage for over a year without losing its potency;
the *laricis*, whose near proximity threw people into fits, causing them to take
on the roles of prophets, merchants, or soldiers; the *cohobba* on Hispaniola,
whose vapors alone inebriated and caused convulsions; a plant from an island
off Brazil that blinded people on touch, causing excruciating eye pain; the
tetlatia or *guao* tree in Mexico, which burned on contact and caused people
to fall asleep; and the *teomat* tree in Peru, which induced depression and led
to suicide, among many others. Zahn also noted that the plants of America
were not only poisonous but also treacherous. Like Satan, the trickster,
American plants deceived people into a false sense of security. There was
the case of a tree on Hispaniola that bore a fruit with a deceptively fragrant
odor, but which when eaten caused instant death; even being near this tree
caused people to become blind and go insane. Finally, there was another tree
on Hispaniola whose sweet pearlike fruit brought on sudden sleep and facial
swelling in those who ate it.

Monsters

Just as he thought that demons were capable of causing storms and inhabit-
ing plants, Zahn believed that the devil struck special alliances with animals.
Dormice in Slovenia, for example, were said to meet periodically with Satan
underground and to bear the devil's signatures on their ears, testifying to
their special relation with Lucifer (see fig. 4.3).

Yet for all his interest in demons and animals, Zahn has nothing to say
on the subject when it came to America. Others, however, did. Susan Scott
Parrish has argued that the female opossum was considered to be a monstrous,
demonic animal. According to Parrish, early modern Europeans embraced
such views well into the seventeenth century because the female opossum
seemed to have great, almost demonic generative capacity (it has two vaginas
and two uteruses) as well as to be made of parts of other animals. In the words
of Vicente Yañez Pinzón (1461–ca. 1521), who offered the first account of the

FIG. 4.3. Satan herding dormice in the forests of Slovenia. Johann Zahn, *Specula physico-mathematico-historica* (Nuremberg, 1696), 2: 327. Courtesy of the Huntington Library, San Marino, California.

natural history of Brazil in 1499, the opossum was "[an animal] as strange a Monster, the foremost part resembling a Fox, the hinder a Monkey, the feet were like a Mans, with Ears like an Owl."[51] Had the Europeans judged exotic animals as satanic simply because they looked as though they were made of parts of animals from the Old World, then they would have seen America as indeed populated with scores of devilish monsters. The Jesuit Nieremberg, who thought that the king of Spain had supernatural powers over Satan, for example, described the *su* of Patagonia in 1635 in the same terms used by Yañez Pinzón to depict the opossum, namely, as a monstrous composite of animal parts from the Old World. Of the *su* he said that "in the first part of its mouth it to a certain extent resembles a lion — or a man, for it is bearded from the ear, with not very long hair, and a long, broad tail like a squirrel."[52]

Yet Europeans typically did not associate the monstrous with the demonic in the New World. Most immediately realized that the "monsters" they encountered so often were simply linguistic artifacts, the unintended consequence of a forced cultural translation by observers who lacked any other way of describing new animals. To describe the new, observers simply had to resort to analogies with parts of animals they already knew (see fig 4.4). To be sure, European observers did find a handful of "monsters," as was the case

CAPVT LXXIII.
De animali quodam piloso.

INuenitur in agro tezzcocano animal pi-
losum valdè, vocatum *tlalcoyoti*, duas
longum fpithamas, vnguibus melis aur

quauhpecotli fimilibus, & cruribus breui-
bus, & nigro veftitis pilo, breuiffimâ caudâ
corpore toto & albo in fuluum vergente, fed
dorfo ac fupernâ parte capitis & colli nigris,
lineaque diftinctis candenti. Capur eft par-
uum, roftrum tenue & longiufculum, exer-
ti canini, ac vita victuiique eadem quæ
quauhpecotli.

S V.

CAPVT LXXIV.
De fu animali.

CAPVT LXXV.
De glire Chiappæ.

---

carnem anguillarem rata, anxie appetiit, abominabilium rerum appetitum com-
avidè comedit, & unâ fimilium rerum eftionemque à *Brachmane* patre fuo,
appetitum fœtui impreffit. Verùm cum domo ejufdem profcriptumque, vitam
de hifce quàm fuiffimè in IX. *Libro* fuam in campis, ferpentum cætero-
Mundi Subterranei de Venenorum origine dif- rumque animalium virulentorum vena-
cufferimus, eò Lectorem remittimus. ru, nulla aliorum ciborum folitorum
Addidit autem Pater Puerum, ob tam alimonia fuftenaffe.

Vefpertilio qui ob corporis molem Cattus Volans dicitur.

of the "hawk of Chiapas." According to Nieremberg the "accipiter Chiappa" had "monstrous legs: one of a goose, the other of an eagle, with one it swims, with the other it captures prey."[53] But even these monsters could not be explained as the product of Satan's sovereignty over America. The "monstrosity" of these animals, as Johann Faber, the German cleric in Rome who befriended Galileo at the Academy of the Lynx, contended, was simply a label slapped on them by provincial European observers. In his commentaries on the work of Francisco Hernández, Faber, for example, sought to make sense of the *maquiztetzauhvatl*, or "Amphisbaena Mexicana" (a snake with a head at each end of its body) (see fig. 4.14), and of the *quauhtlacoymatl quapizotl*, or "Aper Mexicanus" (a wild boar with the "navel" located on its back, in all likelihood a peccary, which has a musk gland on its back). "It so pleased the Creator," Faber argued, "to fashion the amphisbaena and to mold a navel for our Mexican boar not in the stomach but on the back, and to create various different beasts of the New World with other shapes and ways of life, all of which [beasts], when compared with ours, seem monstruous."[54] The animals of the New World, Faber thus forcefully maintained, were God's perfect creations. It was only under the provincial eye of the European observer that they were transmogrified into monsters.

In a field cluttered with descriptions of monsters and oddities, Faber saw himself as a clear-eyed observer determined to set the record straight. According to Faber, the undeserved reputation of America as land of monsters was, paradoxically, the doing of the devil himself. Such was the case, for example, with descriptions of *Picus Americanus*. Rumor had it that this American bird collected in its nest a rare herb that could bend iron on contact. Faber thought this was nonsense, but noted, "I think that a larger beak is to be found in no other bird [*rostrum in ave nulla maius reperiri existimo*]." The devil was also behind the rumor of a gifted bird capable of identifying a marvelous herb: "But if it's a matter of murmured words and gossip, then those things become suspect as a result of the devil's dealings, aid, and suggestion. Indeed, I know that most men are not easily content with things that are common and every-

FIG. 4.4. *(opposite)* The Patagonian *su* that looks like a lion-squirrel and the Chinese bat that looks like a flying cat. From Juan Eusebio Nieremberg, *Historia naturae* (Antwerp, 1635), and Athanasius Kircher, *China monumentis* (Amsterdam, 1667). Courtesy of the Huntington Library, San Marino, California. Both animals seem to be made up of pieces of other animals (lions and squirrels in the case of the *su*; bats and cats in the case of the Chinese bat). Their monstrous aspect did not necessarily make them demonic. The monstrousness simply stemmed from the intrinsic cultural linguistic limitations of European observers.

day anywhere you like, but they very readily believe, seek out, and embrace those [out-of-the-way things]. Silly stories [*fabulae*], old women's ravings, and superstitious rites thought up by the cunning of the devil are so very readily disseminated throughout the whole world as to finally make their way even to our Americans and Antipodeans."[55] Fortunately for both the Amerindians and Faber, the detached European observer, the devil was now on the defensive, as his tyranny and frauds in the New World were challenged by the light of the Gospel. But the old master, Faber warned, was still very much capable of rekindling the smoldering ashes of deceit among the Amerindians.[56]

Satanic Snakes

Juan Eusebio Nieremberg had an uncanny ability to find the occult in animals. His book on marvels in the Indies is full of cases of oils or powders derived from animal bodies that had great preternatural powers. The spines of the porcupine (*animalibus spinosis*, or *hoitzlaquatzin*), for example, could penetrate skin and leather on their own, without anyone having to push them into the flesh.[57] Extracts made from the tail of the opossum cleared stones in urinary tracts, fixed fractures, calmed cramps, and stimulated sexual desire, lactation, menstruation, and labor.[58] The list is long, yet in this list there are only a handful of cases that point to overt connections between animals and Satan in the New World.[59] In fact, often the connections demonstrate that American animals could be used to exorcise demons, as was the case of the of "hornblower duck" (*anatibus cornicinibus*), whose bugle calls drove evil spirits away.[60]

But it was the snakes that in Nieremberg's eyes typified Satan's hold over America (see fig. 4.5). Nieremberg had a knack for finding analogies between animals and peoples of the same geographical region. For example, he found striking similarities between the Andean llamas and the Amerindians, for both were stubborn, dumb-looking, and resistant to bodily punishment, yet willing to obey after gentle persuasion.[61] By the same token, the voracious doglike *rossomaka*, a scavenger in the forests of Muscovy and Lithuania, reminded Nieremberg of the eating habits of the Russians, whom he thought ate and vomited at their parties until they passed out.[62] This penchant for analogies prepared Nieremberg to associate the snakes of the New World with Satan's hold over the Amerindians.[63]

For all his attempts both to undermine the devil's rumors in the New World and to end classifications that took American animals to be satanic monsters, Faber also could not deny that there were indeed animals that belonged to Lucifer. Snakes, he thought, were Satan's pets. How could it be that "Nature, God's creation that feeds and sustains us, has produced a crea-

IOANNIS EVSEBII NIEREMBERGII

EX SOCIETATE IESV

HISTORIÆ NATVRÆ

LIBER DVODECIMVS.

DOMINA SERPENTVM, siue TEVHTLACOCAVHQVI.

CAPVT PRIMVM.

De dominâ serpentum.

 O N sine naturæ vsu reptilia sunt : nec minùs maiestaté Creatoris humilitate suâ exaggerant, non minùs bonitatem peste suâ. Scit pessimis Deus iuuare , scit veneno mederi: liberalem medicina opem è noxijs istis vsurpat. Exordium occupet atrox

genus serpentum, Teuhtlacocauhqui, seu dominam serpentum Barbari vocant, viperam Hispani, siuè ob similitudinem capitis, siue pestis. Anguis hic quaternos pedes aut amplius longus, & humanum, vbi mediocriter crassus est, latus : dorso eminenti , viperino capite, ventre ex albo pallescente, lateribus opertis, candentibus squamis, fascijs tamen pullis per interualla intermixtis: dorsum fuscum est, luteis tamen lineis sese in ipsâ spinâ secantibus insigne. Multæ sunt eius serpentis differétiæ, non plurimùm inter se distantes.

FIG. 4.5. Teuhtlacocauhqui, or Domina Serpentum. From Juan Eusebio Nieremberg, *Historia naturae* (Antwerp, 1635). Courtesy of the Huntington Library, San Marino, California. The alleged proliferation of snakes in the New World was presented in early modern European sources as evidence of Satan's sovereignty over the land.

ture that we hate and fear so much?" The answer, Faber replied rhetorically, lay in the biblical story of Eve and paradise (Gen. 3:14–15). God had punished the demonic serpent for its deceit and treachery: "And God said to the serpent: for what you have done you are cursed among all the animals and beasts of the earth: [you are condemned] to advance crawling and eat dirt all the days of your life."[64] Moreover, God had sown the seed of hatred toward snakes in Eve and her descendants, condemning serpents to be crushed in time.[65] The curse of the snakes in the Pentateuch, Faber argued, had metaphorically been fulfilled in Our Lady of the Immaculate Conception, for "by this woman I understand the most greatly blessed Virgin Mary, a juster Eve to us, who through and with her seed Jesus Christ has worn down the head of the Devil, that ancient serpent, our most implacable foe.[66]

Like Faber, Nieremberg was also puzzled by the contradictory existence of evil, rapacious, wrathful, deathly, and flesh-eating (*rapacia, iracunda, exitalia et carnivora*) animals, who were originally created by God for man to keep as pets. Like Faber, Nieremberg understood original sin to be the cause of evil in Nature, and particularly of the treachery of snakes. The poison in the snakes was clearly a postlapsarian phenomenon, Nieremberg concluded, for the blessed and the holy not only were impervious to the bites of snakes but had command over these animals.[67] In fact, Nieremberg argued, demons had adulterated the original mild snake poisons created by God in order to keep humans terrified and under demonic control.[68] And these humans in the Americas were indeed terrified.

It would be tedious to go over the vast amount of evidence in sixteenth- and seventeenth-century European sources presenting the New World as a land infested by satanic snakes. Suffice it say that this perception colored even the most naturalistic representations of America offered by clear-eyed European observers. Take, for example, the case of Frans Post (1612–80), allegedly one of the first Europeans in the New World ever to portray Nature accurately. It is often argued that this Dutch painter captured images of the alien Brazilian landscape that bear uncanny resemblance to reality. Post, a member of the entourage of John Maurice of Nassau (1604–79), who ruled part of northeastern Brazil for the Dutch from 1636 to 1644, indeed created scores of celebrated landscapes. Yet for all the realism of his compositions, one can usually find lurking at the margins of Post's paintings the ubiquitous snake; in figure 4.6, it sticks its head out of the thick tropical undergrowth to swallow a small hare whole.[69]

That America was in the hands of serpentine demons was widely believed. On June 5, 1662, five squadrons of knights, representing the armies of five nations, rode past the palace of the Tuileries in Paris into the main plaza,

FIG. 4.6. Frans Post, Franciscan cloister in Igaraçú, Brazil (ca. 1655). Courtesy of the Historisches Museum, Frankfurt a/M.

where hundreds of distinguished spectators, including the queens of France and England, had gathered to see the pageant. Leading them were, respectively, the king himself, Louis XIV, and the four most powerful grandees in the kingdom. Ten other knights surrounded each squadron's leader. In addition, the squadrons had dozens of spare horses, squires, pages, grooms,

Chapter 4

FIG. 4.7. The duc de Guise as an American king (left) and American livery servants, squires, and grooms (right). Charles Perrault, *Courses de Testes et de Bague Faittes par Le Roy, et par les Princes et Seigneurs de sa Cour en l'Anne 1662* (Paris, 1670).

trumpeters, drummers, and livery servants. The Romans, led by Louis XIV himself, were furnished with striking shields and armor; so too were the Persians (led by Louis's brother), the Turks (led by the prince of Condé), and the Indians from India (led by the duc d'Anguien). The fifth and last "army" represented "sauvages de l'Amerique" and was led by the duc de Guise. This army, however, was strange. Along with each of the ten knights in the formation came four pages dressed as satyrs. The trumpeters and many of the grooms were "savages" wielding clubs and wearing tiger furs; the drummers came dressed as Tritons and the pages as bacchants. Twelve out of the twenty-four liveried servants were bears, and the rest were black slaves with monkeys on their shoulders. Each squire and page wore a "dragon" head for a helmet, and their uniforms were studded with "dragon's eyes." The ten heroes wore multicolored feathers from American birds, scales of gold, and animal pelts also studded with the "eyes of dragons." On their shoulders, they also carried the heads of tigers, and their saddles were made of panther skins. Leading this terrifying parade was the duc de Guise, the *Roy Ameriquain*, dressed as the devil himself. His armor was made of the pelt, heads, and tails of "dragons." The helmet was adorned with the most exquisite American feathers and the head of a golden dragon. The saddle was made of tiger pelts, and snakes dangled from it. "On the horse's crupper, a large dragon snout vomited a stream of snakes, which formed its tail."[70] Finally, the hero carried a club with a stuffed serpent curled around it.

Catholic Providence in Nature

Sixteenth- and seventeenth-century Catholic observers in the New World were not willing to concede the realm of Nature to the devil. For them signs of the epic Christian struggle against Lucifer also spilled over into the natural world. Europeans were confident that Nature itself was adapting to the arrival of the Gospel in America.

Saints

The first sign that changes in Nature were imminent was the appearance of a host of holy men. Just as the devil held extraordinary influence over Nature, the blessed and holy in Catholic America in particular were thought to have equally great preternatural powers. Thus in Iberian America there emerged a tradition of holy men capable of controlling Nature as they struggled against Satan. Take, for example, the case of Fray Pedro de Córdova, the Augustinian who had managed to escape an attack by Amerindians on Margarita Island by holding tight to his crucifix. After the attack, Córdova and his companion, lone survivors of the slaughter of the first party of Spanish settlers on Margarita, ran to the beach and found a boat with a mast. Unfortunately for the friars, the vessel was leaking and had no sail. Undaunted, the two friars jumped on the boat, sailed for hundreds of miles, and a few days later arrived unscathed in Hispaniola. This feat of navigation, the Augustinian chronicler Agustín Dávila Padilla (1562–1604) explained in his posthumous 1626 hagiography, had been possible only because "water and wind obeyed this servant of God, and he calmed the seas, and all creatures were subject to him, without even the devil himself daring to challenge him."[71]

There is also the case of the "spiritual conqueror" of Paraguay, the Jesuit Marciel de Lorenzana, a typical early modern spiritual knight in America, who spent his life battling the devil on the banks of the River Plate. Lorenzana arrived in Paraguay in 1609 with a crucifix as his sole weapon, "hoisting the sacred wood of the Cross to scare off the devil."[72] He converted even the most powerful shamans, who in league with the devil could trigger earthquakes. With his prayers, Lorenzana was capable of "keeping the devil at bay, sending him back into the air disheartened after having visibly appeared to the Parana Indians."[73] This knight of Christ had the power of healing the sick and of multiplying honey stored in barrels. The poison of serpents had no effect on him.[74]

Far more remarkable than either Córdova or Lorenzana, however, was the Portuguese Jesuit José de Anchieta. Anchieta was born in the Azores, studied in Coimbra, and was sent to Brazil in 1553 as a recently ordained Jesuit to recover from a wasting illness. In Brazil, Anchieta flourished and became a tireless soldier of Christ in the struggle against the devil, as well as an accomplished Latinist. Among the many works he penned, his *De gestis Mendi de Saa* (1563) stands out, for it is the first epic poem to cast the European colonial expansion in the New World in Homeric language and the conquest in demonological terms (see Chapter 2). Besides honing his poetical skills and developing grammars and texts in Tupinamba, Anchieta soon came to be known for his holiness and his ability to predict the future, cure the sick, and levitate. When praying, he gave off a shining light, even becoming invisible.[75]

Anchieta's power over the sphere of air was as extraordinary as that of his contemporary Jesuit Francisco Xavier (1506–52) in India, who acquired a following among Muslim "and other infidel" merchants in the Indian Ocean because of his ability to calm storms at sea. Xavier also once dissolved lightning threatening to strike the village of Tolo in Malacca and saved sailors from dying by making seawater potable. Even "filthy spirits" obeyed him, his hagiographers asserted. "Several times he cast them out of possessed human bodies and from places they threatened to destroy."[76]

Anchieta, for his part, was once able to keep rain from falling during a storm long enough to allow the Amerindians to put on a Christian play. In another occasion, he fell into a profound mystical trance while praying on the beach. When the tide came in, his companions found him surrounded by a wall of seawater, perfectly dry and still in deep meditation. His power over Nature did not stop with the elements; he also controlled animals. In one occasion, he was on a barge under a sun so intense that he asked a flock of *guarace* birds passing by to shelter him from the burning rays. The red birds, which had been addressed by Anchieta in the Brazilian language, willingly acquiesced. On another occasion, he politely addressed a flock of birds scavenging on the fish that a party of Jesuits had just caught. Anchieta asked the birds to leave and come back later for the leftovers, which they dutifully did. Anchieta had such extraordinary power over birds that he had them chirp songs to praise the Lord. His control over monkeys was also legendary. Once a dominant old ape fell off a tree and a band of monkeys gathered around to grieve. The Amerindians, however, attacked the primates to eat them. Anchieta ordered the Amerindians to stop and then told the panicking monkeys to come back and bury the dead. Again, the monkeys obeyed.[77]

A full account of Anchieta's preternatural powers over Nature could fill several pages. But it is the purpose of these skills that should preoccupy us. Anchieta dominated Nature, his hagiographers declared, in order to "proclaim in the New World the greatness of the Creator."[78] Thus Anchieta ordered the monkeys to return to grieve not so much because he cared for the primates as because he wanted to teach the Amerindians a lesson: "Father Joseph was not moved by pity for those animals, but by the desire to awaken veneration and respect for the Creator in the slow intellect [*entendimiento*] of the Indians. [Anchieta by so doing] was demonstrating to [the natives] that every creature abides by the wishes of the creator and is subjected completely to the laws and desires of God."[79]

In fact, the ultimate goal of Anchieta's constant display of mastery over Nature was to teach the Tupinamba a lesson about the predictable triumph of God over Satan. No wonder then that Anchieta was fond of walking barefoot in the jungle, where he took pleasure in being bitten by serpents and emerging unscathed. When he came upon snakes while walking in the wilderness, Anchieta stepped on them, ordered them to crawl onto his lap, petted them, and then let them go. He used such occasions to teach the Tupinamba a lesson on "the omnipotence of God, showing them that all things surrender to those who serve [God]."[80]

Holy men like Córdova, Lorenzana, and Anchieta brought extraordinary preternatural powers to bear in the European struggle to wrestle control of America's natural world away from Satan. What made these men so effective was their sanctity. Miguel Sánchez, the foremost exegete of the cosmic significance of the miracle of Our Lady of Guadalupe (see Chapter 2), argued in 1648 that the body of saints gave off a spiritual fragrance that made demons flee. Just as the fragrance of aromatic plants could drive demons out of the sphere of air, the bodies of saints had a concentrated smell of holiness that even impregnated their clothes.[81] It is no wonder, then, that when holy men and women died in colonial Spanish America, crowds lined up not only to bid them farewell but also to obtain pieces of their bodies (preferably earlobes, fingers, and noses) or, more commonly, pieces of their clothing. When she died in 1617, people thronged to see the corpse of the *beata* Rosa de Lima (canonized in 1671). One chewed off one of Rosa's fingers, but most of the members of the crowd were content with the rags of Rosa's worn habit. The demand was so great that Rosa had to be dressed six times.[82]

If the fragrance of relics warded off the assault of Lucifer, the holy fragrance of miraculous images guaranteed the believer even greater protection. Images of the Virgin Mary were particularly effective. The image of Our Lady of Guadalupe of Extremadura in the sanctuary of Guapulo, near Quito in today's Ecuador, for example, was known for exorcising demons from the bodies of possessed Amerindians.[83] But the most effective exorcist of them all was the image of Our Lady of Guadalupe in Mexico (see fig. 4.8). Sánchez explained this property both within the context of the image's larger cosmic significance and as a result of the holy fragrance that the canvas itself had acquired after the miracle. Since the image was the historical fulfillment of the battles of the woman of the apocalypse against the multiheaded dragon of Revelation 12, according to Sánchez, the whole purpose of her miraculous appearance in Mexico was to destroy the devil.[84] In any case, the image of Our Lady of Guadalupe kept Mexico from being assaulted by demons. As late as 1749, the Jesuit Francisco Carranza assured his audience in a sermon in Mexico City that under the patronage of Our Lady of Guadalupe, Mexico was no longer plagued by demons: cases of possessed people were no longer being reported, and those who came from Spain already possessed were freed from demons as soon as they landed.[85]

The culture of piety and sanctity brought by the Iberians to the New World, a land infested by demons, had literally contributed to its transformation. The conviction that Nature underwent changes as the result of the struggle between the armies of God and the armies of the devil moved Nieremberg to ascertain that the element water had been tamed by Christ's baptism, for the scale and number of floods and deluges had diminished right after Christ stepped into the waters of the Jordan to be baptized by John the Baptist. By the same token, olive trees became stronger after Christ chose olive oil as one of the sacraments. According to Nieremberg, the Adriatic had become a calmer sea after St. Helen dropped one of the nails with which Christ had been crucified into it. The opposite was also true: crocodiles in the Nile became nastier and bigger after Islam triumphed in Egypt. For Nieremberg, shipwrecks were simply a reflection of the sinfulness of the crews; thus praying was the best strategy for sailors whose vessels were in danger of sinking. A century before Nieremberg, the naturalist Fernández de Oviedo had already made all these views public, and his detailed account of shipwrecks in the Atlantic and miraculous tales of survival had the pedagogical purpose of demonstrating that sinful crews had a greater likelihood of experiencing shipwrecks, and that praying to Our Lady Mary helped many to survive. Fernández de Oviedo and Nieremberg both believed that the arrival of Christianity in the Americas had changed Nature itself: hur-

Mexicum totum, Patrocinio Virginis, demonio obses is Semper liberum iisdem peregrè advenientibus Salu

F I G . 4 . 8 . Our Lady of Guadalupe drives away demons who cause tempests (eighteenth century). Copperplate engraving by Nicolo Mogalli of a drawing by Filippo Vangelisti. One of a set of twelve *Escenas de la tradicion guadalupana*. Courtesy of the Museo de la Basílica de Guadalupe, Mexico City.

ricanes in the Caribbean had become less threatening, because the armies of demons stalking the seas were in retreat.[86]

Flora and Fauna

But God did not only act through holy intermediaries, relics, and images. As the Iberian colonization of the New World proceeded, it became clear to observers of Nature that there were plants and animals that God had chosen as allies in the struggle to oust the devil from the continent.

Sixteenth- and seventeenth-century Catholic clerical writings on New World flora and fauna are usually filled with references to Christian lessons to be gained from Nature. Take, for example, the case of Pérez de Ribas, whose 1645 history of the Jesuit missions in Sinaloa described the gruesome cannibal dismemberment of his colleague Tapia. Despite, or perhaps because of, the epic tone of his narrative, Pérez de Ribas managed to introduce snippets of the natural history of the region from which to draw religious lessons. According to Pérez de Ribas, the *tucuchi* tree of Sinaloa (most likely a variety of ficus tree with aerial roots, or a mangrove), for example, had branches supported by small trunks. It was therefore difficult to know whether the trunks grew down from the branches or up from the roots. Pérez de Ribas found in the tree a theological lesson about the mystery of the Trinity: "It can be said that God wished to leave in Nature a trace of how the Holy Spirit emanates from both the Father and the Son."[87] In this arboreal play of the Trinity, the branches and the roots stood for the Father and the Son and the trunks for the Holy Spirit.

Also edifying was the case of the ants of Quito. On January 19, 1649, the inhabitants of that city awoke to the news that thieves had stolen a ciborium full of consecrated wafers from a church. Although the vessel itself could not be recovered, the wafers were found in a ravine, and when people rushed to recover them, they found them surrounded by a sea of ants forming a wall in the shape of a gigantic monstrance: Nature had intervened on the side of the Lord. The city built a church on the site of the miracle: la Iglesia del Robo, the Church of the Robbery.[88]

Perhaps the most influential work in the genre of Catholic natural history was Juan Eusebio Nieremberg's *Historia naturae* (1635). In it, Nieremberg not only identified species that belonged to the devil but also those positioned to teach Christian lessons. For example, Nieremberg describes the case of a lion in North Africa that when about to be killed by a dragon was saved by a Spanish knight. From that day on, the grateful lion followed the knight like a pet. And when the knight sailed back to Spain, the lion drowned itself in the sea. Nieremberg used this chivalric tale to shed light on the nature of the soul. The soul, he argued, was like a lion threatened by the dragon of Satan, and God was the liberating knight to whom the soul should be grateful, even at the risk of self-immolation: "What do you do, O soul, when liberated from the jaws of the infernal dragon by that most noble knight who rides the white horse of his most pure humanity? How can you not run after your liberator? How can you not fly to him, even though you need to contend with the waves of the sea?"[89] Nieremberg also told of a dog that had forced its master not only to get up and attend mass but to wake up every time the doors of the church were left unlocked. The dog also made horses and mules, and those mounting them, genuflect as they passed in front of the church, and obliged the sick who visited the church to behave and dress decently. And Nieremberg told as well how, when fleeing with an image of the baby Jesus stolen from a church in 1628, thieves had encountered a flock of geese, which had mercilessly attacked them and alerted the locals, who caught the robbers.[90]

Not surprisingly, Nieremberg also found animals and plants that bore liberating messages in the New World. One was the *hoitzitziltototl* (hummingbird), which was said to use its beak (or its claws, depending on the contradictory statements of witnesses) to hang from tall trees, where it fell into a catatonic state, only to "resurrect" six months later. Like Christ, the bird thus "died" on a wooden cross and was "small yet capable of victory over death." Its life cycle therefore shed light on the mysteries of both the Passion and the Resurrection.[91] Nieremberg also cited the case of the male *ñandu*, or "ostrich" of the Pampas (*Rhea americana*). Rounding up twenty to thirty females, the male forces them to lay their eggs in a single spot and takes over hatching the eggs himself. Then the male sacrifices an egg to attract insects around the nest, so that later the chicks will have vermin to eat. According to Nieremberg, the behavior of the Rhea "settled the contradiction that Sacred Scripture accuses the ostrich of lack of parental feeling toward its offspring, while [secular] authors praise them for parental feeling: that is, the males are lovers of their offspring; the females show contempt for them."[92]

The Passionflower

But of all things allied with Christ in America, the passionflower possessed the greatest pedagogical potential. It clearly represented the whip and the pillar, Christ's red wounds and blood, the three nails of the Crucifixion, the crown of thorns, and the lance that pierced Christ's side, according to

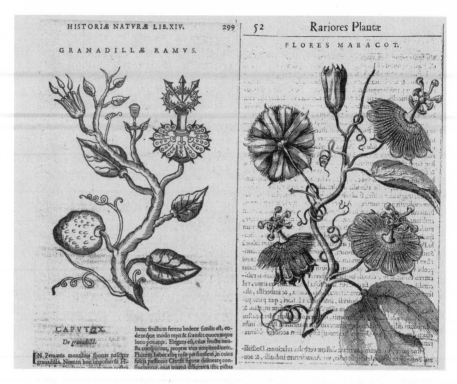

HISTORIÆ NATVRÆ LIB.XIV.   299   52   Rariores Plantæ

GRANADILLÆ RAMVS.   FLORES MARACOT.

FIG. 4.9. Passionflower (left) and vine (right). Juan Eusebio Nieremberg, *Historia naturae* (Antwerp, 1635), and Pietro Castelli, *Exactissima descriptio rariorum quarundam plantarum* (Rome, 1625). Courtesy of the Huntington Library, San Marino, California. The passionflower allegedly represents the instruments of the Passion of Christ, including the crown of thorns, the nails, the pillar, the lashes, the lance, and the wounds. Notice also the heartlike shape of the fruit on the vine (left) and the trilobate shape of the leaves (right). Interest in the theological meaning of the flower began in Rome around 1609 under the papacy of Paul V.

Nieremberg. The plant also bore the "fruit" of resurrection, delicious with sweet nectar. Both the flower and the fruit, he said, were contributing to the spread of the Gospel, encircling the earth with word of the liberation brought about by the Passion and Resurrection of Christ.[93] This last point was not an exaggeration, for the Jesuits had already taken the flower and its liberating meaning into the Ottoman empire.[94]

Given Nieremberg's fascination with the occult and the allegorical in fauna and flora, it is a little surprising to find that the Jesuit did not fully explore the theological meaning of a plant that hailed from a continent long in the hands of Satan. It fell to others to elaborate on this mystery. Monardes was perhaps the first naturalist to call attention, in 1574, to the Christian symbols in the flower.[95] Then between 1607 and 1610, several pamphlets on the meaning of the passionflower suddenly appeared in Italy.[96] The Jesuit Giovanni Botero (1540–1617), author of *Della ragione di stato* (1594), wrote a poem in 1607 wondering how a holy flower could have originated on a continent so distant from where the impious and inhumane Jews had committed their crime against Christ.[97]

It was the German theologian Jakob Gretser (1562–1625), however, who in 1610 first tackled the contradiction identified by Botero. After translating Simone Parlasca's Bolognese pamphlet on the passionflower, *Il fiore della Granadiglia* (1609) into Latin, Gretser went on to offer in poetic form a theological interpretation of every detail of the flower, including the meaning of the spearlike shape of the leaves, the thorns in the petals, and why the flower seemed to have only three nails instead of the four used in the Crucifixion (the fourth nail had been used to tack up the placard identifying Christ as king of the Jews). Since the flower itself symbolized Christ's reign in Nature, he reasoned, the fourth nail was superfluous. Gretser then went on to explore new territory, posing such questions as why the flower had surfaced in the Southern Hemisphere, and specifically in Peru. As heresy spread in Europe, Providence had selected America as the place for the passionflower to be discovered.[98] According to Gretser, the flower was poised to bring Peruvians back from darkness and away from their crimes and sin, making the victory of the Cross all the more impressive.[99] Employing a trope typical of the age, Gretser explained that the plant's lancelike leaves announced that Satan would be ousted from his kingdom by Spanish armies wielding instruments of war.[100] The symbols of the Cross and the Passion would migrate from the New World to help put down heretical outbreaks in the Old.[101]

With so much at stake, it is little wonder that the study of this marvelous text in Nature became a craze among learned clerics in the Atlantic Catholic world. In his 1625 description of rare plants cultivated in the botanical gardens of Cardinal Farnese in Rome, Pietro Castelli (1570–1657) vividly captured the excitement that his contemporaries felt: "This [is the plant which has been] most diligently sought out by the inquisitive because of its rarity. This, sung about by poets with divine praises. This, celebrated by orators in every species of eloquence. This, thoroughly investigated by philosophers with very subtle arguments. This, wondrously commended by doctors for its very salubrious powers. This, long demanded by the sick. This, admired by theologians, venerated by pious Christians. In a word, this has been remarkably desired and long sought out (and still is) by all peoples of whatever nature or condition for the elegance of its shape, its mysteries, its powers, and other qualities."[102]

In addition to recycling well-worn interpretations, Castelli advanced a few of his own: inter alia, that the white petals of the passionflower represented the white cloth worn by the Savior; that the hornlike tips of the white petals stood for the faith that penetrates like a sting; that the trilobate leaves of the vine stood for the mystery of the Trinity; and that the vine and its trellis represented the need Christians had for the institutional support of the Church to ascend to heaven.

Giovanni Battista Ferrari (1584–1655), gardener to Pope Urban VIII, the same pope who sent a relic of Christ's Cross to Peru, was also taken by the passionflower. In his *De florum cultura libri IV* (1633), the learned Ferrari, professor of rhetoric, Syriac, and Hebrew at the Jesuit college, found in the flower the lance-sponge filled with vinegar with which a Roman soldier had maliciously sought to quench Christ's thirst. Ferrari believed it very significant that the flower's fruit had the shape of the heart, "the heart [itself] of a loving God."[103] Moreover, he saw as revealing of the nature of the Church that the vine's roots grew so aggressively that when confined in a jar, they sent shoots through the smallest of holes down into the soil. Like Castelli, Ferrari insisted that the plant had come to Rome from the remotest corners of Mexico and Peru to inspire both poets and preachers.[104] Finally, in his *Annotationes et additiones* to the 1651 Academy of the Lynx edition of Francisco Hernández's natural history of Mexico, Fabio Colonna (1557–1660) maintained that the flower was ideal for keeping evil spirits away and countering sorcery.[105]

Protestant sources blamed the devil for the new craze for the passionflower. The great English gardener-naturalist John Parkinson (1567–1650) argued in 1629 that it was Satan and the Jesuits, his minions, who had spread the idea that "in the flower of this plant are to be seene all the markes of our Saviours Passion . . . as thornes, nailes, speare, whippe, pillar, & etc." These were, Parkinson maintained, "advantageous lies (which with [the Jesuits] are tolerable, or rather pious and meritorious) wherewith they use to instruct their people; but I dare say, God never willed his Priests to instruct his people with lyes: for they come from the Diuell, the author of them."[106]

Despite Protestant skepticism about Catholic reports of natural marvels in the New World, the marvels kept on surfacing. In 1634, for example, in the valley of Limache near Santiago, Chile, workers on a hacienda felled a tree in which the body of the crucified Christ was clearly sketched (fig. 4.10). The owner of the hacienda built a chapel for the tree, and soon the bishop of Santiago came to honor this marvel of Nature and to reflect on its meaning.

Vera Efigies cuiusdam Arboris, quæ in hunc modum et figurā crucis et Crucifix
creuiße inuenta eſt in Regno Chilēnſi in America, vbi in Valle Limache colitur
magna populi dèuotione ab anno Dñi 1634 .

FIG. 4.10. Tree in the shape of a crucified Christ, valley of Limache, Chile.
Alonso de Ovalle, *Histórica relación del reino de Chile* (Rome, 1646). Courtesy of the
John Carter Brown Library, Brown University, Providence, R.I.

"As our faith is beginning to set roots in the New World," the bishop declared, "the creator of Nature has caused this grand and new argument to emerge in the trees themselves, not simply as hieroglyph but as a true representation of the death and passion of our Redeemer, as the only and most efficient way to plant [the faith]."[107] Many years later, a similar phenomenon occurred in the province of Michoacán, Mexico, but this time not one but many crucified Christs appeared in logs floating down the rivers; Christs also appeared sketched on burned logs. It was, the Dominican Matías de Escobar argued, as if Nature in the New World, once home to a multitude of evil spirits, "now gave birth to any number of holy images, be they Christ or Mary."[108]

Protestant Providence in Nature

John Parkinson's angry denunciation of "Jesuit," satanic readings of the passionflower seems to epitomize Protestant traditional criticism of Iberian Catholic attitudes toward the natural world. Protestants decried as instrumentalist and impious the claims of Catholic holy men like Anchieta and Xavier to exert preternatural control over Nature. Central to the Protestant critique of Rome was the alleged desire of Catholics to claim for themselves powers that belonged exclusively to the Almighty. The doctrine of salvation through good works, for example, demonstrated the "demonically" inspired Catholic confusion that assumed that humans could buy their way to grace. The behavior of Anchieta and Xavier, according to Protestant doctrine, reflected the same human hubris that claimed for man powers that belonged exclusively to God. Not surprisingly, New England did not witness the rise of levitating saints with preternatural powers over either storms or birds.

This absence ought not to be interpreted to mean that Puritans in New England were less "superstitious" or more inherently endowed with a "scientific" outlook than their Iberian cousins to the south, for, as David Hall and Robert Godbeer have shown, Puritans had as much a knack for finding marvels in Nature as Catholics did. In fact, countless men and women were found in New England with as great command over Nature as Anchieta displayed in Brazil or Xavier did in India. In the Puritan imagination, however, these individuals did not belong to the community of the elect but were the devil's minions. There were in New England plenty of Amerindian shamans capable of unleashing storms and of petting snakes. There were also scores of wayward witches of European descent with great preternatural powers. In short, there were numerous Anchietas and Xaviers in New England, but they were all demons.[109]

But what of the Puritan attitude toward allegorical interpretations of New World plants and animals? If we are to believe Protestant denunciations of allegorical readings of the passionflower as demonic, it would appear that the Puritans in New England stood apart from the Iberian tendency to read New World plants and animals symbolically. After all, it was John Calvin (1509–64) who denounced the Catholic fondness for allegory as a satanic plot. The quadriga (the fourfold method of reading Scripture, including literal, allegorical, tropological, and anagogical meanings), Calvin argued, was a "licentious system" devised by Satan "to undermine the authority of Scripture and to take away from the reading of it the true advantage. . . . For many centuries no man was considered to be ingenious, who had not the skill and daring necessary for changing into a variety of shapes the sacred word of God."[110] Yet for all the Calvinist determination to stick to literalist interpretations, Puritans did have recourse to allegorical readings of both Scripture and Nature.

As Thomas H. Luxon has elegantly demonstrated, the Calvinist aversion to allegory was in fact matched by an obsessive reliance on typology. The end result was that Calvinists relied on allegorical readings of the Bible every bit as much as, if not more than, their Catholic cousins. Calvinist biblical hyperliteralism combined with unrelenting eschatological and typological readings of the English Civil War, for example, spawned an explosion of allegorical biblical readings that included the claim of thousands to the status of living Christs.[111] It was these same typological and eschatological readings that led the Puritans to interpret the landscape of New England allegorically.

Jonathan Edwards (1703–58) is often cited as having first introduced the typological reading of Nature to early eighteenth-century New England. In Edwards's eyes, all objects in God's original creation were prefigurations of future historical events. Calling Nature a "book" was more than a harmless metaphor to justify Christian natural philosophy. The trope of the book also implied the use of reading techniques on Nature that had long been deployed to interpret the Bible as a coherent whole. Thus typology allowed Edwards to read, say, the moon near conjunction with the sun as a prefiguration of "the decline of the Jewish church from the highest glory in Solomon's time."[112] By the same token, the rainbow was loaded with historical messages of all kinds, including the death and glorious Resurrection of Christ, the loose yet hierarchical nature of the Church, and the millennial community of the saints.[113] Edwards seemed to have carried such typological readings of Nature to extremes. Thus Edwards's much-touted early embrace of

Newtonian physics apparently had more to do with proving that the eternal laws of motion were simply "anti-types" of the Fall than with any genuine experimental pursuits. Edwards determined that no amount of human will could ever be responsible for individual salvation, in the same way that no amount of human desire could ever change the regular motion of the planets. Newton's laws of motion thus served to bolster the unrelenting Calvinist theology of salvation.[114]

According to Janice Knight, Edwards for the first time deployed traditional Calvinist typology in the reading of natural phenomena. There is no denying that Edwards was an exuberant practitioner of typological-allegorical readings of Nature. But he was by no means a lonely pioneer. Take, for example, the case of the radical Dissenter Roger Williams (1604–83), whose antinomian tendencies caused him to be excommunicated and expelled from Boston into the wilderness of Rhode Island. In his *Key into the Language of America* (1643), the feisty Williams denounced his Congregationalist enemies in Boston as hounds, while presenting himself as a sacrificial deer. Persecuted by Boston ministers, Williams found in the predatory behavior of "wolves and swine" in the Algonquian wilderness "a right Embleme of Gods persecuted." In Williams's imagination, the attacking wolves were a type for the Boston clergy, whereas the swine prefigured the behavior of the ministry of both Plymouth and Salem.[115] There is also the case of the poet-cleric Edward Taylor (1642–1729). Like Edwards, Taylor was obsessed with typology and allegorical readings of Nature. Not surprisingly, Taylor wrote poems, say, on the different ways in which a spider went about consuming flies and wasps (easily killing flies, but barely coping with wasps) to shed light on the different ways in which the devil consumes and attacks the sinful and the elect, respectively.[116]

It should surprise no one that Cotton Mather was also another pre-Edwardsian practitioner of typological readings of Nature. Mather read in the behavior of birds not only the Commandments (the stork and the dove as emblems of the right way to treat parents and spouses, respectively) but also the ideal political community.[117] Even more interesting, Mather described parrot-like birds capable of warning the quarrelsome in the Puritan community of the consequences of their behavior. "Look into the third of the *Colossians*, and the sixteenth," these birds parroted to their human audiences, urging Puritans to praise the Lord and not fall prey to the devil.[118]

This Puritan tendency to read Nature not only as a theater of vices and virtues but also as a text that paralleled both biblical and gentile history had repercussions on the interpretation of Nature in the New World. Thus, in

1632, the Puritan congregation of Watertown, near Boston, came together to discuss a most amazing sight: a mouse and a serpent had been locked for days in a struggle near the church. To everyone's amazement, instead of being swallowed by the much larger, treacherous reptile, the small rodent had managed to kill the snake. Fortunately for the perplexed congregation, John Wilson, the pastor, was on hand to explain the event: "That the snake was the devil; the mouse a poor contemptible people, which God had brought hither, which should overcome Satan here, and dispossess him of his kingdom."[119] If Satan's long-held sovereignty in the New World had managed to leave an imprint on the fauna and flora of the Americas, it was clear that the arrival of the Europeans with their message of liberation was bound to manifest itself in the natural world as well.

America as False Paradise

In 1639, the friar Antonio de la Calancha chose a striking image as the frontispiece for his history of the Augustinian order in Peru (fig. 4.11). To the unsuspecting eye, the frontispiece offers a triumphant, even bucolic, interpretation of conversion. With the blessing of the Virgin Mary, the Augustinians substitute the sacraments, the Cross, and the Church for the Andean worship of the sun and the moon. Yet the biblical passages throughout betray a more violent, demonological message. In a characteristic Catholic use of typology, Calancha presents passages in Isaiah, Ezekiel, and Jeremiah as prefigurations of the Spanish conquest. Thus Isaiah 9:2 ("The people that walked in darkness have seen a great light: they that dwell in the land of the shadow of death, upon them hath the light shined"), Isaiah 8:18 ("Behold, I and the children whom the LORD hath given me are for signs and for wonders in Israel from the LORD of hosts, which dwelleth in mount Zion"), Ezekiel 8:16 ("And he brought me into the inner court of the LORD's house, and, behold, at the door of the temple of the LORD, between the porch and the altar, were about five and twenty men, with their backs toward the temple of the LORD, and their faces toward the east; and they worshipped the sun toward the east"), and Jeremiah 44:6 ("Wherefore my fury and mine anger was poured forth, and was kindled in the cities of Judah and in the streets of Jerusalem; and they are wasted and desolate, as at this day") allow Calancha to present the plight of the Amerindians under the colonial regime as God's act of rightful retribution. Ezekiel 8, for example, is a reference to the prophet's vision of the Temple of Jerusalem in which even the priests worship idolatrous images to the sun. In Ezekiel 9, God accordingly sends

CHRONICA

MORALIZADA DEL
ORDEN DE S. AVGVSTIN
en el Peru, con sucesos ex.
emplares vistos en esta
Monarchia
Tomo primero

Por el P.e M.ro F. ANTONIO
DE LA CALANCHA Doctor
Graduado en la Vniuersidad de
Lima ycriollo de la Ciudad de la plata.

DEDICADA A NRÂ. S.a DE
GRATIA VIRGEN MARIA
MADRE DE DIOS Patrona de la
Religion de Nro. P.e S. AVGVSTIN.

Messis quidem multa operarij autem pauci: quia non sicut vtæ.

six men, each carrying "a slaughter weapon in his hand," to slaughter the idolaters and orders them to "let not your eye spare, neither have ye pity. Slay utterly old and young, both maids, and little children, and women" (Ezek. 9:5–6). Jeremiah 44 describes how the exiles from Judea in Egypt have taken to the idolatrous worshipping of Isis. God promises the idolaters: "they shall even be consumed by the sword and by the famine: they shall die, from the least even unto the greatest, by the sword and by the famine" (Jer. 44:12). The passages from Isaiah are no less violent, referring to God's plans to use the Assyrians to destroy the Israelites for having engaged in idolatry.

It is very telling that at the bottom of the composition, Calancha has a friar harvesting wheat, followed by two natives, one male and one female. The couple, the tree, and the serpent suggest an Edenic-demonic setting. An army of Amerindians hide behind the wheat field. Biblical references around this composition clarify its meaning: Matthew 8:29 ("Venisti huc ante tempus torquere nos" [Art thou come hither to torment us before the time?]); Matthew 13:25/39 ("Inimicus seminavit zizania, in medio tritici" [The enemy who planted the tares among the wheat is the devil]); and Matthew 9:37 ("Messis quidem multa operarii autem pauci" [The harvest is so great, but the workers are so few]). These are passages in which demons berate Christ for having expelled them from two men, a farmer decries his enemies for having introduced tares in his wheat field, and Jesus complains about the lack of sufficient followers, while promising to remove "from my kingdom everything that causes sin and all who do evil."

A gardening metaphor organizes the entire composition. Calancha's reliance on Isaiah, for example, is deliberate. Isaiah is a prophetic book in the Old Testament that describes the history of Israel as that of a plantation. Israel first becomes a thriving plantation by embracing God as its sole master. Soon, however, Israel falls back into idolatry, God punishes it with foreign invasions and collective forced exile, and the plantation becomes a barren desert. Isaiah now makes his appearance and prophesies a prosperous new future for Israel if it will abandon idolatry and embrace monotheism. The subtle subtext in Calancha's frontispiece is thus made clear: the conquest of America, which was violent, if justifiable, turned a false paradise into a barren land, but the spiritual conquest of America spearheaded by the Augustinians is transforming the desert into a blooming spiritual plantation. These were

FIG. 4.11. (*opposite*) The weeds of idolatry are rooted out from the Peruvian garden. Frontispiece and detail from Antonio de la Calancha's *Chronica moralizada* (Barcelona, 1639). Courtesy John Carter Brown Library, Brown University, Providence, R.I.

mainstream views. As we saw in the Introduction, the playwright Calderón
de la Barca wrote in 1651 an *auto sacramental* in which of all continents it was
the New World that could uniquely be identified as a deceptively beautiful
land, a false paradise firmly in control of the Devil yet about to be destroyed.
In the following pages, I trace this idea back to a wider early modern intellectual milieu and show how the European intelligentsia came to represent
the New World as a false paradise that to be saved needed to be destroyed.

Renaissance Epics

Modern interpreters of Edmund Spencer's *The Faerie Queene* (1590) such
as Stephen Greenblatt have argued that Spencer's early modern epic poem
about Elizabethan knights behaving virtuously includes veiled references to
the English Protestant colonization of Ireland, for Spencer himself lived as
an English landlord in Ireland and wrote extensively about the English exploits there. Greenblatt has argued that the destruction of the "bower of bliss"
in the *Faerie Queene* is an oblique allusion to English colonial violence.[120]
More recently, David Read has suggested that the second book of Spenser's
epic poem, where the reference to the destruction of the enclosed garden
takes place, is in fact a full-fledged metaphorical allusion to the European
conquest of the New World. According to Read, Spenser conceived Sir
Guyon, the knight of Temperance, the main character in the second book, as
the antithesis of the Spanish conquistador. Unlike Spanish conquistadors in
America, who gave in to each and every temptation, raping and plundering as
they went along, Guyon, the Puritan knight, remains impervious to the allure
of gold and the desires of the flesh.[121] As the adventure unfolds, Guyon arrives
in a garden-island "pickt out by choice of best alive, that natures worke by
art can imitate: in which what ever in this worldy state is sweet, and pleasing
unto living sense." Once there, Guyon confronts the seductress fay Acrasia, a
beautiful sorceress whose sensual charms do to heroes what Omphale once

FIG. 4.12. *(opposite)* Sir Guyon, the Knight of Temperance, slays the Dragon
of Vice and Temptation in Edmund Spenser's *The Faerie Queene* (London, 1590).
Courtesy of the Huntington Library, San Marino, California. Guyon confronts
the seductress Acrasia and destroys a garden, the bower of bliss, she has created
to seduce and hold captive emasculated knights. Like America, Acrasia's island is
surrounded by demonic monsters capable of unleashing fog and whirlpools. Guyon
has to confront monsters guarding the approach to the island, as in the case of the
Hesperides and America.

did to Hercules, namely, emasculate them. Yet Acrasia fails to lure Guyon. In a flight of rage, Guyon, the master of temperance, proceeds to destroy all the sources of temptation, including the garden itself. From the "tempest of his wrathfulnese," he turns "blisse" into "balefulnesse" by felling groves, spoiling trees, defacing the garden, burning houses, and razing buildings. By such acts of physical destruction, Guyon manages to turn "the fairest" into "the fowlest place."[122] "With rigour pitiless," Guyon wipes out the bower of bliss.

Although both Greenblatt and Read draw clear analogies between colonialism and the destruction of the bower of bliss, in their interpretations, Guyon's violence is aimed at the sensuality and wantonness of either colonized natives or degenerate Spanish anti-heroes, not Nature itself. Yet, as A. Bartlett Giamatti has shown, by the time Spenser published his *Faerie Queene*, European audiences had become accustomed to viewing all earthly blissful gardens with suspicion, for pastoral spaces could potentially become corrupting, emasculating spaces where Christian heroes surrendered to the temptations of the flesh. These false paradise gardens were in fact the devil's haven, a place not to be admired but denounced.[123] I want to suggest here that in Spenser's poem, Guyon seeks to destroy not only Acrasia's victims of sexual-sensual excesses but also the satanic landscape itself. Just as Iberian and Puritan settlers had to confront tempests unleashed by demons in their Atlantic crossings, Guyon fights fog and whirlpools to reach the island. In the same way that demons and monsters kept the liberating Christian knight from fully possessing the American landscape, monsters keep Guyon from landing. The "bower of bliss," like the New World, is a treacherously pleasant space ruled by demonic creatures for the early modern Herculean hero to slay.

This sensibility toward the American landscape can also be found in another towering Protestant intellectual, Theodore de Bry (1528–98). In the frontispieces to de Bry's translation of Girolamo Benzoni's *La historia del mondo nuovo* (1565), the Dutch printer seeks to make sense of the Spanish conquest of the New World as narrated by the Italian soldier of fortune (fig. 4.13). Benzoni (b. 1519) was one of many German, Italian, Greek, and Iberian warrior-entrepreneurs who with the sanction of the Spanish Crown came together in private armies over the course of the first half of the sixteenth century to scour America in search of booty, slaves, and vassals. De Bry was a Dutch Protestant printer who had been uprooted from the Low Countries in the wake of the wars fought by Dutch patriots against Habsburg rule. Scholars have argued that de Bry published Benzoni's tales of reckless "Spanish" violence not only to get even but also as part of a larger national-religious campaign to soil the reputation of Spain by means of a "black legend."[124] The Dutch in particular had inextricably linked their own emerging

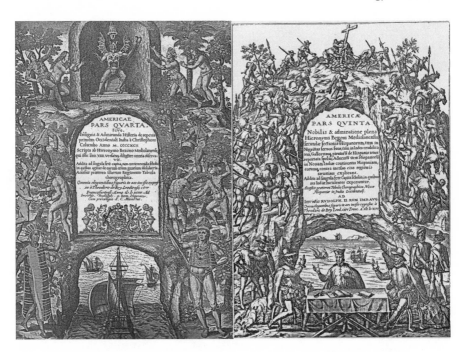

FIG. 4.13. Substituting the Cross for the devil. Theodore de Bry, *America* (Frankfurt a/M, 1595–97), vols. 4–5. The images correspond to the frontispieces to volumes 1 and 2 of de Bry's translation of the travels of Girolamo Benzoni (b. 1519) in Peru. Although the frontispiece to volume 1 is a pastoral representation of America prior to the Spanish arrival, de Bry had no doubts that Satan ruled there. His view of the Spanish conquest, as represented in the frontispiece to vol. 2, is more difficult to interpret. Like other Protestant critics of the brutality of the Spanish conquest, de Bry seems to have believed that, for all its brutality, the conquest was the first step toward vanquishing the devil in the New World. Thus the sequence of images could be read as a narrative of deliverance, in which the Spaniards, by planting the Cross, rightfully destroy a false paradise presided over by Satan. By the same token, de Bry, following Bartolomé de las Casas (1474–1566) (whom de Bry also translated), could also have intended this pictorial narrative as an ironic commentary on the Spanish conquest. Las Casas maintained that America had once been a prelapsarian paradise, which the conquistador-demons had managed to transform into hell.

national identity to the fate of the natives in the Spanish colonies. Both the "Indians" and the Dutch became victims and imagined allies in a narrative of transcontinental struggles against a common Catholic overlord.[125]

At first sight the frontispieces to the first two volumes of Benzoni's 1595–97 edition seem to confirm current scholarly consensus on de Bry, for these images appear to depict the wanton destruction of the Indies by the Spaniards. The first volume opens with an image of a verdant mountain with scantily clad natives frolicking as they pick fruits from a luscious orchard. Sailing through an opening at the foot of the mountain, Spanish vessels "penetrate" and "possess" the continent, ominously announcing the end of this idyllic world. In the frontispiece to volume 2, the garden is no more; it has been replaced by a bleak and barren landscape. These two images seem to parrot Ovid's story of the transformation of the Golden Age. In the first, America stands for a place where, in Ovid's terms,

Trees had not yet
Been cut and hollowed, to visit other shores. . . .
And Earth, untroubled,
Unharried by hoe or plowshare, brought forth all
That man had need for, and those men were happy,
Gathering berries from the mountain sides.

In the second, the greedy conquistadors and their retinue of African slaves have let loose all evil:

The pines came down their mountain-sides. . . .
The rich earth
Good giver of all the bounty of the harvest,
Was asked for more; they dug into her vitals,
Pried out the wealth a kinder lord had hidden. . . .
And war came forth. . . . Bloody hands
Brandished the clashing weapons. Men lived on plunder.[126]

Yet for all its coherence, this interpretation of the images fails to persuade, for it misses crucial elements in the composition. So, for example, the Ovidian reading overlooks the fact that a winged monster wielding a pitchfork presides over the natives cavorting in the luscious orchard. As it turns out, the frolicking natives have gathered to worship Satan. The meaning of the second image, then, is far more ambiguous; for if, on the one hand, the orchard is no more, on the other hand, the Cross has now replaced the devil.

It is perfectly possible that de Bry intended these two images to be ironic. As a translator of Bartolomé de las Casas's *Brevíssima relación de la destrucción de las Indias* (1552), de Bry was surely familiar with how Las Casas inverted the demonological discourse to indict the conquerors as demons themselves (see Chapter 2). De Bry might, therefore, have inserted these images to mock the crusading discourse of the conquest, thus suggesting that America had been better off under Satan than it was under the Cross. As de Bry explains in the preface to his edition of Benzoni's travels, the devil was more present in the Spaniards' relentless pursuit of riches, greed, and ambitions than in the demonic religion of the Amerindians. "This book," de Bry argues, "describes how the Spaniards with their military forces and armies penetrated the various provinces and corners of the continent feigning to seek to implant and impose the name of Christ, when in fact . . . all they were looking for was gold and silver, and great riches," that is, the devil himself.[127] But this seemingly persuasive reading of the images also fails to make sense of all the available evidence.

Like so many of his contemporaries, de Bry took the devil very seriously and thought that Satan had reigned undisturbed in America for centuries. Images of demons and many-headed hydras abound in the many volumes of de Bry's *America* (see, e.g., fig. 4.1). More important, de Bry thought that the areas of the New World under Spanish rule were particularly infested by demons. "Reader you will find in these images . . . the mores, customs, and religion of the inhabitants of this land [Spanish America]," de Bry says in the preface to his edition of Benzoni's account. "You will be able to deduce from them the great differences regarding the practice of religion between the inhabitants of the places described in previous volumes and those discussed here. Unlike the peoples of the island of Virginia who worship God the Creator of all things through a wooden idol, or the peoples of Florida who do so through the moon and the sun, or the Brazilians who worship Maralea, the people here worship the devil himself."[128]

It is not clear why de Bry singled out the Caribbean, Peru, and Mexico prior to the European arrival as havens for Satan. It is clear however, that he thought these places still to be threatening. In the same pages in which he characterizes the places colonized by the Spaniards as uniquely given to worshipping the devil, de Bry argues that there are other forms of paying homage to Satan. The voracious pursuit of material wealth is the most conspicuous of them all. Like the natives, he argues, the Spaniards had fallen prey to Lucifer. Moved by "insatiable avarice," they had used "horrible and tyrannical means" to deal with the local inhabitants. "Prompted by their absurd greed," Spaniards had even been willing to slit each other's throats. That their polities in America had been wrecked by civil wars and ransacked by pirates was just recompense for the pact that the conquistadors had struck with the devil.[129] Yet de Bry did not seek to denounce the Spaniards as a whole, but rather to condemn the effects of avarice and cupidity on the soul, for he thought that any form of greed was itself demonic. The speculative shenanigans and usurious lending of Dutch merchants at home were also manifestations of satanic gluttony in his opinion.[130]

For de Bry, America is first and foremost a demonic space because it

FIG. 4.14. America as a false paradise. Anonymous painter, *From Spaniard and Chamiza, Barcino. Water* (ca. 1770–80). Private collection. Many thanks to Ilona Katzew for securing permission for publication from the collector. This painting comes from a series of eighteenth-century Mexican *casta* paintings. Like other *casta* paintings, this one represents the mixture of two different races in the colonial period: a Spaniard and a Chamiza, the latter the offspring of a "Coyote" (Indian and Mestizo mixture) and an Indian. What is interesting about this painting, however, is the garden and the surrounding grotesquerie. The enclosed garden and the fountains suggest a paradisiacal setting with allusions to the sacred and the Church via the Song of Songs 4:12 ("You are like a private garden, my treasure, my bride! You are like a spring that no one can drink from, a fountain of my own"). But the grotesque motifs suggest a demonic garden. Presiding over the entire composition is a red, devil-like creature. To the left of the Chamiza woman and her Barcino baby is an "amphisbaena," the snake with two heads that the seventeenth-century German cleric-naturalist Johann Faber refused to call a "monster" (see p. 135). The head of Neptune with two snakes

(continued)

threatens to corrupt the souls of all Europeans (see fig. 4.14). The devil is just as present in the religion of the Amerindians as in the bountifulness of the mines of America. The gold, silver, and riches of America are simply tricks used by Satan to seduce Europeans into the greedy, unrelenting pursuit of power. What is needed to fight Lucifer at home is to "contain our appetite and satisfy ourselves with the munificence and grace of God, having no more than what is strictly needed to feed and clothe ourselves."[131] It was as if the American garden needed to be stripped bare of all its abundant commercial resources to save European souls from corruption.[132]

There is also evidence that de Bry interpreted the "discovery" of the New World as part of a much larger apocalyptic narrative. In his posthumous 1599 edition of the travels of the German Ulrich Schmidel (1510–79), a warrior-entrepreneur who participated in the "Spanish" conquest of the River Plate region, de Bry argued that God had allowed the New World to remain hidden until the last age of the world (*postrema mundi aetate*) for a reason. The discovery of the New World, he maintained, was part of a much larger cosmic plan by God to give Europeans one last chance to create a truly pious society. God had intended the piety of the natives, albeit misdirected toward Satan, to be a source of inspiration. Europeans needed to do unto Satan what Satan had done unto God in America, namely, ape and mimic the piety of the Amerindians for the millennium to come.[133]

Like many of his contemporaries, de Bry associated the imminent arrival of the millennium with outbreaks of demonism and witchcraft, which he saw as last-ditch efforts by Satan to avoid the second coming of Christ.[134] It is therefore plausible to argue that the two images I have sought to interpret were in fact intended to be read as a narrative of spiritual, millennial liberation. Like his contemporary Spenser, de Bry seems to have believed the New World to be a "bower of bliss," a false paradise, a source of wealth and corruption that the spiritual hero needed to wipe out to hasten the arrival of the millennium.

We are left with only indirect clues suggesting that Spenser and de Bry thought that the New World was a false paradise. Others, however, were not oblique at all. Take, for example, the case of Torquato Tasso (1544–95), who in his epic poem *Gerusalemme liberata* (1581) explicitly locates an island

FIG. 4.14 (*continued from previous page*)
protruding from it and the two Leviathan-type creatures sticking out grotesquely into the pool where it rests are related to early narratives of Atlantic crossings plagued by tempests unleashed by demons. It is not clear whether the late eighteenth-century painter was conscious of all these earlier colonial associations.

FIG. 4.15. Ballet at the court of Louis XIII representing the captivity of Rinaldo in Armida's false paradise. From *Discourse au vray du ballet danse par le roy* (*La Délivrance de Ranaud*) (Paris, 1617). At the upper left hand, Rinaldo has fallen asleep at the foot of the mountain-paradise. This false paradise is presided over by twelve demons, one of which Louis XIII himself impersonates. In the upper right-hand

(continued)

Demonology and Nature

in America, a place deep "in the vast ocean, where our voyaging seldom or never ventures, utterly beyond our shores," whose luscious gardens are a demonic trap. Building on the well-established medieval and Renaissance trope of an emasculating false paradise, Tasso locates his garden in a "secret world ... [where] the tribes differ ... [where] some adore beasts, others the stars and sun; and some heap high their wicked tables with cruelty and abomination." The plot is simple. Tasso has fay Armida, a Muslim sorceress, lure Rinaldo, a hero whose crusading army is seeking to restore Christian rule over Jerusalem, into the temperate summit of a "witch mountain" in an Atlantic island, a "garden where love appears to breathe from every leaf." Two Christian knights, Charles and Ubaldo, are dispatched to liberate Rinaldo. As they fight their way up the mountain, the knights confront poisonous wells, seductive whores, pythons, wild boars, and great bears. After defeating a lion, a dragon, and a "gigantic army ... of all monstrous things that breed between the Nile and the shores of the Atlantic," the warriors make it to the summit only to find Hercules pitifully emasculated: "gossiping with servant ladies, spinning. He who had harrowed hell and borne the stars now turned his loom." Deep inside the garden, within a maze built by "demons," the warriors locate an effete Rinaldo and set him free.[135]

Tasso's *Gerusalemme liberata* was instrumental in popularizing the trope of America as a false paradise ruled by demons. In 1617, at the court of Louis XIII, for example, the story of Rinaldo's captivity was adapted as a ballet production in which Louis XIII and a host of retainers took to the stage to recreate Tasso's America. The ballet opened with Rinaldo sleeping at the foot of the mountain-garden where Armida, the temptress, had taken him. Like paradise, the mountain is near the stars and therefore immune to processes of generation and corruption typical of terrestrial physics.[136] Louis XIII and eleven other high-ranking members of the French nobility sat in niches within the mountain dressed as "demons" of fire, water, air, war, vanity, and

F I G . 4.15 *(continued from previous page)*
corner, Charles and Ubaldo arrive in the garden to liberate Rinaldo. A nymph seeks to seduce them, but to no avail. In the lower left hand, Armida, the Muslim sorceress, enraged upon noticing that Rinaldo has escaped, surrounds herself with "demons," snails, tortoises, and lobsters. The image in the lower right represents the liberation of Rinaldo from the false paradise. Charles and Ubaldo shatter the chains that had held captive the emasculated Rinaldo, who, unlike the other two heroes, carries no shield and wears no armor.

167

other vices and human passions. The emasculated Rinaldo surrenders to the sensual pleasures of the island, but not so Charles and Ubaldo, who on their way to liberate Rinaldo avoid falling prey to the seductions of nymphs who seek to lure the knights into enclosed gardens. After fighting all sorts of monsters, Charles and Ubaldo encounter a pitifully effeminate Rinaldo with no shield and armor and set him free. In a fit of rage, Armida summons the demons of the island. Some are humans with the faces of dogs; others are lobsters, tortoises, and snails.

This tradition of knights slaying demons and of a false paradise guarded by monstrous animals and located on an island seems to have become a commonplace among early modern Europeans as they sought to interpret the New World. The images used by the Dutch printer Levinus Hulsius (d. 1606) to illustrate his 1599 edition of Ulrich Schmidel's *Neuwe Welt* (1567) typify this tradition (fig 4.16). A mercenary from Bavaria, Schmidel set sail in 1535 with Pedro de Mendoza to settle in South America. After an eventful trip that included the foundation and settlement of Buenos Aires and the colonization of the Brazilian interior, Schmidel returned to Antwerp in 1554 and published an account of his trip in 1567. In the opening image accompanying Schmidel's text, Hulsius has Schmidel step over a ferocious-looking tiger and stand defiantly next to a coiled snake. Schmidel appears clad in armor and wielding a pike, with his coat of arms as background to this scene of chivalric valor.

Hulsius thought of travelers' accounts of America as useful not only because they were entertaining adventures (*non tantum iucundae*), but also because they were necessary for Christians to read (*sed etiam christianis lectu, necessariae sunt*). America, Hulsius maintained, shed light on the nature of the Fall. America was filled with "how many infinite thousands of men [who] have lived and continue to live like wild beasts, deprived of any knowledge of God and His commandments, lacking uprightness of life, marriage, learning, and laws, brought up in horrible idolatry, baseness, shameful lusts, drunkenness, and a more than barbaric gluttony for human flesh." It was clear that God had privileged Europe, and that Christians had a role to play as knights in America vanquishing the devil.[137] It was also clear that Hulsius considered Schmidel another Rinaldo: a knight who had encountered a false paradise.

Flying in the face of all available contemporary geographical evidence, Hulsius represented the land Schmidel explored as an island. Hulsius's map of South America seems lifted from a contemporary chivalric romance. It is peppered with illustrations of Amazons, Patagonian giants, and the monstrous medieval races that Walter Raleigh allegedly encountered in Guyana.

FIG. 4.16. Ulrich Schmidel as a knight in Amercia (left) and Brazil as an island paradise (right). Ulrich Schmidel, *Vera historia admirandae* . . . (Nuremberg, 1599). Courtesy of the Huntington Library, San Marino, California.

In keeping with his chivalric view of the land, Hulsius represented Brazil as an island, because Brazil had in fact been the name of a magical isle in Arthurian romance.[138] For his knight to be on an island, Hulsius postulated a connection between the rivers Amazon and Plate deep inside the continent, thus severing Brazil from the mainland. Hulsius's map is chock full of references to Brazil as a paradise. Brazil appears on it as a triangular island at whose base four rivers converge (two other rivers also come together at the point where La Plata and the Amazon meet). Hulisus's paradise, however, is false: a threatening space inhabited by monstrous races and demonic animals, which the knight should confront.

This type of discursive structure, of heroes battling demons in the New World, helps us make sense of Peter Paul Rubens's design for the Arch of the Mint, a triumphal arch intended to celebrate the 1634 arrival in Antwerp of

FIG. 4.17. *(above and opposite)* America as a garden with golden apples for Hercules to pick and a Golden Fleece for Jason to carry off. Front and rear faces of Peter Paul Rubens's design for the Arch of the Mint in Antwerp. In Jean Gaspard Gevaerts, *Pompa introitus . . .* (Antwerp, 1635). Courtesy of the Houghton Library, Harvard University.

PRETIVM NON VILE SVORVM

VLTRA ANNI

SOLISQ VIAS

OCEANVMQ

VLTRA

MONETA
DEO FVNDAMENTVM GENERIS HVMANI
VITÆ ET INDVSTRIÆ RERVM
IPSO TERRARVM LOCVPLETATRIX
OMNIVM CONSERVATRIX

ARCVS MONETALIS
PARS ANTERIOR

PERVVIVS

RIO
DE LA
PLATA

P. P. Rub Invent.

the new governor of the Spanish Netherlands, Ferdinand of Austria. Paid for and built by the officers of the Royal Mint, and part of a much larger city extravaganza that included the erection of various other porticos, stages, and altars, the arch celebrated the sources of Habsburg power and wealth, namely, the New World. For his design (fig. 4.17), Rubens (1577–1640) drew on the twin traditions of the chivalric and the demonic. Both the front and rear faces of the arch represent the mountain of Potosí, the source of Spanish silver and wealth.

Rubens has the Amerindians hard at work, either carrying loads of ore out of shafts or digging new ones. Although the landscape is barren, the anthropomorphic representation of four New World rivers (Peruvius, Plate, Maragnon, and Condorillus) at the foot of the mountain suggests that Rubens took America to be the original location of paradise. Precisely at the time that Rubens was designing the Arch of the Mint, Antonio León Pinelo in Spain was writing a lengthy treatise linking the waterways of the Magdalena, Orinoco, Plate, and Amazon to the rivers of Eden and thus arguing that paradise had originally been located on the eastern slopes of the Andes. Rubens's allusion to the former bountifulness of an America now turned into a quarry might have tempted some viewers to think that his arch conveyed an Ovidian narrative of decline and plunder.

Yet the arches are a narrative of the valor of Spanish knights delivering America from satanic monsters. At the top of the mountain, Jason and Hercules trample serpents and battle dragons to claim what is properly theirs, namely, the Golden Fleece and the golden apples in the garden of the Hesperides. The reference to Jason the Argonaut and Hercules allowed Rubens to put the Spanish conquest of America in the appropriate chivalric context: the Spaniards in America had stepped into a false paradise ruled by demons. The gold and silver they found was simply for them to keep, God's reward for their heroic exploits.[139]

Lest there be a temptation to assume that Rubens's interpretation was not truly representative, consider another frontispiece, that which introduces volume 11 of Joan Blaeu's monumental *Geographia* (1662–65).

Here a bare-breasted woman wearing a feather skirt and holding a bow and arrow stands for America. Silver ingots and an exotic reptile lie at the feet of this scantily clad Amazon. A mountain to her right is being mined,

F I G . 4 . 1 8 . *(opposite)* America rescued by a knight from the clutches of the devil, in Joan Blaeu, *Geographia* (Amsterdam, 1662–65), vol. 11. Courtesy of the New York Public Library.

this time, however, by blacks, not Amerindians. An epic narrative of sorts unfolds in the clouds to her left, where a native genuflects before the Cross held by a woman sitting opposite and above a demonic creature with claws and wings, who is being driven off by a knight wielding a sword. It is not clear in this frontispiece whether Blaeu (1596–1673) sought to represent the Dutch or the Spanish conquests in America. It is clear, however, that he used the conventions of chivalric Christian romance to represent the early modern European expansion into the New World.

Epic and Epistemology

I want to conclude this chapter by suggesting that this widespread early modern understanding of the American landscape as a false paradise to be conquered, destroyed, or possessed had a lasting impact on the way herbals and natural histories came to represent the task of the European observer in the New World. From the 1500s well into the eighteenth century, herbals and natural histories represented the art of collecting and knowledge gathering as a Herculean task, a knightly adventure into newly discovered territories guarded by satanic forces.

The four images in figure 4.19 are taken from two sixteenth-century herbals, a seventeenth-century gardening treatise, and an eighteenth-century natural history. They all include a Herculean hero clubbing a dragon to death. These images were not mere humanist acknowledgment of the myth of Hercules in the garden of the Hesperides. That they actually sought to represent a colonial attitude to the landscape is confirmed by the exegesis of one of the images offered in 1646 by Giovanni Battista Ferrari, the same learned Jesuit gardener who found in the vine of the passionflower a commentary on the aggressive nature of the Church. The myth of Hercules in the Hesperides, he argued, illustrated the struggle to domesticate Nature. The sentinel dragon who kept the golden apples from being taken by outsiders represented the seemingly insurmountable difficulties of the task. Hercules' club and his slaying of the Nemean lion and the hundred-headed dragon of the Hesperides stood for the triumph of colonization over the wilderness.[140] By the eighteenth century, the triumph over Nature was defined as technical. In the frontispiece to Linnaeus's *Hortus Cliffortianus* (1737), Python is slain. In this case, the Herculean hero is Apollo, standing for the technical prowess of Europe, which has learned to use glass, fire, and water to defeat the elements and create artificial gardens in which to grow all the plants of the world.[141]

against the devil in the New World as a struggle over the control of Nature. Yet while both the Puritans and the Spanish Catholics found Satan everywhere in the American wilderness, they also turned to Nature for providential signs to carve holy lands out of local landscapes. The next chapter describes how Puritans and Spanish Catholics managed to transform formerly demonic spaces into New Jerusalems.

Colonization as Spiritual Gardening

Catalina de Jesús María Herrera (1717–95) woke up one night wondering whether she should have gone to Lima. Although her Dominican convent in Quito had not yet succeeded in producing any spiritual flower, Lima had already produced Saint Rose of Lima (1586–1617), whom Pope Clement X canonized in 1671. Catalina de Jesús doubted whether her convent in Quito was in fact the spiritual garden she had once imagined it to be. Could a flower ever have flourished there? Catalina suddenly had a vision: out of a cell in the convent emerged a nun of blinding radiance: it was the deceased Juana de la Cruz. Catalina persuaded five other nuns to go to the convent's catacombs and disinter Juana. After several nights of prying open vaults containing decomposed corpses and of fighting off demons who sought to keep them locked, Catalina and her religious sisters finally came across a wooden coffin that smelled of roses, with an intact body inside it. Since the coffin bore numerous small cruciform marks, it was clear that the body was that of Juana of the Cross. The body was intact and covered with a glowing powder that resembled stars. It also gave off sweet smells. Despite the efforts of the devil to keep the nuns from knowing the truth, Catalina had found a flower in her convent, a nun of such remarkable virtue that her body defied corruption. Catalina noticed that this powerful body was missing a shoe and reasoned that the priest who had buried Juana of the Cross had taken it; the body and garments of spiritual flowers like Juana were suitable as relics: it was the body of a saint.[1]

The story of Catalina's search for "flowers" in her convent in early eighteenth-century Quito is typical of the Christian Atlantic world. For every fortification Satan had in the New World, Christians built one of their own. The barricades Puritans and Spaniards erected in the Indies were churches and saints. Yet saints and churches were imagined as walled gardens, not ramparts: beautiful plantations with hedges to keep assailants and weeds out. Historians have thought of the term "plantation" in strictly economic terms: land on which to grow cash crops to be sent to Europe. But the

FIG. 5.1. Sor Catalina de Jesús María Herrera (1717–95). Frontispiece to José María Vargas, O.P., *Sor Catalina de Jesús María Herrera*. Catalina herself is presented as a lily, a flower of the Church.

historical actors themselves thought that plantations meant something else, namely, well-tended gardens in the hostile environment that was the satanic wilderness. In the pages that follow, I explore the discourse of colonization as spiritual gardening.

Gardening as Type and Metaphor

Christianity had for centuries defined God and Christ as gardeners, and the soul and the Church as gardens. As the Church came of age under persecution in the Roman empire, martyrs came to be considered flowers, the most beautiful crop of the Church's plantation (see fig. 5.2).[2] The garden-

ing metaphor was in turn linked to the exegesis of the Song of Songs. This odd text describes male and female lovers as flowers and trees, gardeners and gardens.[3] Theologians came to identify at least three lovers of God as they sought to make sense of the Canticles: the soul, the Church, and the Virgin Mary. Exegetes interpreted the soul as fertile ground for the flowers of spiritual virtue to blossom, a garden for the individual to tend. Thus it is not surprising that in sixteenth-century Spain, Saint Teresa of Avila (1515–82) not only wrote an interpretation of the Song of Songs but also conceived of her mystical union with God in gardening metaphors: "It was delightful for me to think of my soul as a garden where God strolled. I prayed for the fragrant little flowers of virtue that, it seemed, were beginning to sprout [in me] for the glory of God to be tended by him."[4]

The closer the individual soul was to sanctity, the more it resembled a flower. Moreover, saintly figures seemed to have enjoyed fertilizing power: through their prayers they had the ability not only of lifting souls to heaven but also of communicating a flowery character to those in purgatory. Take, for example, the case of María de San José (1656–1719), a virtuous nun who

FIG. 5.2. *(Preceding page)*: Fresco of anonymous martyr, Oratory of Abou-Girgeh, Egypt (ca. third century CE?). *(This page)*: Miracle of the Martyrs of Gorcum in Jan Boener, *Waerachtighe ende levende figuren van de H. Martelaers van Gorcum* ('s Hertogenbosch: Antonius Scheffer, 1623), sig. G4v. From Brad S. Gregory, *Salvation at Stake*, 311. In July 1572, eighteen Franciscans and their Dominican confessor were taken from the town of Gorcum by Dutch Calvinists and hanged in Briel after having refused to recant their Catholic beliefs. A flower with three blossoms was found on the burial site in 1615 and kept in a box for two years. When the box was open, the flower not only was still fresh but also had nineteen blossoms, the exact number of the martyrs of Gorcum.

founded the first convent of the Augustinian Recoletas in Mexico City. As a typical veiled nun with extraordinary virtues, María de San José devoted an inordinate amount of energy to writing diaries and autobiographies addressed to her confessor in which she explored the inner recesses of her soul. She also spent her days praying, trying to keep souls from going to purgatory. One day, María de San José lost her beloved confessor, Manuel Barros. Although María thought that confessors were gardeners sent by God to keep the souls of nuns free of weeds, so that Christ could have tidy gardens to visit, it turned out that Barros's own soul was not a garden cultivated well enough for him to go straight to heaven. In a vision, María de San José saw Barros's soul ascending to purgatory for further cleansing. So, using all her accumulated sanctity, María de San José single-handedly managed through prayer to release Barros's soul, which ascended to heaven bejeweled and surrounded by white and red roses.[5] María Anna Agueda de San Ignacio, another mystical nun who achieved a following and great notoriety in early eighteenth-century Puebla, also assisted her own deceased sister, the nun Anna de San Juan, to escape purgatory and reach heaven "through a path of roses."[6]

In the second reading of the amorous metaphors of the Song of Songs, not only the individual soul, but the Church as a whole was the lover of God. It was as though the Song of Songs had anticipated or plotted the loving relationship between God and His Church through history (this became a particularly influential tradition among seventeenth-century Puritans—see more on this below). The Church was therefore expected to be a well-tended garden with no weeds (see fig. 5.3). The mural paintings of the Augustinian convents in Actopan (state of Hidalgo) and Malinalco (state of Mexico) dramatically demonstrate how much this particular belief helped to shape the "spiritual conquest" of the New World. In Actopan, for example, one of the murals describes the goals of the eremitic life for the new native converts: hermits living in the wilderness are harassed by eerily Indian-looking devils yet manage to turn the wilderness into a garden. In Malinalco, the message is starker. The walls and vaults of the lower cloister are covered with an exuberant display of local (and some European) fauna and flora, a paradise mural garden of sorts. As art historian Jeanette Favrot Peterson has persuasively shown, the Augustinians in Malinalco not merely sought to offer a dazzling visual rendition of the Garden of Eden using symbolic idioms adjusted to expectations of Malinalcans, who had long been known in the Aztec empire for their mastery of herbal cures and witchcraft. The friars also sought to represent the millennial Church they wished to establish in the New World. The metaphor of the missions as utopian Christian gardens proved to be a disappointment, and by the early seventeenth century the Augustinians had whitewashed their own murals. The Jesuits, however, did not give up as easily. Charged with the conversion of the natives along the Orinoco River and challenged by a shortage of missionaries, the Jesuit José Gumilla (1687?–1750) argued in 1741 that the Jesuit gardens in the tropics did not depend on access to "water" (missionaries) to flourish but on the "depth of the roots of the flowers." There were two types of missions, he concluded, those with easy access to "water" and those that suffered prolonged droughts. The well-watered missions more often than not withered as soon as the priests left. The missions that suffered "droughts," those in which the Jesuits in the Orinoco had specialized, on the other hand, were rarely "watered" (not visited for years at a time). Yet these gardens had been cultivated in such a way that the natives had unconsciously developed deep roots in the faith. Even though during droughts these spiritual plantations appeared scorched and dead, they greened and blossomed every time the Jesuits managed to return.[7]

The third typological reading of the Song of Songs interpreted the Virgin Mary as the female lover of God. Every detail of the Canticles seemed to

FIG. 5.3. José de Ibarra (eighteenth century), *Christ with Flowers in the Garden of the Church*. Courtesy Instituto Nacional de Antropología e Historia, Museo Nacional del Virreinato, Tepotzotlán, Mexico. The laity and clergy, both males and females, cultivated their souls to become flowers, part of the larger garden of the Church, where Christ took strolls and lay down.

have been a type of the virtues of the Virgin, particularly her immaculate conception. The idea that the Virgin herself, not only Christ, had been conceived without sin found support in this text, for the male lover of the Song of Songs presents his female lover as a sealed, walled garden, free of corrupting weeds: "You are like a private garden, my treasure, my bride! You are like a spring that no one else can drink from, a fountain of my own. You are like a lovely orchard bearing precious fruit, with the rarest of perfumes. . . . You are a garden fountain, a well of living water, as refreshing as the streams from the Lebanon mountains" (4:12–15). Once the female lover of the Song of Songs came to be seen as a type of the Virgin Mary and the walled garden as a prefiguration of the Virgin's immaculate conception of Jesus, the idea of Mary as a bouquet of flowers soon followed, for the female lover of the Canticles clearly refers to herself as a flower: "I am the rose of Sharon, the lily of the valley" (2:1).[8]

In the Middle Ages, the trope of Mary as a rose flourished. It not only affected architectural design in the form of rose stained-glass windows in Gothic churches.[9] It also affected the very ritual of the Catholic Church. The cult of the Virgin Mary came of age in the tenth and eleventh centuries, along with a new sense of God as a suffering deity. After 1,000 CE, when the millennium failed to materialize, a God who had been seen as a rigorous, distant magistrate who would mete out justice at the Last Judgment was slowly transformed into a suffering deity who had assumed a human body and endured pain for the salvation of humankind. Both the laity and the clergy developed ritual practices and theologies that encouraged a sympathetic, even tender relationship with the Christ of the Passion. The Virgin Mary became central to the new religious sensibility: the mental reenactment of the joyful, luminous, sorrowful, and glorious mysteries of the life of Christ and his suffering mother was crystallized in the rosary: a bouquet of twenty roses offered to the mother of God.[10]

These gardening ideas, ritual practices, and theologies were bound to have an effect on the colonization of the New World, which historians have not sufficiently explored. As the story of Catalina de Jesús in Quito reveals, the Christian ideas that I have briefly outlined took on a vigorous life in America, but with a twist. Although Catalina acknowledged that flowers had blossomed in Peru, she was not quite sure that this was the case in Quito. She had to take extreme measures to find out whether there were flowers in her convent. The laity and clergy of Spanish America felt pressured to demonstrate the spiritual bountifulness of their local kingdoms, something Europeans took for granted. More often than not this defensive posturing led to paradoxical results: the local kingdoms were found to be blossoming spiritual plantations, thus pointing to some type of providential election.

The other element in Catalina's story that is peculiar to the New World is the role of the devil. Upon arrival, Europeans thought the New World to be firmly in control of Satan, a tyrannical lord who had enjoyed absolute sovereignty over the peoples and nature of America for at least 1,500 years. When the Gospel began to spread in Eurasia, the devil and a handful of his minions had fled to the New World. In the Indies, the devil had introduced the institutions of hell, particularly the dismemberment of bodies, causing can-

FIG. 5.4. The mysteries of the rosary. From Andrea Gianetti da Salò, *Rosario della sacratissima Vergine Maria, raccolto dall'opere del R.P.F. Luigi di Granata* (Venice, 1587), fol. 73v. Courtesy of the Newberry Library, Chicago. The rosary is a Psalter in which "aves" substitute for the 150 psalms. The beads are mnemonic devices. Usually, for every ten small beads (five in the illustration above), there is a larger bead standing for one of the twenty mysteries (a typical rosary has only five large beads). The joyful mysteries recount the Annunciation and the birth and infancy of Christ; the luminous mysteries describe the life and miracles of the mature Christ, from baptism to the Last Supper; the sorrowful mysteries recapitulate his Passion and death; and the glorious mysteries invite reflection on his Resurrection and Ascension and on the Assumption and Coronation of Mary. The worshipper is encouraged to reenact each mystery using his or her imagination.

nibalism to become widespread. Mockingly, he also established inverted versions of Christian rituals and sacraments among the Amerindians. Tending spiritual gardens in the New World was doubly challenging, because the laity and clergy alike had to face a resilient enemy that had had time to build bulwarks and fortifications. Texts in the Bible, such as Matthew 13 and

Luke 8: 4–15, on the parable of the farmer scattering seed on different types of soil, and their attendant typological readings made it almost impossible to separate the discourse of gardening from that of the satanic epic during the colonization of the New World. It should be recalled that Calderón de la Barca used Mathew 13 in his work *La semilla y la cizaña* (The Seed and the Tare) to argue that of all the continents it was the New World, deceivingly paradisiacal, that was firmly in control of the devil (see Introduction). The metaphor of the garden took on added dimensions in the New World as spiritual gardening became part of a larger epic war of attrition against the devil.

Although it would appear that these were exclusively Catholic typological readings, the metaphor of colonization as spiritual gardening was in fact a Christian idea. Calvinists in New England, for example, also understood colonization as setting up spiritual plantations in a particularly hostile environment. In the pages that follow, I seek to explore how the horticultural language of virtue and sanctity was subtlely transformed in the New World, and how Creole settlers came to see their new societies as providential "gardens." Spaces that had traditionally been thought to be controlled by the devil came to be seen as sacred. Notwithstanding all the literature on the Reformation, the commonalities that I explore here stemmed from common traditions of interpreting and wielding the Bible to make sense of colonization. Like many other Christian holy warriors of the past, the Europeans in the New World managed to transform local demonic landscapes into New Jerusalems, new holy lands.[11]

Flowers and Patriotic Anxieties in Spanish America

Catalina de Jesús need not have been anxious, for in the mid-seventeenth century, a flower of sorts did blossom in the capital of the viceroyalty of Quito: Mariana de Jesús (1618–45), the Lily of Quito. Mariana was born a year after Rose of Lima passed away. Like Rose, the Lily of Quito modeled her life as that of a *beata* (beguine), living a life of mystical retreat without the institutional support of a convent. Like St. Catherine of Siena, both Rosa and Mariana sought to reach God through a compassionate, everyday reenactment of the Passion. To reenact the Crucifixion, they wore hair shirts and crowns of thorns, underwent regular bloodletting (lilies are said to have blossomed from a pail filled with Mariana's blood, thus her name), endured self-flagellation, and slept hanging from a cross. They made of point of living off the Lord: their food consisted only of consecrated wafers. To reenact the

LA AZVZENA D QVITO LA VENERA-
BLE MARIANA DE IESVS.

F I G . 5.5. Anonymous painter (late eighteenth or early nineteenth century), Mariana de Jesús, the Lily of Quito. Courtesy
of the Banco Central del Ecuador, Quito. Already by the mid
seventeenth century, Mariana de Jesús (1618–45) became a
symbol for the laity and clergy of Quito demanding that Rome
acknowledge the spiritual gardens of their local kingdom. The
painting makes reference to Mariana's efforts to sympathetically
gain insights into the nature of a suffering God by reenacting
Christ's Passion and Crucifixion. It also refers to the origin of
her name: lilies are said to have miraculously flourished from
a pail filled with Mariana's blood, which she obtained through
periodic bloodletting.

Fɪɢ. 5.6. Rosa de Lima. Frontispiece to Luis
Antonio de Oviedo y Herrera, *Vida de Santa Rosa
de Lima: Poema heroico a Santa Rosa* (Madrid: Juan
García Infanzón, 1711). Courtesy of the John Carter
Brown Library, Brown University, Providence, R.I.
Rosa is represented as a rose, and a rose blossoms
out of the coat of arms of Lima. America stands to
her right, while the author, the count of la Granja,
scribbles down his poem. St. Rosa is surrounded by
cherubs offering her roses as she ascends to heaven,
as in the Virgin Mary's Assumption. In her right
hand, she holds the anchor of Lima (she keeps the
capital from sinking), and in her left, she holds a
garland of flowers, the typical representation of the
sainthood of martyrs, which she also wears.

humiliations of a God who became human and endured torture to bring about the salvation of humankind, Rosa and Mariana drank the blood and pus of the sick. Their rigid asceticism and passionate, sympathetic insights into the life of a suffering God made them particularly powerful. Since they were close to God, their prayers, to which they devoted most of their time while tending small walled gardens in their homes, freed hundreds of strayed souls from purgatory. Their visions and prophetic powers repeatedly urged the faithful to obedience, to avoid God's wrath, which was often manifested through plagues and earthquakes. They remained powerful after death. Their corpses were considered to have defeated corruption, typical of bodies stained by original sin.[12] Rosa's body was disinterred two years after her death to be transferred to Lima's cathedral and was found intact. It is no wonder that these formidable athletes of the soul, whose bodies almost resembled the immaculate nature of the Virgin Mary, were considered flowers of God.[13] As Manuel de Ribero Leal argued in 1675 in a sermon commemorating the canonization of Rose: "Her virtuous fragrances have converted into paradise of holy delights the previously barbarous jungle of our South America."[14]

Yet despite their similarities, Rosa went on to become the first saint of the Americas, while Mariana remained an obscure *beata*. These radically different paths in their afterlife careers were the cause of much anger and frustration in Quito. Rosa was beatified in 1668, declared patron of Lima by Clement IX in 1669 and patron of the Americas by Clement X in 1670, and finally canonized in 1671. This all happened while the equally remarkable spiritual achievements of Mariana languished in obscurity. From 1670 to 1678, the Jesuits of Quito interviewed witnesses and assembled a file on the life and miracles of Mariana. Nothing seems to have come of this effort. Many Jesuits also wrote epic poems in honor of Mariana, which appear to have been lost. The only document that has come to light is a hagiography by Jacinto Morán de Butrón (1668–1749), completed in 1697 and published in Madrid in 1724 (it first appeared as a short compendium in Lima in 1702).

Morán de Butrón's hagiography is a patriotic effort to prove that Mariana was a flower of the Church as remarkable as Rosa of Lima. In it, Mariana appears as a second new blossom in the bountiful garden of the Indies, for God had wished since creation that a lily flourish in the Indies along with a rose. Morán de Butrón interpreted 4 Ezra 2:16–19 ("And those that be dead will I raise up again from their places, and bring them out of the graves. . . . I have sanctified and prepared for thee twelve trees laden with divers fruits,/ And as many fountains flowing with milk and honey, and seven mighty mountains, whereupon there grow roses and lilies, whereby I will fill thy children with joy") as evidence that roses and lilies were meant to emerge *together* in the Andes, which were no other than the seven mighty mountains of 4 Ezra. Since this passage linked the blossoming of roses and lilies with the Last Judgment and the Resurrection, Morán de Butrón managed to put the lives of Rose and Mariana into a much larger eschatological framework. These two saints and the Andes of Quito and Peru appeared central to any narrative of universal salvation.[15]

Yet the life of Rose was known and publicly honored by Rome, whereas that of Mariana languished in oblivion. According to Morán de Butrón, it was time to correct this oversight: "A whole century after St. Rose's death, [in which] her name has been dispersed all over the globe and the scent of her virtues has been diffused, it appears that the cultivating hand of God has disposed that the time has come for the Lily [of Quito] to be celebrated and [receive] applause and to spring out of the pit of oblivion, the last corner of the earth, and be appreciated."[16] To highlight the providentially significant role of Mariana, Morán de Butrón organized his hagiography as a horticultural treatise on the lily: its blossoming in the prairies (*collados*) of Quito (family, birth, growing up); its ripening elicited by thorns (penitence and sufferings); its multiplying power and its beauties and scents (virtues of the saint); its growth thanks to the showers of God (Mariana's powers and miracles); its short lifespan (death and afterlife miracles).

Morán de Butrón's anxieties managed to turn Quito's marginality into providential election. There was, of course, nothing unique about this horticulturalist patriotism. A contemporary of Morán de Butrón's, the Czech Jesuit Bohuslav Balbinus published a map in 1677 in which the kingdom of Bohemia appears as a rose at the center of the Holy Roman Empire (fig. 5.7). In the imagination of this clerical intellectual, Bohemia itself was a spiritual flower. Balbinus's map came out at about the same time that the composer Heinrich Ignaz Franz von Biber (1644–1704), another famous son of Prague, delivered his "Rosary Sonatas," a bouquet of twenty sonatas, one for each mystery of the rosary.

In the Indies, this type of patriotism took on greater significance, because the spiritual plantations of the colonies were not sufficiently appreciated by either Madrid or Rome. Take, for example, the case of another colonial flower, Felipe de Jesús, a Franciscan who was crucified along with twenty-five other martyrs in Nagasaki on January 5, 1597. Felipe was a youth born in Mexico whose Franciscan vocation had been cut short by the opposition of his parents. He was sent to the Philippines to become a merchant and to

FIG. 5.7. Bohemiae Rose (The Rose of Bohemia). From Bohuslav Balbinus, S.I., *Epitome historica rerum Bohemicarum* (Prague: Jan Mikulas Hampel, 1677). Reproduced with the permission of the Strahov Library, Royal Canonry of the Premonstratensians, Prague. Each of the eighteen districts of the kingdom is presented as a petal of the rose, which rises from the Danube. It does not represent romance or pageantry, for it sprang from the blood spilled in war: "Haec Rosa non Veneris, sed crevit sanguine Martis." Thanks to Vit Ulnas for facilitating my access to the image.

take care of the family's import business. After living a life of debauchery in Manila, Felipe felt drawn to the Franciscans once again and entered the convent of St. Gregory in Manila. After Felipe left the Philippines to be ordained in Mexico, however, his ship was wrecked off the coast of Japan near Nagasaki, and he went to the Franciscan convent in Kyoto. Unfortunately, this was a time when the dozens of Jesuits and Franciscans operating in Japan had begun to weary the strongman Toyotomi Hideyoshi, whose anger mounted when he found that the wrecked ship had been carrying soldiers, canon, and ammunition. Everyone in the convent at Kyoto was arrested, including seventeen Japanese tertiaries, six Franciscan friars (including Felipe), and three guests, namely, the Japanese Jesuit Paul Miki and his two servants. After subjecting the prisoners to torture, including cutting off their ears and humiliating them in public on their way to Nagasaki, Hideyoshi ordered all 26 martyrs to be hanged on crosses and pierced with spears. Their bodies were left to rot for months until Spanish Augustinians and local converts took them down, recovering hands and feet that would later circulate as relics. Marcelo de Rivadeneyra, a Franciscan from the convent of Nagasaki, witnessed the martyrdom and left an account of it: three shafts of light had come down from the sky to shine over the martyrs, he wrote; their bodies did not corrupt, and vultures did not pick out their eyes.[17] The martyrs were beatified by Urban VIII in September 1627.

The relics of Felipe, one of the flowers of the fertile garden of the Franciscan order (*hortus minorum fertilis*), arrived in Mexico City in 1629, and the city council (*ayuntamiento*) declared him patron of the city. Yet the cult of Felipe never really caught on. The great seventeenth-century Mexican theologian Miguel Sánchez, whom we met in Chapter 2, in a sermon delivered in 1640, ascribed the lack of enthusiasm for Felipe in Mexico to a cabal of peninsulars who refused to believe that seeds of sanctity could flourish in the Indies. These were critics "who are not persuaded that [this land] could ever have anything good to it."[18] So they charged that Felipe was not a saint but a "coward exile, a fearful fugitive."[19] Mexico, Sánchez argued, resembled the statue Nebuchadnezzar had dreamt of (Dan. 2:31–35). Like the statue, Mexico had a head of gold (it was full of saintly, virtuous, intelligent people), chest and arms of silver (it breast-fed the world with silver), belly and thighs of bronze (like a womb in labor, it was capable of putting up with great pain), legs of iron (it was strong in its faithfulness to the king), and feet of clay (its much-maligned land). Mexico's sanctity, wealth, endurance, and faithfulness meant nothing to the critics who attached the clay, that is, the land itself. Like the rolling stone that struck the feet of Nebuchadnezzar's

FIG. 5.8. *(Top) The Fertile Garden of the Franciscans*. Engraving by Manuel Peleguer from a drawing by José Camarón, 1794. Courtesy Instituto Nacional de Bellas Artes, Museo Nacional de Arte, Mexico City. The engraving was based on images circulated in the Spanish empire from 1600 to 1627 to support the canonization of the twenty-three Franciscan martyrs of Nagasaki and provides the names and background of the six Franciscan friars and the Christian names of the seventeen Japanese tertiaries. Four angels descend from heaven to crown the heads of the martyrs with garlands. The angels praise the saints for making the heavens happy,

(continued)

imaginary statue, bringing it down, the critics went after the spiritual accomplishments of the kingdom of New Spain by targeting the clay of Mexico, namely, the soil from which her sons sprouted (Sánchez, *Sermón de San Felipe de Jesús*, 13v–14r).

Sánchez rejected the critics by lionizing Felipe in a sermon organized around the trope of gardening. According to Sánchez, the Book of Ruth prefigured the life of Felipe. After having recently lost their husbands, Ruth and mother-in-law Naomi go back to Naomi's hometown, Bethlehem, to rebuild their lives. To help the elderly Naomi survive, the foreigner Ruth gleans leftover grain in the fields of Boaz, a rich landowner. Boaz allows the young Ruth to do so, and in gratitude Ruth asks old Boaz to marry her. For Sánchez, Ruth was the type (prefiguration) of Felipe. Like Ruth, Felipe left for a foreign land, where he was invited by the Lord to the garden of the Franciscan cloister. The grateful Felipe accepted Christ as his bridegroom in the ultimate sacrifice of martyrdom.

According to Sánchez, the life of Felipe itself was a story of changes in the nature of the soil in which the seed of the Cross blossoms. Felipe alone had enjoyed the four soils described by Luke 8:4–8: the soil of the footpath where the seed of the Cross is trodden underfoot and eaten by birds (his growing up); the shallow soil in rocky land where seeds flourish temporarily only to wither (when he first took up the Franciscan habit in Mexico but quit to go to Manila as a merchant); the soil full of thorns and weeds where seeds choke (Felipe's debauchery in Manila); and the fertile soil where harvests multiply abundantly (his return to the Franciscan cloister in Manila, leading eventually to his martyrdom) (6v). The shipwreck Felipe experienced and the torture he endured were the water and the plowing his soul needed for the seed of the Cross to blossom: "As soon as the soil of Felipe was watered [by the shipwreck], it began to be tilled by the tips of plows of the Japanese executioners."[20]

F I G. 5.8 *(continued from previous page)*
(*beata nobis gaudia*), and for seizing on a life of holiness (*vitam beatam possident*), declaring them eternal gifts to God (*aeterna Christi munera*). The martyrs, for their part, maintain that they have preached the word and glory of Christ through their own crucifixion: "Predicamus Christum crucifixum/Nos autem gloriari oportet in cruce" (We preach Christ crucified, but we ourself ought to glory in the Cross). The Franciscan emblems crown the engraving, amid a large bouquet of flowers (see detail). "Hortus minorum fertilis," the garden of the Franciscan order, has flourished, the Latin inscription declares.

Sánchez turned Felipe into the central character in the story of the twenty-six martyrs of Nagasaki. Despite being the youngest of the Franciscan friars, he was the first to volunteer to be pierced by spears, leading the way of martyrdom for the rest to follow. This excellence, in turn, had to do with the source and origins of the soil of Felipe's soul: Mexico. Sánchez ended his defense of Felipe by turning the tables on the critics. If a small piece of Mexican soil had blossomed, what could the nation as a whole produce? (13r). Notwithstanding its critics, Mexico was a soil propitious for many saints to flourish in: "Giving us hope that if a piece of this land was capable of yielding [such] fruits, [the whole] of the land could do the same."[21]

Like Morán de Butrón, Sánchez not only managed to give horticultural and biblical meanings to the life of a colonial saint, he also presented America as land of providential election, destined to harvest vast spiritual plantations. This is precisely the theme of one little-read text, *La grandeza mexicana* (Mexican Greatness) (1604) by Bernardo de Balbuena (ca. 1568–1627). The Castilian Balbuena arrived as a child in Mexico, where he became a secular priest and a poet. Although also a practitioner of the bucolic and the lyric, Balbuena excelled in the epic genre. Written in the 1590s during his stint as parish priest in a dusty frontier town in northern Mexico but published only in 1624, after Balbuena was named bishop of Puerto Rico, *El Bernardo, o la Victoria de Roncesvalles* was his magnum opus, an epic on the defeat of the Carolingian knight Rolando in the battle of Roncesvalles in 778 CE at the hands, not of the Muslims, but of a Spanish Visigothic knight, Bernardo del Carpio. This epic, which resembles those of Matteo Maria Boiardo (ca. 1440–94) and Ludovico Ariosto (1474–1533), has the heroes fly magically across continents to meet an Amerindian sorcerer from Tlaxcala, who predicts the future triumph of the Spanish universal monarchy in America.[22] This work prepared Balbuena to write his 1604 paean to the city of Mexico. In *La grandeza mexicana*, Balbuena praised the Spanish colonization of Mexico as a battle against the devil that had first begun with the original crossing of the Atlantic.[23] Yet Balbuena made Mexico City itself the hero, "awe-inspiring and worthy of Homer."[24] In the poem, Mexico City comes across as an emporium located in the "center and heart of this great ball [the world]" and thus supplied with commodities from all corners of Asia, Europe, and Africa; a land of horses and knights that dwarfed in beauty and valor those described by Boiardo and Ariosto; a polis that enjoys perpetual, equatorial spring and whose artisans produce a cornucopia of goods.[25] But for Balbuena, the true greatness of Mexico City lay in its piety, for it was "populated with more than human giants of

learning, sanctity, exemplariness, living, doctrine, perfection, and Christian hearts," "whose heroic deeds [were] worthy of Homer's pen."[26] For Balbuena, the "true treasure" of the city lay not in its silver mines but in its twenty-two religious orders, one hundred churches, and forty-two convents.[27] Balbuena presents Mexico as a spiritual plantation crowded with "lush gardens full of roses, wallflowers, hyacinth, jasmines, lilies, and carnations."[28] In short, Mexico City was "a new Rome," sporting bouquets of spiritual flowers.[29]

It was the great Mexican baroque polymath Carlos Sigüenza y Góngora (1645–1700) who fleshed out the trope of Mexico as a spiritual plantation in his *Paraíso occidental* (Western Hemispheric Paradise) (1683).[30] *Paraíso occidental* was commissioned to celebrate the centenary of the foundation of the Convento Real de Jesús María, a nunnery established in Mexico not by a religious order, but by Philip II himself, who bestowed a few relics from his

F I G . 5.9. *(opposite)* True treasures of the Indies. Title page from Juan Meléndez, *Tesoros verdaderos de las Indias* (Rome, 1681). Courtesy of the John Carter Brown Library, Brown University, Providence, R.I. The first seven Dominican apostles to Peru (from right to left: Martín de Esquivel; Reginaldo de Pedraza; Alfonso de Montenegro; Vicente Valverde; Thomas de San Martín; Domingo de Santo Tomás; and Pedro de Ulloa) gather around St. Dominic of Guzmán (ca. 1170–1221), the original founder of the order, who wielded the banner of the Cross during the crusade against the Catharist heretics of southern France. Drawing on a hymn from Venantius Fortunatus's *Vexilla regis prodeunt*, St. Dominic therefore calls on the friars to "preach to the people, because God ruled from the Cross" (Dicite in nationibus, quia Dominus regnavit a ligno). The Latin banner on top, which summarizes the spirit of the frontispiece, is drawn from Prov. 8:19 and Eccl. 24:23 (Vulg. 24:17): "My fruit is better than gold and a precious stone; my progeny better than choice silver." "My blossoms (were) a harvest of honor" (Melior est fructus meus auro et lapide pretioso. Et genimina mea argento electo. Flores mei fructus honoris). The fruits of the Dominican garden in Peru were numerous, including St. Rose of Lima, who was a Dominican tertiary, and St. Luis Beltrán (1526–81), who preached in Nueva Granada, Colombia, and was beatified in 1608 and canonized in 1671. Their portraits stand next to the figure of John the Baptist, carrying Christ, the sacrificial lamb. The friars are presented as the shepherds that would guide the nations of Peru into the celestial kingdom: "Isti sunt patres tui (O Peru) verique pastores, qui te regnis celestibus inferendum condiderunt" (These are your fathers, O Peru, and your true shepherds, who have established you to be brought into the celestial kingdoms). Below the two Dominican saints, there are also images of Charles V and Francisco Pizarro. The Dominicans have created a Church that is a sealed garden of virtue and sanctity of a distinctly American character, for the passionflower dominates the composition.

vast collection on the convent to get it off to a good start. Since saints were the flowers of the Church, and their relics bouquets, it is not surprising that the nunnery went on to produce flowers.

The bulk of Sigüenza's treatise is simply a compilation of the autobiographies and diaries of a handful of exemplary nuns. The trope that organizes the text is that of the garden. Drawing on the writings of SS Augustine and Ambrose, Diego de Malpartida Zenteno, the dean of Mexico City's cathedral chapter and the censor of Sigüenza's book, for example, argued that the description of Paradise in Genesis 2:9–14, with the tree of life, the tree of knowledge of good and evil, the spring from which four rivers flow, and several other trees yielding delicious fruit, is simply a prefiguration of the saints, their deeds, Christ, and the four gospels: "The Church is Paradise; the four rivers are the four Gospels; the fruit trees are the Saints and their fruits the Saints' works; the tree of life is Christ, Saint of Saints."[31] Malpartida Zenteno accurately summarized the thrust of Sigüenza's work in calling the Convento Real

FIG. 5.10. Christ as the Tree of Life in the Garden of the Church. (Left) Anonymous nineteenth-century painter. Courtsey of the Instituto Nacional de Antropología e Historia, Museo de Arte Religioso de Santa Mónica de Puebla, Puebla, México. (Right) Juan Schorquens's engraving for Melchor Prieto's *Psalmodia eucharistica* (Madrid, 1622). Clearly, the Puebla painter copied the 1622 engraving. Christ occupies the position of the tree of life right at the center of paradise. He is the fountain of life, the source of the four rivers of paradise. Opposite Adam, Eve, the serpent, and the tree of knowledge of good and evil stand the Cross, the chalice, and the host. The basic narrative of Christian salvation is thus made clear: original sin can be overcome by imitating Christ's passion and sacrifice. The trees and fruits of paradise are Christ's blood and body (chalices and consecrated hosts stand on top of the trees in every corner). The hedge of the enclosed garden, curiously, is made up of vines, flowers, and fruits of the passionflower, a quintessentially American plant. Citing Song of Songs 4, the inscriptions in the painting and the engraving refer to the hedge as pomegranate: "Paradisus Malorum Punicorum. Paradisus Dei Mei" (Paradise of pomegranates. Paradise of my God).

de Jesús María a garden in the middle of the Western Hemisphere, which had already produced a fabulous harvest of flowers (as revealed in the nuns' lives Sigüenza compiled). Mexico had a great many of these plantations.

All over Spanish America, virtuous nuns and priests considered themselves to be flowers. Every time a virtuous nun was ordained or died, she was crowned with flowers to signify her potential or actual sanctity. It is not clear whether this tradition was also typical of Catholic Europe. What is clear, however, is that the genre of paintings of garlanded nuns during ordination and at funerals originated in Spanish America, not Spain.[32]

If in Spanish America there was struggle to position each kingdom at the center of any narrative of universal Christian salvation, the discourse of horticultural providential election did not always come wrapped in hagiographies of the virtuous and the saintly. In Mexico, for example, claims that took the kingdom to be a providential plantation were best articulated through the exegesis of the miracle of Our Lady of Guadalupe.

FIG. 5.11. (*Preceding page*) Portrait of Maria Josefa de San Felipe Neri, anonymous painter, n.d., Museo Nacional de Historia, Mexico City. (*This page*) Portrait of the Carmelite Francisco Santa Ana, anonymous painter, 1754, courtesy of the Instituto Nacional de Antropología e Historia, Museo Nacional del Virreinato, Tepotzotlán, Mexico. More often than not, it was nuns who were featured crowned with flowers. But occasionally priests were also depicted with a flower crown, as in the case of Francisco Santa Ana, who is also wearing a white scapular (a cape similar to that which the Virgin Mary allegedly wore), typical of the Carmelite order. The language of the virtuous as flowers was not gendered and applied equally to men and women.

Our Lady of Guadalupe appeared three times in 1531 to a Nahua commoner, Juan Diego, near the hill of Tepeyac, a few miles to the north of Mexico City. The Virgin asked the Amerindian to inform the bishop that the Virgin wanted a shrine. The bishop and his aides twice brushed Juan Diego aside. The third time, however, the Virgin had Juan Diego go to the top of the barren hill, collect flowers, put them in a cape, and give the flowers to the bishop. When he unrolled the package in front of the weary bishop, and as the flowers fell down, the image of Our Lady of Guadalupe appeared stamped on the cape. Legend has it that the bishop started the cult of the image right away and built the Virgin a shrine. The cult seemed indeed to have begun in the sixteenth century, but it was one of many among both Amerindians and Creoles. It was only in the wake of the publication of Miguel Sánchez's interpretation of the image in 1648 that the cult began to take on new dimensions, cutting across racial and class differences and becoming a distinctly Mexican national symbol. The evolution of the cult and the role of Sánchez are well known.[33] What is not well known, however, is the importance of the metaphor of gardening to the theology of national election that Sánchez put forth.[34]

The key to understanding Sánchez's influence is the image itself, a typical representation of the Immaculate Conception in which the Virgin stands on top of a moon (often trampling a dragon), clad with stars and the sun. A well-established Church tradition held the Immaculate Conception to be the fulfillment of the vision in Revelation 12 of a woman in labor clothed in sun and stars who is threatened by a multiheaded dragon.[35] God takes the newborn to his side, protects the woman by airlifting her into the desert, and sends the archangel Michael to oust the dragon from heaven. The dragon falls to earth but continues to harass the woman, seeking to drown her and her descendants.

Sánchez took this typical interpretation one step further. In his *Imagen de la Virgen María Madre de Dios de Guadalupe* (1648), he asserted that St. John's vision was in fact a prefiguration, not of the Immaculate Conception, but of the conquest and colonization of the New World in general and of Mexico in particular. According to Sánchez, for example, the angel holding the Virgin up in the image was the same archangel, Michael, who had ousted the dragon from heaven. The dragon itself represented the sovereignty the devil had long enjoyed in the New World prior to the arrival of the Christian warriors. Sánchez insisted that the Spanish conquest did not guarantee that the devil had been beaten. Christianity in Mexico, he maintained, was still engaged in an ongoing epic struggle against Lucifer. He thus took the very critics he chastised in his sermon on Felipe to be the new embodiment of Satan in Mexico. Like the dragon, these outsiders sought to "drown" the descendants of the woman, the children of Mexico. The satanic epic narrative of the history of Mexico allowed Sánchez and his clerical followers to claim a central role in universal history for Mexico. Far from being a development at the margins of the Catholic world, the miracle of our Lady of Guadalupe in Mexico had extraordinary universal import. Crucial episodes of the confrontation between good and evil described by St. John in Revelation were taking place in Mexico. Moreover, since Sánchez understood the encounter of Juan Diego and the Virgin at Mount Tepeyac to be the anti-type of that of Moses and God at Mount Sinai, the image of our Lady of Guadalupe became the Mexican version of the tablets of the Ten Commandments, a holy object documenting the covenant of God with the newly elect. "Non fecit taliter omni nationi," drawn from Psalm 147:19–20 ("Qui adnuntiat verbum suum Iacob iustitias et iudicia sua Israhel./Non fecit taliter omni nationi et iudicia sua non manifestavit eis. [He sheweth his word unto Jacob, his statutes and his judgments unto Israel./He hath not dealt so with any nation: and as for his judgments, they have not known them]), was the motto that ever since the late seventeenth century accompanied most illustrations of the images of Our Lady of Guadalupe. The image and the motto documented the special relations of the Lord with his new Israelites.[36]

Since flowers are central to the story of the miracle, it is not surprising that horticultural metaphors dominate Sánchez's exegesis. It would be tiresome to describe them all. Suffice it say that Sánchez cast precolonial Mexico as a barren hill (like Tepeyac), where in the wake of the defeat of the satanic Aztecs, countless flowers of sanctity had blossomed. Sánchez took biblical passage after biblical passage to be prefigurations of the new spiritual plantation that was Mexico. Ezekiel 17:1–6 is typical of his approach. An eagle carries a branch of a cedar tree into a faraway city and plants it in fertile ground next to a broad river. The seedling grew "and set it as a willow tree. And it grew, and became a spreading vine of low stature, whose branches turned toward him, and the roots thereof were under him: so it became a vine, and brought forth branches, and shot forth sprigs." Sánchez presents this passage as a type (prefiguration) of Mexico becoming a thriving spiritual plantation after Mary the eagle planted the seedling of faith.[37] Sánchez does the same with Isaiah 35:1–3 ("The wilderness and the solitary place shall be glad for them; and the desert shall rejoice, and blossom as the rose. It shall blossom abundantly, and rejoice even with joy and singing: the glory of Lebanon shall be given unto it, the excellency of Carmel and Sharon, they shall see the glory of the LORD, and the excellency of our God. Strengthen ye the weak hands, and confirm the feeble knees").[38]

It is not surprising that the trope of Mexico as barren land that turned into a leading spiritual plantation became a staple of the clerical colonial imagination. Take, for example, the case of *Primavera indiana*, a poem published to great acclaim in 1668 by Sigüenza y Góngora. Sigüenza was enamored of gardening metaphors; he applied them to the history of the royal nunnery and, to be sure, to the interpretation of the miracle of Our Lady of Guadalupe. The poem presents Mexico as a barren, spiritually desolate land that originally was in the hands of Satan (xiv). Then suddenly, in December, when bleak winter shrivels everything in sight (viii), the Virgin Mary, herself a sealed garden and flower (x; lxxvi), descends like the spring from the empyrean to resurrect a moribund Mexico (xix). Cortés had managed to defeat Pluto (xxiv), leaving Mexico for dead, empty of its satanic soul but begging to be revived (xlv). Mary swoops down spreading the sweet smells of flowers (xxvii), causing the hills to be covered by blossoms (xxix). She appears to Juan Diego and explains her mission: she wants the bishop to build her a church right where "Pluto, whose horror my feet trample by [unleashing] a tempest of flowers, had his lair" (xlix). After Juan Diego visits the bishop twice, the Virgin has Juan Diego climb the barren cliffs of Tepeyac. On top, he finds that flowers have sprouted in the rocky soil in winter (lv). Juan Diego takes the flowers to the bishop, unfolds the cape, and roses cascade down and an image suddenly appears (dyed red with carnations, white with jasmine and lilies, and blue with lilies) (lviii). But why would Mary turn Mexico, long ruled by Satan, into a spiritual plantation? A white angel with red cheeks, ivory neck, and golden hair descends from heaven to explain (xxxiv–xxxvi): God has looked all over the Catholic world for a nation to bring closer to the empyrean, but has found that Bohemia and Austria are cowed by the Protestants, that France is in the hands of an impostor, while indulging in atheism, and that England, where piety once used to have her temple, is now controlled by the Hydra (xxxvii–xxxix). Understandably, God then turns to Mexico. Mexico has been elected to a seat next to the throne of the Lord (xli).[39]

The horticultural interpretation of the miracle was in turn linked to the literature on the passionflower (see Chapter 4). A debate broke in late seventeenth-century Mexico over the nature of the flowers that had dyed the image of Our Lady of Guadalupe. Clerical intellectuals like Sánchez and Sigüenza were content with the original story: roses, jasmines, carnations, and lilies had dyed the image. In 1668, however, in the preface to his *Estrella del Norte de Mexico* (Pole Star of Mexico), the Jesuit Francisco de Florencia (1619–95), one of the foremost contemporary champions of the cult, challenged an anonymous Spanish priest who had suggested in a sermon that the image belonged more to Spain than to Mexico. According to Florencia, the clinching argument of the sermon was that the roses of the miracle were Castilian roses, and that the only indigenous botanical contribution to the miracle was the material of Juan Diego's cape, namely, a fiber drawn from cactus. Florencia rejected this logic and insisted that the flowers that had sprouted on the barren hill of Tepeyac hailed both from the Old and New Worlds. Florencia did not specify the types of local flowers.[40] But the great Mexican Latinist and poet José Antonio de Villerías (1695–1728) did. In his *Guadalupe quatour libris* (completed in 1724), Villerías describes the flowers of the miracle in some detail, including not only the ubiquitous roses, carnations, and lilies, but also New World flowers such as *Tigridia pavonia* (the Mexican shellflower) and *Hymenocallis amancaes* (the spider lily). Villagrá also describes *Passiflora incarnata*, the wild passionflower, whose striking resemblance to the instruments of the Passion (see Chapter 4), he argued, served "as a reminder of our cruelty."[41] As early as 1622, the passionflower and its vine came to be seen as the hedge of the sealed plantation that was the garden of Church (see figs. 5.9 and 5.10).

The horticultural and providential theology behind the clerical interpretation of the miracle blended nicely with the Marian ritual tradition of the rosary. Most sermons on Our Lady of Guadalupe of the colonial period consciously seek to add to the list of Old Testament prefigurations of Mary typical of the litanies with which the rosary ends: *arca Dei* (Ark of God); *ignis columna* (pillar of fire); *rubeus in flammis* (burning bush); *stilla maris* (drop of the ocean); *stella maris* (star of the sea); rod of Jesse; tower of David; sealed fountain and garden; tower of ivory; house of gold; rose of Sharon; and so on. Clerics created novenas that resembled the structure of the rosary. Finally, as Florencia pointed out, the very shrine of Our Lady of Guadalupe was laid out as a rosary, with twenty shrines (*humilladeros*) connecting the capital with Tepeyac, standing for the twenty mysteries of the rosary.[42]

Puritan "Plantations"

The reader might be tempted to believe that this language of spiritual gardening was typical only of the Iberian colonies, a world trapped in superstition, backwardness, and hubris. But horticultural imagery also flourished in the English colonies. Consider, for example, the Great Seal of Connecticut.

Created in 1636, six years after the *Arbella* arrived with her first cargo of Puritans for Massachusetts, the Connecticut State Seal bears the motto "Sustinet qui transtulit" (He who brought us here sustains us), suggesting providential election, and originally had fifteen grapevines on it (fig. 5.12), reduced to three on the present seal. Like Spanish Americans, the Puritans considered colonization an act of spiritual gardening. The seal speaks volumes about the motivations behind the new colony, founded when the Puritan theologian Thomas Hooker (1586–1647) took a group of disenchanted Newtown colonists to establish Hartford along the banks of the Connecticut River. The migration was prompted by land shortages but also by theological concerns.[43] Hooker and his followers thought that Puritan ministers of Massachusetts like John Cotton had limited membership in the Church only to those who could prove they had been touched by the inscrutable grace of God.[44] Hooker sought to enlarge membership by emphasizing the act of "preparation" of the soul prior to the reception of grace. According to Hooker, the soul needed to be plowed prior to its "ingrafting" into "the

FIG. 5.12. The original Connecticut Seal.
Fifteen grapevines crawl up arbors, while a hand
holds a banner with the motto "Sustinet qui transtulit" (He who brought us here sustains us).

tree of Christ." Hooker articulated his views on preparation repeatedly in
horticultural terms in such treatises as *The Soules Ingrafting into Christ*
(1637) and *The Soules Implantation into the Naturall Olive* (1640).[45]

Hooker may have been right to complain that ministers like Cotton sought
to build Christian communities solely with those who had been blessed by
the unpredictable touch of God, but he was not alone in the use of horticultural metaphors. Cotton himself saw conversion (God's sudden and unpredictable gift of grace) as an act of complete agricultural transformation.[46] In
his posthumous *Treatise of the Covenant of Grace* (1659), Cotton argued that
the "covenant" of law (God's commitment to Abraham and his people in
exchange for their pledge to live by the Mosaic commandments) caused the
soul to flourish only temporarily, yielding a harvest of only one season. It was
the "covenant of grace," however, that truly transformed the soul into a land
in perpetual spring.[47] This difference in the condition of the soul had to do
with the radical transformation that grace brought to the "soil." Deploying
the same horticultural metaphors that Hooker had used to describe the process of "preparation" as soul "plowing" and ground "breaking," Cotton envis-
aged the arrival of grace as the clearing of brush from the soul by fire: "And

so the Lord cometh to leave a man neither Root not Branch: For by a spirit of Bondage the Lord blasteth all flesh; but when it cometh unto the goodliness of flesh, that is consumed by a spirit of Burning."[48]

The examples of Hooker and Cotton, two of the most distinguished first-generation theologians in New England, show that "gardening" tropes were as central to Puritan pietism as they were to Catholic mysticism. Puritans spent inordinate amounts of energy and time discussing the various stages of salvation, including (but not exclusively) "preparation," "justification" (the signs of the arrival of God's grace), and "sanctification" (the behavioral transformation brought about by conversion). All these debates, in turn, were carried out using gardening metaphors. Thus in a sermon in 1651 in Concord, New England, Peter Bulkeley, like Hooker, likened the act of "preparation" to planting. "[The] Lord," Bulkeley argued, "usually scattereth some little seeds of faith in the hearts of those that he will bring unto himselfe; which seed being sowne, doth sometimes quickly put forth." Even though the sudden, inscrutable touch of God's grace (justification) corresponded to a radical alteration of the nature of the soil (in fact, a new creation), he warned, planting or "preparation" was nevertheless needed: "Though our planting into Christ, be a new creation of us, yet this hinders not but there may be a preparation thereto by faith."[49] The notion of "preparation" as the planting in the soul of tiny seeds of grace was a widespread Puritan idea, first introduced in 1611 by the English theologian William Perkins in *A Graine of Musterd-seede, Or, The Least Measure of Grace that is or can be effectual to Salvation*. On the title page of this treatise (see fig. 5.13), the nourishing soul of Cambridge (*Alma Mater Cantabrigia*) is depicted pouring light and rain over two trees, surrounded by the motto "Hinc lucem et pocula sacra" (Hence light and a sacred drinking cup).

This pietistic, horticultural theology colored the way Puritans came to see their mission in the New World. Historians have privileged the mercantilist meanings of the term "plantation," but the historical actors themselves thought they were doing more than just growing cash crops to ship back to England.

For the Puritans, establishing "plantations" in the New World meant establishing walled "gardens," from which heretics would either be excluded or easily uprooted.[50] In fact, in the debate between John Cotton and Roger Williams conducted in Massachusetts in the 1630s, the separatist Williams cited Matthew 13:24–25 as a key biblical passage to sanction religious tolerance: A servant informs his master that tares sowed by his enemies are about to take over the wheat fields. The master replies that the tares should not

A
GRAINE OF
MVSTERD-SEEDE
Or,
THE LEAST MEA-
sure of grace that is or can be
effectuall to Saluation.
Corrected and amended by W. Perkins.

Printed at London by *Iohn Legate,*
Printer to the Vniuersitie of
Cambridge. 1611.
And are to be soid in Pauls Church-yard
as the signe of the Crowne by
Simon Waterson.

FIG. 5.13. Title page from William Perkins's A *Graine of Musterd-Seede* (Cambridge, 1611). For the Puritans, God dispensed grace in horticultural terms: grace grows inside the soul as God showers light and rain on the garden.

be harmed, because pulling them up would also destroy the wheat. Lest we exaggerate William's tolerance, it is worth mentioning that the master in Matthew's parable commands the tares to be burned after the wheat is harvested. According to Williams, heretics would burn in hell, but only on Judgment Day.[51] Cotton, to be sure, believed that the congregational churches could not wait for Christ to burn the heretics at the end of times. The Church was a garden where weeds needed to be systematically and routinely uprooted. "What if the weeds grow so neere the inclosure (or hedge) round about the garden," Cotton asked Williams rhetorically, "that they easily creep into the Garden, and . . . choack the good herbes?" In this debate, Cotton won, and Williams was expelled to Rhode Island.[52]

Puritans regarded the Catholic and Anglican churches as baroque, overwrought, demonic "gardens," full of "ornamentations"—that is, institutions not mentioned in Scripture—and sought to replace them by creating "simple" ones in the "wilderness." The very name "Puritan" derived from their attempts to "purify" the garden of the Church by purging these demonic inventions.[53] As the Anglican theologian Robert Sanderson observed in 1621 during a debate with John Cotton held in Boston, Lincolnshire, over the nature of the Church of England, Puritans sought to return "to the *infancy* of the Church" and create gardens from scratch. Puritans thought that the Church should model itself on that of Moses in the wilderness, Sanderson noted, but since it was in fact already "*possessed* of the Land, and *growne* to years of better strength," it made no sense to pretend to go back to the original wilderness and be fed with Mosaic manna. The Church was a well-kept garden, and its parishioners needed no manna; it sufficed them to "*eate* of the fruit of the Land" harvested from the plowing and sowing the land of the Church.[54]

Puritans also understood religious and civil authority in horticultural terms. Almost every annual election-day sermon delivered in Boston urged elected officials to be responsible gardeners. In his sermon of 1638, the fiery and intolerant Thomas Shepard (1605–49) celebrated the departure of Governor Sir Henry Vane (a radical Puritan aristocrat who had sided with "Antinomians" like Cotton and Anne Hutchinson in the free-grace controversy) with a horticultural sermon on the dangers of having "bramble trees" for leaders. Drawing on Judges 9:7–15, Shepard argued that churches who elected "olive trees" (prudent men "whose oyle in the lamp give light to all the house"), "figs" (rich men who "helpe without taxes and prefer and give gifts" and who "grow in most base and baren soyle . . . and scatter [their] roots and out of every th. fetcheth moisture"), and "grape vines" ("holy men") were bound to flourish. But polities that elected leaders like Vane, a "bramble," could easily go up in flames. Like thornbushes in the wilderness, brambles seduced other plants to take cover under their shadow. But when lightning struck, not only the bramble itself burned, but all the other plants as well. The lesson was clear: "bramble" leaders could single-handedly destroy a "plantation."[55] In his 1682 sermon, Samuel Willard defined "wilderness" as a land "that was not sown" spiritually. Magistrates were gardeners who kept weeds and beasts out, watchmen in the tower to "look out and espy all approaching dangers." It was the role of magistrates to be like Jeremiah and warn that plantations could easily be destroyed by God. Like Micah, magistrates needed to warn the new "Zion" that it could be "ploughed over" by God and thus destroyed.[56]

In his election sermon of 1670, "New England's Errand into the Wilderness," Samuel Danforth argued, citing Matthew 11:7–9, that magistrates needed to be prophets like John the Baptist, who were not "reeds shaken with the wind" but stout trees. Like John, local magistrates should not be afraid of speaking truth to power. John the Baptist had gone to the "wilderness" to avoid the bustle of city life and courtly culture and thus to gain spiritual insight. Magistrates, therefore, could not allow themselves to grow soft and "wear soft clothing" as "in king's houses."[57] The latter was tantamount to degeneration, which was rife in New England: "The vineyard is all overgrown with thorns and nettles cover the face thereof, and the stone wall thereof is broken down," Danforth warned, citing Proverbs 24:31.[58] Puritans had forgotten that what "distinguisheth New England from other colonies and plantations in America" was not "our transportation over the Atlantic Ocean, but the ministry of God's faithful prophets and *the fruition* of his holy ordinances."[59] It was the duty of settlers to cultivate the gardens of their souls and those of their children: "Gleaning day by day in the field of God's ordinances, even among the sheaves, and gathering up handfuls, which the Lord let fall of purpose for you, and at night going home and beating out what you had gleaned, by meditation, repetition, conference, and therewith feeding yourselves and your families."[60] Setting up plantations implied at least three things: electing robust "trees" for leaders, tending the individual garden of the soul, and gleaning and threshing the kernels of the word of God.

Puritans often articulated their hopes and frustrations regarding Native American religious conversions in gardening terms as well. Thomas Shepard, famous for his unrelenting stance toward heretics like Anne Hutchinson, argued that the Amerindians were often thought to be "woody and rocky soile," and that Puritans had therefore "been discouraged to put plow to such dry and rocky ground." He, however, held some hope that "some few [natives] it may bee . . . are better soile for the Gospel then wee can thinke."[61] These metaphors became pervasive as Puritans set out to expand the boundaries of the garden into the "wilderness," Native Americans notwithstanding.[62]

Like their Iberian cousins to the south, Puritans developed a sophisticated discourse of colonization as spiritual gardening, but unlike the former, they came up with historicist readings of the Song of Songs. John Cotton, for example, delivered a series of sermons in Boston, Lancashire, from 1621 to 1623 (published as A *Briefe Exposition of the Whole Book of canticles, or the Song of Solomon* in 1648) that transformed the language of lovers, seal fountains, and gardens of the Canticles into "a divine abridgment of the Acts and Monuments of the Church": a history of the Church from the time of Solomon to the Apocalypse. Cotton interpreted Canticles 1:5 ("I am black but comely"), for example, as a description of the fall of the Israelite Church from its glory and piety under Solomon to its "deformity . . . by idolatrous worship" under Rehoboam. Canticles 2 became a type of the history of the Israelite Church from the time of Josiah to the captivity in Babylon to the days of the Maccabees. The verse "I am the rose of Sharon and the lily of the valleys" (2:1), which for Catholics prefigured the purity of the Virgin Mary, was transformed by Cotton into a reference of the restoration of the Church under Josiah at a time "which wanted culture, ordering and dressing, thornes and bryars growing up in the Church, and not weeded out." Cotton continued his narrative with an interpretation of the rise of the Apostolic Church, the post-Carolingian popish Antichrist, and the Reformation. Canticles 7 and 8 became prefigurations of the conversion of Jews and pagans prior to the arrival of the millennium.[63]

Using these reading techniques, Puritans in New England came to claim a central role in the history of salvation. Cotton delivered his sermons on the Song of Songs prior to the great Puritan migration, so he did not look in the Canticles for references to the colonization of America. But as the Puritans began to move in droves to Massachusetts, Cotton began to use typology (the technique of reading the Old Testament as prefiguring current events) to endow the colonization of the New World with cosmic significance.

In his sermon "Gods Promise to His Plantation" (1630), delivered on occasion of the departure of the *Arbella* for Massachusetts, Cotton sought to put the foundation of the Reformed churches of England in the New World into a much larger cosmic narrative. There were several types of migrations, Cotton argued: those triggered by the search for land, economic betterment, knowledge, personal fulfillment, and propitious religious and political regimes; those elicited by the need to flee "evil" (religious persecution, collective national debauchery and sin; ill reputation due to debt and bad credit); and those prompted by the order of superiors, human or godly. The migrations of the Puritans belonged to the latter kind, being a migration ordained by God.

Since the only other providentially ordained migration had been that of the Israelites to Canaan, it made sense for Cotton to draw lessons from the Pentateuch. According to Cotton, God had "made room" for the Israelites by enabling them to conquer and expel their enemies through war, by causing the conquered to sell their lands, and by leading the elect into "empty" territory (or causing populated territories to be emptied for the elect to take).[64] Cotton thought these were also forms Puritans were using to settle the New World, although in all fairness to him, he discouraged the new migrants from engaging in "conquest," for he sought to distance Puritans from the crimes committed by the Spanish Antichrist in the Indies. Since Cotton conflated the Puritans with the Israelites, he thought that the former were also entitled to God's promise to David: "I will appoint a place for my people Israel and will plant them, that they may dwell in a place of their own, and move no more" (2 Sam. 7:10). Cotton's text demonstrates how Puritans read the Israelite colonization of Canaan as a prefiguring of their own colonization of the Americas. Puritans believed that it was God's plan to "plant" them firmly, never to be removed. But there were dangers, for Cotton knew that a few generations after God had made his promise to David, the Israelites were, in fact, uprooted and sent packing to Assyria.

Cotton used his sermon to give the Puritans tips on how to avoid the fate of the Israelites. The solution consisted in turning the colonies into *permanent* spiritual plantations. God wanted plantations to last, so He had made sure that populations and territories matched: "I will make them to take roote there; and that is, where they and their soyle agree well together, when they are well and sufficiently provided for, as plants suckes nourishment from the soyle that fitteth it." "By planting the Ordinances of God," plantations were destined to become "trees of righteousness." By not "trespassing against God" and thus not "exposing themselves to affliction," Puritans would continue to be "a noble Vine, a right seede." Cotton was certain that God would not harm good plantations: "You shall never finde that God ever rooted out a people that had the Ordinances planted amongst them, and themselves planted into the Ordinances: never did God suffer such plants to be plucked up." Knowing the fate of the Israelites, the Puritans were a step ahead and had a better chance of succeeding.[65]

Like their Iberian cousins, the British-American Puritans both tied the language of spiritual gardening to a discourse of providential election and wove the history of their spiritual gardens into millenarian narratives.

Millennialism was in fact a Puritan obsession, a longing for a time when the primitive structures of the Apostolic Church would finally be restored by the second coming of Christ. The connections between millennialism and the discourse of spiritual gardening can be seen in the writings of the great eighteenth-century theologian Jonathan Edwards, allegedly an Enlightenment figure.

Edwards emerged out of Northampton, Connecticut, to become one of the most important and influential preacher-theologians of the evangelical movement of the mid-eighteenth-century British Atlantic. As the successor of the formidable Solomon Stoddard, his grandfather, Edwards had witnessed how Stoddard had on several occasions produced "harvests" of souls in the parish of Northampton through the sheer persuasion of his preaching, causing some individual souls to convert. Stoddard himself had cultivated the reputation of being, like John the Baptist, a stout tree, not a bending reed. William Williams likened the passing of Stoddard to "the felling of mighty spreading Tree in a Forest [that caused] all the trees about it to shake."[66] It is not surprising therefore that Edwards would describe his own experience of being suddenly touched by the grace of God in the spring of 1721 in horticultural terms. Like St. Teresa of Avila, Edwards felt holiness "of a sweet, pleasant, charming serene, calm, nature." Being touched by God's grace felt like "an inexpressible purity, brightness, peacefulness and ravishment of the soul." His soul was "like a field or garden of God, with all manner of pleasant flowers."[67] But Stoddard's harvests and Edwards's experience were ultimately about individual conversions.

By the 1730s, however, a new phenomenon began to occur in New England, namely, mass conversions. The "Great Awakening" first began in Edwards's parish in 1734, when the rather dull Edwards managed to touch the soul of the loitering youth of Northampton. The youth began to attend church in droves and declare their passion for Christ. Things got even more dramatic in the 1740s, when itinerant preachers began to crisscross the Atlantic, unleashing massive conversations in open-air revivalist meetings. The "Great Awakening" spread over Scotland, England, and the British colonies like wildfire. The scenes of collective conversation convinced Edwards that he was witnessing the beginning of the millennium, for it was "probable this work will begin in America."[68]

The sudden, massive transformation of hundreds of souls into gardens was a sign that the experiences of Creole British America were central to any narrative of universal salvation (and damnation). Soon, however, Edwards came to realize that many of these conversions were not really manifestations of God's grace (which should have led to permanent changes of behavior). Edwards was disappointed. But even when it became clear that the Great Awakening had been a passing, even misleading, event, Edwards hung on to both his millenarian and horticultural hopes. In his *Treatise Concerning the Religious Affections* (1746), Edwards likened the Awakening to the blossoms in the spring: "It is with professions of religion, especially such as become so in a time of outpouring of the Spirit of God, as it is with the blossoms in the spring." All blossoms "look fair and promising; but yet very many of them never come to anything." All blossoms smell sweet and "look beautiful and gay as the others," so it was impossible through the use of the senses alone to "distinguish those blossoms which have in them the secret virtue, which will afterwards appear in the fruit." It was "mature fruit which comes afterwards, and not the beautiful colors and smells of the blossoms," Edwards argued, that should help one assess whether the Reformed churches had become plantations and whether the millennium was indeed near.[69]

Conclusions

The literatures on British and Spanish colonial America have gone their own separate ways. Behind this history of parallel historiographical trajectories lies the assumption that the United States and "Latin America" (that opaque and seemingly homogeneous space south of the Rio Grande, comprising dozens of nation-states and peoples) are in fact *ontologically* different. In the following chapter, I explore how this dichotomy of nations has been justified, and the political work carried out under its assumptions. But the story I have presented here speaks for itself: Puritans and Spanish American elites articulated their clerical visions in remarkably similar ways, the literature on the Reformation notwithstanding. The early modern eschatological imagination helped local colonial clerical elites both in the north (New England) and south (Spanish America) to present their peripheral societies as gardens that were at the center of any narrative of universal salvation.[70] In this chapter I have shown how the typological reading of gardening texts in the Bible allowed the holy warriors to turn local landscapes that they themselves had originally deemed satanic into New Jerusalems, new Holy Lands. The commonalities between Puritan and Spanish Catholic discourses of gardening and the satanic epic are striking. These commonalities show, in turn, that a common pan-American narrative that incorporates all levels of historical analyses (culture, religion, economics, geopolitics) is not only possible but imperative.

Toward a "Pan-American" Atlantic

The Atlantic paradigm seems finally to have put an end to the long-standing tendency of U.S. colonial historiography to explain the genealogies of precious national institutions, namely, democracy and freedom, in self-referential, even provincial, terms. The comparative and the transnational, Jack Greene has suggested, are the best antidote to teleological narratives of the nation.[1] But for all the new emphasis on the global and the transnational, the teleological and the national have yet to loosen their grip on U.S. colonial historiography. The transnational and the global may simply be a new response to the pedagogical and ideological demands of a nation that is, in fact, a global empire. The historiography on the Atlantic is very much organized around the study of the empires created by the early modern national dynastic states (British, Spanish, Portuguese, Dutch, etc.). My previous work has sought to break the grip that the nation has had on Atlantic historiography by making colonial Spanish America "normative" (in the sense of both normal and central).[2] This book seeks to place the Spanish Atlantic at the center of U.S. colonial history. I have not only suggested reading Milton's *Paradise Lost* and Shakespeare's *The Tempest* in the context of rich early modern Iberian traditions of the satanic epic and demonology but have also argued that the literature on Puritan studies stands to benefit from sustained attention to Iberian sources and historiographies. And the opposite is true: I have shown that the literature on typology has the potential of transforming our understanding of such very well known Iberian colonial texts as Juan de Torquemada's *Monarquia indiana*. I have argued that the striking resemblances between Spanish and Puritan discourses of colonization as "exorcism" and as spiritual gardening point to a common Atlantic history, one rooted in a centuries-old shared Christian tradition of battling holy wars against demonic enemies and transforming satanic landscapes into occupied holy lands. These resemblances suggest that we are better off if we simply consider the Puritan colonization of New England as a continuation of Iberian models rather than a radical new departure, as the recent historiography on traditions of legal possession of territory seems to suggest.[3] The Puritans saw themselves as building radically different societies from those instituted in America by the brutal Spanish Antichrist. Nonetheless, as I hope to have shown in the preceding pages, Puritan and Iberian America had enough in common with each other for a single Atlantic narrative to be possible.

Why, then, have historians failed to see the commonalities? Why have U.S. colonial historians failed to see the Iberian colonization of the New World as also normative? The reason is to be found in powerful ideologies and epistemologies that cause scholars to believe that the United States and Latin America are two ontologically different spaces, the former belonging to the "West" and the latter to "Third World." In the following pages, I call into question these ideologies and epistemologies.

Bolton's Legacy

Some seventy years after it was first proposed, Herbert Eugene Bolton's "Epic of Greater America" is enjoying something of a revival. In 1933, Bolton (1870–1953) invited other historians to write a history of the Americas that would supersede traditional national narratives. Although his approach was somewhat narrow and did not pay attention to the lives and deeds of Amerindians, save as passive beneficiaries of European civilizing practices, Bolton's "Epic" still reads today as a farsighted historiographical proposal yet to be fulfilled.[4] For one thing, Bolton anticipated many of the current debates on Atlantic history. His critique of colonial British American historiography as narrowly wedded to a study of the thirteen colonies, to the total exclusion of events and developments in other territories that had once belonged to France, Spain, Holland, and Britain itself (i.e., Canada and the Caribbean), still rings true. There was something visionary in Bolton's proposal. His struggle to bring Spain into the fold of North American colonial history was daring in itself. U.S. historiography had long been colored by what Richard Kagan has characterized as Prescott's paradigm. Historians like William Hickling Prescott (1796–1859) located a treasure chest of tropes in the age-old Protestant "black legend" to help them explain Spain's alleged decline in the early modern period and the United States's meteoric rise. By finding the origins of decline in the choking grip of the Inquisition over innovative thought and in the centralizing, authoritarian Habsburg assault on Spain's medieval democratic traditions, historians also worked out the causes of the alleged U.S. "exceptionalism."[5]

Bolton helped create the climate that led the next generation of historians to abandon some of these simplistic characterizations, particularly as they applied to Spain's activities in the New World. Historians like Arthur S. Aiton, Lewis Hanke, John T. Lanning, Irving Leonard, Lesley B. Simpson, Frank Tannenbaum, and Arthur Zimmerman offered sympathetic accounts of Spain's empire in the Indies.[6] Two of Bolton's students, Lanning and Leonard, found vibrant communities in colonial universities and courts where only barren intellectual landscapes characterized by an inquisitorial style of scholasticism had been identified before.[7] Hanke found wrenching debates over the justice of conquest and colonization at the highest echelons of power. In Hanke's hands, Bartolomé de las Casas became not an anomalous figure in a desperate cry in the wilderness but a well-connected and powerful bishop whose agenda of reform eventually became official imperial policy.[8] Lesley Byrd Simpson discovered a generation of conquistadors not merely bent on pillaging and plundering but also devoted to building paternalistic institutions under the watchful eye of an activist Crown.[9] Aiton and Zimmerman found enlightened Spanish viceroys where other historians had only found corruption and sycophancy.[10] Finally, writing under the spell of Gilberto's Freyre's rosy representation of Brazil as a cauldron of racial democracy, Tannenbaum discovered in Latin America a history of more benign slave-holding societies than in the United States.[11]

If Bolton's insights on colonial Spanish America were well received and further elaborated, his call to study U.S. history as part of a larger narrative of continental America that would include both Canada and Latin America went unattended, when it was not dismissed outright.[12] The new pan-Americanism of the 1920s and 1930s was largely responsible for supporting a new intellectual climate that not only led to the far less aggressive "good neighbor" rhetoric in foreign policy but also to Bolton's generous historiographical proposal.[13] Although Bolton's sympathetic new view of colonial Latin America proved influential, his call to write a new history of the United States that would put Latin America at the center of any comparative or transnational analysis never flourished. The normative historiographical status of Europe in the U.S. scholarly community has continued unabated. Europe has remained the standard against which the narratives of American exceptionalism and Latin American dystopia continue to be imagined.[14]

The "Atlantic" paradigm has been hailed as a multicultural return to Bolton's "Epic." Like Bolton, Atlanticists see colonial British America with more cosmopolitan eyes, refusing to subscribe to the time-honored idea that U.S. colonial history should simply be a study of events in the thirteen "original" colonies. Atlanticists, like Bolton, remind us that British America alone was a composite of settlements spanning all the way from Nova Scotia to the Caribbean, and that North America was a territory colonized and contested by several European powers, including France, the Netherlands, Spain, and Russia. Atlanticists argue that colonial British American history is the history of greater Atlantic migrations and multicultural contact that brought Europeans, Amerindians, and Africans together into a tangle of commercial, ideational, cultural, and political circuits that defy any narrow, territorially based approach.[15]

Journals catering to U.S. colonial historians such as the *William and Mary Quarterly* now regularly feature articles and reviews that survey historiography from the Andes to the Appalachians and from Brazil to Charleston.[16] In the pages of this important quarterly, calls to completely revamp the teaching of the history of colonial North America (in which New England partially gives way in college textbooks to developments in, say, Arizona and California) have been featured prominently.[17] These calls have finally become a reality with the publication of Alan Taylor's *American Colonies* (2001), a study of truly continental scope.[18] Leading historians have used the pages of the *American Historical Review* to openly debate the virtues of crafting a new "greater American" narrative to colonial history.[19] Bolton's ghost is presiding over a sea change of seemingly global proportions.

The new Atlantic historiography has, then, been willing to do away with historiographies modeled along national narratives. Yet for all the greater global awareness on the part of U.S. colonial historians, the fact is that their Atlantic remains very much "British."

The National and the Global

If the recent survey of Atlantic history edited by David Armitage and Michael J. Braddick is any indication, the vast and expansive geographic category of the Atlantic is often seen in terms of national categories: British, Spanish, Dutch, French, Portuguese.[20] It is true that different European empires created somewhat different settler and plantation societies, but these national "Atlantics" had a good deal in common. John H. Elliott has long been advocating a pan-American view of the Atlantic, one that engages seriously in a comparative study of at least the British and Spanish empires.[21] With a few exceptions, particularly among those studying the history of the African diaspora in the New World, Atlanticists have paid only lip service to Elliott's urgent calls, however, even though Elliott himself has demonstrated that the institutions and character of, say, the British Atlantic World can only be explained within a much wider geographical perspective.[22]

But even a wide Atlantic perspective could be distorting, for most of the early modern European empires were in fact global ones. There is indeed no reason not to fold the Spanish American Pacific into the geographies of the Spanish American Atlantic, since the colonization of the Philippines was directed from and through Mexico, not Madrid. The Portuguese and Dutch empires are also cases in point; their colonization of the Americas was marginal and subordinate to their adventures in the Indian Ocean and the China Sea. It was only after their displacement by Ottoman, Mughal, Japanese, and Dutch traders in South Asia that the Portuguese merchants and bureaucrats turned to Brazil in the late seventeenth century, particularly after the discovery of gold in Minas Gerais.[23] As Serge Gruzinski has shown, the Iberian empires in the fifteenth century first set in motion the processes of cultural and racial hybridization of global proportions, not solely Atlantic, that typify our modern world.[24]

The tendency to focus on the British Atlantic not only has to do with the origins of the category of the Atlantic itself, a Cold War construct that naturally took the North to be both the norm and the focus of any trans-oceanic historiography. It is also related to the national teleologies that still organize most historiographies. Despite the efforts to enlarge U.S. colonial narratives to encompass regions other than the thirteen original colonies, Atlantic history seems to be a multicultural, international version of a new *national* narrative, in an age in which we need to be mindful of the rights of the minorities and of the needs of global capital. Thus the new version of U.S. colonial history seeks to give blacks, Hispanics, and other minorities their due, as opposed to the narrow, exclusionary version of the colonial past that focused exclusively on the lives of Protestant whites, particularly the Puritans. Earlier histories of the Pilgrims and Puritans of New England have given way to new narratives in which the slave societies of Virginia and the wider British Caribbean, as well as the Spanish borderlands, are featured prominently.

There are two problems in this approach. One is that "Hispanics" enter into the new Atlantic narratives as enfranchised "minorities" whose histories need to be acknowledged. Their histories, however, remain marginal to events and institutions of the Anglo-American core. The very marginality of these narratives is revealed in the term historians have chosen for them: "borderlands." Borders by definition are margins. They are invoked to spice up the "white" narratives of the past with multiculturalism. Borderlands (e.g., the Spanish Atlantic) do not exist to call into question normative narratives (e.g., the British Atlantic). Second, the new emphasis on globalization seems also to reflect the new ideological needs of an aggressively expansionist nation whose corporations have now decided that everyone else's national boundaries should be thrown open or simply abolished.[25]

The Comparative and the Transnational

But how to break the hold that the nation has on the historiographical imagination? In a recent essay, David Armitage has put forth a heuristic model of three distinct approaches to the (British) Atlantic according to whether the methodological emphasis falls on the transnational, the comparative, or the local. He calls these the circum-, trans-, and cis-Atlantic perspectives. Yet there is nothing intrinsic in any of these three approaches that would help us escape the gravitational pull of the nation. In fact, the comparative approach lies at the very heart of the doctrine of "American" exceptionalism, which is by definition a comparative category and finds even developments in Europe (to this date still the norm of any narrative of universal history) wanting. We have been told that the United States is exceptional in that since at least the eighteenth century, the nation has seemed to escape the social pathologies (rigid social hierarchies; class warfare; fascism) attendant on the development of capitalism in Europe.[26] In fact, Ian Tyrell has argued that comparative histories tend to reinforce narratives of U.S. exceptionalism. But he also suggests that transnational approaches ought to work as an antidote.[27]

But the transnational is no antidote, as Thomas Bender makes clear in his edited volume *Rethinking American History in a Global Age* (2002), where he argues for a new relational, transnational, global narrative, saying: "Attention to the relational aspects of historical phenomena is the key, and it differentiates this approach from most comparative history, which not only tends to reaffirm the nation as a natural category, but more important, seldom explores causal links between the two national experiences being compared."[28] According to Bender, the relational and the transnational should help historians escape the tyranny of geographical enclosure, be it the nation or the Atlantic. So historians are invited to imagine social worlds of different geographical scales (local, national, regional, global) "interacting with one another and thus providing multiple contexts for lives, institutions and ideas." This is all to the good. The catch, however, is that this is to be done ultimately to revitalize the historiography of the *nation*, to bring strangeness and unfamiliarity to narratives that are now well trodden and predictable.

The aim of the relational and the transnational turns out to be simply "to contextualize the nation."[29]

Sudden Divergence

One of the reasons why the British Atlantic has remained normative is simply linguistic: historians of United States, by and large, get away with studying sources only in English. As François Weil has argued, this parochialism (and intense specialization) of U.S. historiography is linked to the very continental scale of the nation itself, which makes self-referentiality not only possible but almost unavoidable.[30] But the other reason why Spanish America has been relegated to the status of the "borderland" of U.S. historiography has to do with a narrative of Anglo "triumphs and successes," along with one of Hispanic "failures and poverty."

In his *The Americas: A Hemispheric History* (2003), however, Felipe Fernández-Armesto offers a bold, sweeping narrative from the precolonial period to the present that upsets this stereotype. Fernández-Armesto sees the continent as whole and finds the South dominating the North demographically, politically, and culturally for most of its history, especially in the precolonial period and during most of the colonial period, when Spanish America developed a considerable number of cities, vast inter- and intracolonial trading circuits, and large internal economies. According to Fernández-Armesto, it was only in the eighteenth century that British America began to catch up with Spanish America: receiving large numbers of immigrants, settling the interior, and developing a brisk trade among colonies that had hitherto remained largely isolated. Then, with the breakdown of the empires (1760s–1820s), British and Spanish America suddenly began to diverge.

Unwittingly, Fernández-Armesto builds on a thesis that Jaime Rodríguez has been eloquently defending for years.[31] Having witnessed no wrecking wars of attrition to gain independence in an age not yet in thrall to the gospel of free trade, British America was able to build on the transatlantic and intercolonial trading circuits of the past and industrialize. Not so Spanish America, where all sorts of centripetal forces tore apart the previous networks and infrastructures of the Spanish empire as a whole (hence the secular political and economic crisis of Spain itself during the nineteenth century). Additionally, the doctrine of free trade (backed by the military might of Britain and the United States) induced the Latin American economies to produce raw materials for exports. For Fernández-Armesto, the cause of *sudden divergence* is to be found in how and when the wars of independence were fought in British and Spanish America, not in any culturalist and dependentist explanations.[32]

Fernández-Armesto finds the essentialist explanations that attribute development in British America to its Protestant work ethic and rugged individualism misguided. In his book, the Catholic South appears as more secular and individualistic than the Protestant North.[33] By the same token, theories that see dependency as the cause of the Spanish America's under-development have failed to notice that the United States was as much visited by "plundering" foreign capital as Latin America.[34] But sudden divergence there was.

For all his brilliant and forceful critique of theories of underdevelopment, however, Fernández-Armesto finds only negative commonalities between North and South after independence: a common history of slavery (and emancipation) and frontier violence (with Amerindians slaughtered on the prairies and the pampas alike). The historical narratives of Latin America and the United States from the early nineteenth century on do not seem to have much in common, except to describe the underbelly of modernity, or when they overlap as the result of U.S. imperial expansion to the South.

Bolton would have been puzzled had he known that Atlantic history is now synonymous with British American *colonial* history, for his "Epic of Greater America" explicitly sought to extend the continental perspective to the late nineteenth and twentieth centuries as well. This important aspect of Bolton's thesis has curiously gone unmentioned. Although there are an increasing number of Atlantic narratives of the national period, most of them leave Latin America out.[35] Daniel T. Rodgers's approach is paradig-matic. He has demonstrated the deep Atlantic roots of ideas and institutions of the Progressive era, which historians had long attributed to a distinctively "American" mind. Yet the focus of his Atlantic remains the North. Rodgers's *Atlantic Crossing: Social Politics in a Progressive Age* (1998) is first and fore-most an analysis of fin de siècle urban social policies in North America and manages to ignore developments in major South Atlantic metropolises such as São Paulo and Buenos Aires.

A brief comparative analysis of articles published in the pages of the *William and Mary Quarterly* (a journal that specializes in colonial British America) and the *Journal of the Early Republic* over the past ten years is telling. Whereas the former has published repeatedly on topics ranging geographically from Canada to the Caribbean to Africa to Spanish and Portuguese America, the latter has remained centered on the traditional northeastern sections of the United States, aside from a special spring 1999 issue on the southwestern and southeastern borderlands.[36] To be sure, historians of the early national period such as Richard White have made exceptional contributions to the greater America paradigm.[37] But it is fair to argue that the Western Hemisphere begins to shrink as soon as coverage of the British-American colonial period ends. These shifts in geographical perspective become even more pronounced when one moves beyond the historiography on the antebellum United States, in which slavery studies have helped maintain a wide comparative Atlantic focus.[38]

Could Spanish America Ever Be Normative?

U.S. colonial historians seem to be comfortable with transnational approaches. Yet it is clear that this global orientation has not done much to make Spanish America more than a background to narratives of the British Atlantic. This refusal to treat the South as normative is even more pronounced in narratives of the U.S. national period, historians of which do not see much point in seeking expertise on Latin American postcolonial history. Frontier and immigration histories, in which adopting a broad hemispheric perspective would seem logical, since similar processes of massive immigration and frontier expansion occurred all over the Americas, have been slow to turn to Latin America for insights.[39] New immigration historians have embraced a cosmopolitan perspective, but they nevertheless hold on firmly to a spatial frame of reference that puts Europe right at its center.[40] New historians of the Western frontier have also sought to explain "frontier" developments in the larger context of the nineteenth-century world economy. Mexico appears in these narratives as the passive victim of U.S. imperial expansion, however, not as a place to find historiographical guidance.

In their efforts to overturn the agrarian myths first peddled by Frederick Jackson Turner (1861–1932), these new frontier historians could easily have turned to the scholarship on nineteenth-century Mexico for inspiration.[41] They could have found in Mexico a long-established tradition of inquiry into how frontiers developed through the actions of federal governments, whose armies and bureaucracies "pacified" and colonized Amerindian territories, and of land speculators and mining and railroad interests, whose actions were linked to the demands of the global economy. The scholarship on the Porfiriato (1876–1911) could have long ago taught the new Western historians that the nineteenth-century conquest of the American "wilderness" was never the result of measures taken by rugged individuals fleeing the stench of federal government in order to tame "virgin lands." That the revisionist historians of the western frontier never turned to Mexico to help them frame their critiques of Turner's agrarian myth suggests that for them the U.S. West and the Mexican North are two ontologically different spaces.[42] When it comes to postcolonial Latin America, the new global historiography has turned to the region mostly for insights into slavery and racism, the underbelly of modernity.[43] But to invite Latin Americans solely through this door might paradoxically be helping to reinforce notions of spatial incommensurability and difference.

Other areas of the Latin American experience have failed to attract much attention. A greater hemispheric narrative of, say, nineteenth-century liberalism and nation building could equally be the focus of the global imagination.[44] There is really no reason why historians of antebellum United States in search of comparative perspective should not turn to the past of a country like Colombia, for example, for in Colombia, just as in the United States, the origin of protonational regional discourses was linked to the development of political-party identities.[45]

The Exclusionary Force of the Narrative of "Western Civilization"

In addition to the isolation of colonial from national history, the category of the "Atlantic" itself helps explain why dichotomous geographical approaches to Latin America have emerged. Just as Bolton's "Epic of Greater America" was made possible by the intellectual atmosphere created by the pan-Americanism and the "good neighbor" foreign policy of the 1920s and 1930s, the concept of an "Atlantic" space originated in the Cold War. Since the late nineteenth century, black U.S. intellectuals have tinkered with wider Atlantic narratives and have implicitly explored the "Black Atlantic," yet in mainstream historiography, the category of the Atlantic had to wait for the shifting geopolitical alliances of the post–World War II era to develop.[46] The Cold War dramatically redrew the cultural geographies of the "West" by bringing Germany back into the allied fold. In both world wars, Germans had been cast as eastern "Huns" threatening the most cherished institutions of the West. With the onset of the Cold War, however, these categories no longer applied and the enemies of the past became allies. The fight against the Soviet Union, itself a former ally, justified the switch. The category of a common "Atlantic" civilization, first coined in the United States by conservative Catholic intellectuals, was at the center of this imaginative redrawing of the West and of the reshuffling of alliances that ensued.[47] But the notion of a common Atlantic civilization linking western Europe and the United States both militarily and historically has had contradictory consequences for the development of pan-American continental narratives. The concept of "Western Civilization" has authorized a most puzzling development. On the one hand, through the category of the Atlantic, it has made the histories of the European colonial powers in the New World part of a common narrative. On the other hand, in university curricula, it has pegged Latin Americans in a vague non-Western space. How has this been possible?

To make sense of such puzzles, we need to understand how the concept of the "West" tends to operate in U.S. public opinion. It is clear that the media have historically fostered a utopian image of Western civilization as the cradle of reason, liberty, democracy, and economic prosperity. For this manicured and misleading image to work, however, the public has indulged over the years in the massive, willful redrawing of geographical and cultural boundaries. Thus, for example, when Germany under Hitler created an irrational, murderous regime of eugenic terror, the media cast Germans as Huns, quintessential barbarians from the East. When Russia turned to Marxism, that most Western of ideologies, the vicious Stalinist regime that ensued was pigeonholed by both the public and academics as a cultural manifestation of Oriental despotism.[48]

The category of the "West" has managed to exclude from the narratives of the origins of modernity entire provinces of the human past. We know, for example, that the architecture of Renaissance Venice, that cradle of Western civilization, owes as much to Islamic Ottoman institutions as to Greek Mediterranean classical models.[49] The Ottoman "Turks" are constantly cast in historiography as being paradigmatic of the "East," heirs to the Islamic Caliphate and the Mongols. Yet after their conquest of Constantinople, the Ottomans, in fact, saw themselves as the rightful heirs to the cultural heritage of Rome.[50] I could multiply my examples of how the historiographical category of the West has served us poorly endlessly; suffice it so say that the most aggressive "anti–Western civilization" movements of the past one hundred years have in fact been built by Arab and Japanese ideologues out of "Western" building blocks.[51]

Faced with the paradigm of "Western civilization," Latin America consistently comes up short. Seen as an area ridden by poverty, corruption, and violence, modern Latin America, like Africa, acts in public opinion as the inverted mirror image of the West, namely, as a dystopic space. Contemporary Latin America thus upsets the aseptic images of the West that the public has learned to cherish. A model denizen of the Third World,

Latin America is therefore safely classified today in the curriculum of U.S. universities as a non-Western other.

Historiographical Barricades

To engage the histories of the North and South in a constructive dialogue, Atlanticists and neo-Boltonians need first to acknowledge that the historiographies of these two regions have followed different trajectories. At this level, the Atlantic paradigm has yet to become truly hemispheric. It is curious that recent histories of the "idea of Atlantic history" manage to survey the literature without once referring to the history of Latin American colonial historiography, because Latin American historians have long operated with large continental and transcontinental perspectives.[52] This oversight is emblematic of what Christopher Schmidt-Nowara, borrowing a phrase from the nineteenth-century Cuban nationalist leader José Martí (1853–95), has called a "'barricade of ideas' that obscures borderlands of historical interpretation."[53] Praising the recent historiographical proposal of Jeremy Adelman and Stephen Aron that has called for a "greater America" continental history attuned to the peculiarities of Amerindian and European interactions in borderlands once held by the British, French, and Spaniards, Schmidt-Nowara has argued that neo-Boltonians tend to ignore alternative Latin American historiographical traditions.[54] Schmidt-Nowara briefly reviews the case of nineteenth-century Cuban scholars, for example, whose complex historiographical views on the interactions of the British, U.S., and Spanish empires in the Caribbean have gone completely unnoticed in any discussion of empires and borderlands. Schmidt-Nowara is not alone in his call for a broad continental historiographical dialogue. Some eighteen years ago, Steve Stern took the world-system theorist Immanuel Wallerstein to task for summarily ignoring the historiography fostered by Latin American theorists, who had long anticipated many of Wallerstein's insights.[55] Frustrated by Wallerstein's silence on this and other charges, Stern bemoaned the "one hundred years of solitude" to which Latin Americans had been condemned, in the Nobel laureate Colombian novelist Gabriel García Márquez's phrase.[56] More recently, Walter Mignolo has taken issue with postcolonialists who despite all their anti-essentialist claims have managed to transform the Anglo-British colonial experience into the normative paradigm.[57] "Barricades of ideas" seem to be built everywhere in U.S. academia. Reviewing Stephen Greenblatt's much-acclaimed book *Marvelous Possessions: The Wonder of the New World* (1991), the critic Roberto González Echeverría took Greenblatt to task for having broached a continental subject without much awareness that the subject of colonialism and the marvelous has long been a staple of Latin American literature.[58]

For the Atlantic paradigm to be truly hemispheric, the generous spatial-historical perspective of today needs to evolve into awareness that alternative historiographies have been circulating around the Atlantic for centuries. A pan-American Atlantic history of ideas is therefore of the essence.

Ideas . . . Where?

The history of ideas in Latin America has long failed to attract U.S. historians of the region, let alone Atlanticists. It could be argued that the turn to social history is to blame, for ideas are widely seen as belonging to "elites," and the "new social history" promotes a view of history that sees the past from the bottom up. This argument clearly does not explain much, however, for intellectual history has not only survived but also thrived under the auspices of the "linguistic turn." Now intellectual historians identify and take "discourses" apart as they confidently go about reconstructing past cultural sensibilities.[59] A "linguistic turn" notwithstanding, the historiography in the United States on elite intellectual discourses among Latin American historians is dismal. In 1985, two separate surveys of one hundred years of U.S. historiography on Latin America concluded that there was a near complete absence of writings in this field.[60] Twenty-one years later, things do not seem to have improved much. One can only speculate as to why this is the case: the same cultural geographies that locate Latin America in the "non-Western" world might well be behind such a historiographical dearth. The category of the "West" carries with it an aura of intellectual agency. Unflagging commitment to innovative thought through open intellectual debate and endless mental curiosity leading to original ideas are often seen as key cultural properties of the West, the source of its power and technological edge. By the same token, the closer one gets to modernity, the more the non-Western world is perceived as derivative and unoriginal. Histories of absences clearly cannot be written.[61]

The turn to multiculturalism in U.S. academia has only contributed to popularizing perceptions of Latin America as a non-Western space. Take, for example, the most recent edition of Thomas E. Skidmore and Peter H. Smith's *Modern Latin America*, one of the most widely read introductions to modern Latin American history in U.S. universities. The image on the book's cover (fig. 6.1) unsubtly conveys the message that "Latin Americans" (an extraordinarily variegated bunch, most of whom are urbanites) are Amerindians in colorful ethnic costumes, who are engaged in subsistence economies, and whose technologies are limited to carrying handicrafts and agricultural staples on their backs and heads.

This is certainly one of the many worlds tourists encounter in their visits to Latin America. But the choice of artwork is telling. Although the text itself describes the extraordinary political, cultural, and social transformations that some one hundred years of industrialization, urbanization, and massive European, Asian, and Middle Eastern migrations have brought to Latin America, the message students first encounter is a pictorial narrative of "tradition," of Amerindians doing and wearing "authentic" things: a manufactured "non-Western" space for U.S. multicultural consumption. In fact, as George Yúdice has suggested, the turn toward multiculturalism in the United States has encouraged representations of Latin Americans as "non-Western" others.[62] An intellectual history *of the West* that includes Latin America seems ludicrous at this stage.

It is unfortunate, however, that the intellectual history of Latin America has failed to attract many adepts. For one thing, it has made the hemispheric historiographical dialogue suggested above unlikely. For another, it has impoverished the intellectual history of the West. An Atlantic history of ideas that takes Latin America (and Africa) seriously has much to offer. I have argued that such iconic English works as Milton's *Paradise Lost* (1667) and Shakespeare's *The Tempest* (ca. 1611) make sense only within the wider traditions of the Iberian satanic epic. Important ideas attributed to Europeans were in fact part of larger Atlantic dialogues.

I do not seek to present Latin America as a continent of lonely, misunderstood intellectual pioneers. I seek to do away with historiographies that are content with tracing how ideas allegedly first coined by North Atlantic intellectuals are consumed and digested everywhere else.[63] This tendency has even affected how the history of European Mediterranean modernity is remembered. Elsewhere, I have shown how the Iberian roots of the so-called scientific revolution have been largely ignored.[64] My critique seeks simply to make obvious the dangerously misleading, flattened images that our impoverished historiography tends to promote.

Take, for example, the case of nineteenth-century Latin American art,

FIG. 6.1. *(opposite)* Traditional Indians as modern Latin America. Thomas E. Skidmore and Peter H. Smith, *Modern Latin America*, 6th ed. (New York: Oxford University Press, 2005), cover. Courtesy Oxford University Press.

THOMAS E. SKIDMORE

PETER H. SMITH

Modern Latin America

SIXTH EDITION

lying silently between the baroque exuberance of colonial sacred architecture and the modernist *indigenismo* of twentieth-century muralism. Dozens of nineteenth-century landscape painters have proven insufficiently exotic to attract the attention of U.S. scholars, so much so that the body of literature in the English language on talented artists who developed sophisticated pictorial languages of their own, like José Maria Velasco (1840–1912; Mexico), Francisco Oller (1833–1917; Puerto Rico), Rafael Troya (1845–1920; Ecuador), Antônio Parreiras (1860–1937; Brazil), and Prilidiano Pueyrredón (1823–70; Argentina), to name only a few, is so thin as to be almost undetectable. Wouldn't our vision of the French and U.S. pasts be terribly diminished had historians never identified such nineteenth-century artistic movements as Impressionism and the Hudson River school of painting? This historical blind spot, I argue, stems largely from the fact that U.S. Latin Americanism has been complicit in fomenting stereotypes of Latin America as a region solely given to crises and petty "revolutions," producing only narratives of secular historical failure.

Should Latin Americans Embrace the Atlantic?

The trajectory of the historiography on colonial Latin America seems to be following directions opposite to those being transited by U.S. colonialists, namely, away from the Atlantic. As mentioned above, historical narratives of Latin America have long been written with the "Atlantic" in mind. Since perhaps as early as the 1940s, Latin American economists and social scientists began to submit modernization theories to the scrutiny of transcontinental historical developments. To be sure, the historiography these scholars produced—overly concerned with economic processes—can hardly be compared with the historicist and culturalist emphases that dominate the new Atlantic scholarship. Yet, like today's, this scholarship sought to put local events in much larger contexts.

In the 1940s, motivated by the Argentine Raúl Prebisch's insightful critique of David Ricardo's classical theory of international trade (comparative advantages allegedly benefit both trading partners), many economists associated with the UN Economic Commission for Latin America (ECLA, or Comisión Económica para América Latina, CEPAL) turned to history to show that Latin America's secular export vocation was largely responsible for the region's underdevelopment. In the narratives of economists-turned-historians like Celso Furtado, Aníbal Pinto Santa Cruz, Aldo Ferrer, Osvaldo Sunkel, Pedro Paz, and René Villareal, Latin America appeared as long having taken part in Atlantic commercial circuits. These circuits, they charged, had halted the region's development, keeping its internal markets from growing and thus thwarting its industrialization.[65] This narrative soon came to dominate how the history of the region was written in both Latin America and the United States.[66]

It did not take Latin American historians long to realize that "dependency theory," as the type of analysis sketched above came to be known, had the potential for turning past complexities into simplistic formulas.[67] For at least two decades now, historians have been moving away from the dependency paradigm and concomitantly away from the Atlantic. As Stuart B. Schwartz has recently recognized, the historiography of colonial Brazil has lately been busy discovering societies with dynamics of their own, with markets and institutions that were not after all entirely shaped by the Atlantic circuits.[68]

There is more in this turn away from the Atlantic than meets the eye. Some historians of Latin America seem to be rejecting the entire paradigm on epistemological grounds. Take, for example, the case of the historian of late colonial Mexico Eric Van Young, who argues that the fashionable paradigm of an "Age of Revolution" forces the Latin American experience into Euro- and Anglo-centric periodizations. The historiographical construct of the "Age of Revolutions," an old favorite with Atlantic historians, postulates a radical break between two periods: an ancien régime and a new liberal order. The trope of discontinuities introduces intolerable distortions when it comes to Latin America, however, where the ancien régime might have lasted considerably longer. By buying into the narrative of the dawn of a new age, historians of the region find themselves having to grapple with questions of decline and failure.[69]

Precisely at the time that U.S. colonial historians have been doing away with narrowly provincial narratives, Latin American historians have been turning inward. These two approaches, of course, are not incompatible. A deeper understanding of local phenomena is most likely to enhance our comprehension of the webs of transnational connections. And the opposite is also true. The best local and national histories are those written with a global awareness.

Away from Tragic Narratives

There are other asymmetric trajectories in historiography that Atlanticists and Latin Americanists in the United States would do well to recognize. Perhaps the most significant one has to do with the radically different plots of U.S. and Latin American historical narratives. Whereas U.S. historians struggle mightily to bring a dose of skepticism to the annoyingly optimistic narratives of "American exceptionalism," Latin American historians are saddled with plots seething with tragedy, failure, and dystopia. This, to be sure, is not new. As I have shown in this book, as early as 1615, the Franciscan friar Juan de Torquemada argued that the history of Mexico was the inverted mirror image of that of Israel. Although both Jews and Aztecs claimed providential narratives for themselves, Torquemada contended, the Israelites were truly God's elect, while the Aztecs were the devil's chosen.

The impartial observer cannot help being astonished by the radically different ways in which the peoples of the Americas have chosen to imagine their pasts. Whereas people in the United States have historically been prone to see their country's past as the fountainhead of everything good and righteous, people in Latin America have more often than not turned to the future for inspiration in order to craft optimistic patriotic narratives. As mentioned above, the historiography on the frontier is a case in point. When U.S. historians were busily developing Turner's agrarian myth, with its happy resolutions, Latin American historians were developing tragic readings of Mexico's Porfiriato. By the same token, whereas revisionist U.S. historians have proposed more tragic narratives for the western borderlands, Latin American historians have yet to find comedic readings of the nineteenth-century Mexican frontier.[70]

Tragic narratives abound in Latin American historiography. Countries like Argentina, whose historical trajectory resembles that of the United States in more ways than one, have only occasionally produced short-lived narratives of national exceptionalism.[71] Popular texts of history have imagined the past through corpse metaphors. In 1971, the Uruguayan Eduardo Galeano's *Las venas abiertas de America Latina* (translated as *The Open Veins of Latin America*) narrated the tragedy of a Latin America bled white by imperialist pillage since the conquest.[72] Dystopic narratives colored by the "black legend" have haunted Latin American historiography since its inception. Nineteenth-century liberals found the root cause of Latin America's secular plight in the region's past, namely, in the Spanish legacy of command economies, intolerance, and Amerindian and clerical corporate rights.[73] Twentieth-century social scientists, in turn, extended the same tragic reading to the deeds of those very nineteenth-century liberals who had sought to correct the "colonial" legacy. Dependency theory dismissed the triumph of nineteenth-century liberalism in Latin America as underdevelopment actively promoted by the local comprador bourgeoisie. Unlike in the United

States, where colonial and national narratives have been conveniently severed, in Latin America, the trope of colonial legacies burdening the present continues to frame the way historians imagine the past.[74]

When these tragic narratives migrate to the United States, they become deadly. They certainly do not help to counter patronizing U.S. perceptions of Latin America as destitute and effete, a land inhabited by superstitious peasants and well-mannered aristocrats, a barely transformed "wilderness" rightfully there for the picking.[75] U.S. scholars have themselves been instrumental in helping to shake many of these perceptions. Historians, for example, have profoundly altered the way colonial Latin America has traditionally been imagined. Thanks to their efforts, we now know that haciendas were not fiefs inhabited by emasculated Amerindian serfs but spaces with as many forms of labor relations as they had variegated landholdings, always catering to local urban markets. For the view of colonial silver mines worked solely by Amerindian forced labor, historians have substituted one of mines where technical innovation, daring entrepreneurs, and wage laborers prevailed. Images of a predominantly rural colonial Latin America are now untenable, because the central role of cities to the lives of both Amerindians and Spaniards has been made explicit. We now know that the *repartimiento de comercio*, the alleged "forced" system of commercial distribution (controlling both production and consumption in the countryside) was in fact the preferred mechanism of credit of the rural poor. And the list goes on.[76]

But for all these contributions, most historical syntheses of the region tend ultimately to harp on exploitation and revolution.[77] Tragedy seems to dominate the field. *Born in Blood and Fire: A Concise History of Latin America*, a textbook by the influential young historian John Chasteen, published by W. W. Norton & Company in 2001, is a case in point. A title like this only reinforces the stereotypes that most U.S. students already have about Latin America. For a historiographical dialogue to take place and a continental narrative to be developed, U.S. historians need to find a balance between the patriotic excesses that characterize the historiography of the North and the tragic visions that dominate the historiography of the South. A middle course needs to be struck, one that finds stories of both misery and redemption throughout the Western Hemisphere. This book is an effort to strike such balance.

Notes

Chapter 1. Introduction

1. Villagómez, ch. 67, p. 176. See also Dacosta, 13. "Levate signum in gentibus" is from Jer. 51:27: "Set ye up a standard in the land, blow the trumpet among the nations" (levate signum in terra clangite bucina in gentibus). "Ecce Crucem Domini, fugite partes adversae" is based on Ps. 68(67):1(2): "Let God arise, let his enemies be scattered: let them also that hate him flee before him" (exsurgat Deus et dissipentur inimici eius et fugiant qui oderunt eum a facie eius). Pope Sixtus V (r. 1585–90) had St. Antony of Padua's brief carved as an exorcism at the base of the Egyptian obelisk in Saint Peter's Square in Rome:

> Ecce Crucem Domini!
> Fugite partes adversae!
> Vicit Leo de tribu Juda,
> Radix David! Alleluia!

> > (Behold the Cross of the Lord!
> > Flee ye enemies!
> > The Lion of the tribe of Judah [Christ],
> > The root of David [Christ] has conquered! Alleluia!)

All my citations of the Bible in English come from the King James Version. Latin citations in Spanish sources derive from the Vulgate. On the seventeenth-century campaigns of extirpation of idolatries in Peru, see Mills, *Idolatry*; Duviols; Griffiths.

2. Villagómez, ch. 27, pp. 90–91: "De cetero fratres comfortamini in Domino, et in potentia virtutis eius in duiti vos armaturam Dei, ut possitis stare adversus insidias Diaboli. Quoniam [*sic*] non est nobis coluctatio adversus carnem, et sanguinem, sed adversus principes, et potestates, adversus mundi rectores tenebrarum harum, contra spirituali [*sic*] nequitiae in caelestibus. Propterea accipite armaturam Dei, ut possitis resistere in die malo et in omnibus perfectis stare. State ergo succincti lumbos vestros in veritate, et induti loricam iustitiae, et calciati pedes in praeparatione Evangelii pacis: in omibus sumentes scutum fidei, in quo possitis omnia tela nequissimi ignea extingere [*sic*], et galeam salutis adsumite, et gladium spiritus quod est verbum Dei."

3. Arriaga, 15–17.

4. Villagómez, ch. 65, p. 255: "Exorzizo te immunde spiritus per Deum Patrem omnipotentem, et per Iesum Christum filium eius, et per Spiritum sanctum, ut

recedes ab his famulis Dei, quos Deus et, Dominus noster ab erroribus, et deceptionibus tuis liberare."

5. Dacosta, 7.

6. This was the theme running through Villagómez's pastoral letter. The metaphor, like much in Villagómez's work, originated in fact with Arriaga; see Arriaga, 79–80.

7. Dacosta, 13.

8. Dacosta, 12: "Ecce material iustitiae et iudicii, ecce ad quid ius dicitur huic mundo: ad hoc scilicet ut Diabolus Princeps eijiciatur foras. Non dicit Diabolus, non tentator, non seductor mundi huius, sed Princeps: quia non eijicitur aseducendo, atentando, acalumniando, sed a principatu, non particulari huius, vel illius hominis, civitatis, aut patriae, sed mundi huius. Principabatur enim, & adorabatur, ut Princips mundi huius Diabolus ante mortem Christi communiter a mundo; hoc est, colebatur in omnibus diis gentium. Et ab hoc principatu eijectus est, sublato per Christum cultu Deorum, ablata ex mundo (quamuis non es singuli partibus simul) Idololatria."

9. Villagómez, ch. 51, p. 187.

10. Villagómez, ch. 26, p. 87: "corrijan los yerros, convirtiendo en llanuras las asperezas de los corazones montaraces y costumbres incultas, que hallaran en los Indios."

11. Villagómez, ch. 29, p. 97: "para la cultura desta heredad, que Dios plantó en el desierto estéril, seco y fuera del camino"; "[para] helar, secar y destruir el jugo y la virtud de la santificación que fertilizaba y debe fertilizar la tierra de los corazones y almas de nuestros Indios, donde se ha sembrado la semilla de la palabra divina."

12. Villagómez, ch. 30, pp. 102–3.

13. Subrahmanyam, *Career and Legend*; Fernández-Armesto, *Columbus*; Russell.

14. Goodman, 104–33; Fernández-Armesto, *Before Columbus*, 11–12, 131, 155, 167, 221; Thornton, 23 (on the Genoese Lanzarote Malo Cello, who led the colonization of the Canary Islands between 1312 and 1335) and 37 (on Lanzarote de Lago, who in 1444 led raids in Senegal).

15. Kagan, "Prescott's Paradigm."

16. Edward Johnson, 7.

17. Ibid., 10.

18. Ibid., 8, 24.

19. Ibid., 30–31.

20. Ibid., 24, 104; see also 39.

21. Ibid., 50–51.

22. Ibid., 114.

23. Ibid., 112.

24. Ibid., 115.

25. Ibid., 113–14.

26. Ibid., 112.

27. Ibid., 26.

28. Ibid., 14–17.

29. Ibid., 25.

30. Well arm'd and strong with sword among, Christ armies marcheth he,
    Doth valiant praise, and weak one raise, with kind benignity
    To lead the Van, 'gainst Babylon, doth worthy Winthrop call,
    Thy Progeny, shall Battel try, when Prelacy shall fall

    (ibid., 48)

31. Ibid., 111.

32. *News from New England*, 6 (my emphasis).

33. On early modern demonology, Stuart Clark's groundbreaking *Thinking with Demons* is indispensable. I have also found Pagels and Forsyth particularly illuminating.

34. On a distinctly New World demonological discourse as it relates to colonization and European-Amerindian interactions, I have profited greatly from Pioffet; Goddard; Reff; David Lovejoy; McWilliams; Norton; Bond; Mello e Souza; Fernando Cervantes; MacCormack; Pino; Duviols; Molinié-Bertrand.

35. See, e.g., Seed, *Ceremonies of Possession* and *American Pentimento*; Pagden; Muldoon.

36. Greene, *Pursuit of Happiness.*

37. Bond (I am grateful to James Sidbury for this reference).

38. My views on Puritan seventeenth-century theology in the New World rely on the superb scholarship of Bozeman; Morgan; Perry Miller; Winship; Holifield, *Theology in America.*

39. Morgan.

40. "Possession" was by definition a violent hijacking of the body, not the will, by the devil. The devil caused the body of the possessed to move, often violently, and to speak. Witches were not possessed but knowingly and willfully surrendered to the devil. Elizabeth Reis has argued that this representation of the devil as an aggressive external force caused Puritans to assume that the weaker female bodies were less capable of resisting Satan's harassment. The souls of females more easily surrendered to sin and temptation as well, because the soul was housed in the body. In the wake of the Salem witchcraft crisis, Puritans felt the need to deemphasize the external physical presence of the devil and turn him into a metaphor for temptation. See Reis.

41. Slotkin, 69–78.

42. Gregory.

43. I take the idea of a transatlantic bazaar of ideas from Bender, "Strategies."

44. Knight, *Orthodoxies*; Winship.

45. Holifield, *Theology*, 51–52.

46. Fernando Cervantes; Clark, pts. 2 and 4. On these transitions, see Bossy, "Moral Arithmetic"; Daston and Park.

47. For a synthesis of recent scholarship on the history of printing in Spanish America, see Calvo. On the complex interaction of the oral, the visual, and the written in early modern Europe, particularly Spain, see Bouza. On the scribal and oral culture of colonial Chesapeake, see Hall, *Cultures of Print*, 97–150. On the centrality of images in Puritan piety, see Bozeman, 32–49.

48. Benavente, bk. 1, ch. 14, par. 139 (p. 128): "estos indios que en sí no tienen estorbo que les impida para ganar el cielo, de los muchos que los españoles tenemos y nos tienen sumidos."

49. Zumárraga quoted in Hanke, *Spanish Struggle*, 175.

50. On Spanish millennial thought in the Indies, see Columbus, Milhou, Watts. On the Franciscan millennium, see Baudot; Brading, *First America*, ch. 5; Phelan. On the evolution of the figure of the Antichrist as increasingly resembling an inverted Christ, see McGinn. On the millenarian logic behind the Franciscan (as well as Dominican and Augustinian) religious compounds and murals, see Lara; Edgerton.

51. Calderón de la Barca, *La semilla y la cizaña* (I am grateful to John Slater for pointing out this reference to me). Another example of the global satanic epic imagination appears in the Hall of Realms (Salón de Reinos) of Philip IV's Buen Retiro Palace, built in Madrid between 1630 and 1640. Calderón, who wrote a play to commemorate the opening of the palace, most likely found the paintings of the Hall of Realms to his liking. Built as the throne room, the hall was covered with grotesquerie and the coats of arms of the twenty-four kingdoms that made up the Spanish monarchy, including the lands controlled by the Portuguese empire. It is no wonder, then, that Philip IV went by the name of "Planet King." Hanging from the walls there were twelve paintings commemorating recent battles against Dutch and British Protestants, including the recovery of Bahia (Brazil), Puerto Rico, and San Cristobal (St. Kitts) in the New World. Interspersed between these twelve paintings, there were ten of the twelve labors of Hercules, including the hero's battles against the Lernean Hydra, the Cretan Bull, the Erymanthean Boar, the Nemean Lion, Cerberus, and the giant Antaeus. The visitor was introduced in another room to paintings of the four Furies. An epic narrative of battles fought on a planetary scale against demonic enemies comes across unmistakably. For a cultural history of the palace, see Brown and Elliott. On demonology in early modern Spain, see Tausiet and Amelang.

52. Lope de Vega, *La Dragontea* (the references are to canto and stanza). In *Mimesis and Empire*, Barbara Fuchs successfully demonstrates the global dimension of the epic genre in Spain. She persuasively shows the importance of Moriscos and Turks in both Spanish and Amerindian representations of the Spanish colonization of the New World.

53. By Francis Drake (1542–96), John Hawkins (Juan de Aquines) (1532–95), and Joris van Speilbergen (1568–1620), who attacked Callao in 1615.

54. Oviedo y Herrera.

55. The documents relative to this episode are in the National Historical Archive (AHN), Madrid, ramo Inquisition, libro 1003 and Inquisition legajo 1650/1. The lengthy documentation has been reproduced in Huerga, 315–504. To appreciate perceptions of the virulence of the devil in the Indies, it is perhaps useful to compare the case of María and her exorcists in Peru with that of her contemporary Lucrecia de León. Lucrecia was a maiden living in Madrid who one day in 1587 found herself having dreams announcing the impending arrival of the millennium in a Spain ruled by an inept and corrupt Philip II. The powerful Alonso de Mendoza, canon of the cathedral of Toledo, member of one of the most prominent families in Spain, and, like de la Cruz, a dabbler in alchemy, talismanic magic, and astrology, got wind of Lucrecia's dreams and, with the help of the head of Madrid's Franciscan convent, Fray Lucas de Allende, transcribed and interpreted all 415 of them over the course of some two years. The Inquisition stepped in as the popular and elite following that developed around Lucrecia began to make plans to welcome and hasten the arrival of the millennium, one that left no room for Philip II and the Habsburgs. As in María's case, the Inquisition ruled that Lucrecia's dreams had been inspired by the devil, not God, as Mendoza and Allende had been led to believe. Despite the openly subversive nature of this episode of demonic deception, the Inquisition was slow to prosecute, meting out relatively benign sanctions against those involved. Moreover,

it did not assume that the devil had sought to destroy the Crown and the state. On Lucrecia and the political cabal around the interpretation of her dreams, see Kagan, *Lucrecia's Dreams*.

56. Alberro. On Peru, see Millar.

57. Laura Lewis. On the Spanish Inquisition reining in overzealous reformers who were given to persecuting witches, see Henningsen.

58. On the origins of the art of discerning spirits that visited female mystics, see Caciola; Dyan Elliott.

59. Jaffary.

60. Martínez.

61. Schmidt.

62. See, e.g., the 1596 satanic epic by FitzGeffrey. On Drake's career, see Cummins.

63. Kupperman; Chaplin.

64. Cave.

65. Lepore.

66. Godbeer.

67. Norton.

68. Cave, 6, 139, and passim.

69. Bossy.

70. On the crusades as part of larger traditions of holy wars, see Tyerman; Riley-Smith. On medieval colonial expansions, see Bartlett.

71. Housley; Swanson (I am grateful to Robert Bartlett for this reference).

72. To my knowledge Brading, in *Mexican Phoenix*, is the first to have masterfully demonstrated the importance of typology in the colonial theology on Our Lady of Guadalupe.

CHAPTER 2. THE SATANIC EPIC

1.   His bene perspectis, quisquis verissima pandit,
     Mittit et in lucem, quae sunt detenta tenebris,
     Carminibus comptis, laudis quoque dignus habetur,
     Ut Castellanos hic, qui fortissima bella
     Narrat & eventus, rerum variosque labores,
     Qui superant omnes, quos doctus pingit Homerus,
     Extenuantque viri prorsus discrimina Teucri
     Nam non errores arctos, quos passus Ulises,
     Non freta Troiani fugientis parva recenset,
     Sed neque forma datur triplex pastoris Hiberi,
     Nec ramosa quidem centeni gutturis Hydra,
     Hesperidumque draco, non custos velleris hidrus,
     Sed tamen Oceanus serpens praelongus & ingens,
     Ceruleis mágnum, qui cingit nexibus orbem,
     Victus ab Hispanis, nam iam sunt undique visi
     Aequoris immensi sinus, anfractusque viarum,
     Flumina vasta nimis, montes, amplisima regna,

Gens celeris pedibus, sumptis non tarda sagittis
Et miranda novus, quae continet Indicus orbis,
Nullis visa prius sed cunctis condita priscis.

> (Keeping all these things in mind, whoever reveals utterly true things
> and in polished verses brings to light of day things hidden in darkness
> is also [i.e., as well as Homer and Virgil] deemed worthy of praise, as
> is this Castellanos, who tells of hard-fought battles and events and
> sufferings that surpass those that learned Homer depicts and entirely
> put in the shade the crises of the Trojan hero [Aeneas]. For he doesn't
> recount the narrow wanderings Ulysses endured or the paltry seas
> of the fleeing Trojan, nor is the triple form of the Spanish shepherd
> [Geryon] related, nor even the branching Hydra of a hundred throats,
> nor the dragon of the Hesperides, nor the serpent guardian of the
> Fleece, but instead Oceanus, a serpent very long and vast, who encir-
> cles the great orb with his dark blue coils, conquered by the Spaniards.
> For now everywhere have come into sight the gulf of the huge sea,
> winding pathways, river too wide, mountains, vast kingdoms, a people
> fleet of foot and not slow with the arrows they take up, and marvels
> that the new Indian world contains, never before seen, but hidden
> from all earlier peoples.)

Castellanos, 1–2.

I am grateful to David Lupher and Elizabeth Vandiver for helping me interpret
the frontispiece.

On the trope of Spanish conquerors, poets, and natural philosophers superseding
the ancients, particularly the Romans, see Lupher.

2. Hispanum regnum declarat bellica virgo
Est maris oceani litus & ipse draco.
Hic serpens ingens orbem circundat utrimque
Coniungens caude, perfreta, longa, caput.
Ergo, quicquid erit, quod continet orbis uterque

> (The warlike maiden declares that the Spanish kingdom is the shore
> of the ocean sea and the serpent itself. This huge serpent embraces
> the globe on both sides and joins its head to its tail across vast gulfs.)

Castellanos, n.p.

3. On early modern Iberian American epics, see Pierce and Peña, who curiously
omit those written in Portuguese and Latin. On the relationship between Iberian
epics and empire, see Quint; Nicolopulos; Elizabeth Davis; Avalle-Arce; Murrin.

4. Anchieta describes the transformations brought about by the civilizing mission of the Portuguese (the Amerindians used to live in the wilderness, ate human
flesh, and drank human blood, but now attend masses, and drink and eat the body
of Christ) in a typical passage:

Quae [gens] prius umbrosis degebat condita silvis,
Iam Domini sacras gaudet adire domos;
Quae [gens] rabidis hominum rodebat corpora malis
Mitia iam sancto pectora pane cibat;

Quae [gens] saeva humanum sugebat fauce cruorem,
Iam divina avida flumina fauce bibit

> (The [people] who used to pass their lives in shadowy forests now rejoice to approach holy dwellings; [the people] who used to gnaw on men's bodies with frenzied jaws now feed gentle breasts with holy bread; [the people] who used to suck human blood with savage gullets now drink divine streams with eager throats.)

Anchieta, 72.

For references to Amerindian cannibalism, see also 104, 114, 124, 130, 202, 206.

5. Ibid., 204.

6. Ibid., 84, 78, 136, 176, 260.

7. Ibid., 142 (shamans' loss of preternatural powers); 144 (Cross ousts Satan); 178 (dragons to be slain).

8. Digo que vimos la infelice tierra
Del malvado cacique Canetabo,
Que si crueldad, que si maldad se encierra
En el reino infernal de cabo a cabo,
La suma, el colmo della en paz y guerra
Se vió en aqueste sólo por el cabo,
Horrenda catadura, monstruosa,
Ronca la voz, bravísima, spantosa.

> Dorantes de Carranza, 145.

9. La cara negra y colorada a vetas,
Gruesísimo xipate por extremo,
Difícil peso para dos carretas,
Debió ser su figura Polifemo;
De tizne y sangre entrambas manos prietas,
Bisojo que aun soñarlo agora temo;
Los dientes y la boca como grana,
Corriendo siempre della sangre humana.

> Dorantes de Carranza, 145.

10. Con Tosco pedernal en él golpea,
sacole el corazon vivo del pecho
y ofrenda a los demonios del ha hecho . . .
¿Qué demonio podrá ser que reciba
tu noble corazón dado en presente?
Mala quitarán ministros del infierno
El sacrificio hecho a Dios eterno

> Dorantes de Carranza, 146.

11. Cruel Neptuno, dice [Cortés], a quien es dado
destos salados reinos el gobierno,
que hoy contra esta flota te has aunado
con furiosas quadrillas del infierno,
en vano ha de salir lo concertado,
que el Dios de las alturas sempiterno

> quiere a despecho de tus crueles manos
> dar ayuda y favor a sus xpianos.
>
> Dorantes de Carranza, 176.

12. Que de mil y trecientos españoles
que al cerco de tus muros se hallaron,
y matizando claros arreboles
tus oscuras tinieblas alumbraron,
quando con resplandor de claros soles
del poder de satán te libertaron,
contando hijos, nietos y parientes
no quedan hoy trescientos descendientes.

> Dorantes de Carranza, 21.

13. That *Mexicana* was meant to make critics forget his earlier *Cortés valeroso* is the argument of Jerónimo Ramírez's prologue to *Mexicana*; see Lasso de la Vega, 9–10.

14. ¡Sienta tu furia, y la violencia sienta,
del levantado mar ciego, confuso!
Y no permitas que la Cruz sangrienta,
Do el Nazareno sus espaldas puso,
La vea el Indio, ni sembrar consienta
Tu poder cuanto el mío descompuso:
Sus naos esconde en tu profundo centro,
Que este Dios y sus leyes llevan dentro.

> Lasso de la Vega, 1.41 (p. 18) (references are to canto and stanza).

For Cortés as "general de Cristo," see 5.21 (p. 42).

15. On the new tempest off Tabasco and the archangel Michael's providential help, 5.1–29 (pp. 40–42); on the help received by the Spaniards from St. James in a crucial battle against the cacique of Tabasco, 12.1–14, 52–54 (pp. 89–90, 94); on the visions and help received by the ruler of Tabasco, 5.49–62 (pp. 44–45); 6.56–59 (p. 52). On Satan vs. St. Michael in the battles of Tlaxcala, see Lasso de la Vega, cantos 16 and 17 passim.

16. See, e.g., Lasso de la Vega's account of the consumption of five Spanish captives by cannibals in Yucatan and the rescue of the sole survivor, Jerónimo de Aguilar, 3.43–44 (p. 31). See also 4.17 (p. 34); 6.55 (p. 52); 15.26–28 (p. 117); and 22.31–35 (p. 172).

17. Lasso de la Vega, 15.22–63 (pp. 117–20).

18. Lasso de la Vega, canto 21, passim.

19. My description of Saavedra y Guzmán comes from his epic *El peregrino indiano*: self-taught astronomer, 306; *corregidor*, 307; his wife, the grand-niece of Pedro de Alvarado, 393; Creole patriotism, 393–94.

20. Ibid., natives as cannibals, 124, 269, 305, 357, 374, 483, 506; substitution of the cross for the devil, 209, 210, 289, 292, 325, 327, 335–36, 415; conquest as an act of liberation from Satan's tyranny, 256, 336.

21. Ibid., 161, 163, 177, 279, 297.

22. Ibid., 163, 265, 281, 336, 436.

23. Ibid., 281, 305, 436, 483, 506.

24. Como el malvado Lucifer se vido
Del sacro impireo Cielo desterrado,
Y al piélago profundo sumergido,
Por sola su soberbia derribado:
Siempre desde aquel punto ha pretendido
Poblar su reyno, y miserable estado,
Envidioso del Cielo, y su grandeza,
Ensalzando su mísera baxeza.
Luego que conoció el divino fruto,
Que la pujante armada prometía,
Con libertar las almas del tributo,
Que el príncipe malvado posseía:
Por no perder el mísero estatuto
De aquel obscuro Reyno y monarquía,
Convocó sus legiones y potencia,
Para que le hiciesen resistencia.
Movió a los poderosos quatro vientos,
Que unánimes viniesse conjurados . . .
De suerte que la flota sumergida
Desecha fuesse, y del gran mar sorbida.

     Ibid., 94–95.

25. Ibid., 101.

26. Ibid., 274–81.

27. See, e.g., the dedication to Philip III, in which the king's role is presented as providential, promoting the expansion of the Catholic faith against the kingdom of the devil: "para ensalzamiento de Nuestra Fé catholica, y extirpación de los graves errores, y vil idolatría, que el demonio nuestro capital enemigo, siembra y derrama, por estas y otras Regiones." Pérez de Villagrá, *Historia*, "Al rey nuestro señor" (n.p.).

28. See ibid., 15v–21v (canto 4).
The following verse is typical of Pérez de Villagrá's sensibilities:

Sóla una terrible falta hallo,
Christianissimo Rey en vuestras Indias,
Y es que estan muy pobladas, y ocupadas,
De gente vil, manchada, y sospechasa.

    (I find only one fault, O most Christian of kings, with your Indies. And it is that they are populated and occupied by vile people, stained and suspect.)

    Ibid., 20v.

29. See ibid., 3* r–v ("canción pindárica" by L. Trib. de Toledo). Toledo presents Oña as nephew of the governor of New Galicia, Christobal de Oña, relative of Moctezuma. See also 27r (canto 6).

30. Marchando así estos pobres reprobados
Delante se les puso aquel maldito [demonio],

En figura de vieja rebozado,
Cuya espantosa y gran desemboltura,
Daba pavor y miedo imaginarla . . .
Desmesurados pechos, largas tetas,
Hambrientas, flacas, secas y fruncidas . . .
Sumidos ojos de color de fuego,
Disforme boca desde oreja a oreja
Por cuyos labios secos desmedidos,
Quatro solos colmillos hazia fuera.

Ibid., 4v, 5r.

31. Ibid., 4v–6v, on Satan's appearance; 7r, on the exorcism of the mound.
32. Ibid., 19v–20r.
33. Quint, 131–85.
34. Nicolopulos. Seeking to resolve the historiographical tension between those who read *La Araucana* as an epic of the defeated and those who see it as bolstering an imperial agenda, Craig Kallendorf offers a very provocative reading of the poem in the light of recent scholarship on Virgil's *Aeneid*. Kallendorf argues that Ercilla, like Virgil, saw *furia* as the key vice separating the barbarian from the civilized. For all their praise of the Italians and the Araucans, Virgil and Ercilla, respectively, present the enemies of the Trojans and the Spaniards as unable to control their passions, always overtaken by fury. Although at times the Trojans and the Spaniards submit to fury, the true heroes of the *Aeneid* and *La Araucana* live according to *pietas*, the virtue opposite to *furia*. As a Virgilian text, *La Araucana* is indeed an imperial poem. See Kallendorf.
35. Ercilla: cannibal scenes in which Amerindians dismember bodies or chew off bodily parts during battle, 46, 57, 89, 95, 100, 135, 247, 312, 315, 369; diabolical fury, 43, 47, 68, 315, 324, 391, 417; satanic Amerindians and communication with Satan/ Eponamón, 22, 117–18, 121, 124–25, 159, 200; Araucanian demonic self-consciousness determined to take Spaniards to hell, 114, 115, 175; souls of dead Amerindians go to hell, 200, 204; Tucapel as the embodiment of Lucifer, 134, 118, 119, 156, 276, 282, 310, 356, 403, 406, 409; demonically induced storms, 124–25, 218–22, 229; Fitón's cave as hell, 325–26; foundational covenant with Satan, 21–22.
36. Gente es sin Dios ni ley, aunque respeta
aquel que fue del cielo derribado,
que como a poderoso y gran profeta
es siempre en sus cantares celebrado:
invocan su favor con falsa seta
y a todos sus negocios es llamado,
teniendo cuanto dice por seguro
del próspero suceso o mal futuro.

    Y cuanto quieren dar una batalla
con él lo comunican en su rito:
si no responde bien, dejan de dalla
aunque más les insista el apetito;
caso grave y negocio no se halla
do no sea convocado este maldito;

llámanle Eponamón, y comúnmente
Dan este nombre alguno si es valiente.
> Ercilla, 21–22.

37. en esto Eponamón se les presenta
en forma de un dragón horrible y fiero
con enroscada cola envuelta en fuego
y en ronca y torpe voz les habló luego
diciéndoles que apriesa caminasen
sobre el pueblo español amedrentado.
> Ercilla, 124–25.

38. Besides *La Araucana*, I have identified the following epic poems describing the Chilean frontier wars: Pedro de Oña, *Arauco domado* (Lima: Antonio Ricardo de Turin, 1596); Diego Arias de Saavedra, *Purén indómito* (1605–17), ed. Mario Ferreccio Podestá and Mario Rodríguez Fernández (Concepción: Biblioteca Nacional/Universidad de Concepción, 1984); Fernándo Alvarez de Toledo, *Araucana II*, which has survived in excerpts in Alonso de Ovalle, *Histórica relación del reino de Chile* (Rome, 1646); Diego de Santiestevan Osorio, *Quarta, y quinta parte de la Araucana* (Salamanca: Juan y Andrés Renaut, 1597); Lope de Vega, *La Araucana*, in *Dos obras de Lope de Vega con tema americano* (Auburn, Ala.: Auburn University, 1968); Lope de Vega, *El arauco domado* (1625), in *Parte veinte de las comedias de Lope de Vega Carpio:Procurador Fiscal de la Cámara Apostólica. Dividida en dos partes* (Madrid: Viuda de Alonso Martín, 1625); Melchor Jufré del Aguila, *Compendio historial del descubrimiento del reino de Chile* (Lima, 1630; Santiago: Imprenta Cervantes, 1897); Juan de Mendoza Monteagudo, *Las Guerras de Chile: Poema histórico* (1660) (Santiago: Imprenta Ercilla, 1888).

39. Quando la tierra estava ya de suerte,
Que no dava lugar al baptizado
A donde estar un punto asegurado
Dela espantosa imagen de la muerte
Prostrado ya su muro, y casa suerte . . .
Alzando al cielo, llamas del infierno
> Oña, 5v.

40. Por la caliente sangre que vertemos
Con que el sulcado rostro rociamos,
Y por la que a vosotros consagramos
Después que asi espumosa la bevemos,
Y por la humana carne que comemos,
Humildes todos juntos suplicamos
> Ibid., 29r.

41. O falso Eponamón allá con otros
Que tengan de tus artes menos ciencia;
No pienses con tus frívolas razones
Obstupecer tan bravos corazones
> Ibid., 31v.

42. On the tempests as caused by demons, see Oña 46r, 50v, 53r, 66rv.

43. Tucapel as Satan, Oña, 87v; souls to hell, 130; warriors possessed, 75r; cannibalism, 26v, 29r.

44. Zuázola.

45. Barco Centenera.

46. On the atrribution of the poem, see Gil, who supplies an annotated translation of the poem (pp. 240–51). The poem was first published as an appendix to F. Pinel y Monroy, *Retrato del buen vasallo, copiado de la vida y hechos de D. Andrés de Cabrera, primer marqués de Moya* (Madrid, 1677). For Columbus as Christumferens, see Isabelle's discourse prompting Columbus to take to the sea to defeat Satan and to fulfill the symbolism of his name: "Perge modo exultans atque omina nominis imple, tecum forte gerens Christum veramque salutem" (lines 131–32).

47. On the complex, morally ambiguous meaning of classical deities, see Lefkowitz.

48. Gambara; Stella. On Stella's and Gambara's poem, Gil.

49. Quirós. On Quirós, see Pimentel. *Testigos*, ch.2.

50. "Quis potis est dignum pollenti pectore /Carmen condere pro rerum maiestate, hisque repertis?" (Who is able with powerful breast to produce a poem worthy of the majesty of the subject and of these things that have been discovered?)

51. "Christophorus Columbus Ligur terroribus Oceani superatis alterius paene Orbis regiones a se inventas Hispanis regibus addixit."

52. "Americus Vespuccius Florentinus portentosa navigatione ad Occasum atque ad Austrum duas Orbis terrarum partes, nostris oris quas incolimus maiores, et nullis antea nobis notas saeculis, aperuit. Quarum alteram de suo nomine Americam mortalium consensus nominavit."

53. For an interpretation of the bird in this engraving, see Wittkower.

54. "Ferdinandes Magalanes Lusitanus anfractuoso euripo superato, & telluri ad Austrum nomen dedit, eiusque navis omnium prima atque novissima Solis cursum in terras aemulata, terrae totius globum circumiit." (Ferdinand Magellan of Portugal gave his name to the winding channel he'd conquered and the land to the south, and his ship, the first and last of all, emulating the Sun's course over the lands, circled the globe of the whole earth.)

55. On Columbus's "Christum-ferens" signature and self-aggrandizing millenarian dreams, see Watts. Las Casas, *Historia*, 1: 359 (bk. 1, ch. 2) (on Columbus as "Christum-ferens"). Las Casas interpreted Columbus's failure to obtain patronage in European courts for six years as acts orchestrated by the devil: "porque contra los negocios más aceptos a Dios y que más provechosos son a su sancta Iglesia, mayores fuerzas pone para los impedir todo el exército de los infiernos, cognosciendo que poco tiempo le queda ya como se escribe en el Apocalipsis" (*Historia*, 1: 507 [bk. 1, ch. 29]). Las Casas also interpreted the ordeals of Columbus's first Atlantic crossing as demonic traps providentially designed to test the hero; see *Historia*, 1: 536 (bk. 1, ch. 37).

56. Eden, a, iiii, r.

57. Redworth. Redworth misses the chance of studying the impact of the arrival of Philip I and his Spanish courtiers had in the chivalric culture of England. Redworth argues (rather unpersuasively, I might add, given the shallowness of the evidence offered) that the Spaniards when they first arrived in England were in-

capable of distinguishing fact from fiction. Philip II, Redworth rather fantastically maintains, decided to land in Bristol because Amadis himself had landed there. According to Redworth, reality finally sets in and the Spanish courtiers decide to go back home because none could find a beautiful Oriana, Amadis's paramour, in England. This type of argument is typical of studies of early modern Iberian chivalry that condescendingly trivialize the genre. McCoy introduces evidence that points to important Anglo-Iberian chivalric dialogues during Philip's regency; see esp. ch. 2.

58. This account of Drake's careers is based on Cummins.

59. On Spanish views of Drake as Satan's wizard but also as a satanic hero, see Cummins, 176, 258–73; Fuchs, 139–51; Vega Carpio. The quotation comes from the "Dedicatory" by J. Philips to Oliver Cromwell in *Tears of the Indians*, a 1656 translation of Las Casas's *Brevísima Relación*. Philips calls on Cromwell, of "earthly fame" equal to that of the "holy Warrior David," to be inspired both by the "prowess" with which Joshua led "his Armies forth to Battel" and by the zeal of Jehu, "to cut off the [Spanish] Idolater from the earth," quoting Scripture in support: "Therefore thine eye shall have no compassion; but life for life, tooth for tooth, hand for hand, foot for foot" (Deut. 9:1).

60. Fletcher, 53.

61. Peele, 5, 6.

62. On English views of Drake, see Cummins, 273–306. There were numerous other poems written to honor Drake, most of which circulated as manuscripts, including: T. N. Cistrensis, "In laudem Francisci Drake militis" (British Library Egerton MS 2642); William Gager, "In laudem fortissimo viri D. Francisci Draconis" (British Library, Additional MS 22583); N. Eleutherius, "Fortunate Draco," in *Trivmphalia de victoriis Elisabethae Anglorvm, Francorvm, Hybernorvmqve reginae avgvstissimae, fidei defensoris acerrimae, contra classem instrvctissimam Philippi Hispaniarvm regis potentissimi, Deo opt. max. fortvnante felicissime partis, anno Christi nati 1588 Jvlio et Avgvsto* (Germany, 1588); Joannes Hercusanus Danus, *Magnifico ac strenuo viro D. Francisco Draco Anglo Equiti aurato* (London: Excudebat Ioannes Charlewood pro Roberto Wallie, 1587); Henry Robarts, *A most friendly farewell giuen by a welwiller to the right worshipful Sir Frauncis Drake Knight, Generall of her Maiesties nauy, which he appointed for this his honorable voiage, and the rest of the fleete bound to the southward, and to all the gentlemen his followers, and captaines in this exploite, who set sale from Wolwich the xv. day of Iuly, 1585. Wherin is briefely touched his perils passed in his last daungerous voiage, with an incouragement to all his saylers and souldiers, to be forward in this honourable exploite* (London: [T. East for] Walter Mantell & Thomas Lawe, 1585); Thomas Greepe, *True and perfecte Newes of the worthy and valiaunt exploytes performed and done by that valiant Knight Syr Frauncis Drake* (London: John Charlewood, for Thomas Hackett, 1589); and Henry Robarts, *The Trumpet of Fame, or Sir Francis Drakes and Sir John Hawkins Farewell* (London: Thomas Creede, 1595).

63. Chapman, *De Guiana*, Av–A4r.

64. But where the sea in envie of your raigne,
   Closeh her wombe, as fast as this disclosde,
   That she like Avarice might swallowe all,
   And let none find right passage through her rage:

There your wise soules as swift as Eurus lead
Your bodies through, to profit and renowne (ibid., A3r).

65. Chapman, Johnson, and Marston, act 3, sc. 3, line 15 (p. 137).

66. Kemys, F2v.

67. Hakluyt, "Epistle Dedicatory to Sir Walter Raleigh, 1587," in id., *Original Writings and Correspondance*, ed. Taylor, 2: 360 (English trans., p. 367): "a tue Virginiae suavissimis amplexib[us], qua[m] nympha[m] pulcherrima[m] licet, nondum satis plerisq[ue]; bene cognita, munificentissima Regina in sponsam tibi dedit, nullis terroribus, iacturis, infortuniis, posse aut unquam velle amoveri. Hac si constantia paulisper modo usus fueris, novos eosque foecundissimos partus brevi emittet sponsa tua." Hakluyt casts Raleigh as a patron whose efforts in exploration are tantamount to creating a new crew of Argonauts to rival the deeds of the Spaniards and to open gates of the sea locked for millennia. Hakluyt also recommends that Raleigh model himself on Cortés and looks forward to an English Homer singing the praises of the hero Raleigh.

68. Purchas, 19: 242. On these metaphors, more typical of English than of Iberian chivalric-epic discourses on colonization, see Montrose, "Shaping Fantasies" and "Work of Gender."

69. For Totnes's translation of Ercilla, see his *Historie of Araucana*.

70. "Heere follow the names of those worthie Spaniardes that have sought to discover and conquere Guiana, extracted out of the writings of Juan de Castellanos clerigo" (Kemys, appendix, n.p.).

71. On chivalry as a functional early modern institution rather than an anachronism, see Maurice Keen, ch. 13; McCoy; Alex Davis.

72. Leonard, *Books of the Brave*. Among the dozens of studies within this tradition, see Armas Wilson; Rodríguez Prampolini; Alvar; Gilman. On Spanish books of chivalry, see the wonderful collection of essays by Eisenberg.

73. Hakluyt, "Epistle Dedicatory to Sir Walter Raleigh, 1587," in id., *Original Writings and Correspondance*, ed. Taylor, 2: 369–70. See also Hutson; Ramsay. On Elizabethan chivalry as ceremonies to assert aristocratic rights over, rather than rituals of devotion to, the queen, see McCoy. See also Alex Davis.

74. Richard Helgerson maintains that Hakluyt's collection of travel accounts represented a turn in English colonialism away from aristocratic ideals and an embrace of mercantilist ones. Given Hakluyt's constant marshaling of the epic and the chivalric to describe English colonialism, the shift was protracted and convoluted. The pirate in English sources reflected the contradictory attitudes of the English toward commerce, for pirates like Drake were imagined as conquistadors of the sea, epic heroes harassing the Spanish Antichrist, getting honor and riches through plunder, not commerce. On the contradictory figure of the pirate, see Fuchs, ch. 5.

75. Gray, A3v.

76. R. A. Williams, 182.

77. Robert Johnson, C2r–v.

78. Hayes, 680, 696.

79. Waterhouse, 24.

80. Karen Ordhal Kupperman, "Introduction," in Smith, *Captain John Smith*, esp. 20–23.

81. In a tomb on the south side of the Choir of the Church of St. Sepulcher in London, the family and friends of Smith remembered him with the following inscription honoring his crusading and chivalric deeds:

> To the living Memory of his
> deceased Friend, Captaine John
> Smith, who departed this mortall
> life on the 21 day of June, 1631,
> with his Armes, and this Motto,
> *Accordamus, vincere est vivere.*
> Here lies one conquer'd
> that hath conquer'd Kings,
> Subdu'd large Territories,
> and done things
> Which to the World
> impossible would seeme,
> But that the truth
> is held in more esteeme,
> Shall I report
> His former service done
> In honour of his God
> and Christendome:
> How that he did
> divide from Pagans three,
> Their heads and Lives,
> types of his chivalry:
> For which great service
> in that Climate done,
> Brave Sigismundus
> (King of Hungarion)
> Did give him as a Coat
> of Armes to weare,
> Those conquer'd heads
> got by his Sword and Speare?
> Or shall I tell
> of his adventures since,
> Done in Virginia,
> that large Continence:
> How that he subdu'd
> Kings unto his yoke,
> And made those heathen flie,
> as wind doth smoke:
> And made their Land,
> being of so large a Station,
> A habitation
> for our Christian Nation:
> Where God is glorifi'd,

their wants suppli'd,
Which else for necessaries
might have di'd?
But what avails
his Conquest now he lyes
Inter'd in earth
a prey for Wormes & Flies?
O may his soule
in sweet Elysium sleepe,
Untill the Keeper
that all soules doth keepe,
Returne to judgement
and that after thence,
With Angels he may have
his recompence.
Captaine John Smith, sometime Gover-
nour of Virginia, and Admirall
of New England.

> John Stow, *The survey of London: contayning the originall, increase, moderne estate, and government of that city, methodically set downe* (London: Nicolas Bourn, 1633), 779–80.

82. Kupperman, "Introduction," in Smith, *Captain John Smith*, 12.

83. Smith, *Captain John Smith*, 58, 62. This selection in Kupperman's edition corresponds to Smith's *The Generall Historie of Virginia, New England, and the Summer Isles* (1624) in *The Complete Works of Captain John Smith* (1580–1631), ed. Philip L. Barbour, 2: 162–80.

84. Smith, *Captain John Smith*, 63.

85. Ibid., 64.

86. Ibid., 65.

87. Lake.

88. John White, 10.

89. Ibid., 28.

90. Ibid., 39.

91. Ibid., 15 and 39.

92. Tompson, *Sad and Deplorable Newes from New England*, 8.

93. Tompson, *New-Englands tears*, 2–3.

94. Tompson, *Sad and Deplorable Newes from New England*, 15–16.

95. Ibid., 7.

96. Cotton Mather, *Magnalia Christi*, 1: 18.

97. Ibid., 1: 41: "if the *wicked one in whom the whole world lyeth*, were *he*, who like *a dragon*, keeping guard upon the spacious and mighty *orchards* of America, could have such as *fascination* upon the thoughts of mankind, that neither this *balancing half* of the globe should be considered in *Europe*, till a little more than two hundred years ago, nor the *clue* that might lead unto it, namely the *Loadstone*, should be known . . . the devil seducing the first inhabitants of America into it, there in aimed at the having of them out of the sound of the silver trumpets of the Gospel."

98. Ibid., 1: 52: "upon the arrival of the English . . . the Indians employed their sorcerers, whom they call powaws, like Balaam, to curse them and let loose their demons upon them, to shipwreck them, to distract them, to poison them, or any way to ruin them. All the noted powwows in the country spent three days together in diabolical conjurations to obtain the assistance of the devils against the settlement of these our English; but the devils at length acknowledged unto them, that they could not hinder those people from their becoming the owners and masters of the country." Mather contradicts himself a few pages later in chapter 4, however, when he notes how difficult it became for the first colonists to spread their plantations. Colonists were killed and failed repeatedly, so "they began to suspect that Indian sorcerers had laid the place under some fascination; and that the English could not prosper upon such enchanted ground" (ibid., 1: 62).

99. Ibid., 1: 152

100. Ibid., 1: 193.

101. Thunder his musick, sweter than the spheres,
    Chim'd roaring canons in his martial ears.
    Frigats of armed men could not withstand,
    "Twas tried, the force of his one swordless hand:
    Hand, which in one, all the briareus had,
    And Hercules's twelve toils but pleasure made."

        Ibid., 1: 208.

102. Ibid., 2: 440: "the church of God had not long been in the this wilderness before the dragon cast forth several floods to devour it; but not the leas of those floods was one of the Antinomian and familistical heresies."

103. In his "New England Epic," Sacvan Bercovitch has offered a reading of Mather's *Magnalia Christi Americana* as a satanic epic. In keeping with his interest in deconstructing the providential messianic nature of U.S. national identity first manifested in the discourse of the "City upon the Hill," Bercovitch emphasizes the eschatological aspects of Mather's work. The *Magnalia* is an epic in which, after a harrowing oceanic crossing, the Puritan heroes confront the wilderness and transform it into a well-kept plantation (including a garden-university), Bercovitch argues. Yet the perils for the heroes increase as the onset of the millennium draws near.

104. Calvete de Estrella, 45, 53 (storms); 63, 155 (natives and landscapes as demonic).

105. Calvete de Estrella, 57, 81, 87, 99, 115, 121, 125, 143.

106. Inca Garcilaso de la Vega, *Historia general*, dedication (n.p.): "con hazañas proesas más grandiosas y heroicas que las de Alezandros de Grecia y Césares de Roma."

107. Ibid.: "las insignes batallas y victorias de los heroicos Españoles, verdaderos Alcides y Cristianos Achiles."

108. Ibid.: "por salir con favor del cielo vencedores del demonio pecado e infierno."

109. Inca Garcilaso de la Vega, *La Florida*, bk. 2, ch. 20, folio 68r.: "ningunas de los más bravos caballeros, que el divino Ariosto, y el illustrísimo y muy enamorado Conde Mattheo María Boyardo su antecessor, y otros claros Poetas introduzen en sus obras, ygualarán con las deste Indio."

110. Ibid., ch. 21, folio 68v: "Si vosotros fuerades hombres de buen juyzio, vi-erades que su misma vida y obras muestran ser hijos del Diablo, y no del Sol y Luna nuestros dioses, pues andan de tierra en tierra matando, robando, y saqueando quanto hallan, tomando mugeres y hijas agenas."

111. Brading, *First America*, 61.

112. Quoted in ibid., 65, 74.

113. Las Casas, *Historia*, 2: 1467 (bk. 2, ch. 43): "y creo que sobre todas las del mundo, en mansedumbre, simplicidad, humildad, paz y quietud y en otras virtudes naturales, señaladas; que no parecía sino que Adán no había en ellas pecado." See also ibid., 1: 553 (bk. 1, ch. 40).

114. Ibid., 2: 928 (bk. 1, ch. 104): "Esta invención comenzó aquí, e cogitada, in-ventada, y rodeada por el Diablo . . . como otras exquisitas invenciones, gravísimas y dañosísimas a la mayor parte del linaje humano, que aquí comenzaron y pasaron y cundieron adelante para total destrucción de estas naciones."

115. Ibid., 2: 1286 (bk. 2, ch. 1): "todos han bebido su sangre y comido de sus carnes."

116. Ibid., 2: 1160 (bk. 1, ch. 160): "eran de todos los indios, por temor vio-lentísimo, adorados; y como de los demonios, delante dellos temblaban."

117. Quiroga, 98: "halleme tan hombre cuando vi en castilla que luego dije que aquellas tierras criaban hombres, y estas nuestras crian animales irracionales en forma de hombres."

118. Ibid., 84: "todo lo que uno osa pensar todo lo osa hablar y aun hacer atrev-imiento que compite con el del infierno."

119. Ibid., 144: "Espántanse en castilla cuando llegáis de acá cargados de oro y riquezas, y no ven también que vais cargados de pieles de indios como rocines de carnicería y tintos en la sangre de los que por vuestra causa y por vuestra riqueza han perecido."

120. Ibid., 81: "Cierto esta tierra adelgaza los juicios, altera los ánimos, daña y corrompe las buenas costumbres y engendra diferentes condiciones y hace en los hombres otros efectos contrarios de los que primero tenían. Y no solamente en los cuerpos humanos, pero aun en los animales y plantas causa esta tierra mutabilidad de bueno en malo."

121. Dorantes de Carranza, 113. "¡Oh Indias! vuelvo a decir: confusión de tropiezos, alcahuete de araganes, carta executoria de los que os habitan; banco donde todos quiebran, depósito de mentiras y engaños; hinchazón de necios, burdel de los buenos, locura de los cuerdos, fin y remate de la nobleza, destrucción de la virtud, confusión de los sabios y discretos; devaneo y fantasía de los simples y que no conocen."

122. Sánchez, *Imagen de la Virgen*, 174–76.

123. Bauckham; Knapp, 41–44, 65–70.

124. The literature on Our Lady of Guadalupe is immense; I have relied on the well-known works of Brading, *Mexican Phoenix*; Maza; Lafaye; Poole.

125. Warner, chs. 16 and 17; Stratton.

126. Sánchez, *Imagen de la Virgen*.

127. Perry Miller; Bercovitch, *American Jeremiad*.

128. See Smolinski; Bozeman.

129. Evans. Evans takes issue with Quint (*Epic and Empire*), who sees *Paradise Lost* as an anti-imperial epic, a critique of European colonialism in the New World.

130. On Milton's *Paradise Lost* as a satanic epic in which the devil is the main hero, see Forsyth. This is a most stimulating book, from which I have borrowed the title of this chapter. Unsurprisingly, however, it completely ignores the early modern Iberian epic traditions described here.

131. English-speaking scholars tend to put Milton's epic within the context of classical and Renaissance Italian traditions without much awareness that the latter tradition was also indebted to Iberian models, as I have proven above. Not surprisingly, no one has read Milton in the context of Iberian colonial epics. On Milton's classical and Renaissance models, see Blessington; Martindale; Quint.

132. Schmidt.

Chapter 3. The Structure of a Shared Demonological Discourse

1. Olmos, 7: "hacen todo lo que pueden para apoderarse, para hacerse dueños de alguien, para mofarse de él, para gobernarlo, para someterlo para agarrarlo con lazos, en un agujero, en una cuerda."

2. Cotton Mather, *Batteries*, 9–10; emphasis in original.

3. Ibid., 36.

4. Hayes, 680.

5. Tynley, K2r.

6. Copland, 28.

7. Purchas, 19: 231.

8. John White, 22.

9. Eliot, 202.

10. Sewall, 51–52.

11. Bynum, *Resurrection of the Body*.

12. Valadés, 172: "Ille [the Christian God], inquam, sicut nos fecit libere . . . , ut illi sponte nostra libere candideque serviamus, non ea servitute qua vosmet Diabolo subiecti estis qui a vobis exigit omnia ultra citraque rationis fines videlicet, immolationem vestrorum natorum, possessiones, corporis deformationes, & sanguinis profusionem, sicut, omnibus horis inter vos accidit." (I say that just as He made us freely . . . so that we might freely and openly serve him of our own accord—not with that servitude with which you have been subjected to the Devil, who demands of you everything that is beyond and outside the bounds of reason—to wit, the immolation of your children, the [destruction?] of your possessions, the disfigurement of your bodies, and the spilling of your blood, just as happens to you at all hours.)

13. Ibid.: "Eius itaque auctoritate ad vos accessimus . . . instigatione, quo vestrum intellectum radiis divini luminis illustraremus, vestros animos corporaque gravissima subiectione qua opprimebantur liberaremus. Et si enim servitus hominum sit molestissima, intollerabilior tamen est illa, qua vos Diabolus humani generis inimicus devinctos atque adstrictos habet. Venimus itaque ad vos, in vitam novam & libertatem asserendos." (And so we have approached you under his authority and at his prompting, so that we might enlighten your minds with the rays of divine light

and free your souls and bodies from the very heavy subjection by which they were oppressed. For if servitude to men is burdensome, much more intolerable still is that in which the Devil, the enemy of the human race, holds you bound and held fast. So we have come to you in order to free you to new life and liberty.)

14. On cannibalism and colonialism, particularly, but not exclusively, in the early modern New World context, see Lestringant; Hulme; Barker, Hulme, and Iversen.

15. Francisco Angelorum, "Orders Given to 'the Twelve' [1523]," in Mills and Taylor, 64.

16. Olmos, ch. 9, 69: "gentes del pueblo eran asi sacrificadas ante los diablos y colgaban y sangraban como esta escrito. A causa de él, del Diablo, a veces se recuerda que hubo espantosos sacrificios sangrientos, efusiones de sangre, crímenes; mucha sangre se esparcía así en su morada, en México, y por todas partes se hacía cuando llegaron los hombres de Castilla. Juntos comían carne de hombres, la comían delante de la gente."

17. Cieza de León, 1: 25 (ch. 15), 1: 30 (ch. 19); 1: 39 (ch. 26); 1: 40 (ch. 38).

18. Pérez de Ribas, Prólogo, ¶¶ 2: "Peleando y reduciendo gentes al Christianismo mas indómitas que los Leones y ossos que desquixararon David y Sansón. . . . Con los que eran fieros e inhumanos quedaron trocados en mansas ovejas de su rebaño."

19. Ibid., bk. 1, ch. 3, p. 9: "La cabezza o cabellera del enemigo muerto, u otro miembro, como pie o brazo, se ponía en una hasta en medio de la plaza y en rededor se hazía el baile, acompañado de algazara Bárbara, y baldones al enemigo muerto, y cantares que referían la vitoria: de suerte que todo estava manifestando un infierno, con cáfilas de demonios, que son los que governavan esta gentes."

20. Ibid., bk. 2, ch. 7, p. 49: "Pero mientras más iva creciendo esta primitiva Iglesia . . . tanto más crecía la rabia y sentimiento del demonio, enemigo capital del género humano que se veía despojar de almas que tenía tiranizadas y en pacífica possessión de tantos años . . . [niños bautizados] ya no entravan en sus cavernas infernales sino ivan al cielo. . . . Entendiendo pues que si no atajava el curso que llevava el Evangelio presto se vería despojado de todas quantas avía en Sinaloa y que el que principalmente le hazía la guerra como capitán de la conquista era el Padre Gonzalo de Tapia, assestó todos sus tiros a él."

21. Ibid., ch. 8, p. 52: "la pretensión del demonio y su quadrilla era desterrar de Cinaloa la predicación de la santa Cruz y del que murió en ella . . . Pero finalmente no saldrían con su intento sino quedaría triunfante la Cruz de Christo." A year before Pérez de Ribas's *Historia* appeared, Tapia's martyrdom was reported by the Jesuit Nieremberg, who gives details not found in Pérez de Ribas. According to Nieremberg, Nacabeba sought to throw Tapia's head into the fire but the head repeatedly put out the flames. Nacabeba also gave Tapia's torso to the dogs, only to see them explode. See Nieremberg. *Firmamento religioso*, 544–48.

22. A raagged regiment, a naked swarm,
    Whom hopes of boty doth with courage arm,
    Set forth with bloody hearts, the first they meet
    Of men or beasts, they butcher at their feet
    They round our skirts, they pare, they fleece, they kill.
        Tompson, *Sad and Deplorable Newes*, 8

23. If Painter ever track my Pen, let him
    An Olive colour mix, these Elves to trim;
    Of such an hue, let many hundred Thieves
    Be drawn like Scarecrows clad with Oaken leaves,
    Exhausted of their Verdant Life and blown
    From place to place without home to own:
    Draw devils like themselves, upon their cheeks
    Those Banks of Grease and Mud a plat for Leeks;
    Whose dangling Locks Medusa's Snakes resemble,
    With grizly looks would make Achilles tremble
    Limn them besmear'd with Christian blood, and oyl'd
    With fat out of white humane Bodies byld.
    Draw them with Clubs like Mauls, all full of stains;
    Like Vulcan's anvelling New Englands brains:
    Let round be gloomy Forrests and thick Rocks;
    Where like to castles they may hide their Flocks:
    Till opportunity their constant friend
    Shall jogge them Vulcan's Worship to attend
    Show them like Serpents in an avious path,
    Waiting to show the Fire-balls of their wrath.

        Tompson, *New-Englands Tears*, 2–3.

24. From martyr'd towns the Heav'ns for aid invoke;
    Churches, barns, Houses, with most pond'rous things
    Made volatile, flie o're the Land with wings.
    Hundreds of Cattel now they sacrifice
    For aiery spirits up to gormandize [to devour];
    And to the Moleth [one who works in darkness] of their Hellish guts
    Which craves the flesh in gross, their Ale in Butts.
    Lancaster, Mendon, Medfield, wildred Groton,
    With many Villages by me not thought on,
    Dy in their youth by Fire that useful foe,
    Which this grand Cheat the world will overflow.

        Tompson, *Sad and Deplorable Newes*, 15–16.

25. And here, methinks, I see this greasy Lout
    With all his pagan slaves coil'd round about,
    Assuming all the Majesty his throne
    Of rotten stump, or of the rugged stone
    Could yield; casting some bacon-rine-like looks,
    Enough to fright a Student from his books,
    Thus treat his peers, and next to them his commons,
    Kennel'd together all without summons.

        Ibid., 7.

26. Edward Johnson, 100 (ch. 62). On the controversy over the monsters delivered by Hutchinson and Dyer, see Schutte.

27. Cotton Mather, *Bateries*, 46.

28. Mede, *Works*, epistle 43 ("Mr. Mede's answer to Dr. Twisse his fourth letter touching the first Gentile Inhabitants and the late Christian Plantations in America," Cambridge, March 23, 1634/35), bk. 4, p. 800.

29. On the Puritan debate over Mede's demonological theories of American exceptionalism, see Canup, 73–79; Smolinski; and Scheiding.

30. Mede, *Key of the Revelation*. See especially the appendix "Conjecture Concerning Gog and Magog," where Mede argues that Rev. 20:7–9 ("And when the thousand years are expired, Satan shall be loosed out of his prison, And shall go out to deceive the nations which are in the four quarters of the earth, Gog and Magog, to gather them together to battle: the number of whom is as the sand of the sea. And they went up on the breadth of the earth, and compassed the camp of the saints about, and the beloved city: and fire came down from God out of heaven, and devoured them") refers to the American origins of the satanic army: "this army shall come from those nations, which live in the Hemisphere opposite to us, whom the Best and most Great God in his secret judgment, for the most part shall not cherish with the light of his Gospel" (Tr). Mede thought that the reference to armies "going up" referred to the antipodes, where the ancients had "placed the seat of Hel" (Tv). The reference to "compassed the camp of the saints and the beloved city" was also an indication that these armies would attack Eurasia (the seat of the New Jerusalem) from the seas, both the Pacific and the Atlantic oceans. Clearly the typological reading of Rev. 20:7–9 demonstrated that St. John had had America in mind: for America was an antipodean continent from which one could reach Eurasia via either the Pacific or the Atlantic. According to Mede, Amerindians, unlike every other sinner on earth, would be spared the first conflagration brought about by the second coming of Christ and the beginning of the millennium. Only after the final battle between God and the armies of Gog and Magog would the Amerindians finally be destroyed by the second conflagration. The American armies of Gog and Magog would be enticed by Satan to set sail to the Old World to take over the New Jerusalem using the same promise of God to Moses and the Israelites, namely, to settle "a land so blessed a soil and aire, and magnificent happiness that they might live blessedly therein" (T2r). On traditional medieval interpretations of the location (or lack thereof) of the lands of Gog and Magog, see Westrem.

31. Sewall, 8–9.

32. MacCormack, 15–49; Clark, 161–78. On the institutional role of the Church in the art of discerning whether visions were caused by angelic or demonic spirits, see Dyan Elliott.

33. Descartes.

34. Clark, 106–33; Sluhovsky. For the case of the Puritans, see Godbeer; Demos; Karlsen; Reis. Witches had long been considered harmful, but had been tolerated. By the fifteen century, however, the Church began to consider witches as part of a growing and secretive heretical sect. Traditional witches were suddenly seen as learned necromancers had been in the past, namely, as worshippers of Satan. To zealous prosecutors, the sudden emergence of this sect pointed both to the imminence of the Apocalypse and to the need for religious reform; see Bailey.

35. Olmos, ch. 5, 46. On sexual intercourse with demons, see Stephens.

36. Silverblatt. Nicholas Griffiths has reached opposite conclusions to those of Silverblatt; see Griffiths, 248–53.

37. Villagómez, ch. 13, p. 45: "les engaña con grandíssima facilidad, como a tan incipientes, rudos en entender, torpes en discurrir, y faltos de experiencia. Y aun los más dellos careciendo de la dotrina necessaria, asestando todo el orgullo y fuerzas de su malicia, y astucia, y las dichas ventajas que les hace en darse a sentir, y moverse, y en la experiencia mayor de las cosas para inducirlos con sus embelecos superiores a la capacidad destos miserables, (como facilissimamente los induce) a que le tengan por digno de honor divino."

38. Loyola, p. 61, point 141.

39. Lancre, bk. 1, discourse 2, 72 and 79: "les Canadiens ne traitent parmi les Français en autre langue qu'en celle des Basques."

40. Ibid., 80: "Qui me fait croire que la devotion et bonne instruction de plusieurs bons religieux ayant chasse les Démons et mauvais Anges du pays des Indes, du Japon et autres lieux, ils se sont jetés à foule en la Chrétienté: et ayant trouvé ici et les personnes et lieu bien disposes, il y ont fait leur principale demeure, et peu à peu se rendent maîtres absolus du pays, ayant gagné les femmes, les enfants et la plupart des Prêtres et des Pasteurs; et roué moyen de reléguer les pères et les maris en Terre-Neuve et ailleurs où la religion est du tout inconnue, pour plus facilment établir son règne." On the Spanish side of the trials of Basque witches, the Inquisition restrained overzealous reformers. In the Spanish empire, by and large, witches were not seen as members of a threatening heretical sect of devil worshippers, akin to learned necromancers, but rather as traditional suppliers of amorous and harming spells. See Henningsen.

41. Mede, *Works*, epistle 43, bk. 4, p. 800.

42. Hubbard, 26: "when the devil was put out of his throne in the other parts of the world, and that the mouth of all his oracles was stopped in Europe, Asia, and Africa, he seduced a company of silly wretches to follow his conduct into this unknown part of the world, where he might lie hid and not be disturbed in the idolatrous and abominable, or rather diabolical service he expected from those his followers; for here are no footsteps of any religion before the English came, but merely diabolical." Cotton Mather, *Bateries*, 20: "When the Silver-Trumpets of the Lord Jesus were to sound in the other Hemisphere of our World, the devil got a forlorn Crue over hither into America, in hopes that the Gospel never would come at them here; and he still gets incredible multitudes and myriads of People elsewhere to live like our Indians."

43. Cotton Mather, *Magnalia Christi*, bk. 1, ch. 1, 1: 41 (emphases in original): "If the *wicked one in whom the whole world lyeth*, were *he*, who like *a dragon*, keeping guard upon the spacious and mighty *orchards* of *America*, could have such as *fascination* upon the thoughts of mankind, that neither this *balancing half* of the globe should be considered in *Europe*, till a little more than two hundred years ago, nor the *clue* that might lead unto it, namely the *Loadstone*, should be known. . . . The devil seducing the fist inhabitants of America into it, there in aimed at the having of them out of the sound of the silver trumpets of the Gospel."

44. James I, *Daemonologie*, bk. 3, ch. 3, p. 68 (emphases in original).

45. Cotton Mather, *Magnalia Christi*, bk. 2, ch. 7, 2: 389 (emphases in original): "Who can tell whether the envy of the Devils at the favour of God unto men, may not provoke them to affect retirement from the sight of populous and prosperous regions, except so far as they reckon their work of tempting mankind necessary to be carry'd on? Or, perhaps, it is not every countrey, before which the Devils prefer the desarts. Regions in which the devils are much serv'd by those usages . . . which are pleasant to them, are by those doleful creatures enough resorted unto . . . [there] Devils entreat that may *not be sent thence into the wilderness* [where God is constantly prayed to like in the land of Israel] the devils often recede much from thence into the wilderness. . . . The christians who were driven into the *American desert*, which is now call'd New-England, have to their sorrow seen Azazel dwelling and raging there in very tragical instances. The devils have doubtless felt a more than ordinary vexation, from the arrival of those Christians with their sacred exercises of christianity in this wilderness: but the sovereignty of heaven has permitted them still to remain in the wilderness, for our vexation, as well as their own."

46. Noyes, 75: "It is certain, Antichrist boasted in his American ΕΥΡΗΚΑ [eurēka], and Conquest when he began to be routed in Europe by the reformation. And who can blame him to provide a New World against the lost his Old One. But the Son of God followed him at the heels and took the Possession of America for Himself."

47. Dávila Padilla, bk. 1, ch. 42, p. 138: "longe ampliores ad Indias terminos a diabolo arripiamus, quam ipse cum Mahumetanis suis, nobis subducat ex Europa. Duplici daemonum muros ariete quatiamus, ut hinc ab eorum possessione antiqua eruamus."

48. Torquemada, bk. 4, prologue, 1: 340: "para turbar el Mundo y meter debaxo de la vandera del Demonio a muchos de los fieles que de padres y Abuelos y muchos tiempos atrás eran católicos; y este Christiano Capitán, para traer al Gremio de la Iglesia católica Romana, infinita multitud de Gentes, que por Años sin cuento avían estado debaxo del Poder de Satanás . . . De suerte que por una parte se perdía, se cobrase por otra en mas u menos numero según la cuenta de Dios."

49. Ramos Gavilán, bk. 2, ch. 9, 248: "Y parece que a esta gente de Inglaterra, se puede acomodar aquello del Evangelio, yo os digo de verdad que os será quitado el Reyno de Dios, y dado a gente que haga sus frutos [Matt. 21:43]. Pues vemos este assiento de Copacabana, y sus islas, que antes eran habitación de demonios, medrados ya en la religión, y aquella de Inglaterra, tan desmedrada como otra Babylonia; receptáculo infidelidad; confusión, y muerte. Razón es que pensemos que las Imágines se les quitaron para concedérselas a estos venturosos Indezuelos."

50. Mede, *Works*, epistle 43, bk. 4, p. 800.

51. San Pedro, 161: "El demonyo que es como ximia de dios les dixo Esto y esta falsíssima Trinidad" (the deity was Ataguju, who, feeling alone, created two others similar to himself: Sugadzavra and Ucumgarvrad).

52. Cotton Mather, *Wonders*, 140.

53. Ibid., 141.

54. Olmos, ch. 3: "De como ay sacramentos en la yglesia cathólica y en la diabólica execramentos."

55. Acosta, bk. 5, ch. 11 and chs. 23–25. Most of book 5 in fact is devoted to exploring the way the devil sought to mimic God in America by instituting churches, holy

sacrifices, penitence, nunneries, priests and monasteries, inverted versions of the sacraments (baptism, confession, Eucharist, priestly anointing), the doctrine of the Trinity, and the celebration of Jubilee.

56. San Pedro, 208: "Cosa es de espanto que estos yndios también tenyan confesión vocal."

57. Ibid., 190: "En todos los pueblos desta provincia les suadió el demonyo que tuviesen guarda común de todo el pueblo comos theólogos dizen que ay ángel que le guarda particularmente a cada república y pueblo. Que como digo el demonyo imita lo que vee y se procura de transfigurar en ángel de luz. Aunque en esto se transfigura en piedra y es que en cada pueblo avía una guaca o ydolo que hera un gran piedra."

58. Garcilaso de la Vega, *Primera parte de los comentarios reales*, bk. 2, ch. 7.

59. MacCormack, 113, 250.

60. Cieza de León, 1: 181 (ch. 30). See also MacCormack, 106. On the cult of saints and their relics, see Peter Brown; Bynum, *Fragmentation and Redemption*, ch. 2.

61. ¡Válgame Dios! ¿Qué dibujos,
    qué remedos o qué cifras
    de nuestras sacras Verdades
    quieren ser estas mentiras?
    ¡Oh cautelosa Serpiente!
    ¡oh Aspid venenosos! ¡Oh Hidra,
    que viertes por siete bocas,
    de tu ponsoña nociva
    toda la mortal cicuta!
    ¿Hasta dónde tu malicia
    quiere remedar de Dios las sagradas Maravillas?

    De la Cruz, *loa* 261–71 (references are to verse lines in either the *loa* or the *acto*, not pages). I follow the text's translation.

62. Acosta, bk. 4, ch. 1, p. 304: "Mas en fin ya que la idolatría fue extirpada de la mejor y más noble parte del mundo, retirose a lo más apartado, y reynó en estrota parte del mundo, que aunque en nobleza muy inferior, en grandeza y anchura no lo es."

63. Acosta, bk. 7, ch. 4, pp. 459–60.

64. Gregorio García, bk. 3, ch. 3, sec. 3, fol. 234.

65. Ibid.: "¿Quién no dirá, que parece esta salida, y peregrinación de los Mexicanos, a la salida de Egipto, y camino que hicieron los Hijos de Israel? Pues aquellos, como estos, fueron amonestados a salir y buscar Tierra de Promisión, y los unos y los otros llevavan por Guía su Dios, y consultaban el Arca, le hacían Tabernáculo, y así les avisaban, y daba Ley, y Ceremonias, así, los unos, como los otros, gastaron gran número de años en llegar a la Tierra prometida, que en todo estos, y en otras muchas cosas, a semejanza de lo que las Historias de los Mexicanos refieren, de lo que la Divina Escritura cuenta de los Israelitas."

66. On typology in general, see Dawson; Frye.

67. For Spanish America, see Brading, *Mexican Phoenix*. For Puritan America, see, e.g., Brumm; Bercovitch, ed., *Typology*; Lowance; Hammond; Lewaski; Knight; Rowe.

68. Torquemada, bk. 2, ch. 3, 1: 83: "que es lo mismo que le sucedió al Pueblo de Israel, corriendo por la soledad del Desierto, en cuio discurso y camino murieron

Moisés y Aarón que fueron los que los sacaron de Egipto y acaudillaron por el desierto." On Huitziton as Moses, see 1: 80.

69. Ibid., ch. 1, 1: 78–79: "Entonces el Demonio les dijo: Ya estáis apartados y seggregados de los demás, y así quiero, que como escogidos míos, ya no os llaméis Aztecas sino Mexicas."

70. Ibid., 1: 79: "vencer muchos enemigos y hacerse Señores de Grandes Provincias y Reinos."

71. Ibid., bk. 2, ch. 2, 1: 81: "¿Qué así quieren traspasar y poner objección a mis determinaciones y mandamientos? ¿Son ellos por ventura maiores que yo? Dezidlos que yo tomaré venganza de ellos . . . porque no se atrevan a dar parecer en lo que yo tengo determinado y sepan todos que a mi sólo han de obedecer."

72. Ibid., ch. 4, 1: 83: "como al pueblo de Israel bajo el Faraón."

73. Ibid., 1: 84: "Metidos en este lugar tan estrecho y chico consideraban su aflicción y mala ventura, y lloraban su apretada y estrecha suerte."

74. Ibid., ch. 9, 1: 90: "No tengáis pena, Mexicanos . . . que yo os aiudaré."

75. Ibid., ch. 15, 1: 100: "Yo los sacaré de esta pesadumbre y aflicción. Yo lo haré todo mui fácil y llano."

76. Ibid.: "esto me parece cosa más que Humana, porque quando yo lo mandé lo tuve por imposible; . . . quiero que entendáis que estos son favorecidos de su Dios y por esto han de venir a ser sobre todas la Naciones."

77. Ibid., 1: 100–101: "Pero así como en el reino de Egipto no se contentaba Faraón de los Pechos y Tributos ordinarios que los Hijos de Israel le daban sino que viéndoles tan multiplicados le añadía mal a mal y carga a carga, así este Rei Tirano que deseaba oprimir a esta pobre gente."

78. Ibid., ch. 43, 1: 151: "De las primeras cosas en que se ocupó este valeroso Rei, fue una, hacer Templo y Casa al Demonio." Torquemada also draws parallels between Moctezuma Ilhuicamina and Numa Pompilius, the second king of Rome. Ibid., ch. 54, 169.

79. Ibid., ch. 63, 1: 186.

80. Ibid., ch. 47, 1: 159.

81. Ibid., ch. 64, 1: 188 and chs. 77–78 passim. There are also the wizards of the Cuitlachtecas, who also read the signs correctly and foretell the destruction of the Aztecs by an army of knights in armor. Sensing the near end of their Mexica opressors, the Cuitlachtecas chase out the Aztecs' tax collectors (bk. 2, ch. 78). Of Nezahualpilli, Torquemada says: "He did not adore God as sole and true deity; [Nezahualpilli] mixed his worship of God with that of the devil. His piety was therefore in vain. For this reason he is in Hell" ("no le adoró como a Solo y verdadero, y mezclo su adoración con la del demonio y así fue vano su servicio, y por esto está en el Infierno" [1: 217]). Yet "Nezahualpilli was "a man of great Heart and determination. He did not fear [and understood] prophetic visions" ("porque era Hombre de gran Corazón y esfuerzo y no temía semejantes Visiones" [1: 238]). See also 1: 230.

82. Ibid., ch. 90, 1: 233: "Como la República de Israel, a quien en mucho, los hemos comparado en diversos lugares de esta historia."

83. According to Torquemada, the signs leading to the destruction of Jerusalem were a comet that lasted for a year; a light that came down from the sky during a service at the Temple; a cow brought to the Temple to be sacrificed that gave birth

to a sheep; the sudden opening of the great, heavy bronze doors of the Temple by the wind; an army besieging the city seen in the skies at dusk; voices of angels heard in the Temple announcing their departure; and a man called Jesus who went mad prophesying the destruction of the Temple for seven years. Ibid., passim.

84. Ibid., 1: 235: "Faltó un Joseph, como lo tuvo Faraón, y un Daniel, como lo tuvo el Rei Balthasar, que fueron Declaradores Verdaderos de los sueños, que avían soñado, y cosas que avían visto, que todos los otros Hechiceros, fueron Hombres torpes y ciegos, y como tales, pedían que declarase el Rei, lo que avía visto. Así que careció Motecuhzuma de uno de esos Santos Varones que le certificasen la Verdad."

85. Ibid., ch. 91, 1: 239: "El cielo le embiaba [señales] pa disponerse de mejor Vida y Costumbres de las que usaba; porque como dice del Pueblo Judáico, Josepho, muchas veces acostumbraba Dios a embiar señales, por las quales los Hombres buelvan en si y considerándolas busquen los medios de su Redempción."

86. Ibid., bk. 4, ch. 28, 1: 417: "porque Dios que tiene Poder para atar las Bocas de los leones que quieren despedazar a sus santos . . . ata las Lenguas delos Demonios, y no deja decir nada en ofensa de sus Siervos." Moctezuma tries again to send wizards to detain Cortés; this time they bump into Tezcatlipoca, a Mexica deity, in the road. After presenting the wizards with a vision of Tenochtitlán in flames, Tezcatlipoca, drunk and naked from the waist up, orders them to go back and be resigned (ibid., ch. 44).

87. Ibid., bk. 3, ch. 30, 1: 312: "y que no sólo le debieron perseguir en el cielo (con celo de tan conocida justicia) sino que en la Tierra era razón, que le hiciesen Guerra, llevando siempre adelante y no decayendo un punto."

88. Ibid., ch. 26, 1: 302: "y que en los mismos lugares que ha puesto su Trono [el demonio] sea destruido y levantado el Estandarte de sus gloriosas Victorias."

89. Ibid., 1: 303–4: "Y si en aquel tiempo gentilicio allí eran sacrificados Cuerpos de Hombres al Demonio, ahora es ofrecida en Hostia aplacable la carne y Sangre de Jesu-Christo . . . Y concluió con decir que tiene ahora más Ángeles buenos que la defienden y amparan y socorren en sus peligros, que Ángeles malos y Demonios fueron en otros tiempo contra ella para derribarla en ofensa y errores."

90. Ibid., 1: 303: "¿Cómo han de levantar esta Cruz estado asido de ella el que esta? . . . Apártate maldito, levantaran la Cruz de Jesu-Christo y el estandarte de la Fe será enarbolado."

91. San Pedro, 190: "Destas se quitaron por los dichos padres y en muchas partes. En su lugar pusieron cruces."

92. Pérez de Ribas, bk. 2, ch. 4, p. 43: "El padre junto la gente que pudo, hizo aderezar una hermosa cruz y cantando la Doctrina Cristiana, fue allá; hizo derribar el arbol y plantar en su lugar el preciosisimo dela santa Cruz. Bendixo El aquel lugar, con que se borraron las memorias del otro arbol y de aquellas supersticiones."

93. Dávila Padilla, bk. 1, ch. 40, p. 120: "Quando los Españoles no tenían ya en que huyr, mandó el demonio a los indios, que los matasen a todos. . . . Murieron todos los Españoles, y no quedaron sino el padre fray Pedro de Córdova y su compañero. Los dos religiosos estavan con sendas Cruzes de madera en las manos, y milagrosamente salieron dentre las de los Indios, y se fueron azia la playa."

94. Ibid., bk. 2, ch. 79, pp. 611–13.

95. Olmos, 4: "¿Si en el arbol verde tales cosas acaecen que será del seco? Si la

vieja cristiandad se quema, no es de maravillar que arda la nueva, pues el enemigo no menos envidia, enojo y rencor tiene destos que poco hace se le escaparon de las uñas que de los que ya ha mucho tiempo se le escaparon de las manos."

96. Pérez de Ribas, 17: "Porque como ve el demonio que con la luz del Evangelio y doctrina . . . se deshazan y desvanecen todos sus embustes y enredos y pierden autoridad . . . aquí pone toda su diligencia esse enemigo del género humano por medio de hechizeros para persuadir a los pueblos que se levanten, abrasen las iglesias y se vuelvan a los montes y vivan a sus anchuras."

97. Clenddinnen, pt. 2.

98. On the Portuguese use of crosses in ceremonies of possession, see Russell-Wood, *Portuguese Empire*; Seed, *Ceremonies of Possession*, 100–148.

99. Barros, 174–75: "Per o qual nome Sancta cruz foy aquela térra nomeáda os primeiros annos: e a cruz arvoráda alguns durou naquelle lugar. Porém como o demônio per o final da cruz perdeo o domínio que tinha sobre nós, mediante a paixão de Christo Jesus consumada nella: tanto que daquella térra começou de vir o páo vermelho chamado brasil, trabalhou que este nome ficasse na boca do povo, e que se perdesse o de Sancta Cruz. Como que importava mais o nome de hum páo que tinge panos: que daquelle páo que deu titntura a todolos sacrementos per que somos salvos, per o sangue de christo Jesu que nelle foy derramado. E pois em outra cousa nesta parte me nam pósso vingar do demónio, amoesto da párte da cruz de Christo Jesu a todolos que este lugar lerem, que dem a esta térra o nome que con tanta solenidade ilhe soy posto, sob pena de a mesma cruz que nos há de ser mostráda no dia final, os acusar de mais deuvótos do páo brasil que della." On brazilwood as "deceitful dye," see Greenfield, 28–29.

100. Lope de Vega, 53: "hizo un mundo sin cimiento en su ingenio singular, como Molino de viento, y este mundo va a buscar." Lope de Vega's play *El nuevo mundo* was written a few years before the publication of the first part of Miguel de Cervantes's *El ingenioso hidalgo Don Quixote de la Mancha* (Madrid, 1605).

101. Devil:
> ¡Oh, que gracioso que estás
> con esa amistad fingida!
> Estos, codiciando oro
> De tus Indias, se hacen santos,
> Fingen cristiano decoro,
> mientras vienen otros tantos
> que llevan todo el tesoro.

Dulcan:
> ¡Oh gente vil, inhumana,
> fieras de piedad desnudas,
> con pieles de ley cristiana!

Lope de Vega, *El nuevo mundo*, 138–40.

102. Providence:
> Dios juzga de la intención:
> si El, por el oro que encierra,
> gana las almas que ves, en el cielo hay interés.

Ibid., 33.

103. Devil:

> Vencido soy, venciste, Galileo.
> Venciste Cristo, resistime en vano;
> Tuya es la gloria, el triunfo y el trofeo.
> Ya que en el blanco pan bajar te veo
> A tomar posesión del reino indiano,
> Cedo el derecho a tu divina mano
> Y bajo a las prisiones del Leteo.
> Como en puercos estaba entre esta gente,
> Que así me lo mandaste, y ya me arrojas
> Desde sus cuerpos a otro mar profundo.
> No me llame su dios eternamente.
> Pues hoy del nombre y reino me despojas,
> Tuyo es el mundo; redimiste al mundo.
>
> Ibid., 141.

104. Chaplin, 49 (on erecting Cross), 55 (quotations), 58 (later Inuit uses of the Cross).

105. Smith, *Captain John Smith*, 100: "In all those places and the furthest we came up the rivers, we cut in trees so many crosses as we would, and in many places made holes in trees, wherein we writ notes, and in some places crosses of brasse, to signifie to any, Englishmen had beene there."

106. Chaplin, 66.

107. Walsh, 84–85.

108. Bremer, 5–22.

109. Godbeer.

110. For an account of this episode, see Reis, 91.

111. Hall, *Worlds of Wonder*, 25 (quotation); see also Cressy.

112. Lepore, 54, 269.

113. On the confrontation between Morton and the Puritans, see Canup, 105–25.

114. Walsh, 85 (on Winthrop), 89–92 (on the sacralization of particular spaces, notwithstanding Puritans' disclaimers to the contrary).

115. Tyerman; Riley-Smith; Barlett

116. Housley.

117. Swanson.

CHAPTER 4. DEMONOLOGY AND NATURE

1. Fernando Cervantes, 24–31; MacCormack, ch. 6.

2. Clark, pt. 2.

3. On these revolts, see Linebaugh and Rediker, ch. 1.

4. See Shakespeare, *The Tempest*. I have used the Folger Shakespeare Library's edition.

5. There is much debate on whether *The Tempest* is about America in the first place and representative of English views of the Amerindians. For skeptical views see Willis; Marshall. For postcolonial readings of *The Tempest*, see Paul Brown;

Cheyfitz; Greenblatt, *Learning to Curse*, 16–39; Hulme; Knapp. For an interesting history on the literature of Caliban as either a Wild Man or an Amerindian, see Vaughan and Vaughan. On Sycorax as an "Amerindian" witch, see Purkiss, ch. 10.

6. On Caliban as the son of the devil, see Latham.

7. Purchas, 19: 6–12. On the tradition of claiming Strachey as the source of Shakespeare's account of the tempest, see Marx, 40–41; Shakespeare, 192–94; Linebaugh and Rediker, 14.

8. Idolatry [Devil]:

> con el mágico horror de mis horrores
> pertuban de manera
> de tierra y mar oy una y otra esfera,
> que el mar, antes que desta hallada playa
> a aquel baxel con las noticias vaya,
> le embata, le çoçobre y le persiga. (129)

On the devil's location in the sphere of air, see Calderón de la Barca, 141–42.

9. *Relations des Jésuites*, 1: 3 (1632): "Je viens icy comme les pionniers qui marchent les premiers pour faire les tranchées, et par apres les braves soldats viennent assieger et prendre la place."

10. Ibid., 2: 1–2 (1638): "grandes machines de guerre [ou] batteries qui détruiront l'empire de Sathan."

11. Ibid., 64 (1641): "voir rentrer les Demons dans leur empire."

12. Ibid., 2–3 (1640): "quelque grand bien de ce passage [les demons] . . . susleverent tout l'ocean, deschainerent les vent, exciterent des tempestes si horribles et si continues. . . . Les Anges conservoient nostre Flotte par les mesmes tempestes que les demons excitoient pour la perdre."

13. Ibid., 77 (1639): "un donjon des Demons."

14. Ibid., 5: 2 (1657): "ces grandes forests estant gardées pendant L'Esté des petits Dragons volans, je veux dire par un millon d'escadrons de Mousquittes, de Maringoins ou de Cousins tres avides d'un sang qu'ils n'avoint jamais gousté."

15. Master Welles quoted in Carroll, 37.

16. Cotton Mather, *Magnalia Christi*, 2: 312 (bk. 6, ch. 3), and 1: 65, 69, 109, 529. See also Wharton.

17. Cotton Mather, *Magnalia Christi*, 2: 313 (bk. 6, ch. 3).

18. Ibid., 404 (bk. 6, ch. 7).

19. Hakluyt, *Principall Navigations*, 7: 397; 9: 382, 11: 106–7; *Present State of New England with Respect to the Indian War*, 15; Increase Mather, *Relation of the Troubles*, 20; Cotton Mather, *Magnalia Christi*, bk. 7, 107; *Beginning, Progress, and Conclusion of Bacon's Rebellion*, 19; D. S. Lovejoy, 609–11.

20. Zahn, 1: 346 (1.2.6): "Mirabilium Ventorum ac horrendarum tempestatum ope Daemonis & a[rt]e magica productarum Exempla ex variis authoribus proferuntur & recensentur." (Examples of marvelous winds and horrid tempests produced by the help of the Devil and the art of magic are offered and recorded by various authors.)

21. Zahn, 1: 357 (1.3.1). Zahn also argues that demons and magicians can cause meteors as well.

22. Nieremberg, *Curiosa filosofía*, bk. 1, ch. 50 (36v–37r): "por qualquier parte

que la partan tiene formada una Cruz estremadamente hecha . . . y no me espantara que el demonio por esta causa huyesse de esta yerva porque será huir de la Cruz."

23. Ibid., ch. 51, 37v: "[los ángeles malos piensan algunos] les atrae el cabello compuesto y hermoso permite esto dios por el sobrado cuydado que en aderezarse ponen [las mujeres] por el peligro en que han querido poner a los hombres, provocándoles con su vista, y por la gloria vana que en esto tienen, para deseen las mugeres de querer agradar a los hombres, con aquello le agradan alos demonios."

24. Ibid., ch. 52.

25. Ibid., chs. 47–48.

26. Ibid., ch. 49, 36r: "condicione el ayre y al espacio medio que no quede a propósito para que el demonio se vista de figura alguna."

27. It is strange that this obvious connection between plants and demonology has not attracted much scholarly attention. To my knowledge, only Osvaldo F. Pardo has written on this topic. Yet Pardo's focus is on the epistemological connections between New World botany and demons. Spaniards, he argues, considered the Amerindians too simple-minded to admit that the natives on their own had amassed a large body of sophisticated botanical knowledge. So the Spaniards repeatedly suggested that Amerindian knowledge of plants came from the whisperings of a much more intelligent devil; see Pardo.

28. Hernández, bk. 3, ch. 17, p. 56: "Fama est apud indigenas Cacodaemones hanc arborem pertimescere ac fugere, & fascino adversari."

29. Ibid., bk. 1, ch. 5, p. 6: "arbor insaniae dicta, quia daemones pellendo, & fascinum inhibendo eos curat, qui horum pravitate insaniunt."

30. Ibid., bk. 10, ch. 17, p. 340: "Nec non alius Crystallo simillimus . . . facultate, si vere narrant, mirabili praeditus, ut qui daemones fugiat, serpentes, & quiduis venenatum arceat."

31. San Pedro, 197: "Que luego se le encogían los brazos y piernas y quedavan tollidos y por esto no osavan llegar a Ella y así quando los padres la fueron a quemar no la osavan mostrar de myedo y así más por fuerza que de voluntad llevaron dos yndios para mostrar y se quemó contra la voluntad de los yndios y el demonio no tuvo fuerza para hazernos el mal que hazia a los yndios."

32. Ibid., 211.

33. Ibid., 212: "super aspidem et basiliscum ambulabis et conculcabis leonem et draconem."

34. Cárdenas, bk. 3, ch. 15, p. 268: "avemos absolutamente de negar que las yerbas ni medicamentos puedan hazer obra alguna que exceda y pase el límite de obrar naturalmente."

35. Ibid., p. 273. "Pero que mediante la yerba se hagan las bruxas invisibles y que se vayan en un momento por todo el mundo y que penetren los cuerpos y tornen a bolver al lugar do salieron, todo esto se ha de presumir antes ser por arte del demonio que por virtud que aya en la yerba, y dezir otra cosa es yerro."

36. Ibid., pp. 274–76.

37. Fernández de Oviedo, 3: 32. See also 1: 116–17.

38. Aguilar y Leiva, fols. 4v–5v.

39. Hurtado, fols. 34r–42r.

40. James I, *Covnterblaste to Tobacco*, C3r.
41. Ibid., C4r.
42. Ibid., C4v.
43. Ibid., B2r.
44. Ibid., D2r.
45. Monardes, *Segunda parte*, fol. 91r–93r; Faber, 830 ("Carolus Clusius sibi ab hortulano Regis Hispaniarum missos fuisse fructus quosdam nominee Dragonatis, qui Bruxellae terrae commissi prodierint, foliis iridis oblongis, viridibus, per oras rubris. Fructu Cerasi magnitudine fuisse, sed pelle sublata, animalis nulla, nedum Dracunculi effigies visa fuit").
46. Bustamante de la Cámara, n.p.: "Haec enim planta altissimas radices immittit, pertingentes intima vasa seminaria animantis huius, lumbis adnata, per quos seminis ductus decurrunt, semen ut trahere possint formatum, prolificum, efficere potens Draconem verum, formetq[ue] ut illum foliis primo: Draconibus inserta ortu accepta virtute: servataq[ue] imposterum terrae commissa, loco fruticis, quae nullum alium fructum gerunt unquam, quam foliis Draconem efformatum (mirabile satis!)." (For this plant sends down deep roots, reaching into the deepest seminal receptacles of this animal, which grow upon its genitals, through which ducts of semen run down, so that they [the roots] may draw up the seed already formed, fruitful, able to make an actual dragon, and so that it may form it first in the leaves, having taken up power through its origin in having been implanted in dragons and preserved afterwards committed to the earth, in the place of the trunk, which never bear any other fruit than a dragon formed on the leaves (sufficiently marvelous!).)
47. Faber, 799–830; Freedeberg.
48. Faber, 815, 820.
49. Natural histories of dragons remained a staple of natural history well into the late seventeenth century; see, e.g., Zahn 2.3.7, entitled: "De Draconibus, bestiis serpentiformibus maxime stupendis varia notabilia & mirabilia adducuntur" (433–39). Zahn covers such themes in the lives of dragons as:

Sec. 1: De Draconibus quaedam in genere producuntur
- draconis quid sint
- eorum exortus
- loca & regio [regions of warm skies like the Middle East, although they have been spotted in Switzerland]
- forma
- color
- fortitudo & astucia
- visus et auditus
- quomodo ignem spirare videantur
- mores draconum
- aetas

Sec. 2: De Draconibus quibusdam in specie & memorabilium casuum circa ipsos exemplis
- Draco apud Babylonios
- Draco Cracoviensis

- Dracones variis in locis visi diversae magnitudinis
- Draco ingens apud Chios
- Circe turim Babe & in desertis illic plures habitant Dracones
- Draco in Gallia interemptus
- Draco Mediolanensis
- Draco mirabiliter caesus ab Heraldo
- Draco in insula Rhodo
- Casus mirus in Dracone Bernensi hominem deglutiente
- Admiranda historia de Vietore cum duobus draconibus habitante.
- Dracone igniti
- Dracones tantum grandioris vulturis magnitude.

Sec. 3: Mirabilium quarundam operationum in Draconibus exempla
- Draco S. Mariae Magdalenae et Marthae obsequeus
- Draco thesauri custos a S. Hypatio abactus
- Draco Alevam pastorem amans
- Puella a dracone adamata
- Gratitudo draconis
- Vindictae & Ultionis explum in Dracone
- Dracones pellaei valde mansueti
- Draco Epidaurius

Sec. 4: De Draconibus mirabilia quaedam miscellanea recensentur
- Draconites gemma
- Lapis a Dracone dimissus mirabilis virtutis
- Incendii portentum a dracone
- Romae Draco visusin inundatione, quam pestis subsecuta
- Auspicia & prodigia ex Draconibus

50. Zahn 2.2.15: "Admirabiles quaedam virtutes, vires ac operationes quorundam Vegetabilium recensentur" (243–47).

51. Vicente Yañez Pinzón quoted in Parrish, 485.

52. Nieremberg, *Historia naturae*, bk. 9. ch. 74, p. 189: "Prima oris acie quodammodo leonem emulatur, aut hominem, nam ab aure barbata, haud promissis valde pilis . . . cauda ampla & long sciuri instar."

53. Nieremberg, *Historia naturae*, bk. 10, ch. 51, p. 223: "monstrosos pedibus: unus anserinus, alter aquilinus: uno innatat, altero raptat praedam."

54. Faber, 797: "Ita Creatori placuit Amphisbaenam effingere, & Apro nostro Mexicano insculpere umbilicum, non in ventre, sed in dorso, & varias aliis figuris, modisq Novi orbis bestias producere, quae omnes ad nostras comparatae, monstrosae videntur." References to a two-headed snake in the New World were not unique to the "Catholic" imagination. As late as 1760, the British-American Creole Edward Bancroft refers to them outside a demonological context. See Bancroft, 131, 214–15. He actually uses the image of the two-headed snake in the frontispiece to his *Essay on the Natural History of Guiana.*

55. Faber, 704: "Quod si admurmuratis verbis cantilenisque agitur, iam illa de diaboli commercio, auxilio, & suggestione suspecta fit. Scio equidem, plerosque hominum non facile contentos esse, iis, quae ubiuis obvia, & quotidiana sunt: sed [illeg-

ible Greek word here] illa libentissime credere, appetere, & amplecti. Adeo fabulae, deliramenta anilia, & superstitiosae, Cacodaemonis astu excogitatae ceremoniae, per universum orbem facillime disseminantur, ut ad Americanos & Antipodes nostros quoque iam olim penetraverint." In South Africa, pied crows (*Corvus albus*) sometimes weave their nests out of fence wire, and tales of a bird that could bend iron might have been based on similar phenomena (I am grateful to Peter Dreyer for this reference).

56. Ibid.: "Et quidni? Cum enim luce Evangelica variae orbis nostri cogniti regiones essent illustratae, & fraudes Sathanae ideo detectae migrandum sibi putavit ad gentes novi orbis barbaricis ritibus plenissimas & veri DEI cultu orbatas. His cum superbiam, arrogantiam, & tyrannidem suam diu misere exercuit, apud has idolatriam perfide fixit, ut licet iam bona pars earum CRISTI doctrinam amplexata fuerit, remanserint tamen antiquarum superstitionum fomites quidam, e quibus continuo adhuc idolomanie igniculi exhalant." (And why not? For when the various regions of our known world have been enlightened by the light of the Gospel and the frauds of the Devil have been laid bare, he thought it was time for him to move on to the people of the New World, full of barbarian rites and deprived of the worship of the true God. Since he wretchedly practiced his pride, arrogance, and tyranny upon them for a long time and faithlessly established idolatry among them, even though now a good part of them may have embraced the teaching of Christ, there nonetheless remains some tinder of ancient superstition from which little fires of idol-madness constantly shoot forth even now.)

57. Nieremberg, *Historia naturae*, bk. 9, ch. 2, p. 154: "etiam postquam ab aminantis cute est divulsa, occulta virtute, etiam cum a nemine urgeatur, sponte penetrat carnem." (Even after it has been torn from the skin of the animal, it penetrates flesh of its own accord, through a hidden power, even when it is not pushed by anyone.)

58. Ibid., ch. 4, p. 157: "intra corpus sumpta . . . urinae meatus obstruunt extrahit. Venerem excitat, generat lac, & medetur fractis & colicis. Partum accelerat, menses elicit. Tusa & imposita, extrahit aculeos infixos, ventremque; emollit." (Taken into a body it removes [stones that] obstruct the passage of urine; it stirs up sexual desire; it produces milk; it heals those with broken bones and colic; it hastens childbirth; it calls forth menstruation. Ground and applied, it pulls out lodged arrowheads, and it soothes the stomach.)

59. Armadillo shells possess occult powers associated with maleficence, Nieremberg asserts, for instance. Shamans put soil or objects touched by thieves inside an armadillo shell and add *chicha*, fermented maize liquor. Pustules appear on the cheek of the thief when he drinks from this container, revealing his identity: "Conchulis huius animalis utuntur Indi in maleficis, praecipue ad explorandos et puniendos fures. Tangunt prius cum concha terram a fure calcatam, sive aliud quidquid ille attigerit : implet maxilam potione quam chihcahm vocant : tympanis deinde circumsonant, concha interim sponte subsultante et tripudiante. Hoc veneficio notatur vultus furis, pustula in genis quae per utramque maxillam serperet, nisi maleficium diligenter dissolvatur." Nieremberg, *Historia naturae*, bk. 9. ch. 6, p. 160. Elsewhere, under the rubric "De tigribus indiarum," Nieremberg discusses a tiger capable of distinguishing between Spaniards and Amerindians, which spares the former but goes after the latter: "Mira tigridi discretio gentium: parcit Hispanis, inaudit

Indos, ut inter multos Europaeos barbarum internoscens, impetum in illum desti-
net." The Amerindians fear this animal more than any other, and the devil speaks
to them in the form of a tiger ("Daemon illis saepissime specie tigridis loquebatur")
(bk. 9. ch. 15, p. 166). Finally, under the rubric "De rubetis lactifluis," Nieremberg
tells of a toad whose secretions are used in sorcery ("harum lac posteriore fusum
veneficium") (bk. 11, ch. 29, p. 256).

60. Nieremberg, *Historia naturae*, bk. 10, ch. 25, 215.

61. Ibid., bk. 9, ch. 53, pp. 182–83.

62. Ibid., ch. 69, p. 188. Nieremberg finds in Potosí a parrot exquisitely capable
of reading social hierarchies among the Amerindians. The parrot denounces those
Amerindian commoners who in the anonymity of the city pretend to descend from
noble indigenous lineages. See bk. 9, ch. 63, p. 229 ("De ingenio psittacorum").

63. Ibid., bk. 4, chs. 32–33; bk. 5, ch. 23; bk. 9, ch. 96.

64. Faber, 776: "Et ait Dominus ad serpentem: Quia fecisti hoc, maledictus
es inter omnia animantia, & bestias terrae: super pectus tuum gradieris, & terram
comedes cunctis diebus vitae tuae."

65. Ibid.: "INIMICITIAS ponam inter te, & mulierem, & semen tuum, &
semen illius; ipsa conteret caput tuum, & tu insidiaberis calcaneo illius."

66. Ibid.: "per faeminam hanc, maxime Beatissimam Virginem MARIAM aequi-
orem nobis Evam intelligi [sic], quae per semen & cum semine suo IESU CHRISTO,
contriuit caput Diaboli, antiqui illius serpentis, hostis nostri infensissimi."

67. Nieremberg, *Historia naturae*, bk. 4, ch. 32, p. 69: "Ut taceam quod multis
sanctorum Christi servorum non solum innocuous, sed etiam obedientes legamus
fuisse serpentes." (And I'll pass over in silence the fact that we read that snakes were
often not only harmless but even obedient to many of Christ's holy servants.)

68. Ibid.: "sed reptio ista nihil horroris haberet, si non illa diabolus ad mortem
domini eius, hominis, usus fuisset. Multo magis vero nec virus pestifeum vomeret,
nec in se ipso haberet, si non illud idem creaturae Dei adulteror veneficus illo suae
malitiae veneno polluisset et per os suum homini mortem insibilasset." (For that
reptile would have nothing of horror in it, had not the Devil made use of it for the
death of its master, man. Nay, rather, it would not be spewing pestiferous poison nor
have it in itself if the poisonous spoiler of God's Creation had not befouled that very
thing with the poison of his malice and had not through its own mouth hissed death
to man.)

69. On Frans Post, see Schmidt, 290–91, 311–12; Sousa-Leão.

70. Perrault, 59v : "un gros muffle de dragon vomissoit sur la croupe quantite de
couleuvres qui en formoient la queue."

71. Dávila Padilla, 120: "a este siervo de dios obedecían el agua y el viento, y se le
quietava la mar, y le estavan subjetas todas las criaturas, sin que se le atreviese aun
el mismo demonio."

72. Nieremberg, *Firmamento religioso*, 241: "partiose sin más armas ni más per-
trechos de guerra, que su Cruz en la mano. . . . Va enarbolando el sagrado madero
de la Cruz, para el espanto del demonio."

73. Ibid., 254: "su oración enfrenó y tuvo a raya . . . al demonio, que se aparecía
visiblemente a los Indios Paranás . . . que despachado se desapareció por el aire,
amenazándoles con su ira."

74. Ibid., 243.

75. Nieremberg, *Ideas de virtud*, 513–57.

76. Nieremberg, *Honor del Gran patriarca*, 207: "reconocían el orden de San Francisco, los espíritus inmundos, echándolos diversas vezes de los cuerpos humanos, de que estavan apoderados, y también de lugares que destruían."

77. Nieremberg, *Ideas de virtud*, 519 (stops storm), 539 (catatonic mediation), 538 (flock of *guaraces*); 538–39 (birds disrupting fishing); 543 (birds singing on demand to praise the Lord); 540–41 (monkeys grieving). In his *Historia naturae*, Nieremberg offers a long list of holy men known for their ability to control animals; see bk. 9, ch. 95, pp. 202–3.

78. Nieremberg, *Ideas de virtud*, 540: "porque parece que escogió nuestro Señor al padre Ioseph para Autor de prodigios, y maravillas, que declarasen a aquel Nuevo mundo las grandezas del Criador."

79. Ibid., 541: "No hizo esta acción el Padre Ioseph, movido tanto de lástima de aquellos animals . . . quanto deseoso de acreditar así la ley de Dios, y despertar los entendimientos tardos de los Indios, a la veneración y respeto de su criador; pues así les mostrava que todo obedecía al hazedor de todas las cosas, y que todas servían al que enteramente se sujetava a las leyes de Dios."

80. Ibid., 524: "mandó a la vívora que le viniesse a las manos; obedeció ella y el siervo de Dios muy contento se sentó con mucho espacio, regalándola y passándola la mano por encima, como si fuera un perrito de falda, y aprovechándose de la ocasión comenzó a hablar de la omnipotencia de Dios, mostrando como todas las cosas se rinden a los que le sirven." See also Nieremberg, *Historia naturae*, bk. 9. ch. 96.

81. Sánchez, *Imagen de la Virgen*, 259.

82. Mujica Pinilla, 154.

83. Rodríguez Castelo, 72.

84. Sánchez, *Imagen de la Virgen*, 259 (on the holy fragrance of the canvas); 169, 238, 254–55, 259 (Our Lady of Guadalupe as main enemy of the devil).

85. Carranza, 18.

86. Nieremberg, *Curiosa filosofía*, 13r–16v. Fernández de Oviedo, 13: 243–76 and vol. 14 passim (on shipwrecks and praying); 1: 300–302 (scale and number of hurricanes diminished in Hispaniola after consecrated wafers are put in monstrances in churches and monasteries).

87. Pérez de Ribas, bk. 1, ch. 1, p. 5: "y podemos dezir que quiso Dios en esto dexar en la naturaleza un rastro de como el Espíritu Santo emana del Padre y del Hijo."

88. Rodríguez Castelo, 50.

89. Nieremberg, *Historia naturae*, bk. 9, ch. 25, p. 170: "Quid tu facis, o anima, a draconis infernalis faucibus per nobilissimum illum Equitem, qui super candidum purissimae, humanitatis suae equum vehitur, liberata? Quomodo post hunc liberatorem tuum non curris? Quomodo ad eum non evolas, etsi vel cum maris undis te conflictare oporteat?"

90. Ibid., bk. 9, ch. 94, pp. 200–202, "De cane quodam Ulyssiponis"; bk. 10, ch. 99, p. 243, "De vig,lia et custodia anserum."

91. Ibid., bk. 1, p. 12: "exigua avis est, sed incredibili providentia moritur victura. . . . In ligno putat se feliciter morituram, unde resurrecturam. Documentum nobis est, astute moriendi saeculo in arbore crucis, unde immortales erimus, si

mundo crucifixione mortuit." (It is a small bird, but through an amazing providence it dies to live again. It thinks it will die happy on the wood from which it will rise up again. This is a sign for us of wisely dying to the world in the tree of a cross, from which we shall be immortal, if it [the hummingbird?] has died to the world by crucifixion.) See also bk. 10, ch. 1, p. 206. Hummingbirds are, in fact, known to hibernate. In his *Sumaria relación*, 126–27, Dorantes de Carranza calls the same bird a *huitzilzil* and the tree a *cacaloxuchitl* (otherwise known as an *amancayo* or *chilacayote*).

92. Ibid., bk. 10, ch. 32, p. 217: "Sic componitur, quod Scriptra sacra accuset impietatis erga prolem struthiones, & Auctores ob pietatem laudent: scilicet mares amantes sobolis sunt, feminae contemnunt."

93. Nieremberg included a poem alluding to the plant as an emblem of the Passion of Christ:

> Pulcher in America Moscho redolentior est flos
> Qui gerit occisi nobile stemma Dei.
> Conscia flagrorum croceo stat in orbe columna;
> Circumstant granis Vulnera quina rubris.
> Cum clavis residet spinosum in vertice sertum;
> Respersus violam pingit ubique cruor.
> Visitur in plantae foliis penetrabile ferrum,
> Sacrum quo fodit lancea dira latus.
> Sed quae vulnifici flores dant poma cadentes!
> Ambrosius miscet nectareusque sapor.
> Patenti novitas, et consona rebus imago
> Adstruit antiquam clarificatque fidem;
> Missaque Pontifici Romano circuit orbem,
> Fertque salutiferae nuntia laeta Crucis.
> Nam Deus omnipotens nostros tulit ipse dolores,
> Ipsius est nobis Crux paradisus. Amen

>> (There is in America a flower more fragrant than musk, which bears the noble pedigree of the murdered God. A column calling to mind whips rests in a yellow orb. Five wounds stand around with red grains. A prickly garland on the top rests on nails. Everywhere scattered gore paints the violet. Piercing iron is to be seen in the plant's leaves, iron with which the dire lance dug into the sacred flank. But what fruits the wounding flowers yield when they fall! Ambrosial and nectarous flavors mingle. A novelty that fits what is already manifest and an image suiting deeds adds to and makes clear ancient faith. Having been sent to the Roman pontiff, it has circled the globe and brought glad tidings of the salvation-bearing Cross. For omnipotent God has himself borne our sorrows. His Cross means paradise for us. Amen.)

> Nieremberg, *Historia naturae*, bk. 14, ch. 10, p. 300.

94. "The Jesuits have brought here [i.e., to Turkey] the picture of a plant which grows in the Indies. In it one sees, designed by nature, all the mysteries of the most Holy Passion of our Lord. For those who do not admit a miracle in the world of nature it is very difficult to accept this drawing." Simon Contarini, Vigne di Pera,

October 3, 1609, to the doge and senate, in *Calendar of State Papers and Manuscripts Relating to English Affairs Existing in the Archives and Collections of Venice and in Other Libraries of Northern Italy*, ed. Horatio F. Brown, vol. 11 (1607–10), 360–61.

95. Monardes, *Primera y segunda y tercera partes de la historia medicinal*, bk. 3, 109r–v.

96. E.g., Donato Rasciotti, *Copia del fiore et fruto che nasce nelle Indie Occidentali, qual di nuovo e stato presentato all Santità di NSP Paolo V* (1609); Parlasca; Bosio.

97. Unde accidit, o sancta, & incomparabilis flos
 Quod in terra nascaris, & climate tam remoto
 Cum indignis tormentis, quae tulit Redemptor
 Ab infido populo, impio, inhumano?

> (How does it happen, O holy and incomparable flower, that you were born in a land and clime so distant, with undeserved torments that the Redeemer endured at the hands of a faithless, impious, inhumane people?)

Juan Botero quoted in Stengel, 370.

98. Cur apud Antipodas Flos Crucis compareat?
 Post se Sol tenebras linquit: qua cedit ab ora
 Umbris opacans hanc tegit caligine
 Hinc syncera Fides retrahit sua lumina : quare,
 Incumbit errorum gravis nox ocyus
 Partibus e nostris sensim demigrat ad Indos
 Gloria Crucis, dum furit, & ardet Haeresis.
 Antipodas sed adit, qui grato pectore Lucem hanc
 Captant, honorant mente pura, & simplice.
 Eminet hinc inter sylvestria germina Flos hic
 Crucifer, & Indo Gratiam monstrat Crucis.

> (Why does the flower of the Cross appear among the antipodeans? The sun leaves darkness behind him when he departs from a shore. Darkening this shore [i.e., Europe] with shadows, he has covered it with gloom. From here the true Faith is withdrawing its light. Therefore the heavy night of errors is settling down more swiftly. Gradually from our regions the glory of the Cross migrates to the Indies, while heresy rages and glows [i.e., here in Europe]. But it approaches the antipodeans, who grasp at it with grateful breast and honor it with pure and simple minds. This cross-bearing flower stands out amid the fruits of the forest and shows the grace of the Cross to the Indian.)

Gretser, pt. 5, sec. 7, 273–94 (emphasis in the original).

99. Ad Peruvvium
 O multum gratare tibi Peruane, Deoque
 Grates innumeras nocte, dieque refer;
 De radiis Fidei, tenebras haec sola fugavit
 Perfidiae, & Vitii: quae tibi numen erant.

De Cruce vera Salus en obtigit. En eadem Crux
Per florem hunc cedit Pignori usque loco.
Crimen abundavit: successit Gratia maior.
Hanc tibi adaugebunt culta Tropaea Crucis.

> (To a Peruvian: Oh, count yourself extremely lucky, Peruvian, and
> offer innumerable thanks to God night and day. From the rays of Faith,
> this alone [sc., the Cross] has put to flight the darkness of falsehood
> and sin, which were divinity to you. Behold: from the Cross true salva-
> tion has come about. Behold: through this flower the same Cross has
> utterly abandoned its place [to serve] as a token. Guilt has abounded;
> Grace has come all the more to take its place. The cultivated trophies
> of the Cross have caused it [Grace] to abound for you.)
> Ibid.

100. Ingeniose frutex, quid in haec miracula surgis?
Nutrisque, hastatas per tua membra comas?
Vidi ego damnatis Hispanica castra sarissis,
Haec arma in gentem vertere saepe tuam.
Nec vero incassum. Castis Victoria; quamque
Ferrea non potuit, lancea sacra dedit.
Et tu degeneres porro vernabis in hastas?
Devictosque, Indos Indicus ipse, voles?
Omen, io, faustum. Cunctis dominabimur Indis.

> (Ingenious bush, why do you rise up into these marvels and nourish
> spearlike stalks in your branches? I myself have seen Spanish camps
> with accursed lances often turn these weapons against you — not in-
> deed in vain. Victory is for the pure, and that which the iron lance can-
> not give, the sacred lance has given. And will you continue to bloom
> into base spears? And will you, Indian yourself, wish the Indians
> defeated? Oh, lucky omen: we shall rule over all the Indians.)
> Ibid.

101. Cur Crucis mysteria ex orbe novo in hoc nostro tandem emergant?
Haeresis heu pridem convicta est argumentis
Impia, mirandis prodigiisque, Crucis.
Et quia de templis insignia sancta Salutis
Sustulit, & pessum, qua potis illa, dedit
En ex Orbe novo mittiit Natura peregre
Nostro Orbi sobolem, munera rara, suam.
Granadilla quidem parva es: sed grandia praestas.
Tu Crucis eloqueris, muta vel ipsa, decus.
Quot folia, & spinae, aut fructus tibi stemmate pendent:
Tot lingua iaculis perfida corda feris.

> (Why do the mysteries of the Cross emerge at last from the New
> World in this world of ours? Impious heresy has long been refuted by
> arguments and by the marvelous wonders of the Cross. And because
> it has removed from the temples [i.e., churches] the holy symbols of

Salvation and destroyed them to the extent that it could, behold: from the New World Nature has sent to our world from abroad her own off-spring, rare gifts. You are indeed but a little granadilla, but you offer great things. Though mute yourself, you proclaim the honor of the Cross. As many leaves, spears, or fruits hang from your stem, with just so many spears as a tongue you strike faithless hearts.)

Ibid.

102. Castelli, ch. 3, p. 49: "Haec a curiosis ob raritatem summe expetita. Haec a poetis divinis laudibus decantata. Haec ab oratoribus omni eloquentiae genere celebrata. Haec a philosophis subtilissimis rationibus percuntatata. Haec a medicis ob saluberrimas vires mire commendata. Haec ab aegrotis diu efflagitata. Haec a Theologis admirata, a piis Christianis venerata. Denique haec ab omnibus cuiusque naturae, et conditionis gentibus, ob formae elegantiam, misteria, vires, et alia, mirum in modum exoptata, et perquisita diu fuit, et adhuc est."

103. Ferrari, *Flora*, 194: "conciosia cosa che dal fiore di quella divina serita ap-parisse, come un vital frutto, il cuore dell'amoroso Iddio."

104. Ibid., 192: "venuto finalmenteda' remotissimi confini del Perù, e del Messico; ricevuto con canore voci da' poeti, con faconde dagli oratori."

105. Colonna, 890: "Flos ipse ob signa Passionis Domini devote in eius memo-riam habitus, & gestatus, immundos spiritus arcere existimatur, atque contra incan-tamenta & veneficia valere." (This very flower, which on account of the signs of the Lord's Passion is kept and carried about in memory of Him, is believed to ward off unclean spirits and to have power against enchantments and poisonings.)

106. Parkinson, 398.

107. Ovalle, bk. 1, ch. 23, p. 80: "y quedó admirado [the bishop of Santiago] y consolado de ver una tan grande y nuevo argumento de nuestra fe, que como co-mienza en aquel Nuevo Mundo a echar raíces, quiere el Autor de la naturaleza que las de los mesmos árboles broten y den testimonios de ella, no ya en jeroglíficos, sino en la verdadera representación de la muerte y pasión de nuestro redentor, que fue el único y eficaz medio con que ella se plantó."

108. Matías de Escobar, *Americana Thebaida: [vitas patrum de los religiosos her-mitaños de N.P. San Augustín de la Provincia de San Nicolás Tolentino de Mechoacán]* (1729–40), quoted in Brading, *Mexican Phoenix*, 143.

109. Hall, "World of Wonders" and *Worlds of Wonder*; Godbeer; Van De Wetering.

110. John Calvin, *Commentaries on the Epistles of Paul to the Galatians and Ephesians*, trans. William Pringle (Edinburgh: Calvin Translation Society, 1854), 135.

111. Luxon.

112. Edwards, *History of the Work of Redemption*, 229, quoted in Knight, "Learning the Language of God," 537. For Edwards's typological readings of Nature and his scientific writings, see Edwards, *Images or Shadows*; *Typological Writings*; *Scientific and Philosophical Writings*.

113. Stein.

114. Lukasik.

115. Cited in Canup, 138.

116. Thou sorrow, venom elf.
        Is this thy play,
    To spin a web out of thyself
        To catch a fly?
            For why?
    I saw a pettish wasp
        Fall foul therein,
    Whom yet thy whorl pins did not clasp
        Lest he should fling
            His sting.
    But as afraid, remote
        Didst stand hereat
    And with thy little fingers stroke
        And gently tap
            His back.
    Thus gently him didst treat
        Lest he should pet,
    And in a froppish waspish heat
        Should greatly fret
            Thy net.
    Whereas the silly fly,
        Caught by its leg,
    Thou by the throat took'st hastily
        And 'hind the head
            Bite dead.
    This goes to pot, that not
        Nature doth call.
    Strive not above what strength hath got
        Lest in the brawl
            Thou fall.
    This fray seems thus to us:
        Hell's spider gets
    His entrails spun to whipcords' thus,
        And wove to nets
            And sets,
    To tangle Adam's race
        In's stratagems
    To their destructions, spoiled, made base
        By venom things,
            Damned sins.
    But mighty, gracious Lord,
        Communicate
    Thy grace to break the cord; afford
        Us glory's gate
            And state.
    We'll Nightingale sing like,

> When perched on high
> In glory's cage, Thy glory, bright,
> And thankfully,
> For joy.

Edward Taylor, "Upon a Spider Catching a Fly," in *The Oxford Book of English Verse*, ed. Christopher B. Ricks (Oxford University Press, 1999), 221. On Taylor, see Rowe; Scheick; Howard; Cherry.

117. Cotton Mather, *Christian Philosopher*, 196, and "New Settlement of Birds."

118. Cotton Mather, *Christian Philosopher*, 197.

119. John Wilson quoted in Winthrop, 1: 83–84.

120. Greenblatt, *Renaissance Self-Fashioning*, 157–92. Greenblatt connects Guyon's destruction of the bower of bliss to European colonialism in America, the English occupation of Ireland, and Protestant destruction of Catholic images during the Reformation.

121. Read.

122. Spenser, *Faerie Queene* 2.12.42, p. 268; 2.12.83, p. 276 (references are to book, canto, stanza, and page).

123. Giamatti.

124. On the Spanish "Black Legend," see Juderías; García Carcel; Gibson, ed.; Maltby. On de Bry and the Black Legend, see Bucher; John H. Elliott, "De Bry y la imagen europea de América," in de Bry, 7–13.

125. Schmidt.

126. Ovid, *Metamorphoses*, trans. Rolphe Humphries (Bloomington: Indiana University Press, 1955), 5–7.

127. De Bry, *América*, bk. 5, p. 188: "Describe luego que los españoles se adentraron en varias provincias y parajes del continente con fuerzas militares y ejércitos fingiendo querer implantar e imponer allí el nombre de Cristo, cuando en verdad, tanto en sus corazones como de facto, buscaban no más que oro y plata y grandes riquezas."

128. Ibid., bk. 4, p. 152: "Y verás también retratos varios . . . en que se manifiestan muchas cosas relativas a las costumbres, vida y religión de los habitantes de esta tierra. Podrás dellos deducir la grande diferencia entre los habitantes de los parajes descritos en los anteriores libros y estos de que tracta el presente sobre todo en lo que a la religión atañe: en particular ya que estas gentes no adoran al Dios y Creador de todas las cosas en una imagen de madera como hacen los habitantes de Virginia, ni el sol y la luna como los floridianos, ni Maralea como los brasileños, sino más bien, al propio diablo que se les aparece y presenta bajo toda suerte de horribles formas, tal y como podrás deducir viendo las figuras y leyendo el libro."

129. Ibid.: "¿No contrariamos también nosotros cristianos públicamente a Dios, obedeciendo y adorando al diablo? ¿Quién no adolece de ese maldito vezo que es la cudicia, llamada idolatría por los apóstoles en referencia al codicioso que oro y plata adora y, en estos, al rey deste mundo? . . . De ahí que el diablo, célere y socarrón, nos muestre este mundo con toda su magnificencia y todos sus bienes, queriendo ansí, por nuestro apetito desas cosas, incitarnos a adorarle, como tentara a Cristo. Verás en este libro qué insaciable cudicia reinaba entre los españoles, a cuánto vezo y oprobio los movia dicha cudicia, con cuán horribles y tiránicos modos tractaron

ellos a los pobres indios, y cómo infamemente se degollaron incluso entre ellos mesmos, incitados por la absurda avidez." See also ibid., bk. 5, p. 186: "Es pues el justo y merecido pago (que los españoles se hallan matado entre ellos y los ataquen piratas) que corresponde a todos quienes se han entregado al maldito Diablo. Porque no cabe la menor duda que la ambición y el afán de poder provienen del diablo."

130. Ibid., bk. 4, p. 154: "Pero más vale que cada cual reflexiones en conciencia sobre los actos de otras gentes de otras naciones, para no imputar tal vergüenza y deshonor sólo al pueblo español. ¿No cometemos día a día actos parecidos? Compramos y acopiamos vino y frutos y los guardamos en nuestras bodegas y graneros traiendo hambre y carestía a los pobres, despojamos a nuestros hermanos de sus bienes y los esmorecemos del todo con engaños, usura y finanzas. Día a día nos asfixiamos los unos a los otros, hechizados por desmedida ambición y cudicia. Por ende no debemos ser tan céleres en reprender a los españoles, sino examinar antes si somos mejores nostros o ellos."

131. Ibid.: "es contener nuestro apetito, y ansi satisfacernos con los regalos de la gracia y bondad de Dios y no de ser más de cuanto nos basta para alimentarnos y vestirnos."

132. Benjamin Schmidt has shown that the Dutch first imagined the New World as a land oppressed by cruel Spaniards. The Dutch therefore sought to hammer out alliances with the natives to oust their common overlords. Later, the Dutch chose to see the New World as a land of abundance, whose riches they had the right to exploit to teach the Spaniards virtue. The final stage, however, was one of disenchantment and lost innocence. As they came to share in the wealth of the continent, the Dutch started to bemoan their own corruption. De Bry seemed to have perceived this threat much earlier. See Schmidt.

133. Theodore de Bry, "Lectori benevolo Theodoricus de Bry salutem," in Schmidel, *Americae pars VII*, 4: "Consideratione autem maxime dignum in historiae huius lectione fuerit, quod Deus mirabilia sua opera non velit aeternum manere abscondita & ignota, sed subinde aliquos excitet, qui ea hominibus patefaciant, & omnipotentiam in eis divinam agnoscant, praedicent, atque mirentur. Fuit equidem non minima isthaec Orbis pars America, parentibus nostris hactenus ignota plane atque incognita; Nobis autem hac postrema mundi aetate, divina gratia patefacta est & manifestata, ut occasionem vel inde etiam aliquam haberemus, Deum praedicandi, & vitam nostram iuxta ipsius voluntatem pie instituendi." (Moreover, in the reading of this history it would be especially worthwhile to consider that God does not wish his marvelous works to remain hidden and unknown, but that from time to time he stirs certain people up to reveal them to men and to acknowledge, proclaim, and marvel at divine omnipotence in them. For indeed not the least [sc., of these marvelous works] is precisely this new part of the world, America, which was utterly unknown and undiscovered right up to the time of our parents. To us, however, in this last age of the earth, it has been revealed through divine Grace so that we might have yet another opportunity even from there to proclaim God and order our life piously in accord with His will.)

134. Stuart, pt. 3.

135. Tasso, *Gerusalemme liberata* 14.69, p. 283; 14.73, p. 284; 14.76, p. 285; 15.51, p. 296; 16.3, p. 300; 16.1, p. 300; 15.27–28, p. 291. That Tasso located his emasculat-

ing island in the New World is already well established; see Tylus; Cachey; Fuchs, 23–34.

136. Singleton.

137. Schmidel, *Vera historia*, 1–2: "Narrationes historicae de novis Regionibus & populis, meo iudicio, non tantum iucundae, sed etiam christianis lectu, necessariae sunt. Si immensa, & miranda Dei opera eiusque; ineffabilem misericordiam considerabimus, quam in nos miseros indignosque; Christianos declaravit, quod non tantum sui noticia nos illustravit, sed etiam Adami culpa exitio destinatos preciosos lytro redemit. Contra vero, qa infinita pene millia hominum, qui ut ferae bestiae, destituti omni veri Dei, & eius mandatorum cognitione, sine vitae honestate, coniugio, disciplina, legibus, in horribili Idolatria, sordibus, turpibus libidinibus, ebrietate, & carnium humanarm plusquam barbarica voracitate educati vixerint, & adhuc vivant: Quis christianus non per se aestimare poterit, quantas & quam multiplices habeamus causas, toto vtae nostrae tempore, Deo pro his beneficiis gratias agendi." (Historical accounts of new regions and peoples are in my opinion not only pleasant but even necessary for Christians to read. If we consider the immense and marvelous works of God and the ineffable compassion that he declares for us wretched and unworthy Christians, in that he has enlightened us not so much for his own fame but so that he might also redeem precious peoples destined to destruction through Adam's sin — and if we consider on the other hand how many infinite thousands of men have lived and continue to live like wild beasts, deprived of any knowledge of God and His commandments, lacking uprightness of life, marriage, learning, and laws, brought up in horrible idoltary, baseness, shameful lusts, drunkenness, and a more than barbaric gluttony for human flesh — then what Christian would not be able to judge for himself how many and how varied reasons we have for giving thanks to God for these benefactions all our lives long?)

138. Williamson, 10. Cortesão, *Nautical Chart of 1424*; id., *History of Portuguese Cartography*, 2: 52–73; J. E. Kelley, 27–33; Morison, 81–111.

139. On Rubens's designs to commemorate the arrival in Antwerp of the new Spanish Habsburg governor, see Gevaerts; and Martin, 189–203 (on the Arch of the Mint).

140. Ferrari, *Hesperides*, bk. 1, ch. 1, p. 1: "Hercules profecto nequaquam fabulous est cultura recentior, fabulae involucris, quasi Leonis exuuiis personata: quae labore omnia peruincente, tanquam domitrice clava, magis metuendum excubitore Dracone, diu ineluctabilis difficultatis monstrum ita infregit, atque mactavit: ut Hesperidium pomaria eduli auro spoliaverit: & felici malo nobiles Medorum silvas, extero in solo pridem indociles hospitari, totius iam fere terrarum orbis effecerit inquilinas: imo vero quot auriferas consevit arbores, totidem victoriae suae splendida & pretiiosa trophea statuerit." (Hercules, indeed, not at all utterly mythical, is [i.e., represents] the cultivation of recent times, masked in the wrappings of fable as in his lion skin. This cultivation, with labor conquering all things like a masterful club, has so shattered and killed a monster of long invincible difficulty, far more fearful than a guardian dragon, that it might rob the Garden of the Hesperides of edible gold and might make the Persians' noble groves with their fertile apples, previously untaught to take up lodging in foreign soil, inhabitants now of almost the whole

world. Indeed, as many as are the gold-bearing trees it has planted, so many are the splendid monuments of its victory that it has set up.)

141. "Verklaaring van de Tytelprent"

> Dus bloeit de HARTEKAMP daar *Pyton* legt gevelt.
> En kruiden, bom, noch mensch met zynen damp meer kwelt:
> Dank zy het *Licht* de ZOON', 't welk nevens dat der MAANE
> De moeder de AARDE ontdekt, opdat ze een doortogt baane
> En, door haar *Sleutelen*, zich voor 't gewas onstuit'
> Dies stort zy eenen *Hoorn* van zeldzaamheden uit:
> AR iert een *Vestingkroon* waar meê zy zit te parlen
> Op't Vorstlyk *Dierenpaar*: Zy laat zich niet bepaalen
> Aan 't geen natuur in elx saizoen of luchtstreek teelt;
> Maar word door ARBEID en door KUNST geprangt, gestreelt
> Tot *Water*, *Vuur* en *Glas*, de broejing en het luchten
> De groei bevorderen aan planten en aan vruchten
> Dus kan EUROPE hier den *Ommenkring* van 't JAAR
> Braveeren met *Feestoen* gevlochten by malkaêr
> Uit de alleredeste *Gewasseb*, *Urugten*, *Bloemen*
> Daar AZIE, AFRYKE en AMERIKA op roemen.
> Dit tuigt inzondeheid de *Pisang*, welke Plant
> Het eerst op deze Plaats gewyd aan Nederland,
> Hier, nevens duizenden, Heer Cliffords yver loonen
> En, door Linnaeus Pen, zich aan de waereld toonen.

> In Linnaeus, *Hortus Cliffortianus* (Amsterdam, 1737).

I am very grateful to Willem Klooster for providing me with the following translation from the original Dutch:

"Explanation of the Frontispiece"

> Thus blooms the DEER FOREST where Python lies slain
> And can no longer hurt herbs, tree, nor men with his vapor
> Thanks to the Light of the SUN, which with that of the MOON
> Discovers [or: Uncovers] mother EARTH, so that it forces its way through
> And, with her Keys [?] for the crops;
> She pours out a horn of rarities:
> [??] a Fortified Crown with which she flaunts
> On the Princely Animal Couple: She will not be led
> By what nature grows in each season or climate
> But she is pressed, caressed by LABOR and ART
> Until Water, Fire, and Glass, the heating and airing
> Promote the growth of plants and fruits
> Thus EUROPE can defy the YEAR's circle
> With a Festoon braided
> From the most noble Crops, Fruit, Flowers
> That ASIA, AFRICA, and AMERICA can boast of
> Especially the Banana, a Plant first

devoted to the Netherlands in this place
They reward, with many thousands, Mr. Clifford's zeal
And show themselves to the world through Linnaeus's Pen.

CHAPTER 5. COLONIZATION AS SPIRITUAL GARDENING

1. Herrera, ch. 60–62, pp. 162–67. On the life of Catalina de Jesús, see Vargas.
2. Patricia Miller.
3. E. A. Matter; Astell.
4. "Vida de Santa Teresa de Jesús y algunas de las Mercedes que Dios le hizo, escritas por ella misma por mandato de su confessor, a quien lo envia y dirige, y dice así," in *Obras completas*, 62 (ch. 14): "Me era un gran deleite considerar ser mi alma un huerto y al Señor que se paseaba en él. Suplicábale aumentase el olor de las florecitas de virtudes que comenzaban, a lo que parecía, a querer salir, y que fuese para su gloria, y las sustentase." There are also countless other passages in the autobiography in which Teresa of Avila conceives of her soul as a garden or flower and God as a gardener; see, e.g., 70 (ch. 16), 73 (ch. 17). See also her exegesis of the Song of Songs, "Conceptos del amor de Dios. Escritos por la beata Madre Teresa de Jesús, sobre algunas palabras de los Cantares de Salomón," in *Obras completas*, 503–35.
5. San José, 106, 108 (vision of Barros), 111 (confessors as gardeners).
6. Villa Sánchez, 25: "havia visto subir a Anna de San Juan al Cielo, por un camino de rosas."
7. Peterson, 165 (on Acolman) and passim (Malinalco). Gumilla, 239–42. On the theatrical function of murals, cloisters, and churches in the early missionary compounds created by the Augustinians, Franciscans, and Dominicans in Mexico, see Lara; Edgerton.
8. Warner, chs. 8, 16, and 20; Falkenburg; Stratton.
9. Cowen.
10. Constable, 143–248; Fulton, *From Judgment to Passion* and "Virgin in the Garden"; Winston-Allen.
11. Swanson; Barlett, 153–55, 190, 262–63.
12. See Mujica Pinilla, 154. On colonial saints in Mexico, see the magisterial work of Rubial García.
13. On St. Rose of Lima, see Flores Araoz et al.; Myers; Graziano. On Mariana's life, I have followed the hagiography by Morán de Butrón. On suffering, relics, and saintliness as the defeat of the corruption of the body, see Bynum, *Fragmentation* and *Resurrection of the Body*.
14. Manuel de Ribero Leal, *Oración Evangélica en la beatificación de Rosa de Santa María* (Lima, 1675), quoted in Myers, 260: "Fragancia de buenos exemplos . . . han convertido en parayso de delicias santas esta selva antes inculta de nuestra Meridional América."
15. Morán de Butrón, 59–64, esp. 63; see also 24–25, 42.
16. Ibid., 42: "Pero parece haber dispuesto la mano agricultora del Altísimo, que después de un siglo entero en que muerta San Rosa, difundídose por todo el orbe su fama y esparcídose el olor de sus virtudes, salga ahora la Azucena para la celebridad

y el aplauso, o del botón de su olvido o de la los últimos fines de la tierra para su mayor aprecio."

17. Rivadeneyra, 499. On the cult of Felipe de Jesús in Mexico, see Estrada de Gerlero.

18. Sánchez, *Sermón de San Felipe de Jesús*, 13r: "Pues no se persuaden, puede tener alguna cosa buena!" Many thanks to Cory Conover for making a copy of the sermon available to me.

19. Ibid.: "retirado cobarde, temeroso fugitivo."

20. Ibid., 7v: "Regada ya la tierra de Felipe, comienzan a surcarla puntas de los arados y Japonés verdugos."

21. Ibid., 16v: "dejándonos esperanzas que si un pedazo de nuestra tierra supo dar frutos, los puede dar la tierra."

22. For a solid but dated analysis of Balbuena's *El Bernardo*, see Van Horne.

23. El bravo brío español que rompe y mide,
    a pesar de Neptuno y sus espantos,
    los golfos en que un mundo en dos divide,
    y aquellos nobles estandartes santos,
    que con su sombra dieron luz divina
    a las tinieblas en que estaban tantos.

    Balbuena, 13.

24. Ibid., 15: "Solo diré de lo que soy testigo,/digno de Homero y de la fama espanto."

25. Ibid., 76: "El centro y corazón de esta gran bola." On the horses and knights of Mexico as superior to Orlando's, see ibid., 22–23.

26. Ibid., 64: "pobladas de gigantes más que humanos/en letras, santidad, ejemplo, vida,/doctrina, perfección, pechos cristianos"; 69: "hazañas dignas del caudal de Homero."

27. Ibid., 68: "Este es pues, señora, el verdadero/tesoro." On the enumeration of religious orders, temples, and convents, see ibid., 64–68, 100.

28. Ibid., 69: "de aquestos amenísimos vergeles,/llenos de rosas, alhelís, jacintos,/jazmines, azucenas y claveles." It was common in Spanish America for religious orders to present their colleges as sealed, blossoming gardens of learning and piety. For a controversy in Cuzco using these metaphors, see Stastny.

29. Ibid., 70: "nueva Roma parece en trato y talle."

30. For an analysis of this text, see Ross. I have used the 1995 edition of Carlos Sigüenza y Góngora's *Paraíso occidental* (1683).

31. Sigüenza, *Paraíso occidental*, 42: "Paradisus est Ecclesia: quatuor flumina sunt quatuor Evangelia: ligna fructifera sunt Sancti; fructus sunt opera Sanctorum; lignum vitae est Christus Sanctus Sanctorum."

32. On this pictorial genre typical of colonial Spanish America, see the beautifully produced exhibition catalogue edited by Miguel Fernández Félix and Sara Gabriela Baz, *Monjas coronadas: Vida conventual femenina en Hispanoamérica*.

33. The literature on Our Lady of Guadalupe is immense; I have relied on the well-known works of Brading (*Mexican Phoenix*); Masa; Lafaye; and Poole.

34. There is one exception; see Osorio Romero, 123–26, 223–35 on the horticultural trope in the colonial poetry to Our Lady of Guadalupe.

35. Warner, ch. 16–17; Stratton.
36. Sánchez, *Imagen*, 153–281.
37. Ibid., 233.
38. Ibid., 230.
39. Sigüenza y Góngora, *Primavera indiana*, 335–58. The Roman numerals refer to the number of the verse in the poem.
40. The edition of Florencia's *Estrella of Mexico* in *Testimonios históricos guadalupanos* (1982) does not reproduce the Preface. For it, I have consulted Francisco Florencia, *La estrella de el norte de Mexico* (1688), n.p.
41. Villerías y Roelas, 354: "memor servat crudelia nostrae."
42. Florencia (1982), 379–80 (on the influence of the rosary in the spatial organization of the cult).
43. On the event that led to the creation of settlements in Connecticut, see Shuffelton, esp. ch. 6; and Lucas.
44. On the incredibly stringent restrictions of Church membership (contingent on proving through public testimony that one had received God's grace) once the Puritans arrived in the New World, see Morgan.
45. Curiously, I have not been able to find any interpretation of the origins of the Connecticut seal.
46. The topic of bodily transformation induced by grace is one that to my knowledge has not been explored. The early modern body was seen as matter that could easily be transformed (both racially and in gender) by dreams, climate, and excretion and circulation of bodily fluids. Puritans understood conversion as though God were a "seal" on human wax.
47. John Cotton, *Treatise of the Covenant*, 32, 215.
48. Ibid., 19.
49. Bulkeley, 335, 371. On the various stages of spiritual life (preparation, justification, and sanctification), see Holifield, *Theology in America*, 42.
50. On hedges protecting the garden-church in the New World, see Carroll, ch. 6.
51. Roger Williams, ch. 28. Rosenmeier, "Teacher and the Witness," dismisses all efforts to cast Williams as a forerunner of religious tolerance.
52. John Cotton, *Bloudy Tenent*, 151, quoted in Carroll, 114. For a summary of the debate in the context of the rise of Puritan millennialism, see Holifield, *Theology in America*, 51–52; see also Rosenmeier, "Teacher and the Witness."
53. On the primitivism of the Puritan Church, see Bozeman.
54. Sanderson, 120 (the third sermon). Italics in the original. On the Sanderson-Cotton debate in England, see Rosenmeier, "Eater and Non-Eaters."
55. Shepard, 362. On Shepard as a polarizing figure in the free-grace (Antinomian) controversy, see Winship.
56. Willard, 99, 90, 98.
57. Danforth, 59.
58. Ibid., 68–69.
59. Ibid., 73 (my emphasis).
60. Ibid., 66.

61. Thomas Shepard, *Day-Breaking, If not The Sun-Rising of the Gospell With the Indians in New-England* ([1647] 1834), 4, quoted in Canup, 164.

62. Carroll, *Puritanism and the Wilderness*, 123–26.

63. John Cotton, *Briefe Exposition*, 9, 14, 53. On Cotton's exegesis on the larger context of Puritan interpretations of the Song of Songs, see Hammond.

64. This sense that Puritans could have it both ways is one of the themes in Lepore. Lepore argues that the Puritans sought to distance themselves from the brutalities of the Spanish Antichrist in the New World while engaging themselves in systematic brutalities of their own. They were successful. Today U.S. colonial historiography seems to be unsure whether the colonization of British America was "conquest" or "settlement"!

65. John Cotton, *Planters Plea*, 14, 15, 16, 18.

66. William Williams, *Death of a Prophet*, 23, quoted in Gura, 57.

67. Edwards, "Personal Narrative," 796.

68. Edwards, *Some Thoughts*, 353.

69. Edwards, *Religious Affections*, 184–85.

70. Similar discourses of soul management as colonization and spiritual gardening appear in the Huguenot colonization of the New World; see Kamil. Kamil gives central place in Huguenot theology to Bernard Palissy, a designer of grottos and gardens.

CHAPTER 6. TOWARD A "PAN-AMERICAN" ATLANTIC

1. Greene, "Beyond Power."

2. Cañizares-Esguerra, *How to Write the History of the New World*.

3. Pagden; Seed, *Ceremonies of Possession* and *American Pentimento*; Chaplin.

4. Bolton. Benjamin Keen has described Bolton's "generous enthusiasm . . . for Spain's daring explorers and missionaries" as a "'white man's burden' defense of Spanish colonialism." See Keen, "Main Currents," 662. For a more sympathetic yet critical assessment of Bolton's Spanish borderland scholarship as worked out by his pupil John Francis Bannon, see Weber, *Myth*, 55–88.

5. Kagan, "Prescott's Paradigm."

6. Keen, "Main Currents."

7. See Lanning, *Academic Culture* and *Eighteenth-Century Enlightenment*; Leonard, *Don Carlos de Sigüenza y Góngora, Baroque Times in Old Mexico*, and *Books of the Brave*.

8. See Hanke, *Spanish Struggle for Justice* and *Aristotle and the American Indians*.

9. See Simpson, *Encomienda in New Spain* and *Studies in the Administration of the Indians*.

10. See Aiton, *Antonio de Mendoza*; Zimmerman, *Francisco de Toledo*. Herbert I. Priestley first initiated the genre; see his *José de Gálvez*.

11. See Tannenbaum, *Slave and Citizen*; Freyre, *Masters*.

12. Bolton's call for a history of continental America was summarily dismissed by historians in the United States and Mexico, who argued that the United States and

Latin America were culturally and historically incommensurable. For two representative articles, see O'Gorman, and Whitaker. Whitaker found the Enlightenment to
be the only period when both societies came together.

13. Pike, 193–296.

14. The Pan American Institute of Geography and History stood behind Bolton's
proposal and even sponsored a History of America program, which shut down in
the early 1960s with little to show in the way of new insights and scholarship. For a
brief overview of this initiative in the context of Bolton's proposal, see Hanke, 3–50.
On the normative role of Europe in history at large, see Chakrabarty. On American
exceptionalism, see Rodgers, "Exceptionalism."

15. Karras; Benjamin; Armitage and Braddick.

16. Kicza.

17. See Hijiya and the series of short replies to his proposal by prominent historians of the West in *William and Mary Quarterly*, 3d ser., 51, 4 (1994): 717–54.

18. Taylor.

19. Adelman and Aron. See also Chase and the AHR Forum, "Revolutions in
the Americas," in *American Historical Review* 105 (February 2000): 93–152, featuring essays by Jack Greene, Franklin W. Knight, Virginia Guedea, and Jaime E.
Rodríguez O.

20. Armitage and Braddick. See also the special issue of *Itinerario* 23, 2 (1999),
featuring articles by David Hancock, Silvia Marzagalli, and Carla Rahn Phillips on
the British, French, and Spanish Atlantic worlds, respectively.

21. See, e.g., J. H. Elliott's gentle yet forceful critique of most of the essays in
Armitage and Braddick's "Atlantic History." See also his *En búsqueda* and *Britain
and Spain.*

22. For wide pan-American narratives, see Blackburn; Eltis; Pagden; and Seed,
Ceremonies of Possession and *American Pentimento.*

23. On the global dimensions of most early modern European empires, see
Ringrose; Subrahmanyam, *Portuguese Empire*; Russell-Wood, *Portuguese Empire*;
Kamen.

24. Gruzinski.

25. L. A. Pérez.

26. Rodgers, "Exceptionalism"; Ross, "Historical Consciousness"; Greene, *Intellectual Construction.*

27. Tyrrell; Karras. That comparative perspectives tend to reinforce the thesis of
"American exceptionalism" can be seen in Morton Keller's 2001 review of James C.
Scott's *Seeing Like a State: How Certain Schemes to Improve the Human Condition
Have Failed* (New Haven, Conn.: Yale University Press, 1998). Among sociologists,
the comparative and the global (world-system) approaches have remained separate
and distinct. Late processes of globalization, however, are forcing sociologists to
reconsider the wisdom of maintaining these boundaries. On this, see Arrighi.

28. Bender, "Historians," 8.

29. Ibid., 12.

30. Weil.

31. Jaime Rodríguez has studied the impact of the wars in far greater detail
and has offered a powerful and persuasive interpretation of the impact of the wars

on nineteenth-century Latin American underdevelopment that parallels some of Fernández-Armesto's interpretations on the causes of sudden divergence. See Rodríguez O., "Emancipation" and *Independence*. Rodríguez demonstrates the "poverty of theory" in recent continental interpretations of the wars such as that offered by Langley.

32. On the wars, see Wood; Langley; and Rodríguez's critique, "Emancipation."

33. For representative studies of these culturalist traditions, see Hartz; Veliz.

34. Fernández-Armesto, *Americas*, builds its critique of culturalist and dependentist explanations of underdevelopment on the brilliant and heterodox insights of Dunkerley.

35. Bender, *Rethinking*; Howe; Rodgers, *Atlantic Crossing*; O'Rourke and Williamson; Gabbaccia.

36. Besides numerous articles on French colonial North America and the British Caribbean and the references on Spanish American historiography cited above, the *William and Mary Quarterly* has published three special issues on Atlantic history since 1990, dealing with colonial encounters (April 1992), race and racial ideologies (January 1997), and African-American slavery (April 1999). Aside from its special spring 1999 issue on borderlands, my review of the *Journal of the Early Republic* yielded only one article remotely resembling an Atlantic perspective: Jack Ray Thomas, "Latin American Views of US Politics in the Nineteenth Century," ibid., 1992, pp. 357–80. See however the push toward the internationalization of the *Journal of American History* launched in 1992; for the rationale behind this push, see Thelen.

37. Richard White, *Middle Ground*. Adelman and Aron's study reaches into the early nineteenth century.

38. See Tannenbaum; Freyre; Degler; D. B. Davis; Thomas; Thornton; Blackburn; Berlin, esp. chapter on "Atlantic creoles"; Eltis; and the AHR Forum, "Crossing Slavery's Boundaries," *American Historical Review*, vol. 105 (April 2000), 451–84, featuring articles by David Brion Davis, Peter Kolchin, Rebecca J. Scott, and Stanley L. Engerman

39. There is, to be sure, a tradition of comparative frontier studies that explore imperial expansions from China to Russia to South Africa to Australia to the New World; see, e.g., Webb; Lattimore; Wyman and Kroeber, eds.; Miller and Steffen, eds.; Savage and Thompson, eds.; Lamar and Thompson, eds. Latin Americanists are becoming increasingly interested in comparative frontier studies; see Baretta and Markoff; Platt and di Tella, eds.; Solberg; Weber and Rausch, eds.; Slatta; Guy and Sheridan. Using Canada and Argentina, Jeremy Adelman has done away with many of the historiographical pieties that have dominated comparative studies of the prairies and the pampas (farmsteads and freeholders in the North vs. haciendas and tenants in the South); see Adelman, *Frontier Development*.

40. Wyman, *Round-Trip*; Hoerder. Some authors, however, have expanded the study of nineteenth-century European migrations within Europe and to (and back from) the New World to include Brazil and Argentina; see, e.g., Nugent; Baily; Moya.

41. Richard White, *"It's Your Misfortune"*; but see chapter by Walter Nugent in Limerick et al., eds., *Trails*, that does bring in Brazil and Argentina.

42. See, however, Bender, *Rethinking*; Howe; Rodgers, *Atlantic*; O'Rourke and Williamson; Gabbaccia for alternative perspectives. For two representative studies of the Porfiriato, see Wasserman; Vanderwood. For a textbook that successfully locates nineteenth-century Mexico in the greater context of the history of the borderlands, see MacLachlan and Beezley.

43. On New World plantation slavery as inextricably linked to the making of modern institutions, see Blackburn; Gilroy, 41–71.

44. Jeremy Adelman has sought to interpret nineteenth-century liberalism in Argentina from a more generous global perspective; see Adelman, *Republic*. See also Dunkerley. For an effort to present Creole Spanish American attempts at nation building as original and even normative (in fact anticipating European ones), see Anderson, ch. 4. For a wonderful study of how women's suffrage first developed outside the North Atlantic, in peripheral settings rather than the metropolitan cores, see Markoff.

45. Some scholars argue that the Civil War was in fact a struggle between two different "nations," whose identities have been linked to the dynamics of antebellum partisan politics. For a synthesis of this literature, see Fredrickson. For a similar narrative of nation building, see Bushnell.

46. R. D. G. Kelley; Gilroy; D. G. White.

47. Bailyn; O'Reilly.

48. Lewis and Wigen. On the category of "Oriental despotism" as a critique of Stalinism, see Karl A. Wittfogel, *Oriental Despotism: A Comparative Study of Total Power* (New Haven, Conn.: Yale University Press, 1957). Russia to be sure had long been cast as "Oriental"; see Wolff. The "Asiatic" character of Russia, for example, allowed Western observers to underreport (and even justify) the 1932–33 famine brought about by the Bolshevik forced collectivization of the Ukrainian countryside. On this, see Engerman. Russians have themselves bought into these constructs; see Kingston-Mann. With the disintegration of the Soviet Union and their integration to the European Union, Polish, Czech, and Hungarian intellectuals have been forced to grapple with similar issues. Czech intellectuals like Milan Kundera insist that "Prague is [intellectually] west of Vienna." Their "West," however, seeks merely to expand the North Atlantic into the former Eastern Europe. Thanks to John Markoff for bringing this to my attention.

49. Jardine and Brotton; Deborah Howard.

50. Goffman.

51. Buruma and Margalit; Ohnuki-Tierney.

52. See, e.g., O'Reilly; Bailyn.

53. Schmidt-Nowara.

54. For a history of Latin American alternative transnational discourses, see Rojas Mix.

55. Stern, "Feudalism."

56. See Wallerstein; Stern, "Ever More Solitary."

57. Mignolo, vii–xvii, 1–25.

58. González Echeverría.

59. Toews.

60. Benjamin Keen, "Main Currents"; J. J. Johnson. The list below does not

seek to be exhaustive and identifies only works in English; the literature in French, Spanish, and Portuguese, of course, is huge. Moreover, I have purposefully excluded the many fine works by literary critics such as Rolena Adorno, Margarita Zamora, Nicolas Shumway, Doris Sommer, and Deborah Poole, as well as those by Anthony Pagden, David Brading, Fernando Cervantes, and other historians based in Britain. The colonial period has, it seems, been the focus of more attention, largely because the subject is still Europe. See the works by Lanning and Leonard cited in the bibliography. See also Grafton; Benjamin Keen, *Essays* and *Aztec Image*; MacCormack; Luis Martín; Phelan. For the national period, see Hale, *Mexican Liberalism* and *Transformation*; Skidmore, *Black into White*; Gootenberg; Stepan; Love, *Crafting the Third World*. I am sure more books ought to be added, but the list would nevertheless remain rather short.

61. For a recent insightful critique of these constructs, see Hart.

62. Yúdice.

63. For an insightful critique of this historiography, see Blaut.

64. Cañizares-Esguerra, "Iberian Science in the Renaissance."

65. See Prebisch et al.; Celso Furtado, *A economia brasileira (Contribução á análise do seu desenvolvimiento)* (Rio de Janeiro: A. Noite, 1954); id., *Uma economia dependente* (Rio de Janeiro: Ministério de Educação e Cultura, 1956); id., *Formação econômica do Brasil* (Rio de Janeiro: Fondo de Cultura, 1959); Aníbal Pinto de Santa Cruz, *Chile un caso de desarrollo frustrado* (Santiago: Ed. del Pacífico, 1959); Aldo Ferrer, *La economía argentina: Las etapas de su desarrollo y problemas actuales* (Mexico City: Fondo de Cultura Económica, 1963); Osvaldo Sunkel and Pedro Paz, *El subdesarrollo latinoamericano y la teoría del desarrollo* (Madrid: Siglo Veintiuno de España, 1970); René Villareal, *El desequilibrio externo en la industrialización de México (1929–75): Un enfoque estructuralista* (Mexico City: Fondo de Cultura Económica, 1976). For a history of the process through which Prebisch's critique was historicized, see Love, "Furtado."

66. See André Gunder Frank, *Capitalism and Underdevelopment in Latin America. Historical Studies of Chile and Brazil* (New York: Monthly Review Press, 1967); Fernando Henrique Cardoso and Enzo Faletto, *Dependencia y desarrollo en América Latina: Ensayo de interpretación sociológica* (Mexico City: Siglo Veintiuno Editores, 1969), translated into English as *Dependency and Development in Latin America* (Berkeley: University of California Press, 1979); Halperín-Donghi, *Historia contemporánea de América Latina*; Stanley J. Stein and Barbara H. Stein, *The Colonial Heritage of Latin America: Essays on Economic Dependence in Perspective* (New York: Oxford University Press, 1970); E. Bradford Burns, *Latin America: A Concise Interpretative History* (Englewood Cliffs, N.J.: Prentice-Hall, 1972); Benjamin Keen and Mark Wasserman, *A Short History of Latin America* (Boston: Houghton Mifflin, 1980); Thomas Skidmore and Peter H. Smith, *Modern Latin America* (New York: Oxford University Press, 1984).

67. See Halperín-Donghi, "'Dependency Theory' and Latin American Historiography." See also Fernando Henrique Cardoso, "The Consumption of Dependency Theory in the United States," *Latin American Research Review* 12, 3 (1977): 7–24.

68. Schwartz. Latin American historians might seem to be departing from the

Atlantic paradigm, but they remain methodologically engaged with U.S. historiography; see Skidmore, "Studying the History."

69. Van Young, "Was There an Age of Revolution in Spanish America?"

70. Richard White, "Trashing the Trails." On tragic and comedic emplotments, see Hayden White. Although frontier images of cowboys, llaneros, and gauchos do sometimes overlap, and although images of the frontier as "wilderness" and invigorating "virgin land," the cradle of nationality, did emerge in Latin America, the historiographies of the frontier in the United States and Latin America took separate paths. On overlapping themes and differences, see Slatta, 3–34; and Guy and Sheridan, 7–12.

71. Halperín-Donghi, "Argentines Ponder the Burden of the Past."

72. Galeano.

73. For a case study of this tendency, see Shumway; Halperín-Donghi, "Argentines Ponder the Burden of the Past."

74. This trope organizes "dependency-theory" historiography. For examples outside the "dependentista" school, see Jacobsen. More recently, Jeremy Adelman has sought to call attention to potential pitfalls of this approach; see his "Introduction: The Problem of Persistence in Latin American History," in id., ed., *Colonial Legacies*, 1–13.

75. For the history and persistence of these stereotypes, see Pike.

76. For historiographical surveys, see Lockhart; Keen, "Main Currents"; Kicza; Russell-Wood, "United States Scholarly Contributions"; Eric Van Young, "Recent Anglophone Scholarship." For a positive view of the *repartimiento*, see Baskes.

77. There are, of course, exceptions; see, e.g., Rodríguez O. and MacLachlan for a deliberate attempt to do away with "prevalent view[s] [that] held that New Spain's experience had been [a] negative [one, of unremitting cruelty and destruction, or a simple and straightforward domination of one group over another]." The authors daringly advance the argument that "New Spain's history represents [in terms of creating a truly hybrid, mestizo culture] a remarkable human achievement, unequaled in other parts of the world" (preface to expanded edition, 1990). I find Mills and Taylor's emphasis on religion particularly insightful.

Select Bibliography

Acosta, José de. *Historia natural y moral de las Indias....* 1590. Madrid: Alonso Martín, 1608.

Adelman, Jeremy. *Frontier Development: Land, Labour and Capital on the Wheatlands of Argentina and Canada, 1890–1914.* Oxford: Clarendon Press, 1994.

————. "Introduction: The Problem of Persistence in Latin American History." In Adelman, ed., *Colonial Legacies,* 1–13. New York: Routledge, 1999.

————. *Republic of Capital: Buenos Aires and the Legal Transformation of the Atlantic World.* Stanford: Stanford University Press, 1999.

————, ed. *Colonial Legacies: The Problem of Persistence in Latin American History.* New York: Routledge, 1999.

Adelman, Jeremy, and Stephen Aron. "From Borderlands to Borders: Empires, Nation-States, and the Peoples in Between in North American History." *American Historical Review* 104, 3 (1999): 814–41.

Aguilar y Leira, Francisco del. *Desengaño contra el mal uso de tabaco.* Córdoba: Salvador de Cea Tesa, 1634.

Aiton, Arthur S. *Antonio de Mendoza, First Viceroy of New Spain.* Durham, N.C.: Duke University Press, 1927.

Alberro, Solange. *Inquisición y Sociedad en México, 1571–1700.* Mexico City: Fondo de Cultura Económica, 1988.

Alvar, Manuel. "Fantastic Tales and Chronicles of the Indies." *Hispanic Issues* 9 (1992): 163–82.

Anchieta, José de. *De gestis Mendi de Saa (poema epicum).* 1563. Edited by José María Fornell Lombardo. Granada: Santa Rita, 1992.

Anderson, Benedict. *Imagined Communities: Reflections on the Origins and Spread of Nationalism.* 1983. Rev. ed. New York: Verso, 1991.

Appleby, Joyce. "A Different Kind of Independence: The Postwar Restructuring of the Historical Study of Early America." *William and Mary Quarterly,* 3d ser., 50 (1993): 245–67.

————. *Inheriting the Revolution. The First Generation of Americans.* Cambridge, Mass: Harvard University Press, 2000.

Armas Wilson, Diana de. *Cervantes, the Novel and the New World.* Oxford: Oxford University Press, 2000.

Armitage, David, and Michael Braddick, eds. *The British Atlantic, 1500–1800.* New York: Palgrave Macmillan, 2002.

Arriaga, Pablo José de. *Extirpación de la idolatría del Piru.* 1621. Edited by Horacio

H. Urtega. Colección de Libros y Documentos Referentes a Historia del Perú. 2d ser. Vol. 1. Lima: San Martí, 1920.

Arrighi, Giovanni. "Globalization and Macrosociology." In Janet Abu-Lughod, ed., *Sociology for the Twenty-First Century: Continuities and Cutting Edges*, 117–33. Chicago: Chicago University Press, 2000.

Astell, Ann W. *The Song of Songs in the Middle Ages*. Ithaca, N.Y.: Cornell University Press, 1990.

Avalle-Arce, Juan Bautista. *La épica colonial*. Pamplona: Universidad de Navarra, 2000.

Avila, Saint Teresa de. *Obras completas*. Edited by Luis Santullano. Madrid: M. Aguilar, 1951.

Bailey, Michael D. *Battling Demons: Witchcraft, Heresy, and Reform in the Late Middle Ages*. University Park: Pennsylvania State University Press, 2003.

Baily, Samuel L. *Immigrants in the Land of Promise: Italians in Buenos Aires and New York City, 1870–1914*. Princeton, N.J.: Princeton University Press, 1999.

Bailyn, Bernard. "The Idea of Atlantic History." *Itinerario* 20, 1 (1996): 19–44.

Balbuena, Bernardo. *Grandeza mexicana*. Mexico City: Universidad Nacional Autónoma de México, 1941.

Bancroft, Edward. *An Essay on the Natural History of Guiana, in South America*. London: T. Becket and P. A. De Hondt, 1769.

Barco Centenera, Martín del. *Argentina y conquista del Río de la Plata*. 1602. Edited by Silva Tieffemberg. Buenos Aires: Universidad de Buenos Aires, 1998.

Baretta, Silvio Duncan, and John Markoff. "Civilization and Barbarism: Cattle Frontiers in Latin America." *Comparative Studies in Society and History* 20 (October 1978): 587–620.

Barker, Francis, Peter Hulme, and Margeret Iversen, eds. *Cannibalism and the Colonial World*. Cambridge: Cambridge University Press, 1998.

Barlett, Robert. *The Making of Europe: Conquest, Colonization and Cultural Change*. Princeton, N.J.: Princeton University Press, 1993.

Barros, Joam de. *Asia: Dos feitos que os portugueses fizeram no descobrimento e conquista dos mares e terras do oriente, primera decada*. 1552–53. Edited by António Baião. 4th ed. Scriptores Rerum Lusitanarum, ser. A. Coimbra: Imprensa da Universidade, 1932.

Baskes, Jeremy. *Indians, Merchants, and Markets: A Reinterpretation of the Repartimiento and Spanish-Indian Economic Relations in Oaxaca, 1750–1821*. Stanford: Stanford University Press, 2000.

Bauckham, Richard. *Tudor Apocalypse: Sixteenth-century Apocalypticism, Millennarianism and the English Reformation*. Oxford: Sutton Courtenay, 1978.

Baudot, Georges. *Utopia and History in Mexico: The First Chroniclers of Mexican Civilization, 1520–1569*. Translated by Bernard R. Ortiz de Montellano and Thelma Ortiz de Montellano. Niwot: University Press of Colorado, 1995. Originally published as *Utopie et histoire au Mexique: Les Premiers Chroniqueurs de la civilisation mexicaine, 1520–1569* (Toulouse: Privat, 1977).

The Beginning, Progress, and Conclusion of Bacon's Rebellion in Virginia in the Years 1675 and 1676. American Colonial Tracts Monthly, no. 8 (December 1897).

Behar, Ruth. "Sex and Sin, Witchcraft and the Devil in Late-colonial Mexico." *American Ethnologist* 14 (1987): 34–54.

Benavente, Toribio de. *Historia de los Indios de Nueva España.* Ca. 1550. Edited by Claudio Esteva Fabregat. Colección Crónicas de América. Madrid: Dastin, 2001.

Bender, Thomas. "Historians, the Nation, and the Plentitude of Narratives." In Bender, ed., *Rethinking American History in a Global Age,* 1–21. Berkeley: University of California Press, 2002.

————. "Strategies of Narrative Synthesis in American History." *American Historical Review* 107 (2002): 129–53.

————, ed. *Rethinking American History in a Global Age.* Berkeley: University of California Press, 2002.

Benjamin, Thomas, Timothy Hall, and David Rutherford. *The Atlantic World in the Age of Empire.* Boston: Houghton Mifflin, 2000.

Bercovitch, Sacvan. *American Jeremiad.* Madison: University of Wisconsin Press, 1978.

————. "New England Epic: Cotton Mather's 'Magnalia Christi Americana.'" *English Literary History* 33 (1966): 337–50.

————, ed. *Typology and Early American Literature.* Amherst: University of Massachusetts Press, 1972.

Berlin, Ira. *Many Thousands Gone: The First Two Centuries of Slavery in North America.* Cambridge, Mass: Belknap Press of Harvard University Press, 1998.

Blackburn, Robin. *The Making of New World Slavery: From the Baroque to the Modern, 1492–1800.* London: Verso, 1997.

Blaeu, Joan. *Geographia, quae est cosmographiae Blauianae.* 11 vols. Amsterdam: Joan Blaeu, 1662–65.

Blaut, J. M. *The Colonizer's Model of the World: Geographical Diffusionism and Eurocentric History.* New York: Guilford Press, 1993.

Blessington, Francis."*Paradise Lost" and the Classical Epic.* London: Routledge & Kegan Paul, 1979.

Bolton, Herbert Eugene. "The Epic of Greater America." *American Historical Review* 38 (1933): 448–74. Reproduced in Hanke, ed., *Do the Americas Have a Common History?* 67–100. New York: Knopf, 1964.

Bond, Edward L. "Source of Knowledge, Source of Power: The Supernatural World of English Virginia, 1607–1624." *Virginia Magazine of History and Biography* 108 (2000) 2: 105–38.

Bosio, Iacomo. *La trionfante e gloriosa croce.* Rome: A. Ciacone, 1610.

Bossy, John. *Christianity in the West, 1400–1700.* Oxford: Oxford University Press, 1985.

————. "Moral Arithmetic: Seven Sins into Ten Commandments." In Edmund Leites, ed., *Conscience and Casuistry in Early Modern Europe.* Cambridge: Cambridge University Press, 1988.

Bouza, Fernando. *Communication, Knowledge, and Memory in Early Modern Spain.* Philadelphia: University of Pennsylvania Press, 2004.

Bozeman, Theodore Dwight. *To Live Ancient Lives: The Primitivist Dimensions in Puritanism.* Chapel Hill: University of North Carolina Press, 1988.

Brading, David. *The First America: The Spanish Monarchy, Creole Patriots, and the Liberal State.* Cambridge: Cambridge University Press, 1991.

———. *Mexican Phoenix: Our Lady of Guadalupe. Image and Process.* Cambridge: Cambridge University Press, 2001.

Bremer, Francis J. "Endecott and the Red Cross: Puritan Iconoclasm in the New World." *Journal of American Studies* 24 (1990): 5–22.

Brown, Jonathan, and John H. Elliott. *A Palace for the King: The Buen Retiro and the Court of Philip IV.* Rev. expanded edition. New Haven, Conn.: Yale University Press, 2004.

Brown, Paul. "'This thing of darkness I acknowledge mine': The *Tempest* and the Discourse of Colonialism." In Jonathan Dellimore and Aland Sinfield, eds., *Political Shakespeare: New Essays in Cultural Materialism*, 48–71. Ithaca, N.Y.: Cornell University Press, 1985.

Brown, Peter. *The Cult of Saints: Its Rise and Function in Latin Christianity.* Chicago: University of Chicago Press, 1981.

Brumm, Ursula. *American Thought and Religious Typology.* Translated by John Hoogland. New Brunswick, N.J.: Rutgers University Press, 1970. Originally published as *Die religiöse Typologie im amerikanischen Denken: Ihre Bedeutung für die amerikanische Literatur- und Geistesgeschichte* (Leiden: Brill, 1963).

Brunfels, Otto. *Herbarum vivae eicones ad naturae imitatione.* . . . Strasbourg: Ioannem Schottum, 1532.

Bry, Theodore de. *América (1590–1634).* Translated by Adán Kovacsis. Edited by Gereon Sievernich. Madrid: Siruela, 1992.

Bry, Theodore de, et al., eds. *Americae pars I–XIII.* Frankfurt a/M, 1590–1634.

Bucher, Bernardette. *Icon and Conquest: A Structural Analysis of the Illustrations of de Bry's Great Voyages.* Chicago: University of Chicago Press, 1981.

Bulkeley, Peter. *The Gospel-Covenant; or the Covenant of Grace Openend.* Enlarged 2d ed. London: Mathew Simmons, 1651.

Buruma, Ian, and Avishai Margalit. *Occidentalism: The West in the Eyes of Its Enemies.* New York: Penguin Books, 2004.

Bushnell, David. *The Making of Modern Colombia: A Nation in Spite of Itself.* Berkeley: University of California Press, 1993.

Bustamante de la Cámara, Juan. *De animantibus Scripturae Sacrae. Tomus Primus: De reptilibvs vere animantibvs Sacrae Scripturae.* Alcala de Henares: Juan Gracian, 1595.

Bynum, Carolyn Walker. *Fragmentation and Redemption: Essays on Gender and the Human Body in Medieval Religion.* New York: Zone Books, 1992.

———. *The Resurrection of the Body in Western Christianity, 200–1336.* New York: Columbia University Press, 1995.

Cachey, Theodore. "Tasso's Navigazione del Mondo Nuovo and the Origins of the Columbus Encomium." *Italica* 69, 3 (1992): 326–43.

Caciola, Nancy. *Discerning Spirits: Divine and Demonic Possession in the Middle Ages.* Ithaca, N.Y.: Cornell University Press, 2003.

Calancha, Antonio de la. *Chronica moralizada del orden de San Augustin en el Peru, con sucesos egenplares en esta monarquia.* Barcelona: Pedro Lacavalleria, 1639.

Calderón de la Barca, Pedro. *La aurora en Copacabana.* 1672. Edited by Ezra S. Engling. London: Tamesis, 1994.

———. *La semilla y la cizaña.* In id., *Autos sacramentales,* 3: 817–93. Edited by Enrique Rull Fernández. 7 vols. Madrid: Fundación José Antonio de Castro, 2002.

Calvete de Estrella, Juan Cristóbal. *Elogio de Vaca de Castro.* Translated and edited by José López de Toro. Madrid: Consejo Superior de Investigaciones Científicas, 1947.

Calvo, Hortensia, "The Politics of Print: The Historiography of the Book in Early Spanish America." *Book History* 6 (2003): 277–305.

Canup, John. *Out of the Wilderness: The Emergence of and American Identity in Colonial New England.* Middletown, Conn.: Wesleyan University Press, 1990.

Cañizares-Esguerra, Jorge. *How to Write the History of the New World: Histories, Epistemologies, and Identities in the Eighteenth-century Atlantic World.* Stanford: Stanford University Press, 2001.

———. "Iberian Science in the Renaissance: Ignored How Much Longer?" *Perspectives on Science* 12 (2004): 86–124.

Cárdenas, Juan de. *Problemas y secretos maravillosos de las Indias.* 1591. Madrid: Alianza Editorial, 1988.

Carranza, Francisco Xavier. *La trasmigración de la iglesia a Guadalupe.* México City: Colegio de San Idelfonso, 1749.

Carroll, Peter N. *Puritanism and the Wilderness: The Intellectual Significance of the New England Frontier, 1629–1700.* New York: Columbia University Press, 1969.

Castellanos, Juan de. *Primera parte de las elegías de varones illustres de Indias.* Madrid: Viuda de Alonso Gómez, 1589.

Castelli, Pietro. *Exactissima descriptio rariorum quarundam plantarum, qu[a]e contientur Rom[a]e in Horto Farnesiano.* Rome: Iacobi Mascardi, 1625.

Cave, Alfred A. *The Pequot War.* Amherst: University of Massachusetts Press, 1996.

Cervantes, Fernando. *The Devil in the New World: The Impact of Diabolism in New Spain.* New Haven, Conn.: Yale University Press, 1994.

Chakrabarty, Dipesh. *Provincializing Europe: Postcolonial Thought and Historical Difference.* Princeton, N.J.: Princeton University Press, 2000.

Chaplin, Joyce. *Subject Matter: Technology, the Body, and Science on the Anglo-American Frontier, 1500–1676.* Cambridge, Mass: Harvard University Press, 2001.

Chapman, George. *De Guiana, carmen epicum.* In Lawrence Kemys, *A Relation of the second voyage to Guiana,* Av–A4r. London: Thomas Dawson, 1596.

Chapman, George, Ben Jonson, and John Marston. *Eastward hoe. As it was playd in the Black-friers. By the Children of her Maiesties Reuels.* 1605. Edited by R. W. Van Fossen. Manchester: Manchester University Press; Baltimore: Johns Hopkins University Press, 1979.

Chase, Jeanne. "Porous Boundaries and Shifting Borderlands: The American Experience in a New World Order." *Reviews in American History* 26 (1998): 54–69.

Chasteen, John. *Born in Blood and Fire: A Concise History of Latin America.* New York: Norton, 2001.

Cherry, Conrad. *Nature and Religion: From Edwards to Bushnell.* Philadelphia: University of Pennsylvania Press, 1980.

Cheyfitz, Eric. *The Poetics of Imperialism*. Oxford: Clarendon Press, 1991.

Cieza de León, Pedro. *La Crónica del Perú (primera parte)*. 1553. In *Obras completas*, ed. Carmelo Sáenz de Santa María. 3 vols. Monumenta Hispano-Indiana. Madrid: CSIC, 1984.

Clark, Stuart. *Thinking with Demons: The Idea of Witchcraft in Early Modern Europe*. Oxford: Oxford University Press, 1997.

Clenddinnen, Inga. *Ambivalent Conquests: Maya and Spaniards in Yucatan, 1517–1570*. Cambridge: Cambridge University Press, 1987.

Colonna, Fabio. *Annotationes et additiones*. In *Rerum medicarum Novae Hispaniae thesaurus seu plantarum animalium mineralium mexicanorum historia*, 841–99. Rome: Vitalis Mascardi, 1651.

Columbus, Christopher, ed. *The Book of Prophecies*. Ca. 1500. Translated by Blair Sullivan. Edited by Roberto Rusconi. Berkeley: University of California Press, 1997.

Constable, Giles. *Three Studies in Medieval Religious and Social Thought*. Cambridge: Cambridge University Press, 1995.

Copland, Patrick. *Virginia's God be thanked, or A sermon of thanksgiving for the happie successe of the affayres in Virginia this last yeare. . . .* London: Printed by I[ohn] D[awson] for William Sheffard and Iohn Bellamie, 1622.

Cortesão, Armando. *History of Portuguese Cartography*. 2 vols. Coimbra: Junta de Investigações do Ultramar-Lisboa, 1969–71.

———. *Nautical Chart of 1424 and the Early Discovery and Cartographical Representation of America: A Study on the History of Early Navigation and Cartography*. Coimbra: University of Coimbra, 1954.

Cotton, John. *The Bloudy Tenent washed, And made white in the bloud of the Lambe*. London: Matthew Symmons for Hannah Allen, 1647.

———. *A Briefe Exposition of the whole Book of Canticles, or Song of Solomon. . . .* London: J. Young for Charles Green, 1648.

———. *The Planters Plea or the Grounds of Plantations Examined, And usual Objections answered. . . .* London: William Iones, 1630.

———. *A Treatise of the Covenant of Grace, As it is dispensed to the Elect Seed, effectually unto Salvation*. London: Ja. Cottrel for John Allen, 1659.

Cowen, Painton. *Rose Windows*. San Francisco: Chronicle Books, 1979.

Cressy, David. "Books as Totems in Seventeenth-century England and New England." *Journal of Library History* 21 (1986): 92–106.

Cummins, John. *Francis Drake: The Lives of a Hero*. New York: St. Martin's Press, 1995.

Dacosta, Blas. *Sermón en la solemníssima colocación de la sagrada reliquia del Santo Lignum Crucis. . . .* Lima: Luis de Lyra, 1649.

Danforth, Samuel. "A Brief Recognition of New Englands Errand into the Wilderness." In A. W. Plumstead, ed., *The Wall and the Garden: Selected Massachusetts Election Sermons, 1670–1775*. Minneapolis: University of Minnesota Press, 1968.

Daston, Lorraine, and Katherine Park. *Wonders and the Order of Nature, 1150–1750*. New York: Zone Books, 1998.

Dávila Padilla, Agustín. *Historia de la fundación y discurso de la provincia de San-*

tiago de México, de la Orden de Predicadores, por las vidas de sus varones insignes, y casos notables de Nueva España. 1596. Brussels: Ivan de Meerveque, 1625.

Davis, Alex. *Chivalry and Romance in the English Renaissance*. Cambridge: D. S. Brewer, 2003.

Davis, David Brion. *The Problem of Slavery in the Age of Revolution, 1770–1823*. Ithaca, N.Y.: Cornell University Press, 1975.

Davis, Elizabeth B. *Myth and Identity in the Epic of Imperial Spain*. Columbia: University of Missouri Press, 2000.

Dawson, John David. *Christian Figural Reading and the Fashioning of Identity*. Berkeley: University of California Press, 2001.

De la Cruz, Sor Juana Inés. *The Divine Narcissus/El Divino Narciso*. Translated and annotated by Patricia A. Peters and Renée Domeier, O.S.B. Albuquerque: University of New Mexico Press, 1998.

Degler, Carl N. *Neither Black nor White: Slavery and Race Relations in Brazil and the United States*. New York: Macmillan, 1971.

Demos, John. *Entertaining Satan: Witchcraft and the Culture of Early New England*. Oxford: Oxford University Press, 1982.

Descartes, René. *Meditationes de prima philosophia*. . . . Amsterdam: Ludovico Elzevirium, 1642.

Dodoens, Rembert. *A nievve Herball, or historie of plantes: wherin is contayned the whole discourse and perfect description of all sortes of Herbes and Plantes*. . . . London: Gerard Dewes, 1578.

Dorantes de Carranza, Baltasar. *Sumaria relación de las cosas de Nueva España*. 1604. Edited by José María de Agreda y Sánchez. Mexico City: Museo Nacional, 1902.

Dunkerley, James. *Americana: The Americas in the World Around 1850 (or "Seeing the Elephant" as the Theme for an Imaginary Western)*. London: Verso, 2000.

Duviols, Jean-Paul, and Annie Molinié-Bertrand, eds. *Enfers et damnations dans le monde hispanique et hispano-américain*. Paris: Presses universitaires de France, 1996.

Duviols, Pierre. *La Lutte contre les religions autochtones dans le Pérou colonial*. Lima: Institut français d'études andines, 1971.

Eden, Richard. *The Decades of the Newe Worlde or West India*. . . . London: Guilhelmi Powell [for William Seres], 1555.

Edgerton, Samuel Y. *Theaters of Conversion: Religious Architecture and Indian Artisans in Colonial Mexico*. Albuquerque: University of New Mexico Press, 2001.

Edwards, Jonathan. *A History of the Work of Redemption*. Edited by John Wilson. Vol. 9. of *The Works of Jonathan Edwards*, ed. Miller et al. New Haven, Conn.: Yale University Press, 1989.

———. *Images or Shadows of Divine Things*. Edited by Perry Miller. New Haven, Conn.: Yale University Press, 1948.

———. "Personal Narrative." In id., *Works of Jonathan Edwards*, ed. Miller et al., vol. 16: *Letters and Personal Writings*, ed. George S. Claghorn. New Haven, Conn.: Yale University Press, 1998.

———. *The Religious Affections*. Edited by John E. Smith. Vol. 2 of *Works of Jonathan Edwards*, ed. Miller et al. New Haven, Conn.: Yale University Press, 1959.

———. *Scientific and Philosophical Writings*. Edited by Wallace Anderson. Vol. 6 of *Works of Jonathan Edwards*, ed. Miller et al. New Haven, Conn.: Yale University Press, 1980.

———. *Some Thoughts*. In *The Great Awakening*, ed. C. C. Goen. Vol. 4 of *Works of Jonathan Edwards*, ed. Miller et al. New Haven, Conn.: Yale University Press, 1972.

———. *Typological Writings*. Edited by Wallace Anderson, Lowance Mason, and David Watters. Vol. 11 of *Works of Jonathan Edwards*, ed. Miller et al. New Haven, Conn.: Yale University Press, 1993.

———. *The Works of Jonathan Edwards*. Edited by Perry Miller, John E. Smith, Herry S. Stout, et al. 23 vols. New Haven, Conn.: Yale University Press, 1957–.

Eisenberg, Daniel. *Romances of Chivalry in the Spanish Golden Age*. Newark, Del.: Juan de la Cuesta, 1982.

Eliot, John. *Tears of repentance: or, A further narrative of the progress of the Gospel amongst the Indians in Nevv-England. . . .* London: Peter Cole, 1653.

Elliott, Dyan. *Proving Woman: Female Spirituality and Inquisitional Culture in the Later Middle Ages*. Princeton, N.J.: Princeton University Press, 2004.

Elliott, John H. "Atlantic History: A Circumnavigation." In Armitage and Braddick, eds., *British Atlantic*, 233–49. New York: Palgrave Macmillan, 2002.

———. *Britain and Spain in America: Colonists and Colonized*. The Stenton Lecture. Reading, Eng.: University of Reading, 1994.

———. *En búsqueda de la historia atlántica*. Las Palmas de Gran Canaria, Spain: Cabildo de Gran Canaria, 2001.

Eltis, David. *The Rise of African Slavery in the Americas*. Cambridge: Cambridge University Press, 2000.

Engerman, David C. "Modernization from the Other Shore: American Observers and the Costs of Soviet Economic Development." *American Historical Review* 105 (2000): 383–416.

Ercilla, Alonso de. *La Araucana*. 1569, 1578, and 1589. Colección Sepan Cuantos No. 99. Mexico City: Porrúa, 1968.

Estrada de Gerlero, Elena Isabel. "Los protomártires del Japón en la hagiografía novohispana." In *Los pinceles de la historia: De la patria criolla a la nación mexicana, 1750–1860*. Mexico City: Museo Nacional de Arte, Instituto Nacional de Bellas Artes, 2000.

Evans, J. Martin. *Milton's Imperial Epic*. Ithaca, N.Y.: Cornell University Press, 1996.

Faber, Johann. *Aliorum Novae Hispaniae animalium Nardi Antonii Recchi imagines et nomina*. In Francisco Hernández, *Rerum medicarum Novae Hispaniae thesaurus seu plantarum animalium mineralium Mexicanorum Historia*, 456–839. Rome: Vitalis Mascardi, 1651.

Falkenburg, Reindert L. *The Fruit of Devotion: Mysticism and the Imagery of Love in Flemish Paintings of the Virgin and Child, 1450–1550*. Translated by Sammy Herman. Philadelphia: John Benjamins, 1994.

Fernández-Armesto, Felipe. *The Americas: A Hemispheric History*. New York: Random House, Modern Library, 2003.

———. *Before Columbus: Exploration and Colonization from the Mediterranean to the Atlantic, 1229–1492*. Philadelphia: University of Pennsylvania Press, 1987.

————. *Columbus*. Oxford: Oxford University Press, 1991.

Fernández de Oviedo, Gonzalo. *Historia general y natural de las Indias, Isla y Tierra-firme del Mar Océano*. 1535–57. Edited by J. Natalicio González and José Amador de los Ríos. 14 vols. Asunción del Paraguay: Guaranda, 1944–45.

Fernández de Quirós, Pedro. *Memorial*. Madrid, 1609. Reproduced in Carlos Sanz, *Australia: Su descubrimiento y denominación*, 23–26. Madrid: Ministerio de Asuntos Exteriores, 1973.

Fernández Félix, Miguel, and Sara Gabriela Baz, eds. *Monjas coronadas: Vida conventual femenina en Hispanoamérica*. Mexico City: Museo Nacional del Virreinato, 2003.

Ferrari, Giovanni Battista. *Flora, overo cultura di fiori*. 1633. Rome: Pier'Ant. Faciotti, 1638.

————. *Hesperides sive de malorum aureorum cutura et usu. Libri Quatuor*. Rome: Sumptibus Hermanni Scheus, 1646.

FitzGeffrey, Charles. *Sir Francis Drake, His Honorable Life's Commendation, and His Tragical Death's Lamentation*. Oxford: Joseph Barnes, 1596.

Fletcher, Francis. *The World Encompassed by Sir Francis Drake*. 1628. London: Nicholas Bourne, 1652.

Florencia, Francisco de. *La Estrella de el* [sic] *Norte de Mexico. . . .* Mexico City: Por doña Maria de Benavides, viuda de Juan de Ribera, 1688. Reproduced in *Testimonios históricos guadalupanos*, edited by Ernesto de la Torre Villar and Ramiro Navarro de Anda. Mexico City: Fondo de Cultura Económica, 1982.

Flores Araoz, José, Ramón Mujica Pinilla, Luis Eduardo Wuffarden, and Pedro Guibovich Pérez. *Santa Rosa de Lima y su tiempo*. Lima: Banco de Crédito del Perú, 1995.

Forsyth, Neil. *The Satanic Epic*. Princeton, N.J.: Princeton University Press, 2003.

Fredrickson, George M. "Nineteenth-century American History." In Molho and Wood, eds., *Imagined Histories*, 164–84. Princeton, N.J.: Princeton University Press, 1998.

Freedeberg, David. *The Eye of the Lynx: Galileo, His Friends, and the Beginnings of Modern Natural History*. Chicago: University of Chicago Press, 2002.

Freyre, Gilberto. *The Masters and the Slaves: A Study in the Development of Brazilian Civilization*. New York: Knopf, 1946. Originally published as *Casa-grande & senzala: Formação da familia brasileira sob o regimen de economia patriarcal* (Rio de Janeiro: Maia & Schmidt, 1933).

Frye, Northrop. *The Great Code: The Bible and Literature*. New York: Harcourt, 1982.

Fuchs, Barbara. *Mimesis and Empire: The New World, Islam, and European Identities*. Cambridge: Cambridge University Press, 2001.

Fulton, Rachel. *From Judgment to Passion: Devotion to Christ and the Virgin Mary, 800–1200*. New York: Columbia University Press, 2002.

————. "The Virgin in the Garden, or Why Flowers Make Better Prayers." *Spiritus* 4 (2004): 1–23.

Gabbaccia, Donna. "A Long Atlantic in a Wider World." *Atlantic Studies* 1 (2004): 1–27.

Galeano, Eduardo. *Las venas abiertas de América Latina*. Madrid: Siglo XXI de

España, 1971. Translated as *Open Veins of Latin America: Five Centuries of the Pillage of a Continent* (New York: Monthly Review Press, 1973).

Gambara, Lorenzo. *De navigatione Christophori Columbi libri quattuor*. Rome: Franciscum Zannettum, 1581

García Carcel, Ricardo. *La leyenda negra: Historia y opinión*. Madrid: Alianza, 1981.

García, Gregorio. *Origen de los Indios del Nuevo Mundo e Indias Occidentales*. Valencia: Patricio Mey, 1606.

Gevaerts, Jean Gaspard. *Pompa introitus honori Ferdinandi Austriaci Hispaniarum Infantis*. Antwerp: Apud Ioannem Meursium, 1641.

Giamatti, A. Bartlett. *The Earthly Paradise and the Renaissance Epic*. Princeton, N.J.: Princeton University Press, 1966.

Gibson, Charles, ed. *The Black Legend: Anti-Spanish Attitudes in the Old World and New*. New York: Knopf, 1971.

Gil, Juan. "La épica latina quiñentista y el descubrimiento de America." *Anuarios de Estudios Americanos* 40 (1983): 203–51.

Gilman, Stephen. "Bernal Díaz del Castillo and Amadís de Gaula." In *Studia Philologica: Homenaje ofrecido a Dámaso Alonso*, 2: 99–114. Madrid: Gredos.

Gilroy, Paul. *Black Atlantic: Modernity and Double Consciousness*. London: Routledge, 1993.

Godbeer, Richard. *The Devil's Dominion: Magic and Religion in Early New England*. Cambridge University Press, 1992.

Goddard, Peter A. "The Devil in New France: Jesuit Demonology, 1611–50." *Canadian Historical Review* 78 (1997): 40–62.

Goffman, Daniel. *The Ottoman Empire and Early Modern Europe*. Cambridge: Cambridge University Press, 2002.

González Echeverría, Roberto, "Europeans in Wonderland." *New York Times Book Review*, February 16, 1992.

Goodman, Jennifer R. *Chivalry and Exploration, 1298–1630*. Rochester, N.Y.: Boydell Press, 1998.

Gootenberg, Paul. *Imagining Development: Economic Ideas in Peru's "Fictitious Prosperity" of Guano, 1840–1880*. Berkeley: University of California Press, 1993.

Grafton, Anthony. *New Worlds, Ancient Texts: The Power of Tradition and the Shock of Discovery*. Cambridge, Mass.: Belknap Press of Harvard University Press, 1992.

Gray, Robert. *A good speed to Virginia*. London: Felix Kyngston for William Welbie, 1609.

Graziano, Frank. *Wounds of Love: The Mystical Marriage of St. Rose of Lima*. Oxford: Oxford University Press, 2004.

Greenblatt, Stephen. *Learning to Curse: Essays in Early Modern Culture*. New York: Routledge, 1990.

———. *Marvelous Possessions: The Wonder of the New World*. Chicago: University of Chicago Press, 1991.

———. *Renaissance Self-Fashioning: From More to Shakespeare*. Chicago: University of Chicago Press, 1980.

———, ed. *New World Encounters*. Berkeley: University of California Press, 1993.

Greene, Jack P. "Beyond Power: Paradigm Subversion and Reformulation and the Re-Creation of the Early Modern Atlantic World." In *Interpreting Early America: Historiographical Essays*. Charlottesville: University Press of Virginia, 1996.

———. *The Intellectual Construction of America: Exceptionalism and Identity from 1492 to 1800*. Chapel Hill: University of North Carolina Press, 1993.

———. "Interpretive Frameworks: The Quest for Intellectual Order in Early American History." *William and Mary Quarterly*, 3d ser., 48 (1991): 515–30.

———. *Pursuits of Happiness: The Social Development of Early Modern British Colonies and the Formation of American Culture*. Chapel Hill: University of North Carolina Press, 1988.

Greenfield, Amy Butler. *A Perfect Red: Empire, Espionage, and the Quest for the Color of Desire*. New York: HarperCollins, 2005.

Gregory, Brad S. *Salvation at Stake: Christian Martyrdom in Early Modern Europe*. Cambridge, Mass.: Harvard University Press, 1999.

Gretser, Jakob. "Descriptio floris Indici, quem Granadillam vocant. . . ." In *Hortvs S. Crvcis. . . .* Ingolstadt: Adami Sartorii, 1610.

Griffiths, Nicholas. *The Cross and the Serpent: Religious Repression and Resurgence in Colonial Peru*. Norman: University of Oklahoma Press, 1996.

Gruzinski, Serge. *Les Quatre Parties du monde: Histoire d'une mondialisation*. Paris: Martinère, 2004.

Gumilla, José. *El Orinoco Ilustrado: Historia natural, civil y geográphica de este gran río. . . .* Madrid: Manuel Fernández, 1741.

Gura, Philip F. *Jonathan Edwards: America's Evangelical*. New York: Hill & Wang, 2004.

Guy, Donna J., and Thomas E. Sheridan. "On Frontiers: The Northern and Southern Edges of the Spanish Empire in the Americas." In Guy and Sheridan, eds., *Contested Ground: Comparative Frontiers on the Northern and Southern Edges of the Spanish Empire*, 3–15. Tucson: University of Arizona Press, 1998.

Hakluyt, Richard. *The Original Writings and Correspondance of the Two Richard Hakluyts*. Edited by E. G. R. Taylor. 2 vols. London: Hakluyt Society, 1935.

———. *Principall Navigations*. 12 vols. Glasgow: James MacLehose & Sons, 1903–5.

Hale, Charles. *Mexican Liberalism in the Age of Mora, 1821–1852*. New Haven, Conn.: Yale University Press, 1968.

———. *The Transformation of Liberalism in Late Nineteenth-century Mexico*. Princeton, N.J.: Princeton University Press, 1989.

Hall, David D. "A World of Wonders: The Mentality of the Supernatural in Seventeenth-century New England." In David D. Hall and David Grayson Allen, eds., *Seventeenth-century New England*. Publications of the Colonial Society of Massachusetts, vol. 63. Boston: Colonial Society of Massachusetts, 1984.

———. *Cultures of Print: Essays in the History of the Book*. Amherst: University of Massachusetts Press, 1996.

———. *Worlds of Wonder, Days of Judgment: Popular Religious Belief in Early New England*. New York: Knopf, 1989.

Halperín-Donghi, Tulio. "Argentines Ponder the Burden of the Past." In Adelman, ed., *Colonial Legacies*, 151–73. New York: Routledge, 1999.

―――. "'Dependency Theory' and Latin American Historiography." *Latin American Research Review* 17, 1 (1982): 115–30.

―――. *Historia contemporánea de América Latina*. Madrid: Alianza Editorial, 1969.

Hammond, Jeffrey A. "The Bride in Redemptive Time: John Cotton and the Canticles Controversy." *New England Quarterly* 56 (1983): 78–102.

Hanke, Lewis. *Aristotle and the American Indians: A Study in Race Prejudice in the Modern World*. Chicago: Regnery, 1959.

―――. "Introduction." In id., ed., *Do the Americas Have a Common History?* 3–50. New York: Knopf, 1964.

―――. *The Spanish Struggle for Justice in the Conquest of America*. Philadelphia: University of Pennsylvania Press, 1949.

―――, ed. *Do the Americas Have a Common History? A Critique of the Bolton Thesis*. New York: Knopf, 1964.

Hart, Roger. "The Great Explanandum." *American Historical Review* 105 (2000): 486–93.

Hartz, Louis. *The Founding of New Societies: Studies in the History of United States, Latin America, South Africa, Canada, Australia*. New York: Harcourt, 1964.

Hayes, Edward. A *report of the voyage and successe thereof, attempted in the yeere of our Lord 1583 by Sir Humfrey Gilbert knight. . . .* In Richard Hakluyt, *The Principall Navigations, Voiages and Discoveries of the English nation. . . .* London: George Bishop & Ralph Newberie, 1589.

Helgerson, Richard. *Forms of Nationhood: The Elizabethan Writing of England*. Chicago: University of Chicago Press, 1992.

Henningsen, Gustav. *The Witches' Advocate: Basque Witchcraft and the Spanish Inquisition*. Reno: University of Nevada Press, 1980.

Hernández, Francisco. *Rerum medicarum Novae Hispaniae thesaurus seu plantarum animalium mineralium Mexicanorum Historia. . . .* Rome: Vitalis Mascardi, 1651.

Herrera, Catalina de Jesús María. *Autobiografía de la Vble. Madre Sor Catalina de Jesús Ma. Herrera, Religiosa de Coro del Monasterio de Santa Catalina de Quito*. Quito: Santo Domingo, 1950.

Hijiya, James A. "Why the West Is Lost." *William and Mary Quarterly*, 3d ser., 51 (1994): 276–92.

Hoerder, Dirk, ed., *Labor Migration in the Atlantic Economies: The European and North American Working Classes During the Period of Industrialization*. Westport, Conn.: Greenwood Press, 1985.

Holifield, Brooks. *The Covenant Sealed: The Development of Puritan Sacramental Theology in Old and New England*. New Haven, Conn.: Yale University Press, 1974.

―――. *Theology in America. Christian Thought from the Age of the Puritans to the Civil War*. New Haven, Conn.: Yale University Press, 2003.

Hooker, Thomas. *The Soules Implantation into the Naturall Olive*. London: R. Young, 1640.

Housley, Norman. *Religious Warfare in Europe, 1400–1536*. Oxford: Oxford University Press, 2002.

―――. *The Soules Ingrafting into Christ*. London: J. H. for Andrew Crooke, 1637.

Howard, Alan B. "The World as Emblem: Language and Vision in the Poetry of Edward Taylor." *American Literature* 44 (1972): 359–84.

Howard, Deborah. *Venice and the East: The Impact of the Islamic World on Venetian Architecture, 1100–1500.* New Haven, Conn.: Yale University Press, 2000.

Howe, Daniel Walker. *American History in an Atlantic Context.* Oxford University Press, 1993.

Hubbard, William. *A General History of New England, from the Discovery to MD-CLXXX. 1680.* 1848. New York: Arno Press, 1972.

Huerga, Alvaro. *Los Alumbrados de hispanoamérica (1570–1605).* Vol. 3 of *Historia de los Alumbrados (1570–1630).* Madrid: Fundación Universitaria Española, 1986.

Hulme, Peter. *Colonial Encounters: Europe and the Native Caribbean, 1492–1797.* London: Methuen, 1986.

Huntington, Samuel P. *The Clash of Civilizations and the Remaking of World Order.* New York: Simon & Schuster, 1996.

———. *Who Are We? The Challenges to America's National Identity.* New York: Simon & Schuster, 2004.

Hurtado, Tomás. *Chocolate y tabaco ayvno eclesiastico y natvral: si este le quebrante el chocolate: y el tabaco al natural, para la sagrada comunión.* Madrid: F. García, 1645.

Hutson, Lorna. "Chivalry for Merchants; or Knights of Temperance in the Realm of Gold." *Journal of Medieval and Early Modern Studies* 26 (1996): 29–59.

Jacobsen, Nils. *Mirages of Transition: The Peruvian Altiplano, 1780–1930.* Berkeley: University of California Press, 1993.

Jaffary, Nora E. *False Mystics: Deviant Orthodoxy in Colonial Mexico.* Lincoln: University of Nebraska Press, 2004.

James I [king of England]. *A Covnterblaste to Tobacco.* London: R. Barker, 1604. Amsterdam: Theatrum Orbis Terrarum; New York: Da Capo Press, 1969.

———. *Daemonologie, in Forme of a Dialogue. Divided into three bookes.* London: William Aspley and W. Cotton, 1603.

Jardine, Lisa, and Jerry Brotton. *Global Interests: Renaissance Art Between East and West.* Ithaca, N.Y.: Cornell University Press, 2000.

Johnson, Edward. *A history of New-England. From the English planting in the yeere 1628. untill the yeere 1652. . . . .* London: Nath Brooke, 1654.

Johnson, John J. "One Hundred Years of Historical Writing on Modern Latin America by United States Historians." *Hispanic American Historical Review* 65 (1985): 763–64.

Johnson, Robert. *Noua Britannia. Offering most excellent fruites by planting in Virginia. Exciting all such as be well affected to further the same.* London: [John Windet] for Samuel Macham, 1609.

Juderías, Julián. *La leyenda negra: Estudios acerca del concepto de España en el extranjero.* 9th ed. Barcelona: Araluce, 1943.

Kagan, Richard. *Lucrecia's Dreams: Politics and Prophecy in Sixteenth-century Spain.* Berkeley: University of California Press, 1990.

———. "Prescott's Paradigm: American Historical Scholarship and the Decline of Spain." In Molho and Wood, eds., *Imagined Histories*, 324–48. Princeton, N.J.: Princeton University Press, 1998.

Kallendorf, Craig. "Representing the Other: Ercilla's *La Araucana*, Virgil's *Aeneid*, and the New World Encounter." *Comparative Literature Studies* 40, 4 (2003): 394–414.

Kamen, Henry. *Empire: How Spain Became a World Power, 1492–1763*. New York: Harper Collins, 2003.

Kamil, Neil. *Fortress of the Soul: Violence, Metaphysics, and Material Life in the Huguenots' New World, 1517–1751*. Baltimore: Johns Hopkins University Press, 2005.

Karlsen, Carol F. *The Devil in the Shape of a Woman: Witchcraft in Colonial New England*. New York: Vintage Books, 1989.

Karras, Alan L. "The Atlantic World as a Unit of Study." In Alan L. Karras and J. R. McNeill, eds., *Atlantic American Societies: From Columbus Through Abolition, 1492–1888*, 1–15. London: Routledge, 1992.

Keen, Benjamin. *The Aztec Image in Western Thought*. New Brunswick, N.J.: Rutgers University Press, 1971.

———. *Essays in the Intellectual History of Colonial Latin America*. Boulder, Colo.: Westview Press, 1998.

———. "Main Currents in the United States Writings on Colonial Spanish America, 1884–1984." *Hispanic American Historical Review* 65 (1985): 657–82.

Keen, Maurice. *Chivalry*. New Haven, Conn.: Yale University Press, 1984.

Keller, Morton. "Looking at the State: An American Perspective." *American Historical Review* 106 (2001): 114–18.

Kelley, James E., Jr. "Non-Mediterranean Influences That Shaped the Atlantic in the Early Portolan Charts." *Imago Mundi* 31 (1979): 18–35.

Kelley, Robin D. G. " 'But a Local Phase of a World Problem': Black History's Global Vision, 1883–1950." *Journal of American History* 86 (1999): 1045–77.

Kemys, Lawrence. *A Relation of the second voyage to Guiana*. London: Thomas Dawson, 1596.

Kicza, John E. "The Social and Ethnic Historiography of Colonial Latin America: The Last Twenty Years." *William and Mary Quarterly*, 3d ser., 48 (1991): 515–30.

Kingston-Mann, Esther. *In Search of the True West: Culture, Economics, and Problems of Russian Development*. Princeton, N.J.: Princeton University Press, 1999.

Kircher, Athanasius. *China monumentis, qua sacris qua profanis.* . . . Amsterdam: Jacobum à Meurs, 1667. Reprinted Frankfurt a/M: Minerva, 1966.

Knapp, Jeffrey, *An Empire Nowhere: England, America, and Literature from Utopia to the Tempest*. Berkeley: University of California Press, 1992.

Knight, Janice. "Learning the Language of God: Jonathan Edwards and the Typology of Nature." *William and Mary Quarterly*, 3d ser., 48 (1991): 531–51.

———. *Orthodoxies in Massachusetts: Rereading American Puritanism*. Cambridge, Mass.: Harvard University Press, 1994.

Kupperman, Karen Ordahl. *Indians and English. Facing Off in Early America*. Ithaca, N.Y.: Cornell University Press, 2000.

Lafaye, Jacques. *Quetzalcóatl et Guadalupe: La Formation de la conscience nationale au Mexique*. Paris: Gallimard, 1974.

Lake, Peter. "Anti-Popery: The Structure of a Prejudice." In Richard Cust and Ann Hughes, eds., *Conflict in Early Stuart England: Studies in Religion and Politics, 1603–1642*, 72–106. London: Longman, 1989.

Lamar, Howard, and Leonard Thompson, eds. *The Frontier in History: North America and South Africa Compared*. New Haven, Conn.: Yale University Press, 1981.

Lancre, Pierre de. *Tableau de l'inconstance des mauvais anges et demons où il est amplement traicté des sorciers & de la sorcelerie*. 1612. Edited by Nicole Jacques-Chaquin. Paris: Aubier, 1982.

Landsman, Ned C. *From Colonials to Provincials: American Thought and Culture, 1680–1760*. Ithaca, N.Y.: Cornell University Press, 1999.

Langley, Lester. *The Americas in the Age of Revolution, 1750–1850*. New Haven, Conn.: Yale University Press, 1996.

Lanning, John T. *Academic Culture in the Spanish Colonies*. London: Oxford University Press, 1940.

———. *The Eighteenth-century Enlightenment in the University of San Carlos de Guatemala*. Ithaca, N.Y.: Cornell University Press, 1956.

Lara, Jaime. *City, Temple, Stage: Eschatological Architecture and Liturgical Theatrics in New Spain*. Notre Dame, Ind.: University of Notre Dame Press, 2004.

Las Casas, Bartolomé. *Historia de las Indias* (1552–61). Vol. 3 of *Obras Completas*, ed. Miguel Angel Medina, Jesús Angel Barreda, and Isacio Pérez Fernández. Madrid: Alianza Editorial, 1994.

———. *The Tears of the Indians: Being An Historical and true Account of the cruel Massacres and Slaughters of above Twenty Millions of innocent People. . . .* London: J.C. for Nath Brook, 1656. A translation of Las Casas's *Brevísima relación de la destrucción de las Indias* (1552).

Lasso de la Vega, Gabriel Lobo. *Mexicana*. Edited by José Amor y Vázquez. Biblioteca de Autores Españoles, vol. 232. Madrid: Ediciones Atlas, 1970.

Latham, Jacqueline E. M. "*The Tempest* and King James's *Daemonologie*." *Shakespeare Survey* 28 (1975): 117–23.

Lattimore, Owen. *Studies in Frontier History: Collected Papers, 1928–1958*. London: Oxford University Press, 1958.

Lefkowitz, Mary. *Greek Gods, Human Lives: What We Can Learn from Myths*. New Haven, Conn.: Yale University Press, 2003.

Leonard, Irving. *Baroque Times in Old Mexico: Seventeenth-century Persons, Places, and Practices*. Ann Arbor: University of Michigan Press, 1959.

———. *Books of the Brave: Being an Account of Books and of Men in the Spanish Conquest and Settlement of the Sixteenth-century New World*. Cambridge, Mass.: Harvard University Press, 1949.

———. *Don Carlos de Sigüenza y Góngora: A Mexican Savant of the Seventeenth Century*. Berkeley: University of California Press, 1929.

Lepore, Jill. *The Name of War: King Philip's War and the Origins of American Identity*. New York: Knopf, 1998.

Lestringant, Frank. *Le Cannibale: Grandeur et décadence*. Paris: Perrin, 1994.

Lewaski, Barbara Kiefer. *Protestant Poetics and the Seventeenth-century Religious Lyric*. Princeton, N.J.: Princeton University Press, 1979.

Lewis, Laura A. *Hall of Mirrors: Power, Witchcraft, and Caste in Colonial Mexico*. Durham, N.C.: Duke University Press, 2003.

Lewis, Martin W., and Kären E. Wigen, *The Myth of the Continents: A Critique of Metageography*. Berkeley: University of California Press, 1997.

Limerick, Patricia Nelson, Clyde A. Milner II, and Charles E. Rankin, eds. *Trails: Toward a New Western History*. Lawrence: University Press of Kansas, 1991.

Linebaugh, Peter, and Marcus Rediker. *The Many-Headed Hydra: Sailors, Slaves, Commoners, and the Hidden History of the Revolutionary Atlantic*. Boston: Beacon Press, 2000.

Linneaus, Carl von. *Hortus Cliffortianus*. . . . Amsterdam, 1737.

Lockhart, James. "The Social History of Colonial Spanish America: Evolution and Potential." *Latin American Research Review* 7 (1972): 6–45.

Love, Joseph L. *Crafting the Third World: Theorizing Underdevelopment in Rumania and Brazil*. Stanford: Stanford University Press, 1996.

———. "Furtado, Social Science, and History." In Adelman, ed., *Colonial Legacies*, 193–205. New York: Routledge, 1999.

Lovejoy, David S. "Satanizing the American Indian." *New England Quarterly* 67 (1994): 603–21.

Lovejoy, Paul E. *Transformations in Slavery: A History of Slavery in Africa*. 2d ed. Cambridge: Cambridge University Press, 2000.

Lowance, Mason I. *The Language of Canaan: Metaphor and Symbol in New England from the Puritans to the Transcendentalists*. Cambridge, Mass.: Harvard University Press, 1980.

Loyola, Ignacio de. *Spiritual Exercises*. Edited by Louis J. Puhl. Chicago: Loyola University Press, 1951.

Lucas, Paul. *Valley of Discord: Church and Society Along the Connecticut River, 1636–1725*. Hanover, N.H.: University Press of New England, 1976.

Lukasik, Christopher. "Feeling the Force of Certainty: The Divine Science, Newtonianism, and Jonathan Edwards's 'Sinners in the Hands of an Angry God.'" *New England Quarterly* 73, 2 (June 2000): 222–45.

Lupher, David. *Romans in a New World. Classical Models in Sixteenth-century Spanish America*. Ann Arbor: University of Michigan Press, 2003.

Luxon, Thomas H. *Literal Figures: Puritan Allegory and the Reformation Crisis in Representation*. Chicago: University of Chicago Press, 1995.

MacCormack, Sabine, *Religion in the Andes: Vision and Imagination in Early Colonial Peru*. Princeton, N.J.: Princeton University Press, 1991.

MacLachlan, Colin M., and William H. Beezley. *El Gran Pueblo: A History of Greater Mexico*. Englewood Cliffs, N.J.: Prentice-Hall, 1994.

Maltby, William S. *The Black Legend in England: The Development of Anti-Spanish Sentiment, 1558–1660*. Durham, N.C.: Duke University Press, 1971.

Markoff, John. "Margins, Centers, and Democracy: The Paradigmatic History of Women's Suffrage." *Signs: Journal of Women in Culture and Society* 29 (2003): 85–116.

Marshall, Tristan. "*The Tempest* and the British Imperium in 1611." *Historical Journal* 41 (1998): 375–400.

Martin, John Rubert. *The Decorations for the Pompa Introiutus Ferdinandi*. London: Phaidon, 1972.

Martín, Luis. *The Intellectual Conquest of Peru: The Jesuit College of San Pablo, 1568–1767*. New York: Fordham University Press, 1968.

Martindale, Charles. *John Milton and the Transformation of Ancient Epic*. London: Croom Helm, 1986.

Martínez, María Elena. "The Black Blood of New Spain: *Limpieza de Sangre*, Racial Violence, and Gendered Power in Early Colonial Mexico." *William and Mary Quarterly*, 3d ser., 61 (2004): 479–520.

Marx, Leo. *The Machine in the Garden: Technology and the Pastoral Ideal in America*. Oxford: Oxford University Press, 1964.

Mather, Cotton. *Batteries upon the Kingdom of the Devil*. London: Nath. Hiller, 1695.

———. *The Christian Philosopher: A Collection of the best Discoveries in Nature, with Religious Improvements*. London: E. Matthews, 1721.

———. *Magnalia Christi Americana: Eclessiastical History of New England from its first Planting in the Year 1620, unto the Year of Our Lord, 1698 in Seven Books*. 2 vols. First American edition from the London edition of 1702. Hartford, Conn.: S. Converse, 1820.

———. "The New Settlement of Birds in New England." In *Selections from Cotton Mather*, ed. Kenneth B. Murdock, 363–65. New York: Harcourt Brace, 1926.

———. *The Wonders of the Invisible World: Observations as well Historical and Theological upon the nature, the Number, and the Operations of the Devils*. Boston: Benjamin Harris for Sam. Phillips, 1693.

Mather, Increase. *A Relation of the Troubles which have hapned in New England, By reason of the Indians there: From the Year 1614 to the Year 1675*. Boston: John Foster, 1677.

Matter, E. Ann. *The Voice of My Beloved: The Song of Songs in Western Medieval Christianity*. Philadelphia: University of Pennsylvania Press, 1990.

Maza, Francisco de la. *El guadalupanismo mexicano*. 1953. Mexico City: Secretaría de Educación Pública y Fondo de Cultura Económica, 1984.

McCoy, Richard C. *The Rites of Knighthood: The Literature and Politics of Elizabethan Chivalry*. Berkeley: University of California Press, 1989.

McGinn, Bernard. *Anti-Christ: Two Thousand Years of the Human Fascination with Evil*. New York: Harper Collins, 1994.

McWilliams, John. "Indian John and the Northern Tawnies." *New England Quarterly* 69 (1996): 580–604.

Mede, Joseph. *The Key of the Revelation, Searched and demonstrated out of the Naturall and Proper Characters of the Visions. . . . The second edition in English, whereunto is added "A Conjecture concerning Gog and Magog."* London: J.L. for Phil. Stephens, 1650. Originally published under the title *Clavis apocalyptica, ex innatis et insitis visionum characteribus eruta et demonstrata . . .* (1627).

———. *The Works of the Pious and Profoundly-Learned Joseph Mede, B.D. 1663*. London: Roger Norton and Richard Royston, 1672.

Mello e Souza, Laura de. *Inferno Atlântico: Demonologia e colonização, séculos XVI–XVIII*. São Paulo: Companhia das Letras, 1993.

Mesa, José de, and Teresa Gisbert. *Historia de la pintura cuzqueña*. 1962. 2 vols. Lima: Fundación Augusto N. Wiese Banco Wiese Ltdo., 1982.

Mignolo, Walter D. *The Darker Side of the Renaissance: Literacy, Territoriality, and Colonization*. Ann Arbor: University of Michigan Press, 1995.

Milhou, Alain. *Colon y su mentalidad mesiánica en el ambiente franciscanista español*. Valladolid: Casa-Museo de Colón, Seminario Americanista de la Universidad de Valladolid, 1983.

Millar C., René. *Inquisición y sociedad en el virreinato peruano: Estudios sobre el Tribunal de la Inquisición de Lima*. Santiago de Chile: Instituto Riva-Agüero Pontificia Universidad Católica del Perú and Instituto de Historia de la Universidad Católica de Chile, 1998.

Miller, David Harry, and Jerome O. Steffen, eds. *The Frontier: Comparative Studies*. Vol. 1. Norman: University of Oklahoma Press, 1977.

Miller, Patricia Cox. "'The Little Blue Flower Is Red': Relics and the Poetizing of the Body." *Journal of Early Christian Studies* 8 (2000): 213–36.

Miller, Perry. *Errand into the Wilderness*. Cambridge, Mass.: Harvard University Press, 1956.

Mills, Kenneth. *Idolatry and Its Enemies: Colonial Andean Religion and Extirpation, 1640–1750*. Princeton, N.J.: Princeton University Press, 1997.

Mills, Kenneth, and William B. Taylor. *Colonial Spanish America: A Documentary History*. Wilmington, Del.: Scholarly Resources, 1992.

Miramontes Zuázola, Juan de. *Armas antárticas*. Edited by Jacinto Jijón y Caamaño. 2 vols. Quito: Julio Sáenz Rebolledo, 1921.

Molho, Anthony, and Gordon S. Wood, eds. *Imagined Histories: American Historians Interpret the Past*. Princeton, N.J.: Princeton University Press, 1998.

Monardes, Nicolás. *Primera y segunda y tercera partes de la historia medicinal de las cosas que se traen de nuestras Indias Occidentales que sirven en medicina. . . .* Seville: Alonso Escribano, 1574.

———. *Segunda parte del libro que trata de las cosas medicinales que traen de nuestras Indias occidentals: dose escrive de la yerva que llaman tabaco. . . .* Seville: Alonso Escribano, 1571.

Montrose, Louis. "'Shaping Fantasies': Figurations of Gender and Power in Elizabethan Culture." *Representations* 1, 2 (1983): 61–94.

———. "The Work of Gender in the Discourse of Discovery." In Greenblatt, ed., *New World Encounters*, 197–217. Berkeley: University of California Press, 1993.

Morán de Butrón, Jacinto. *La Azucena de Quito que brotó el florido campo de la Iglesia en las Indias Occidentales*. 1724 Madrid edition collated with 1697 original manuscript. Reproduced in *Vida de Santa Mariana de Jesús*, ed. Aurelio Espinosa Polit, S.I. Quito: Imprenta Municipal, 1955.

Morgan, Edmund S. *Visible Saints: The History of a Puritan Idea*. New York University Press, 1963.

Morison, Samuel Eliot. *The European Discovery of America: The Northern Voyages*. Oxford: Oxford University Press, 1971.

Moya, José C. *Cousins and Strangers: Spanish Immigrants in Buenos Aires, 1850–1930*. Berkeley: University of California Press, 1998.

Mujica Pinilla, Ramón. "El ancla de Santa Rosa de Lima: mística y política en torno a la Patrona de América." In José Flores Araoz, Ramón Mujica Pinilla, Luis Eduardo Wuffarden, and Pedro Guibovich Pérez, *Santa Rosa de Lima y su tiempo*. Lima: Banco de Credito del Peru, 1995.

Muldoon, James. *The Americas in the Spanish World Order: The Justification for Conquest in the Seventeenth Century*. Philadelphia: University of Pennsylvania Press, 1994.

Muñoz Camargo, Diego. *Descripción de la Ciudad y Provincia de Tlaxcala de las*

Indias y del Mar Océano para el buen gobierno y ennoblecimiento dellas. Facsimile edition of the Glasgow manuscript. Edited by René Acuña. Mexico City: Instituto de Investigaciones Filológicas, Universidad Nacional Autónoma de México, 1981

Murrin, Michael. *History and Warfare in Renaissance Epic.* Chicago: University of Chicago Press, 1994.

Myers, Kathlen Ann. "'Redeemer of America': Rosa de Lima (1586–1617), the Dynamics of Identity, and Canonization." In Alan Greer and Jodi Lininkoff, eds., *Colonial Saints: Discovering the Holy in the Americas.* New York: Routledge, 2003.

News from New England, being a True and last Account of the present Bloody Wars carried on betwixt the Infidels, natives, and the English Christians, and Converted Indians of New-England. . . . London: J. Coniers, 1676.

Nicolopulos, James. *The Poetics of Empire in the Indies: Prophecy and Imitation in La Araucana and Os Lusíadas.* University Park: Pennsylvania State University Press, 2000.

Nieremberg, Juan Eusebio. *Curiosa filosofía y tesoro de maravillas de la naturaleza, examinadas en varias questiones naturales. . . .* Barcelona: Pedro Lacavelleria, 1644.

———. *Firmamento religioso de luzidos astros en algunos varones de la Compañía de Iesus.* Madrid: María de Quiñones, 1644.

———. *Historia naturae, maxime peregrinae. Libris xvi. . . .* Antwerp: Balthasar Moreti, 1635.

———. *Honor del Gran patriarca San Ignacio de Loyola Fundador de la Compañia de Iesus. . . .* Madrid: María de Quiñones, 1645.

———. *Ideas de virtud en algunos claros varones de la Compañia de Iesus.* Madrid: María de Quiñones, 1643.

Norton Mary Beth. *In the Devil's Snare: The Salem Witchcraft Crisis of 1692.* New York: Knopf, 2002.

Noyes, Nicholas. *New-Englands duty and interest, to be an habitation of justice, and mountain of holiness. . . .* Boston: Bartholomew Green & John Allen, 1698.

Nugent, Walter. *Crossings: The Great Transatlantic Migrations, 1870–1914.* Bloomington: Indiana University Press, 1992.

O'Gorman, Edmundo. "Do the Americas Have a Common History?" *Points of View* 3 (1941): 1–10. Reproduced in Hanke, ed., *Do the Americas Have a Common History?* 103–11. New York: Knopf, 1964.

O'Reilly, William. "Genealogies of Atlantic History." *Atlantic History* 1 (2004): 66–84.

O'Rourke, Kevin H., and Jefrey G. Williamson, *Globalization and History: The Evolution of a Nineteenth-century Atlantic Economy.* Cambridge, Mass.: Harvard University Press, 1999.

Ohnuki-Tierney, Emiko. *Kamikaze, Cherry Blossoms, and Nationalisms: The Militarization of Aesthetics in Japanese History.* Chicago: University of Chicago Press, 2002.

Olmos, Andrés de. *Tratado de hechicerías y sortilegios: Paleografía del texto náhuatl.* Edited by Georges Baudot. Mexico City: Universidad Nacional Autónoma de México, 1990.

Select Bibliography

Osorio Romero, Ignacio. *El sueño criollo: José Antonio de Villerías y Roelas (1695–1728)*. Mexico City: Universidad Nacional Autónoma de México, 1991.

Ovalle, Alonso de. *Histórica relación del reino de Chile*. 1646. Santiago: Editorial Universitaria, 1969.

Oviedo y Herrera, Luis Antonio de. *Vida de Santa Rosa de Lima: Poema heroico*. Reprint of 1711 Madrid original. Mexico City: Viuda de Miguel Rivera de Calderón, 1729.

Pagden, Anthony. *Lords of All the World: Ideologies of Empire in Spain, Britain and France, c. 1500–c. 1800*. New Haven, Conn.: Yale University Press, 1995.

Pagels, Elaine. *The Origin of Satan*. New York: Random House, 1995.

Pardo, Osvaldo F. "Contesting the Power to Heal: Angels, Demons, and Plants in Colonial Mexico." In Nicholas Griffiths and Fernando Cervantes, eds., *Spiritual Encounters. Interactions Between Christianity and Native Religions in Colonial America*, 163–84. Lincoln: University of Nebraska Press, 1999.

Parkinson, John. *Paradisi in Sole Paradisus Terrestris: A garden of all sorts of pleasant flowers which our English ayre will permitt to be noursed vp*. London: Humfrey Lownes & Robert Young, 1629.

Parlasca, Simone. *Il fiore della Granadiglia, o vero della passione di nostro signore Giesu Christo. . . .* Bologna: Bartolomeo Cocchi, 1609.

Parrish, Susan Scott. "The Female Opossum and the Nature of the New World." *William and Mary Quarterly*, 3d ser., 54 (1997): 475–514.

Peele, George. *A Farewell Entituled to the famous and fortunate Generalls of our English forces. . . .* London: John Charlewood, 1589.

Peña, Margarita. "Epic Poetry." In *The Cambridge History of Latin American Literature*, vol. 1: *Discovery to Modernism*, ed. Roberto González Echeverría and Enrique Pupo-Walker, 231–59. Cambridge: Cambridge University Press, 1996.

Pérez de Ribas, Andrés. *Historia de los trivmphos de nvestra santa fee entre gentes las mas barbaras, y fieras del Nueuo orbe. . . .* Madrid: A. de Paredes, 1645.

Pérez de Villagrá, Gaspar. *Historia de la Nueva México*. 1610. Mexico City: Museo Nacional, 1900.

Pérez, Louis A., Jr. "We Are the World: Internationalizing the National, Nationalizing the International." *Journal of American History* 89 (2002): 558–67.

Perrault, Charles. *Courses de testes et de bague faittes par le roy et par les princes et seigneurs de sa cour, en l'année 1662*. Paris: Impr. royale, 1670.

Peterson, Jeanette Favrot. *The Paradise Garden Murals of Malinalco: Utopia and Empire in Sixteenth-century Mexico*. Austin: University of Texas Press, 1993.

Pettit, Norman. *The Heart Prepared: Grace and Conversion in Puritan Spiritual Life*. 2d ed. Middletown, Conn.: Wesleyan University Press, 1989.

Phelan, John. *The Millennial Kingdom of the Franciscans in the New World: A Study of the Writings of Gerónimo de Mendieta (1525–1604)*. Berkeley: University of California Press, 1956.

Phelan, John Leddy. *The Millennial Kingdom of the Franciscans in the New World*. 2d ed. rev. Berkeley: University of California Press, 1970.

Pierce, Frank. *La poesía épica del Siglo de Oro*. Madrid: Gredos, 1961.

Pike, Frederick B. *The United States and Latin America: Myths and Stereotypes of Civilization and Nature*. Austin: University of Texas Press, 1992.

Pino, Fermín del, ed. *Demonio, religión y sociedad entre España y América.* Madrid: Consejo Superior de Investigaciones Científicas, 2002.

Pioffet, M. C. "L'Arc et l'épée: Les Images de la guerre chez le jésuite Paul le Jeune." In Réal Ouellet, ed., *Rhétorique et conquête missionnaire: Le Jésuite Paul Lejeune,* 41–52. Quebec: Septentrion, 1993.

Platt, D. C. M., and Guido di Tella, eds. *Argentina, Australia, and Canada: Studies in Comparative Development, 1870–1965.* London: Macmillan, 1985.

Poole, Stafford. *Our Lady of Guadalupe: The Origins and Sources of a Mexican National Symbol, 1531–1797.* Tucson: Arizona University Press, 1995.

Prebisch, Raúl, et al. *The Economic Development of Latin America and Its Principal Problems.* Spanish ed., 1949. New York: United Nations, 1950.

The Present State of New England with Respect to the Indian War. London: Darman Newman, 1675.

Priestley, Herbert I. *José de Gálvez, Visitor-General of New Spain (1765–1771).* Berkeley: University of California Press, 1916.

Purchas, Samuel. *Hakluytus posthumus, or Purchas His Pilgrimes.* 1625. 20 vols. Glasgow: James MacLehose & Sons for Glasgow University Press, 1905–7.

Purkiss, Diane. *The Witch in History: Early Modern and Twentieth-century Representations.* London: Routledge, 1996.

Quint, David. *Epic and Empire: Politics and Generic Form from Virgil to Milton.* Princeton, N.J.: Princeton University Press, 1993.

Quiroga, Pedro de. *Coloquios de la verdad.* Ca. 1550–70. Edited by Daisy Ripodas Ardanaz. Valladolid: Instituto de Cooperación Iberoamericana/Seminario Americanista, 1992.

Ramos Gavilán, Alonso. *Historia del Santuario de Nuestra Señora de Copacabana.* 1621. Edited by Ignacio Prado Pastor. Lima: Ignacio Prado, 1988.

Ramsay, G. D. "Clothworkers, Adventurers and Richard Hakluyt." *English Historical Review* 42 (1977): 504–21.

Read, David. *Temperate Conquests: Spenser and the Spanish New World.* Detroit: Wayne State University Press, 2000.

Redworth, Glyn. "¿Nuevo mundo u otro mundo? Conquistadores, cortesanos, libros de caballerías y el reinado de Felipe el Breve de Inglaterra." In *Actas del primer congreso anglo-hispano/Asociación de Hispanistas de Gran Bretaña e Irlanda,* vol. 3: *Historia: In memoriam Derek Lomax,* ed. Richard Hitchcock and Ralph Penny, 113–25. Madrid: Castalia, 1994.

Reff, Daniel T. "The 'Predicament of Culture' and Spanish Missionary Accounts of the Tepehuan and Pueblo Revolts." *Ethnohistory* 42 (1995): 63–90.

Reis, Elizabeth. *Damned Women: Sinners and Witches in Puritan New England.* Ithaca, N.Y.: Cornell University Press, 1997.

Relations des Jésuites contenant ce qui s'est passé de plus remarquable dans les missions des pères de la Compagnie de Jésus dans la Nouvelle-France. 1858. 6 vols. Montréal: Éditions du Jour, 1972.

Riley-Smith, Jonathan. *What Are the Crusades?* 3d ed. San Francisco: Ignatius Press, 2002.

Ringrose, David. *Expansion and Global Interaction, 1200–1700.* New York: Longman, 2000.

Rivadeneyra, Marcelo de. *Historia de las islas del archipiélago filipino y los reinos de la Gran China, Tartaria, Conchinchina, Malaca, Siam, Cambodge y Japón.* Barcelona, 1601. Translated as *History of the Philippines and Other Kingdoms* (2 vols.; Manila: Historical Conservation Society, 1971).

Rodgers, Daniel T. *Atlantic Crossings: Social Politics in a Progressive Age.* Cambridge, Mass.: Harvard University Press, 1998.

———. "Exceptionalism." In Molho and Woods, eds., *Imagined Histories,* 21–40. Princeton, N.J.: Princeton University Press, 1998.

Rodríguez Castelo, Hernán. *Literatura en la Audiencia de Quito Siglo XVII.* Quito: Banco Central del Ecuador, 1980.

Rodríguez O., Jaime. "The Emancipation of America." *American Historical Review* 105 (2000): 131–52.

———. *The Independence of Spanish America.* Cambridge: Cambridge University Press, 1996.

Rodríguez O., Jaime E., and Colin M. MacLachlan, *The Forging of the Cosmic Race: A Reinterpretation of Colonial Mexico.* Berkeley: University of California Press, 1980. Expanded ed., 1990.

Rodríguez Prampolini, Ida. *Amadises en América: La hazaña de Indias como empresa caballeresca.* Mexico City: Junta Mexicana de Investigaciones Históricas, 1948.

Rojas Mix, Miguel. *Los cien nombres de América, eso que descubrió Colón.* Barcelona: Lumen, 1991.

Rosenmeier, Jesper. "'Eater and Non-Eaters': John Cotton's *A Brief Exposition of . . . Canticles* (1642) in Light of Boston's (Lincs.) Religious and Civil Conflicts, 1619–22." *Early American Literature* 36 (2001): 149–81.

———. "The Teacher and the Witness: John Cotton and Roger Williams." *William and Mary Quarterly,* 3d ser., 25 (1968): 408–31.

Ross, Dorothy. "Historical Consciousness in Nineteenth-century America." *American Historical Review* 89 (1984): 909–28.

Ross, Kathleen. *The Baroque Narrative of Sigüenza y Góngora: A New World Paradise.* Cambridge: Cambridge University Press, 1994.

Rowe, Karen E. *Saint and Singer: Edward Taylor's Typology and the Poetics of Meditation.* Cambridge: Cambridge University Press, 1986.

Rubial García, Antonio. *La santidad controvertida: Hagiografía y conciencia criolla alrededor de los Venerables no canonizados de Nueva España.* Mexico City: Fondo de Cultura Económica, 1999.

Russell, Peter. *Prince Henry "the Navigator": A Life.* New Haven, Conn.: Yale University Press, 2000.

Russell-Wood, A. J. R. *The Portuguese Empire, 1415–1808: A World on the Move.* Baltimore: Johns Hopkins University Press, 1992.

———. "United States Scholarly Contributions to the Historiography of Colonial Brazil." *Hispanic American Historical Review* 65 (1985): 683–723.

Saavedra y Guzmán, Antonio de. *El peregrino indiano.* Edited by José Rubén Romero Galván. Mexico City: Consejo Nacional para la Cultura y las Artes, 1989.

Sánchez, Miguel. *Imagen de la Virgen María madre de Dios de Guadalupe. . . . 1648.* Reproduced in *Testimonios históricos guadalupanos,* ed. Ernesto de la Torre Villar and Ramiro Navarro de Anda. Mexico City: Fondo de Cultura Económica, 1982.

———. *Sermón de San Felipe de Jesús*. . . . Mexico City: Juan Ruiz, 1640.

Sanderson, Robert. *Three Sermons, Ad Clerum*. . . . London: R.Y for R. Dawlman, 1627.

San José, María de. *A Wild Country Out in the Garden: The Spiritual Journals of a Colonial Mexican Nun*. Translated and edited by Kathleen A. Myers and Amanda Powell. Bloomington: Indiana University Press, 1999.

San Pedro, Fray Juan de. *La persecución del demonio: Crónica de los primeros Agustinos en el norte del Perú*. 1560. Málaga: Algazara, 1992.

Savage, William W., Jr., and Stephen I. Thompson, eds. *The Frontier: Comparative Studies*. Vol. 2. Norman: University of Oklahoma Press, 1979.

Scheick, William. "Typology or Allegory: A Comparative Study of George Herbert and Edward Taylor." *Essays in Literature* 2 (1975): 76–86.

Scheiding, Oliver. "Samuel Sewall and the Americanization of the Millennium." In Bern Engler, Joerg O. Fichte, and Oliver Scheiding, eds., *Millennial Thought in America: Historical and Intellectual Contexts, 1620–1860*, 165–85. Trier: Wissenschaftlicher Verlag Trier, 2002.

Schmidel, Ulrich. *Americae pars VII. Verissima et iucundissima descriptio praecipuarum quarundam Indiae regionum & insularam, quae quidem nullis ante haec tempora visae cognitaeque*. . . . Frankfurt a/M: Theodore de Bry, 1599. Translation by Gotthard Arthus of Schmidel's *Warhafftige und liebliche Beschreibung*.

———. *Vera historia admirandae cuiusdam nauigationis*. . . . Nuremberg: Levini Hulsii, 1599.

Schmidt, Benjamin. *Innocence Abroad: The Dutch Imagination and the New World, 1570–1670*. Cambridge: Cambridge University Press, 2001.

Schmidt-Nowara, Christopher Ebert. "Borders and Borderlands of Interpretation." *American Historical Review* 104 (1999): 1226–28.

Schutte, Anne Jacobson. "'Such Monstrous Births': A Neglected Aspect of the Antinomian Controversy." *Renaissance Quarterly* 38 (1985): 85–106.

Schwartz, Stuart B. "The Colonial Past: Conceptualizing Post-Dependentista Brazil." In Adelman, ed., *Colonial Legacies*, 175–92. New York: Routledge, 1999.

Seed, Patricia. *American Pentimento: The Invention of Indians and the Pursuit of Riches*. Minneapolis: University of Minnesota Press, 2001.

———. *Ceremonies of Possession in Europe's Conquest of the New World, 1492–1640*. Cambridge: Cambridge University Press, 1995.

Sewall, Samuel. *Phaenomena quaedam apocalyptica ad aspectum novi orbis configurata, or, Some few lines towards a description of the new heaven as it makes to those who stand upon the new earth*. Boston: Bartholomew Green & John Allen, 1697.

Shakespeare, William. *The Tempest*. Ca. 1611. Edited by Barbara A. Mowat and Paul Werstine. Folger Shakespeare Library. New York: Washington Square Press, 1994.

Shepard, Thomas. "Election Sermon in 1638." *New England Historical and Genealogical Register and Antiquarian Journal* 24, 4 (1870): 361–66.

Shuffelton, Frank. *Thomas Hooker, 1586–1647*. Princeton, N.J.: Princeton University Press, 1977.

Shumway, Nicolas. *The Invention of Argentina*. Berkeley: University of California Press, 1991.

Sigüenza y Góngora, Carlos de. *Paraíso occidental*. 1683. Mexico City: Consejo Nacional para la Cultura y las Artes, 1995.

———. *Primavera indiana, poema sacro histórico: Idea de María Santísima de Guadalupe de México, copiada de flores*. 1668. Reproduced in *Testimonios históricos guadalupanos*, ed. Ernesto de la Torre Villar and Ramiro Navarro de Anda (Mexico: Fondo de Cultura Económica, 1982).

Silverblatt, Irene. *Moon, Sun and Witches: Gender Ideologies and Class in Inca and Colonial Peru*. Princeton, N.J.: Princeton University Press, 1987.

Simpson, Lesley Byrd. *The Encomienda in New Spain: Forced Indian Labor in the Spanish Colonies, 1492–1550*. Berkeley: University of California Press, 1929.

———. *Studies in the Administration of the Indians in New Spain. Part III. The Repartimiento System of Native Labor in New Spain and Guatemala*. Berkeley: University of California Press, 1938.

Singleton, Charles S. "Stars over Eden." *Annual Report of the Dante Society* 75 (1975): 1–18.

Skidmore, Thomas E. *Black into White: Race and Nationality in Brazilian Thought*. Oxford: Oxford University Press, 1974.

———. "Studying the History of Latin America: A Case of Hemispheric Convergence." *Latin American Research Review* 33 (1998): 105–27.

Skidmore, Thomas E., and Peter H. Smith. *Modern Latin America*. 6th ed. New York: Oxford University Press, 2005.

Slatta, Richard W. *Comparing Cowboys and Frontiers*. Norman: University of Oklahoma Press, 1997.

Slotkin, Richard. *Regeneration Through Violence: The Mythology of the American Frontier, 1600–1860*. Middletown, Conn.: Wesleyan University Press, 1973.

Sluhovsky, Moshe. "The Devil in the Convent." *American Historical Review* 107, 5 (2002): 1379–1411.

Smith, John. *Captain John Smith: A Selected Edition of His Writings*. Edited by Karen Ordhal Kupperman. Chapel Hill: University of North Carolina Press, 1988.

———. *The Generall Historie of Virginia, New England, and the Summer Isles*. 1624. In *The Complete Works of Captain John Smith (1580–1631)*, ed. Philip L. Barbour. 3 vols. Chapel Hill: University of North Carolina Press, 1986.

Smolinski, Reiner. "*Israel Redivivus*: The Eschatological Limits of Puritan Typology in New England." *New England Quarterly* 63 (1990): 357–95.

Solberg, Carl E. *The Prairies and the Pampas: Agrarian Policy in Canada and Argentina, 1880–1930*. Stanford: Stanford University Press, 1987.

Sousa-Leão, Joaquim de. *Frans Post, 1612–1680*. Amsterdam: A. L. van Gendt, 1973.

Spenser, Edmund. *The Faerie Queene*. 1590–96. Ware, Herts, UK: Wordsworth Editions, 1999.

Stastny, Francisco. "The University as Cloister, Garden and Tree of Knowledge: An Iconographic Invention in the University of Cuzco." *Journal of the Warburg and Courtauld Institutes*, 46 (1983): 94–132.

Steele, Ian K. "Exploding Colonial American History: Amerindian, Atlantic, and Global Perspectives." *Reviews in American History* 26 (1998): 70–95.

Stein, Stephen J. "Jonathan Edwards and the Rainbow: Biblical Exegesis and Poetic Imagination." *New England Quarterly* 47 (1974): 440–56.

Stella, Giulio Cesare. *Columbeidos libri priores duo.* Rome: apud Sanctium & Soc., 1589.

Stengel, Karol. *Hortorum, florum, et arborum historia in II tomos distributa.* Editio altera auctior. Augsburg: Andrea Apergeri, 1650.

Stepan, Nancy Leys. *"The Hour of Eugenics": Race, Gender, and Nation in Latin America.* Ithaca, N.Y.: Cornell University Press, 1991.

Stephens, Walter. *Demon Lovers: Witchcraft, Sex, and the Crisis of Belief.* Chicago: University of Chicago Press, 2002.

Stern, Steve J. "Ever More Solitary." *American Historical Review* 93 (1988): 886–97.

———. "Feudalism, Capitalism, and the World-System in the Perspective of Latin America and the Caribbean." *American Historical Review* 93 (1988): 829–72.

Straet, Jan van der. *New Discoveries: The Sciences, Inventions, and Discoveries of the Middle Ages and the Renaissance as Represented in 24 Engravings Issued in the Early 1580's by Stradanus.* Norwalk, Conn.: Burndy Library, 1953.

Stratton, Suzanne L. *The Immaculate Conception in Spanish Art.* Cambridge: Cambridge University Press, 1994.

Subrahmanyam, Sanjay. *The Career and Legend of Vasco de Gama.* Cambridge: Cambridge University Press, 1997.

———. *The Portuguese Empire in Asia, 1500–1700: A Political and Economic History.* London: Longman, 1993.

Swanson, R. N., ed. *The Holy Land, Holy Lands and Christian History.* Rochester, N.Y.: Published for the Ecclesiastical History Society by the Boydell Press, 2000.

Tannenbaum, Frank. *Slave and Citizen: The Negro in the Americas.* New York: Knopf, 1947.

Tasso, Torquato. *Jerusalem Delivered/Gerusalemme liberata.* 1581. Translated and edited by Anthony M. Esolen. Baltimore: Johns Hopkins University Press, 2000.

Tausiet, María, and James S. Amelang, eds. *El Diablo en la edad moderna.* Madrid: Marcial Pons, 2004.

Taylor, Alan. *American Colonies.* New York: Viking Press, 2001.

Thelen, David. "Of Audiences, Borderlands, and Comparisons: Toward the Internationalization of American History." *Journal of American History* 79 (1992): 432–62.

Thomas, Hugh. *The Slave Trade: The Story of the Atlantic Slave Trade, 1440–1870.* New York: Simon & Schuster, 1997.

Thornton, John. *Africa and Africans in the Making of the Atlantic World, 1400–1680. Transformations in Slavery: A History of Slavery in Africa.* Cambridge: Cambridge University Press, 1992.

Toews, John E. "Intellectual History After the Linguistic Turn: The Autonomy of Meaning and the Irreducibility of Experience." *American Historical Review* 92 (1987): 879–907.

Tompson, Benjamin. *New-England's tears for her present miseries, or, A late and true relation of the calamities of New-England. . . .* London: N.S., 1676.

———. *Sad and Deplorable Newes from New England. Poetically Related.* . . . London: H.J., 1676.

Torquemada, Juan de. *De los veinte iun libros rituales i monarchia Indiana, con el origen y guerras, de los Indios Occidentales.* 1615. 3 vols. Madrid: Nicolás Rodríguez Franco, 1723.

Totnes, George Carew. *The Historie of Araucana written in verse by Don Alonso de Ercilla translated out of the spanishe into Englishe prose almost to the Ende of the 16: Canto [Lambeth Palace Library, Ms 688].* Edited by Frank Pierce. Manchester: Manchester University Press, 1964.

Tyerman, Christopher. *Fighting for Christendom: Holy War and the Crusades.* Oxford: Oxford University Press, 2004.

Tylus, Jane. "Reasoning Away Colonialism: Tasso and the Production of the *Gerusalemme liberata.*" *South Central Review* 10, 2 (1993): 100–114.

Tynley, Robert. *Two learned sermons. The one, of the mischieuous subtiltie, and barbarous crueltie, the other of the false doctrines, and refined haeresis of the romish synagogue.* . . . London: W. Hall for Thomas Adams, 1609.

Tyrrell, Ian. "American Exceptionalism in an Age of International History." *American Historical Review* 96 (1991): 1031–55.

Valadés, Diego de. *Rhetorica Christiana ad concionandi, et orandi usum accommodata.* . . . Perugia: Apud Petrumiacobum Petrutium, 1579.

Van De Wetering, Maxine "Moralizing in Puritan Natural Science: Mysteriousness in Earthquake Sermons." *Journal of the History of Ideas* 43 (1982): 417–38.

Van Horne, John. *El Bernardo of Bernardo de Balbuena: A Study of the Poem with Particular Attention to Its Relations to the Epics of Boiardo and Ariosto and to Its Significance in the Spanish Renaissance.* Urbana: University of Illinois, 1927.

Van Young, Eric. "Recent Anglophone Scholarship on Mexico and Central America in the Age of Revolution (1750–1850)." *Hispanic American Historical Review* 65 (1985): 725–43.

———. "Was There an Age of Revolution in Spanish America?" In Victor M. Uribe-Uran, ed., *State and Society in Spanish America During the Age of Revolution,* 219–46 Wilmington, Del.: Scholarly Resources, 2001.

Vanderwood, Paul. *Disorder and Progress: Bandits, Police and Mexican Development.* Rev. ed. Wilmington, Del.: Scholarly Resources, 1992.

Vargas, José María, O.P. *Sor Catalina de Jesús María Herrera: Religiosa Domínica.* Quito: Editora Royal, 1979.

Vaughan, Alden T., and Virginia Mason Vaughan. *Shakespeare's Caliban: A Cultural History.* Cambridge: Cambridge University Press, 1991.

Vega, Inca Garcilaso de la. *La Florida del Ynca. Historia del adelantado Hernando de Soto . . . y de otros heroicos caballeros españoles e indios.* Lisbon: Pedro Crasbeeck, 1605.

———. *Historia general del Perú. Trata el descubrimiento del; y como lo ganaron los españoles.* . . . Córdoba: Viuda de Andres Barrera, 1617.

———. *Primera parte de los comentarios reales, que tratan del origen delos Yncas.* . . . Lisbon: Pedro Crasbeeck, 1609.

Vega, Lope de. *La Dragontea.* 1598. Madrid: Museo Naval, 1935.

————. *El nuevo mundo*. Ca. 1598–1603. Edited by Joaquin de Entrambasaguas. 2d ed. Madrid: Instituto de Cultura Hispanica, 1963.

Vega, Mariano Antonio de la. *La más verdadera copia del divino Hércules del cielo y sagrado Marte de la iglesia, el glorioso archangel señor San Miguel.* . . . Mexico City: Maria de Rivera, 1753.

Veliz, Carlos. *The New World of the Gothic Fox: Culture and Economy in English and Spanish America*. Berkeley: University of California Press, 1994.

Villa Sánchez, Juan de. *Justas y debidas honras, que hicieron, y hazen sus propias obras, a la M.R. M. Maria Anna Agueda de S. Ignacio.* . . . 1756. Mexico: Bibliotheca Mexicana, 1758.

Villagómez, Pedro de. *Carta pastoral de exhortación e instrucción acerca de las idolatrías de los indios del arzobispado de Lima*. 1649. Edited by Horacio H. Urteaga. Colección de Libros y Documentos Referentes a Historia del Perú, vol. 12. Lima: Sanmarti, 1919.

Villerías y Roelas, José de. *Guadalupe Quatuor libris*. 1724. In Ignacio Osorio Romero, ed., *El sueño criollo: José Antonio de Villerías y Roelas (1695–1728)*. Mexico City: Universidad Nacional Autónoma de México, 1991.

Wallerstein, Emanuel, "Comments of Stern's Critical Tests." *American Historical Review* 93 (1988): 873–85.

Walsh, James. "Holy Time and Sacred Space in Puritan New England." *American Quarterly* 32 (1980): 79–95.

Warner, Marina. *Alone of All Her Sex: The Myth and the Cult of the Virgin Mary*. New York: Knopf, 1976.

Wasserman, Mark. *Capitalists, Caciques and Revolution: The Native Elite and Foreign Enterprises in Chihuahua Mexico, 1854–1911*. Chapel Hill: University of North Carolina Press, 1984.

Waterhouse, Edward. *A declaration of the state of the colony and affaires in Virginia.* . . . London: G. Eld for Robert Mylbourne, 1622.

Watts, Pauline Moffitt. "Prophecy and Discovery: On the Spiritual Origins of Christopher Columbus's 'Enterprise of the Indies.'" *American Historical Review* 90 (1985): 73–102.

Webb, Walter Prescott. *The Great Frontier*. Austin: University of Texas Press, 1951.

Weber, David J. *Myth and the History of the Hispanic Southwest*. Albuquerque: University of New Mexico Press, 1988.

Weber, David, and Jane M. Rausch, eds. *Where Cultures Meet: Frontiers in Latin American History*. Wilmington, Del.: Scholarly Resources, 1994.

Weil, François. "Do American Historical Narratives Travel?" In Bender, ed., *Rethinking American History in a Global Age*, 317–42. Berkeley: University of California Press, 2002.

Westrem, Scott D. "Against Gog and Magog." In Sylvia Tomasch and Sealy Gilles, eds., *Text and Territory: Geographical Imagination in the European Middle Ages*, 54–75. Philadelphia: University of Pennsylvania Press, 1998.

Wharton, Donald P. "Providence and the Colonial American Sea-Deliverance Tradition." *Essex Institute of Historical Collections* 119 (1983): 42–48.

Whitaker, Arthur P. "The Americas in the Atlantic Triangle." In *Ensayos sobre la*

Historia del Nuevo Mundo, 69–96. Mexico City, 1951. Reproduced in Hanke, ed., *Do the Americas Have a Common History?* 141–64 (New York: Knopf, 1964).

White, Deborah Gray. "'Yes,' There Is a Black Atlantic." *Itinerario* 23 (1999): 127–40.

White, Hayden. *Metahistory: The Historical Imagination in Nineteenth-century Europe*. Baltimore: Johns Hopkins University Press, 1973.

White, John. *The Planters Plea or the Grounds of Plantations examined and usual Objections Answered. . . .* London: William Jones, 1630.

White, Richard. *"It's Your Misfortune and None of My Own": A New History of the American West*. Norman: University of Oklahoma Press, 1991.

———. *The Middle Ground: Indians, Empires and Republics in the Great Lakes Region, 1650–1815*. Cambridge: Cambridge University Press, 1991.

———. "Trashing the Trails." In Limerick et al., eds., *Trails*, 26–39. Lawrence: University Press of Kansas, 1991.

Willard, Samuel. "The Only way to prevent threatened Calamity: As it was delivered in a Sermon, Preached at the Court of Election, May 24, 1682." In A. W. Plumstead, ed., *The Wall and the Garden: Selected Massachusetts Election Sermons, 1670–1775* . Minneapolis: University of Minnesota Press, 1968.

Williams, Robert A., Jr. *The American Indians in Western Legal Thought*. Oxford: Oxford University Press, 1990.

Williams, Roger. *The Bloudy Tenent, of Persecution, for the Cause of Conscience, Discussed, in a Conference Between Truth and Peace*. London, 1644.

Williams, William. *The Death of a Prophet Lamented and Improved, in a Sermon Preached at Northampton, Feb. 13, 1729*. Boston, 1729.

Williamson, James Alexander. *The Cabot Voyages and Bristol Discovery Under Henry VIII*. Hakluyt Society Works, 2d ser., 120. Cambridge: Cambridge University Press, 1962.

Willis, Deborah. "Shakespeare's The *Tempest* and the Discourse of Colonialism." *Studies in English Literature* 29 (1989): 277–89.

Winship, Michael P. *Making Heretics. Militant Protestantism and Free Grace in Massachusetts, 1636–1641*. Princeton, N.J.: Princeton University Press, 2002.

Winston-Allen, Anne. *Stories of the Rose: The Making of the Rosary in the Middle Ages*. University Park: Pennsylvania State University Press, 1997.

Winthrop, John. *Winthrop's Journal: History of New England, 1630–1649*. Edited by James Kendall Hosmer. 2 vols. New York: Scribner, 1908.

Wittfogel, Karl A. *Oriental Despotism: A Comparative Study of Total Power*. New Haven, Conn.: Yale University Press, 1957.

Wittkower, Rudolf. "'Roc': An Eastern Prodigy in a Dutch Engraving." In id., *Allegory and the Migration of Symbols*, 94–96. Boulder, Colo.: Westview Press, 1977.

Wolff, Larry. *Inventing Eastern Europe: The Map of Civilization on the Mind of the Enlightenment*. Stanford: Stanford University Press, 1994.

Wood, Gordon. *The Radicalism of the American Revolution*. New York: Knopf, 1991.

———. "The Relevance and Irrelevance of American Colonial History." In Molho and Wood, eds., *Imagined Histories*, 144–63. Princeton, N.J.: Princeton University Press, 1998.

Wyman, Mark. *Round-Trip to America: The Immigrants Return to Europe, 1890–1930*. Ithaca, N.Y.: Cornell University Press, 1993.

Wyman, Walker D., and Clifton B. Kroeber, eds. *The Frontier in Perspective*. Madison: University of Wisconsin Press, 1957.

Yúdice, George. "We Are *Not* the World." *Social Text* 10 (1992): 202–16.

Zahn, Johann. *Specula Physico-Mathematico-Historica Notabilium ac Mirabilium Sciendorum in qua Mundi Mirabilis Oeconomia.* . . . 3 vols. in 2. Nuremberg: Joannis Christophori Lochner, 1696.

Zimmerman, Arthur F. *Francisco de Toledo, Fifth Viceroy of Peru, 1569–1581*. Caldwell, Idaho: Caxton Printers, 1938.

Index

Index

black legend, 216, 232; origins of, 160–61
Blaeu, Joan (*Geographia*), 172–74
body: and Amerindian emasculation, 97, 129; animals resembling human, 136; of Christ, 95–96, 199(fig); dismemberment of, 65, 72, 74, 88, 92, 95; and female demonic possession, 237n40; of kings, 126; landscapes as, 58–60; and monstrous births, 93; polity as, 129; of saints, 143, 178, 186, 187(fig), 189, 192; and satanic mockery of the resurrection, 102; and transformation due to conversion, 282n46; and visions, 95–96
Bohemia, 191(fig), 204
Boiardo, Matteo Maria (*Orlando innamorato*), 53, 73, 195
Bolton, Herbert Eugene, 216–18, 222
Bond, Edward L., 14
borderlands, 219–20
Bossy, John, 18, 29
Botero, Giovanni, 149
Bozman, Theodore Dwight, 80
Braddick, Michael J., 218
Brutus, 77
Bry, Theodore, 54–55, 61, 160–63, 165
Bulkeley, Peter, 207
Bustamente de la Cámara, Juan, 130
Bynum, Carolyn Walker, 88

Calancha, Antonio de la, 155–57
Calderón de la Barca, Pedro: *La Aurora en Copacabana*, 114–15, 124; *La semilla y la cizaña*, 23, 158, 186
Calef, Robert, 117
Calvete de Estrella, Juan Cristóbal (*De rebus Vaccae Castri*), 71–72
Calvin, John, 15, 153
Calvinism: theology of salvation, 15, 154, 207; and conversion, 15–16, 205–6; and human nature, 17, 168; and typology, 104, 153. *See also* Puritans
Camões, Luis Vaz de (*Os Lusíadas*), 45, 49, 53
Canaanites/Canaan, 8(fig), 9, 13(fig), 14, 77, 80, 84, 99; Aztecs as, 109; enemies of the Aztecs as, 105–6; Puritans battle, 118; and Scythians, 101; Spaniards as, 57
Canetabo, 41
cannibalism. *See* Satan

Cárdenas, Juan de, 128, 129
Careri, Gemelli, 10(fig)
Carpio, Bernardo del, 195
Carranza, Francisco, 144
Castellanos, Juan de (*Elegías de varones illustres*), 35, 37, 39–40, 60, 71
Castelli, Pietro, 149, 150
Catalina de Jesús, 178, 179(fig), 184, 186
Catherine of Siena, 186
Caupolicán, 45
Cave, Alfred A., 28
Cervantes, Fernando, 4(fig), 18
Chaplin, Joyce, 28
Chapman, George (*De Guiana carmen epicum*), 58–59, 62
Charles I, 64(fig)
Charles V, 197(fig)
Chasteen, John, 233
chivalry: Amerindians as the opposite of, 129–30; critique of, 60–61, 65, 113, 162; in the New World, 7, 61, 168–69, 172, 247n57
Christ. *See* millenarianism
Cieza de León, Pedro, 90–92, 102
Clark, Stuart, 18, 120
Clement VIII, 50
Clement IX, 189
Clement X, 178, 189
Clusius, Carolas, 130
Colón, Bartolomé, 115(fig)
Colonna, Fabio, 150
Columbus, Christopher, 7; as "Christumferens," 48, 51, 52, 53, 73, 246n46, 246n55; critique of, 113
Condé, prince de, 140
Connecticut, seal of, 205–6
Conversos. See Satan
Copland, Patrick, 87
Córdova, Pedro de, 111, 141, 143
Cortés, Hernán, 40, 54, 57, 107; as archangel Michael, 22, 203; as "General of Christ," 19, 20, 41, 42, 100; as model for the English, 61, 65, 248n67
Cortés, Martín, 54
Cotton, John, 18, 205, 206–7, 209, 211–12
Cross, the: carved on trees, 150–52; of De la Vega, 115(fig); demons expelled by, 1, 3, 4(fig), 40, 93, 110–16, 161(fig)–62, 173(fig); and name of Brazil, 112–13; and passionflower, 149; and saints, 186;

Index

Index

71; different strands of, 17–18, 205–6; and epic of Atlantic crossing, 9, 125; reject the cross, 116; and sacralization of space, 116, 118; and spiritual plantations, 205–14; and typological readings of Nature, 153–55; use of images among, 19
Pyrrhonism (skepticism), 96

Quakers, and Satan, 29
Quint, David, 45, 46
Quiroga, Pedro de (*Coloquios de la verdad*), 74–75

Raleigh, Walter, 56, 58–61, 65, 67, 168
Ramos Gavilán, Alonso, 100
Read, David, 158, 160
Reconquista, in Spanish America, 5, 47, 50; in New England, 12, 31, 69
Reformation, the, 15, 29, 76, 77, 82, 186; prefigured in Revelations, 94; reshuffles global balance of demons, 99, 100
Reis, Elizabeth, 237n40
relics, 1, 3, 33, 143, 192; as protection from Satan, 111–12; satanic mockery in Peru of, 102
Ricardo, David, 230
Rinaldo (Roland), 166, 168, 195
Rivadeneyra, Marcelo de, 192
Rodgers, Daniel T., 222
Rodríguez, Jaime, 221, 284n31, 288n77
rosary, 184, 185(fig), 190, 205
Rose of Lima, St., 24, 33, 143–44, 178, 186–90, 197(fig)
Rubens, Peter Paul, 169–72
Rule, Margaret, 117
Russell, Peter, 7

Sá, Mem de, 40
Saavedra y Guzmán, Antonio de (*El peregrino indiano*), 40, 42–43, 77
saints: body parts of, 143, 192; calm the seas, 141, 142; as flowers, 178–79, 186–200; reenact the passion of Christ, 186, 187(fig), 189; unaffected by poisons, 128, 138, 142, 143
Salem: witchcraft crisis, 28–29, 31, 70, 101, 237n40
Sánchez, Miguel: on Felipe de Jesús, 192, 194–95; on Our Lady of Guadalupe, 76–79, 143, 201–3, 204

Sanctification, doctrine of, 16, 207
Sanderson, Robert, 209
sangre de drago, 130
San José, María de, 180–81
San Juan, Anna, 181
San Martín, Thomas de, 197(fig)
San Pedro, Juan de, 101, 111, 127, 128
Santa Ana, Francisco de, 201(fig)
Santiago Matamoros (St. James the Moor-Killer), 2(fig)
Santo Tomás, Domingo de, 197(fig)
Satan: and Algonquians, 66–67; and Amerindian cannibalism, 32, 40, 41, 69–70, 88–93; and Amerindian emasculation, 97; and Antinomians, 29, 68, 70, 93; arrival of to New World, 16, 98–99, 103–4; Aztecs as the elect of, 19, 79, 103–10, 232; and blacks, 27; colonization as deliverance from, 35–37, 54, 62, 69–71, 88; and conquest of Mexico, 202, 203; controls the ocean, 9, 33, 35, 39, 40, 41, 42, 43, 46, 48, 49, 54, 59, 70, 72, 99, 123–25, 165(fig), 250n97; and *conversos*, 22, 26, 44; and Creoles, 94; and dormice, 132, 133(fig); at end of the millennium, 256n30; as Eponamón (Araucanian god), 46, 47, 48; and "excraments," 102; fortifications in New World built by, 12, 13(fig), 16, 87; and French soldiers, 29; geopolitics of, 97–100, 163; and greed, 163, 165; and heretic cannibalism, 93; as hero, 24, 81 (*see also* Drake; Milton; Tucapel); and *hololisque*, 128; as Huizilopochtli (Aztec god), 105–6; illusions caused by, 95–96; and Incas, 24; in Japan, 98; and King Philip's War, 69–70, 71, 93; and King William's War, 71; and Lake of Mexico, 10(fig); lightning caused by, 46, 125; as mastermind of Spanish conquest, 61–63, 71–76, 80, 84, 95, 161(fig), 163; and mestizos (*castas*), 27, 164(fig); in Mexican frontier, 92; and millennium, 9; mocks the Cross, 112–13; mocks the Eucharist, 19, 92–93, 102–3; mocks Leviticus, 20; mocks the Pentateuch, 19, 32, 101, 103–10; mocks Puritan churches, 101; mocks the Trinity, 101; mocks using Nature, 120–21, 132; and monsters, 135–36; monstrous births caused by, 93; and Moors, 23–24, 49, 99; multiple allies of, 14, 17,